Better Homes and Gardens®

AMERICAN CHRISTMAS
CRAFTS AND FOODS

BETTER HOMES AND GARDENS® BOOKS

Editor: Gerald M. Knox
Art Director: Ernest Shelton
Managing Editor: David A. Kirchner

Crafts Editor: Nancy Lindemeyer
Senior Crafts Books Editor: Joan Cravens
Associate Crafts Books Editors: Debra Felton,
Laura Holtorf, Rebecca Jerdee, Sara Jane Treinen

Food and Nutrition Editor: Nancy Byal
Department Head, Cook Books: Sharyl Heiken
Associate Department Heads: Sandra Granseth,
Rosemary C. Hutchinson, Elizabeth Woolever
Senior Food Editors: Julie Henderson,
Julia Malloy, Marcia Stanley
Associate Food Editors: Jill Burmeister, Molly Culbertson,
Linda Foley, Linda Henry, Lynn Hoppe, Mary Jo Plutt,
Maureen Powers, Joyce Trollope
Recipe Development Editor: Marion Viall
Test Kitchen Director: Sharon Stilwell
Test Kitchen Home Economists: Jean Brekke, Kay Cargill,
Marilyn Cornelius, Maryellyn Krantz, Dianna Nolin, Marge Steenson

Associate Art Directors: Linda Ford Vermie,
Neoma Alt West, Randall Yontz
Copy and Production Editors: Marsha Jahns,
Mary Helen Schiltz, Carl Voss, David A. Walsh
Assistant Art Directors: Harijs Priekulis, Tom Wegner
Senior Graphic Designers: Alisann Dixon,
Lynda Haupert, Lyne Neymeyer
Graphic Designers: Mike Burns, Mike Eagleton, Deb Miner,
Stan Sams, D. Greg Thompson, Darla Whipple, Paul Zimmerman

Vice President, Editorial Director: Doris Eby
Executive Director, Editorial Services: Duane L. Gregg

General Manager: Fred Stines
Director of Publishing: Robert B. Nelson
Vice President, Retail Marketing: Jamie Martin
Vice President, Direct Marketing: Arthur Heydendael

American Christmas Crafts and Foods
Crafts Editors: Joan Cravens, Debra Felton, Rebecca Jerdee
Food Editors: Sharyl Heiken, Julia Malloy, Marcia Stanley
Copy and Production Editor: Mary Helen Schiltz
Graphic Designer: Lyne Neymeyer
Electronic Text Processor: Donna Russell

Contributing Crafts Editor: Coleen Deery Bragg

Our seal assures you that every recipe in
American Christmas Crafts and Foods has been tested
in the Better Homes and Gardens® Test Kitchen.
This means that each recipe is practical and reliable,
and meets our high standards of taste appeal.

✻ CONTENTS ✻

CHRISTMAS–
A CELEBRATION
OF
AMERICAN CRAFTS

*Gifts from our hands and hospitality
from our hearts represent the
American holiday tradition. In that spirit,
the loving hands of dedicated crafts people
across the country have joined ours
to bring you ideas to enrich your
Christmas, starting with the appliquéd
scene on the next page. In this section
(and all that follow), you'll find
handcrafted holiday decorations and gifts
to make this Christmas—and many
to come—a special celebration of America's
rich crafts heritage.*

CHRISTMAS—A CELEBRATION OF AMERICAN CRAFTS

Handcrafted Classics— to Make, to Share, to Enjoy

For most Americans, Christmas is a time to celebrate tradition. Year after year, loved ones gather to delight in the special customs of the season and to share in the joy of generations as they craft Christmas ornaments, gifts, and trims for the holidays.

Christmas past lives again in the centuries-old Kentucky home, *opposite,* and throughout this section of handcrafted holiday treasures. A glance around the room reveals ideas that are part of our proud crafts heritage—from the Appalachian cookie cutter designs and angel ornaments that trim the tree to the handmade brooms crafted by Berea College students, *below.* Instructions for all projects begin on page 20.

In these days of mass production, Curtis Alvey, *below,* takes great care as he crafts beautiful baskets from natural materials. You can share that pride in workmanship this holiday season by crafting the Christmas treasures here.

Fashion a festive floral wreath from crepe paper, *below,* or turn simple Shaker-style boxes into great gifts with a dab of paint and a band of potato-printed papers.

Doll fanciers of all ages will delight in the prim and proper aproned doll. She's knitted in stockinette stitches with bits of sport-weight yarn. If cross-stitch is your forte, make a "1, 2, 3"

sampler or its companion "A, B, C" stocking. Both are embroidered on fiddler's cloth with Persian yarn.

To make fetching garments for holiday festivities, fashion a flea market quilt into a colorful country-style skirt, *right,* and a pair of kid-size overalls. Or stitch a wool patch skirt like Grandma's, *opposite,* using randomly cut scraps of plaid fabric. Grandpa's knitted sweater is a variation on a classic reindeer style.

Handcrafted Classics—to Make, to Share, to Enjoy

Simple materials provide the ideal means of recapturing the primitive scene of Christ's birth in the manger. Use natural and dyed corn shucks to create the crèche figures, *opposite*. Craft the stable from the branches and vines you might find on a country stroll.

The manger rests on a homespun cloth enhanced with an edging of crocheted scallops. You also might use this lacy edging to add a festive touch to other seasonal items such as stockings, aprons, place mats, napkins, and more.

Everyone knows that the joy of Christmas stems from giving. But you can add another dimension to that joy by making the gifts you bestow on those you love. Children especially take great pride in crafting personal gifts.

Start your youngsters on easy projects that call for simple materials and few (if any) tools. Try making spiced pomanders; they're a traditional Christmastime trim and a perfect project for beginners. For projects that require more complicated skills, guide your child through each step and stay close at hand when tools are involved.

Handcrafted Classics—to Make, to Share, to Enjoy

Whatever the season, the kitchen is probably one of the favorite gathering spots in your house—and during the holidays, it becomes the heart of the home. What could be more festive than a rousing sing-along, complete with guitar and banjo pickers, homemade biscuits, sorghum molasses, and other freshly baked treats?

Spruce up your kitchen with a tabletop tree trimmed with cookie cutter ornaments and piled high with handmade gifts. Then, craft a grapevine wreath to brighten a window. (For more about these projects, please turn the page.)

Give an old theme a new twist by presenting your friends with jam-packed Christmas baskets. The toys, gifts, and goodies will spread joy today, and the basket will be welcome all year long.

14

C lassic cookie cutter motifs inspire all kinds of Christmasy treats, *opposite*. Craft traditional tree trims and a "ducky" breadboard from pine. Or use these timeless designs to enhance tea towels and downy crib quilts. And why not whip up this cuddly kerchiefed doll for a favorite child?

Add quaint charm to window or wall by creating the grapevine wreath, *above*. Decorate it simply with corn shuck "blooms" you make yourself and streamers of satin ribbons.

16

Handcrafted Classics—to Make, to Share, to Enjoy

A rustic country dining room, *opposite,* is ever-ready for no-fuss entertaining—be it a simple sit-down meal or a seasonal snack of Christmas cookies and coffee. Traditional blue and white spatterware Bybee Pottery is set upon colorful place mats crocheted with strips of fabric. Wooden swallows, crafted from dip-dyed pine and wooden dowels, fly freely among purchased birdhouses. The luminous centerpiece is simply a cluster of candles encircled by a grapevine wreath (see previous page). For more Appalachian flavor, create a pine forest, *below.*

Four generations of Cornelisons have created pottery like the tableware shown here. Today, Walter and sons Buzz and Jimmy, *right,* continue to make this traditional spatterware.

Cookie Cutter Trims
Pictured on page 9

MATERIALS: Tin cookie cutters in shapes and sizes of your choice (optional; see instructions, *below*); good quality (knot free) ½- or 1-inch-thick white pine boards; jigsaw; ⅛-inch-diameter drill bit and electric drill; medium-fine and fine sandpapers; fabric dyes in colors of your choice; waxed paper; dollhouse wallpapers or other small-scale printed papers; white glue; watercolor brush; artist's brayer (optional); clear acrylic spray or polyurethane (optional); lightweight cardboard or plastic lids (optional; see instructions, *below*).

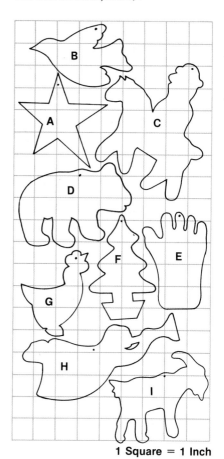

1 Square = 1 Inch

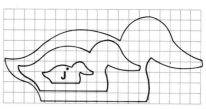

1 Square = 1 Inch

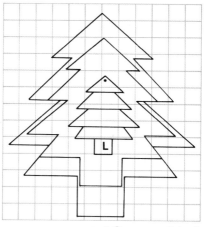

1 Square = 1 Inch

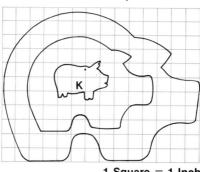

1 Square = 1 Inch

INSTRUCTIONS: To make ornament patterns, trace around tin cookie cutters. Or, enlarge the lettered patterns and the smallest duck, tree, and pig patterns, *left* and *above,* onto cardboard or plastic lids to make templates. (Larger ducks, trees, and pigs will be used for other projects.) Cut out the patterns.

Draw around the patterns onto pine; cut out ornaments using a jigsaw. Using an electric drill, drill holes (see dots on patterns) for hangers. Sand edges smooth.

To color ornaments, mix fabric dyes, according to the manufacturer's instructions, in an enameled kettle or sink.

Before dyeing ornaments, test scrap lumber in dyebaths to determine the amount of time you need to leave wood in the dye to achieve the intensity of color you wish. Then float ornaments in dyebaths, turning them every minute or so until you achieve the desired shade.

Remove ornaments from the dyebath, blotting drips on a rag. Stand ornaments on a waxed-paper surface to dry. Clean sink, kettle, or other surfaces with household cleanser.

To decorate dyed ornaments with papers, draw around dry ornaments onto small-scale dollhouse wall coverings or other printed papers, such as gift wraps. Cut along outlines and glue shapes to ornaments. (Thin white glue with water, then brush it thinly and evenly onto wood before applying paper shapes. Press out air bubbles using an artist's brayer or your fingers.)

Dry ornaments thoroughly. If desired, seal paper surfaces with clear acrylic spray or a coat of polyurethane. When dry, sand edges lightly and puncture holes in paper atop holes already drilled for hanging.

1 Square = 1 Inch

Angel Ornaments
Pictured on page 9

MATERIALS: Scraps of muslin, calico, lace, and gold lamé fabrics; black, white, and gold sewing thread; dressmaker's carbon paper; polyester fiberfill.

INSTRUCTIONS: Enlarge the pattern, *opposite*. (Pattern includes ¼-inch seam allowance all around.)

Cut the body front and back from calico; hand- or machine-stitch the muslin face and hands to the dress front. Transfer the facial details to muslin using dressmaker's carbon, then outline with short machine stitches. Add lace scraps (striped shapes on pattern) to simulate collar, cuffs, and apron.

Cut four wings and two 2-inch-diameter circles (halo) from gold lamé. Cut feet from muslin and stitch embroidery lines on fronts.

To assemble, sew wings, body, feet, and halo fronts to backs with right sides facing. Leave openings for turning. Clip curves, trim seams, and turn all parts right side out. Stuff lightly with fiberfill and blindstitch openings closed. Attach feet, wings, and halo to body.

Floral Wreath
Pictured on page 10

MATERIALS: One package *each* of red, pink, natural, and light and dark green industrial-weight crepe paper (we used Cindus Super-Crepe paper, available in craft and hobby shops); approximately 27 feet of 19- or 20-gauge wire; sewing thread; brown floral tape; glue; macrame hoop (12 or 13 inches in diameter); dried mallow or other natural dried material (flower centers); artificial flower stamens (optional).

INSTRUCTIONS: To make a crepe paper flower, cut a 6-inch length of 20-gauge wire for a stem; fold over one end to make a flat loop. Next, wrap a narrow strip of crepe paper through and around the loop. Wrap the stem of the mallow (flower center) into the loop, then wind thread around the loop and mallow stem to secure.

From crepe paper, cut 12 large petals (see full-size pattern, *below*), and curl their tips by rolling them around a pencil. Stretch and curl the petal centers inward.

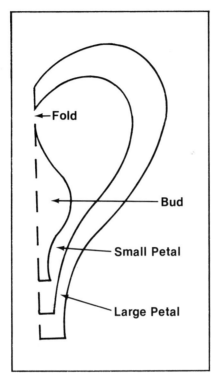

←Fold

Bud

Small Petal

Large Petal

Adding one petal at a time, secure the petals around the stem, wrapping their ends tightly with thread. When all the petals are in place, tie thread off and glue the thread ends. Make eight large flowers and 12 small ones.

To make buds, cut seven or eight bud shapes. Stretch the crepe paper in the center to form a cup shape. Cut wire into 7-inch lengths, make a flat loop in one end of each wire, and wrap it with crepe paper. (The wrapped loop prevents petals from slipping down the stem.)

Add the petals, following the procedure for making blossoms. Then twist the tops of the petals together, adding a dot of glue to hold petals in position.

Next, cut leaf shapes in several sizes from light and dark green crepe paper. Stretch and curl leaves, same as petals.

To assemble flowers and buds, wrap the stem with floral tape, adding light and dark leaves along the stem as you wrap.

Cut 9-inch lengths of wire for six vines. Make a loop on one end, same as for flowers. Then wrap the wire with floral tape, substituting leaves for flowers. (Use smaller leaves at top of wire.)

To assemble wreath, wrap macrame hoop with floral tape, wrapping in the flowers, buds, and vines. Bend stems to shape wreath.

Tulip Shaker Boxes
Pictured on page 10

MATERIALS: Yellow rice paper or construction paper; potato; small, sharp knife; green, yellow, and red drawing inks; Shaker boxes; red enamel, or substitute red latex and polyurethane; white glue; paper towels; newspaper; paintbrushes.

INSTRUCTIONS: Paint boxes with red enamel (or use latex and coat with polyurethane), then cover them with strips of paper decorated with potato-stamped designs.

To make stamps, cut a potato in half with a knife. On the flat side of one potato half, draw a simple plant shape. Using a small, sharp knife, cut away the flesh of the potato *around* the plant. Cut a tulip bloom stamp from the other half of the potato. Blot stamps on paper towels to remove excess moisture.

Practice stamping on newspaper. Brush ink on the raised design and press onto paper to make a print. Experiment with colors, blending two to make new colors. Then print the yellow paper with many prints and decorate the boxes with paper strips glued in place.

Knitted Doll
Pictured on page 10

MATERIALS: Coats & Clark Red Heart Sport Yarn (or a suitable substitute) in the following amounts and colors: 2 ounces of cranberry, 1 ounce *each* of eggshell, camel, black, gray, and blue; Size 3 knitting needles, or size to obtain gauge below; polyester fiberfill.

continued

21

Abbreviations: Page 310.

Gauge: Over st st, 13 sts = 2 inches; 9 rows = 1 inch.

INSTRUCTIONS: Finished size is 18 inches tall.

Body and head: Beg at lower edge with eggshell, cast on 54 sts. Work even in st st (k 1 row; p 1 row) until work measures 4½ inches; drop eggshell, attach cranberry. Work even in cranberry until work is 9 inches; drop cranberry and attach eggshell. Work even in eggshell until total work measures 12 inches. Cast off.

Fold work in half lengthwise and sew back seam; sew lower edge. Stuff firmly, leaving top open. Draw a strand of eggshell through sts of first row of eggshell; pull tightly to form neck and secure.

Hair section: Beg at back of neck with black, cast on 8 sts.

Row 1 (wrong side): K in front and back of first st, k to last st, k in front and back of last st—2 incs made.

Row 2: P in front and back of first st, p to last st, p in front and back of last st.

Rep Rows 1 and 2 alternately until there are 68 sts on needle. Work even in st st for 1 inch more. Break off, leaving a 20-inch tail. Thread this end into a needle and draw the tail through sts on needle. With another strand of black, sew edges of last 1 inch tog.

With seam at center front and cast-on sts ½ inch above the neck, pin hair section in place; sew. Add more fiberfill as necessary to fill in hair section. Draw sts tightly tog and secure. Then wind black yarn into a 1-inch-diameter ball for a bun and tack it in place.

Embroider eyes with black; embroider mouth and cheeks with cranberry.

Leg (make 2): Beg at upper edge with black, cast on 26 sts. Work in st st for 5 inches, ending with a p row. *Now work in pat as follows: Rows 1-2: P across. Row 3: K across. Rows 4-8: P each row. Row 9: * P 2 tog. Rep from * across.* Break off, leaving a 20-inch tail. Thread this end into a needle, draw through remaining sts. Draw tog tightly and secure; then

sew seam, leaving top open. Stuff firmly. Sew top seam tog and sew to body.

Arm (make 2): Beg at top edge with cranberry, cast on 4 sts. Working in st st, cast on 3 sts at end of next 6 rows—22 sts. Work even until work measures 5 inches. Fasten off cranberry; attach eggshell and continue in st st for 1¼ inches more. Break off, leaving 20-inch tail. Thread this end into a needle and draw through sts on needle. Draw tog; then sew seam, leaving top open; stuff. With cast-on sts on top, sew arm opening to body 1 inch below neck.

Bloomers, Front: *First leg section:* Beg at lower edge with camel, cast on 16 sts. *Row 1:* K across.

Row 2: P across.

Rows 3-4: Rep Rows 1 and 2.

Row 5 (1st eyelet row): K 1, * k 2 tog, yo. Rep from * across, ending with k 1.

Row 6: P across.

Rows 7-10: Rep Rows 1 and 2 alternately.

Row 11 (2nd eyelet row): K 2 (k 2 tog, yo, k 3) twice; k 2 tog, yo, k 2.

Row 12: P across. Work even in st st until work measures 3½ inches, ending with a p row. Break off, sl sts to a holder. Make another leg section in the same way; do not break off.

Joining row: K across sts on needle, cast on 4 sts, then k across sts on holder—36 sts. Work even in st st for 3 inches. Cast off.

Back: Work same as for Front. Sew side seams and crotch seam. Fold first 4 rows to wrong side on first eyelet row and sew in place. Pull on bloomers; add more fiberfill to round out body. Sew top edge to body. Thread a needle with a 15-inch double strand of eggshell. Draw through sts of each leg section ¼ inch above 2nd eyelet row, and tie at side.

Petticoat: Beg at lower edge with camel, cast on 116 sts.

Rows 1-10: Work as for Rows 1-10 of Leg Section of Bloomers.

Row 11: K 2, * k 2 tog, yo, k 3. Rep from * to last 4 sts; k 2 tog, yo, k 2. Beg with a p row, work in st st until total length measures 5½ inches. Fasten off, leaving a 20-inch tail.

Thread this end into a needle and draw through sts on needle. Fold first 4 rows to wrong side on first eyelet row and sew in place. Pull on petticoat, draw sts on yarn end tog to fit around body, and sew in place ½ inch above bloomers.

Skirt: Beg at lower edge with cranberry, cast on 124 sts.

Rows 1-4: Rep Rows 1-4 of leg section of bloomers.

Next row: P across for turning ridge. Beg with a p row, work even in st st until work measures 6 inches. Break off, leaving a 20-inch tail. Draw yarn through sts on needle. Turn first 4 rows to wrong side on turning ridge and sew in place. Draw sts on yarn end tog to fit waistline and sew in place.

Apron, Lower part: Beg at lower edge with gray, cast on 46 sts. K 6 rows, then work in pat as follows: *Row 1* (right side): K 4, p to last 4 sts, k 4.

Row 2: K across. Rep Rows 1 and 2 alternately until length is 5 inches. Break off, leaving a 20-inch tail; draw ends through sts on needle.

Upper part: Beg at lower edge with gray, cast on 20 sts. K 4 rows, then work in pat as follows: *Row 1* (right side): K 3, p to last 3 sts, k 3.

Row 2: K across.

Rep Rows 1 and 2 alternately until total length measures 2 inches.

Next 4 rows: K across. Cast off. Draw sts on yarn end of lower part to width of upper part; secure and sew tog. For tie, cast on 90 sts; k 6 rows and cast off. Place center of tie at center of apron on seam; tack in place.

Shawl: With blue, cast on 3 sts.

Row 1: K 2; with yarn in front of needle, sl 1 as to p. Always sl last st in this way.

Row 2: K 1; k in front and back of next st—inc made; sl 1.

Row 3: K 3, sl 1.

Row 4: K 2, inc in next st, sl 1.

Row 5: K 4, sl 1.

Row 6: K 3, inc in next st, sl 1.

Row 7: K 5, sl 1.

Row 8: K to last 2 sts, inc in next st, sl 1.

Row 9: K to last st, sl 1.

Rep Rows 8 and 9 alternately until there are 40 sts on needle, ending with Row 8. Work 3 rows even.

Next row: K to the last 3 sts, k 2 tog, sl 1 st.

Following row: K to last st, sl 1. Rep last 2 rows until 3 sts rem. Cast off. Drape shawl over shoulders, crossing points at front. Tack each point to waist at side. Tie apron at back. Tack each corner of upper apron part to shawl.

Bonnet: Beg at center back with eggshell, cast on 18 sts.

Row 1: K across.

Row 2: P across.

Row 3: Inc one st in each st across—36 sts.

Row 4: P across.

Rows 5-6: Rep Rows 1 and 2.

Row 7: * K 1, inc on st in next st. Rep from * across—54 sts.

Row 8: P across.

Rows 9-12: Rep Rows 1 and 2 alternately. With a different color yarn, make each end of last row.

Rows 13-18: Work as for Rows 7-12—81 sts.

Row 19: Inc one st in first st, * k 1, inc on st in next st. Rep from * across—122 sts. Beg with a p row, work even in st st until total length measures 3½ inches. Break off, leaving 20-inch tail. Draw yarn through sts on needle.

Brim: With eggshell, cast on 66 sts. Work even in st st for 1¼ inches, ending with a p row.

Next row: P across for turning ridge. Beg with a p row, continue in st st for 1¼ inches; cast off. Draw cast-on sts at center back tightly tog and secure. Sew seam to marker. Draw sts on yarn end to length of brim and secure. Fold brim on turning ridge, place gathered end of bonnet bet the two layers of brim and sew in place.

Cord: Cut two 72-inch strands. Twist these strands tightly in one direction, then fold twisted strands in half and twist in opposite direction. Cut in half and knot each end. Tack one cord to each side of bonnet; tie.

Cross-Stitched Stockings
Pictured on pages 10-11

MATERIALS: *For each stocking:* 12x23 inches each of 14-count fiddler's cloth and backing fabric; thread. *For sampler stocking:* 23 yards of red and 15 yards of blue 3-ply Persian yarn. *For ABC stocking:* 23 yards red, 10 yards green, 4 yards brown, and 2 yards yellow Persian yarn.

INSTRUCTIONS: For each design, stay-stitch edges of fiddler's cloth (stocking front) to prevent raveling. Do not cut out stocking until embroidery is complete.

Begin stitching in the center of the fabric and the center of the chart, *page 24.* Work stitches over two threads or squares, making 7 stitches per inch. When completed, carefully steam-press the cross-stitched fabric on the wrong side.

Using the chart as a guide, baste around stocking outline. With right sides facing, sew stocking front to backing fabric along basted lines; leave top open. Trim excess fabric, leaving ½-inch margins beyond the seam. Clip curves and turn stockings right side out. Press.

Cut two lining pieces for each stocking and sew them together. *Do not* turn linings right side out. Slip linings inside stockings. Turn under raw edges of stockings and linings (see fold lines on charts). Press. Blindstitch linings to stockings along folds.

Patchwork Skirt and Overalls
Pictured on pages 10-11

MATERIALS: Old patchwork quilt (see *Note, below*); thread; buttons; zipper, snaps; Vogue pattern No. 7896 (skirt) or Butterick pattern No. 3989 (coveralls), or a suitable substitute.

INSTRUCTIONS: *Note:* We recommend that you make patchwork clothing only of old or damaged quilts that are no longer usable as bed covers and not valuable as art objects or for sentimental reasons.

Following the steps in your patterns, cut and sew clothing, substituting the patchwork quilt for purchased yard goods. (Plan placement of pieces to take advantage of quilted designs.)

Reindeer Sweater
Pictured on page 11

Instructions are for Size 38; changes for Sizes 40, 42, and 44 follow in parentheses. Chest = 40½ (42½, 43½, 45½) inches.

MATERIALS: Unger Skol (1.6-ounce ball), or a suitable substitute: 14 (15, 16, 17) balls natural (MC), 2 (2, 3, 3) balls each dark green (A), and wine (B); Sizes 8 and 10 knitting needles, or size to obtain gauge given below; tapestry needle.

Abbreviations: Page 310.

Gauge: With larger needles over st st, 7 sts = 2 inches; 5 rows = 1 inch.

INSTRUCTIONS: *Note on two-color knitting:* Always twist yarn on the wrong side when working with two colors to prevent making holes in the work. Carry the color not in use loosely across the back, being careful to maintain gauge. Work motifs in duplicate st when pieces are completed.

Back: With smaller needles and MC, cast on 73 (77, 79, 83) sts.

Work in k 1, p 1 ribbing for 3½ inches. Change to larger needles and st st. Work 2 rows even. Now beg pat as follows:

Row 1 (right side): K 4 (6, 7, 1) MC, k 1 A, * k 7 MC, k 1 A. Rep from * across, ending with k 4 (6, 7, 1) MC.

Rows 2, 4, 6: With MC, p.

Rows 3 and 5: With MC, k.

Row 7: K 8 (2, 3, 5) MC, k 1 A, * k 7 MC, k 1 A. Rep from * across, ending with k 8 (2, 3, 5) MC.

Rows 8, 10, 12: With MC, p.

Rows 9 and 11: With MC, k.

Rep Rows 1-12 for pat. Work even until work measures approximately 16-16½ inches, or desired length to underarm, ending with a p row. Place a marker at each end for armholes.

Yoke pat: Row 1 (right side): K 1 MC, * k 1 A, k 1 MC. Rep from * across.

Row 2: P 2 MC, p 1 A, * p 1 MC, p 1 A. Rep from * across, ending with p 2 MC. Fasten off A. With MC only, work 28 rows even in st st. (*Note:* Add duplicate st reindeer and tree to this MC panel later.)

continued

* Rep Rows 1 and 2 of yoke pat, work 2 rows even with MC. Rep from * until armhole measures 9½ (10, 10, 10½) inches, measuring from beg of yoke.

Shoulder shaping: With MC only, cast off 23 (24, 25, 26) sts, work next 27 (29, 29, 31) sts and sl to holder for back of neck; cast off rem 23 (24, 25, 26) sts.

Front: Work same as for Back until work to shoulder is 16 rows less than back.

Neck shaping: Keeping to pat, work 29 (30, 31, 32) sts, sl rem sts to holder. Working left side only,

dec 1 st at neck edge every row 4 times, then every other row twice— 23 (24, 25, 26) sts.

Work to shoulder as for Back. Cast off. Leaving center 15 (17, 17, 19) sts on holder, sl rem 29 (30, 31, 32) sts onto needle.

Attach yarn at neck edge; work to correspond to other side, reversing shaping.

Neckband: Sew left shoulder seam. With MC, smaller needles, and right side facing, pick up 75 (79, 79, 83) sts around neck, including sts on holders. Beg p 1, k 1 and work ribbing for 2¼ inches. Cast off loosely in ribbing. For turtleneck,

work same as above for 6 (6, 6½, 6½) inches.

Sew right shoulder seam and weave neckband or turtleneck seam. For crew neckband, fold in half to inside and sew loosely in place.

Sleeves: With larger needles, MC, and right side facing, pick up 65 (69, 69, 73) sts along armhole edge from marker to marker. Beg with a p row and work st st for 3 rows even. Dec 1 st each end of next row—63 (67, 67, 71) sts. Work 1 row even. Now beg pat as follows:

Row 1: With MC, k 3 (1, 1, 3), k 1 A, * k 7 MC, k 1 A. Rep from * across, ending with k 3 (1, 1, 3).

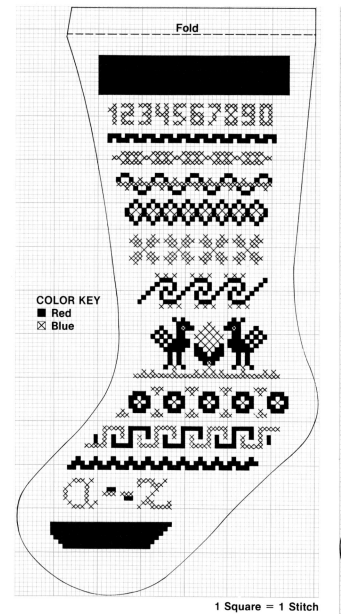

COLOR KEY
■ Red
⊠ Blue

1 Square = 1 Stitch

COLOR KEY
⊠ Green
■ Red
· Yellow
⊽ Brown

1 Square = 1 Stitch

Row 2: With MC, p.

Row 3: With MC, k and dec 1 st each end—61 (65, 65, 69) sts.

Row 4 and 6: Rep Row 2.

Row 5: With MC, k.

Row 7: K 6 (4, 4, 6) MC, k 1 A, * k 7 MC, k 1 A. Rep from * across, ending with k 6 (4, 4, 6) MC.

Continue in pat established, dec 1 st each end every 10th row 6 (7, 7, 7) times, every 8th row 1 (1, 1, 2) time, adjusting pat for decs—47 (49, 49, 51) sts. Work even until 18½ inches from beg, or 3 inches less than desired length, ending on wrong side.

Change to smaller needles and MC. *Row 1:* K across, dec 12 sts evenly spaced across—35 (37, 37, 39) sts. Work k 1, p 1 ribbing for 3 in. Cast off loosely in ribbing.

Duplicate stitch pat: Mark center st of front and back in the 3rd row of MC panel; working from C to D, work tree in duplicate sts (see diagram, *below*) on center of front and back. Beg in 4th row of MC panel and, working from A to B, work left reindeer in duplicate sts on front and back. Reverse pat; work right reindeer in duplicate sts on front and back.

COLOR KEY: O = A   X = B

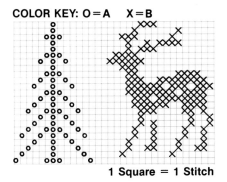

1 Square = 1 Stitch

Finishing: Weave in all ends. Sew undersleeve and side seams. Block lightly to measurements.

Corn Shuck Crèche
Pictured on page 12

MATERIALS: Red, blue, gold, green, and natural-color corn shucks (use fabric dyes for coloring); glycerin (for brittle shucks); cotton balls; 1-inch-diameter foam balls for heads; wire; excelsior (for the crib); 3/16-inch-thick balsa wood (crib and bench); T-pins; white glue; yarn or cornsilk (hair); grapevine; ¼x13x19 inches of plywood (stable); nails.

INSTRUCTIONS: *Note:* Because of their florist's wire armatures, these dolls are not suitable for young children.

Keep corn shucks damp while working with them so they will be less apt to break: Soak in warm water for a few minutes, adding 1 or 2 drops of glycerin if shucks are thick or brittle. Before shucks are dry, bend torsos, arms, and heads into desired positions.

For heads, wrap thread around middle of a 3-inch-wide shuck; place foam ball in center of shuck (thread will be at top of head). Fold shuck over ball; wrap thread around base of ball to form neck. Slide a 6-inch-long wire through neck and head.

For arms, cut a wire 11 inches long for Mary, 11½ inches for Joseph. Bend ends inward ¾ inch to form loops (hands). Thread a ¾-inch-wide strip of shuck through each hand. Wrap strip around loops and to middle of wire, adding strips as necessary. Wrap sewing thread around hands and arms to secure shucks. Remove thread when shucks are dry.

For puffed sleeves, gather 6-inch-wide shucks around each wrist, extending shucks over hand; wrap shucks tightly at wrist using sewing thread. Pull shuck back over arm, shaping puffed sleeve; wrap near center of wire (shoulders). Push head wire through center of arms and wrap.

To form Mary's torso, place two cotton balls side by side in center of a vertically positioned shuck. Fold long sides toward center; fold shuck in half across width. Wrap thread around bottom to form waist. Position this section on front of neck wire ½ inch below neck. Wrap thread over shoulder and around waist to secure.

For Mary's dress bodice, center a 3-inch-wide strip of husk on each shoulder; cross shucks over the bust in front and back, gathering at waist. Secure shucks at waist with thread. Wrap shucks below waist tight to heads; wire; excelsior (for the crib); the wire with thread. Repeat with two more shucks, pleating them across shoulders.

For Joseph's chest, fold sides of a wide husk to the center; pad center with folded paper towel. Wrap string around padding, and again around body of figure to attach padded chest to wire extending from neck. Pad in front and back.

To make Joseph's robe, cut a 15-inch square of heavy paper and wrap it into a cylindrical shape with a 1- to 2-inch-diameter opening at the top; the robe should flare only slightly toward the bottom. Tape edges securely. Trim hemline so figure will stand when assembled.

For lower part of robe, cover half of the cylinder with shucks; overlap them slightly and pin to base of paper. Trim shucks toward the top so they lie flat against cone. Wrap shucks with thread to prevent buckling as they dry. For upper (top) "skirt," gather wide shucks around top of cylinder, using thread; wrap shucks in place until dry.

Insert the chest through opening in cylinder; secure by pushing a long needle through the "skirt" and chest to the other side of "skirt." Glue waist section inside cylinder; remove needle when glue is dry.

To make Joseph's beard, sew a loop through the chin area. Lay a bit of combed natural-color yarn or cornsilk through the loop with bulk of yarn or silk up over the head. Pull the loop taut; fold "hair" back over chin and neck to form beard. Trim into desired shape. Repeat this procedure along forehead for hair.

For flowing robes and drapery around heads, fold damp shucks and arrange them on figures. Pin or tie shucks in place until dry.

For Mary, make figure following procedure above, except make skirt as follows: Omit the cylinder and substitute shucks instead. Gather and lay four shucks (two in front, two in back) around figure's waist so narrow edge is at waist and wide edge goes upward over her head. Wrap string at waist to secure, then flip shucks down; pin in place to form skirt. Using T-pins, secure Mary in a sitting position until dry.

continued

For infant's blanket, drape shucks over edge of a small box until dry.

To make the infant, follow the same steps as for the other figures, except use a ½-inch-diameter foam ball for the head and 3½ inches of wire for arms.

For clothing, cut two 4x6-inch pieces of shuck; taper one 4-inch side of each to 2 inches at top. Gather top of shuck and lay it at the neck with long end up over head. Wrap at neck.

Bring shucks down over body; pin in place to form dress. Fold damp shuck around Baby as a hooded bunting; tie until dry.

For Mary's bench, cut and glue balsa wood into a 2x5-inch seat with 2-inch-tall legs.

For crib, cut two balsa pieces 2¾x6 inches, and four legs, each ⅜x4 inches; glue together.

For stable, nail ¾-inch-thick, mature (not green) grapevine lengths along back and sides of a 13x19-inch plywood floor. Nail wall and roof support beams to floor. With vertical lengths of ½-inch-thick grapevine, build walls and roof. Nail and glue ¼-inch-thick grapevine lengths inside stable for manger.

Tablecloth Edging
Pictured on page 12

MATERIALS: Size 5 DMC pearl cotton (27.3-yard skeins) in color of your choice: one skein for 8½ scallops; Size 7 steel crochet hook, or size to obtain gauge below.

Abbreviations: Page 310.

Gauge: 2 blocks = ¾ inch; 7 rows = 2 inches; 1 scallop = 1⅛x1⅛ inches.

INSTRUCTIONS: The finished edging is approximately 2 inches wide and is worked in a four-row repeat pattern. Make a test swatch of the edging first, then divide the desired finished measurement by the edging width to determine the number of pattern repeats. Instructions for making a corner follow the repeat pattern.

Ch 21. *Row 1:* Dc in 8th ch from hook, ch 2, sk 2 ch, dc in each of next 4 ch, ch 2, sk 2 ch, dc in next ch, ch 4, join with sl st to last ch; ch 2, turn.

Row 2: 7 dc in ch-4 lp, ch 2, sk dc and ch-2 sp, dc in next dc, ch 2, sk 2 dc, dc in next dc, ch 2, dc in next dc, ch 2, sk 2 ch, dc in next ch; ch 5, turn.

Row 3: **Dc in next dc, ch 2, dc in next dc, 2 dc in ch-2 sp, dc in next dc—block (bl) made;** ch 2, dc in next sp, ch 1, sk next dc, (dc in next dc, ch 1) 6 times; dc in top of ch-2; ch 3, turn.

Row 4: Sc in first ch-1 lp, ch 3 (sc in next lp, ch 3) 5 times; sc in next lp, sl st in top of next dc, ch 2, bl, ch 2, sk 2 dc, dc in next dc, bl, ch 2, sk 2 ch, dc in next ch; ch 5, turn.

Row 5: **Scallop pat:** Dc in next dc, ch 2, sk 2 dc, dc in next dc, bl, ch 2, sk 2 dc, dc in last st, ch 4, sc in first ch-3 lp; ch 2, turn.

Row 6: **Rep Row 2.**

Row 7: **Rep Row 3, except sc in 2nd ch-3 lp before final ch-3; turn.**

Row 8: **Rep Row 4.**

Rep Rows 5-8 (scallop pat) until desired length is reached, breaking off thread after sl st.

To work edging around a corner, end with Row 8; ch 1, turn. *Corner row 1:* Sl st in first dc and in next 2 ch, sc in next dc, ch 2, sk 2 dc, hdc in next dc, bl, ch 2, sk 2 dc, dc in next dc, ch 4, sc in first ch-3 lp; ch 2, turn.

Corner row 2: Work same as for Row 2 until 2nd ch-2 has been completed; then sk 2 dc, hdc in next hdc, 2 sc in next sp, sc in next sc, 2 sc in next sp, sc in last st; ch 1, turn.

Corner row 3: Sl st in first 6 sc, sl st in next hdc, 2 sl st in next sp, sl st in next st, sc in next sp, ch 2 sk first dc of cluster, (dc in next dc, ch 1) 6 times; dc in top of ch-2, sc in next lp; ch 3, turn.

Corner row 4: Beg same as for Row 4, working to and including sl st in next dc, ch 4, turn, sc in first ch-3 lp; ch 2, turn.

Corner row 5: 7 dc in ch-4 lp, sk 1 dc, dc in next dc, ch 2, sk 2 sts, (dc in next st, ch 2, sk 2 sts) twice; dc in last st, ch 5, turn.

Next corner row: Rep Row 7, above. Corner has now been turned; continue in scallop pat.

Press and block edging; sew to fabric edge.

Grapevine Wreath
Pictured on page 16

MATERIALS: Several 12- to 20-foot lengths of mature (not green) grapevine; wire or cord; garden clippers.

INSTRUCTIONS: Remove any strands of loose bark along vine; clip side branches away, leaving small tendrils intact. Twine the vines into a wreath shape one at a time, adding vines until the wreath is full. Fasten with wire where necessary to hold shape.

Decorate with crepe paper flowers (how-to instructions, *page 21*) and ribbons.

Christmas Tea Towels
Pictured on page 17

MATERIALS: Purchased kitchen towels; red and green fabric scraps; fabric glue; thread; paper.

INSTRUCTIONS: Use a cookie cutter to make a pattern or enlarge tree pattern (F), *page 20,* onto paper; cut out.

Pin pattern to fabric scraps; cut trees from fabric. Glue appliqués on towel borders with fabric glue. Secure with machine satin stitching along edges.

Cutting Boards
Pictured on page 17

MATERIALS: 1-inch-thick pine boards; medium-fine sandpaper; lightweight cardboard.

INSTRUCTIONS: Enlarge the large- or medium-size duck or pig pattern, *page 20,* onto cardboard. Draw around patterns on pine and cut out on jigsaw; sand.

Kerchiefed Doll
Pictured on page 17

MATERIALS: ⅓ yard of muslin; scrap of brown broadcloth; ⅓ yard of gray pindot fabric; scrap of rose and gray floral print fabric; one small button; thread; ½ ounce of tan yarn; pink and dark brown embroidery floss; polyester fiberfill.

INSTRUCTIONS: Enlarge patterns, *below*. Make additional patterns on tissue paper as follows: 15½x6½ inches (apron skirt), 3x2¼ inches (apron bib), 15½x1⅛ inches (apron sash, straps), 6½x1⅛ inches (dress collar), 1¼x1¼ inches (apron pocket), 6x6 inches (head scarf), and 4⅝x¾ inches (hair guide). (*Note:* All pattern pieces include ¼-inch seam allowances.)

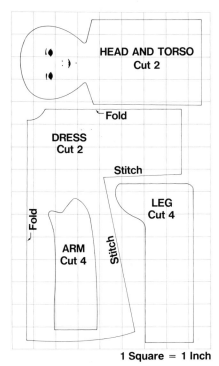

1 Square = 1 Inch

Cut two torsos, four arms, and all apron pieces (except pocket) from muslin. Cut two dress pieces (on the fold of the fabric) and one collar from gray pindot. Cut four legs from brown broadcloth. Cut head scarf and apron pocket from rose and gray floral scrap. (*Note:* Scarf and apron pieces are used with raw edges exposed.)

Trace facial features onto head of doll. Place corresponding pieces of torso, arms, and legs together. Stitch, leaving tops of arms and legs, bottom of torso, and seam at shoulder of torso open. Clip curves, turn, and press. Stuff arms, body, and legs. Insert arms and legs into openings of torso and stitch.

Embroider features with two strands of floss, using brown for eyes and brows, and pink for nose, mouth, and chin. Rub pink powder or colored pencil into cheek.

Cut a piece of fabric for hair guide that closely matches color of yarn for hair. Wind yarn around 12-inch piece of cardboard until hank is 2½ to 3 inches thick. Cut yarn at each end. Center strands of yarn crosswise along fabric strip and distribute strands evenly along its length. Sew along center of fabric strip; fold ends of strip under and stitch along center back of head. For bangs, bring several strands of hair to front of head and tack in place; trim.

Hem short sides and one long side of collar. With wrong side of dress and right side of collar together, sew collar to dress. Clip curves; turn collar through neck opening to front. Sew arm and side seam of dress, right sides facing. Turn; press; hem bottom edge and sleeves.

Hem bottom and sides of apron skirt. Gather top edge, and pin to sash along center 8 inches. (Remainder of sash is used for straps.) Stitch apron skirt to sash. Press seam up, then press remaining raw edge up ¼ inch. Fold opposite raw edge under along entire length. Fold sash in half lengthwise, matching folded edges; topstitch along folds to conceal all raw edges.

Hem top and sides of bib; stitch to apron skirt. Sew pocket in place.

Put dress on doll; secure it at neckline by tying a strip of fabric or yarn directly over collar seam with collar up; knot securely. Tack points of collar in place.

Put apron over dress and secure at back sash with small button tacked through overlapped sash. Criss-cross straps over shoulders; tack in place to wrong side of top edge of apron bib. Fold head scarf in half diagonally and secure in place.

Tabletop Trees
Pictured on page 18

MATERIALS: 1-inch-thick pine boards; medium-fine sandpaper; fabric dyes; lightweight cardboard.

INSTRUCTIONS: Enlarge patterns, *page 20*, onto cardboard.

For smaller tree, draw around pattern on pine and cut out on jigsaw. For larger tree, glue two boards together to make a thicker tree. Trace pattern; cut out on jigsaw. Sand. Dye trees in fabric dye as for dyed tree ornaments (*page 20*).

Wooden Swallows
Pictured on pages 18-19

MATERIALS: ½-inch-thick pine board; ten ¾x2x2-inch pine blocks; five ¼x24-inch dowels; medium-fine sandpaper; red and blue fabric dyes; waxed paper; white glue; lightweight cardboard.

INSTRUCTIONS: Enlarge bird pattern B, *page 20*, onto cardboard; cut out. Draw 10 birds on pine; cut them out with a jigsaw. Sand edges.

Drill holes to fit dowels 1 inch deep into undersides of birds and ¾ inch deep into centers of pine blocks. From dowels, cut two 5-, 7-, 8-, 10-, and 12-inch lengths. Insert dowels in birds and blocks.

Dye birds blue and red; see cookie cutter ornament instructions, *page 20*, for dyeing procedure.

Crocheted Place Mats
Pictured on page 19

MATERIALS: Scraps of muslin and print fabrics; Size 15 wooden crochet hook, or size to obtain gauge below.

Abbreviations: Page 310.
Gauge: 9 sc = 4 inches.

INSTRUCTIONS: Finished size is approximately 12x18 inches.

Preshrink all fabrics and tear them into ¾- to 1-inch-wide strips. Pull raveled threads from strips; press if desired. Roll strips into balls.

To begin, ch 28. *Row 1:* Sc in 2nd ch from hook and in each ch across; ch 1, turn.

Row 2: Sc in 2nd sc from hook and in each sc across.

Rep Row 2 until work measures 18 inches, changing prints and muslin randomly. Fasten off.

CHRISTMAS—
A CELEBRATION
OF AMERICAN
CRAFTS

Dolls and Toys to Treasure

Gifting children with home-spun playthings is one of the special pleasures of Christmas. Not only do they inspire squeals of delight on Christmas morning, but handmade toys and dolls are often among a child's most treasured possessions. When you craft a toy by hand, you're creating a family heirloom that will be enjoyed by generations of youngsters.

This friendly family of country-style dolls is sure to bring smiles to the faces of young and old alike. To stitch these jolly dolls, all you need is a collection of homespun fabrics like calicos, shirtings, and printed wools, plus a few decorative buttons and trims. Cut the faces, bodies, and hands from flesh-colored fabric. Use unspun wool or yarn for hair and man's moustache. Paint facial details with acrylics.

Instructions for the dolls and toys in this section begin on page 34.

Kentucky is an area rich in grass-roots crafts traditions. It is also home to many dedicated crafts people—like Jane DeTeresa, *opposite,* a designer noted for her soft-sculpture dolls. As a special holiday gift, Jane has created a stylized version of Mrs. Claus, *foreground,* for you to duplicate.

Come Christmas morning, youngsters and oldsters alike will find the Kentucky rag doll and her doll chest, *above,* hard to resist. This old-fashioned doll is dressed in Christmasy colors and stitched with linen, cotton, and calico. Build the charming chest with particleboard and hardwood, then finish with dollhouse wallpapers.

Engaging and easy to make, the nut-head dolls, *right,* are updates of the traditional version. The heads are painted pecans. Wire armatures wrapped with batting and nylon stockings form the bodies. Use the six- and nine-inch-tall dolls as stocking stuffers for older children and adults or as delightful decorations for a festive holiday table.

31

Dolls and Toys to Treasure

In times gone by, handcrafted toys were made from simple materials. Bits of fabric and timeworn household linens were saved and transformed into whimsical treasures to enchant the children when Christmas came. It's in that spirit that weaver Minnie Yancey, *below*, creates handwoven clothing and rugs.

You don't have to be a weaver to work with the richly textured fabrics of the barnyard animals shown here. Thrifty dime-store rugs are the basis for the duck and stocking. The cats are stitched from tea towels, the horse and goat are created from table runners, and the goose and rocking horse are worked from fabric scraps or prequilted patchwork fabric.

Family Dolls

Pictured on pages 28-29

MATERIALS: Flesh-tone fabric (bodies); wool and calico scraps (clothing); unspun wool or mohair (hair); buttons, lace, ribbons, leather scraps; acrylic paints; paintbrush; fabric glue; fiberfill; thread.

INSTRUCTIONS: Enlarge patterns, *right* and *opposite*. For bodies, trace outlines of patterns. Sketch faces. For dresses, cut along necklines on main patterns; extend hemlines to 1 inch below boot tops.

For scarves (mother and daughters), cut triangles 7½x7½x10 inches. Cut 2½x12-inch scarves for father and son. Cut 1½x6-inch father's cuffs, 1¼x3¾-inch son's cuffs. Son's pants are 6x6 inches. Patterns include ¼-inch seam margins.

For each doll, cut two bodies and four arms. From wools and calicos, cut fronts and backs for shirts, dresses, sleeves, cuffs, pants, boots, and pig. Cut one apron and one scarf.

Sew aprons to dress fronts; trim with lace. Pin dress, shirt, and boot fronts to body fronts. Pin dress, shirt, and boot backs to body backs. Pin sleeve fronts and backs to arm fronts and backs. Sew body fronts and backs together; leave openings. Repeat for arms. Turn and stuff.

Note: For overhang on dress hem do not sew between boot tops and skirt bottom. Tuck dresses up; sew around boots. See detail on pattern.

Hem dress; trim lower edge with lace. Add sleeve cuffs, lace trims, shirt buttons, and shoelace detail. Sew finger and boot divisions.

For hair, sew wool or yarn along parts on heads; style hair as desired. Using acrylics, paint faces.

Mrs. Claus Doll

Pictured on page 30

MATERIALS: ⅛ yard *each* muslin (face, hands, apron), red and green print (bodice, arms, skirt base), and blue cotton (boots); ¼ yard *each* green velveteen (skirt) and red print (hat); string (hair); 1 yard narrow red ribbon; thread.

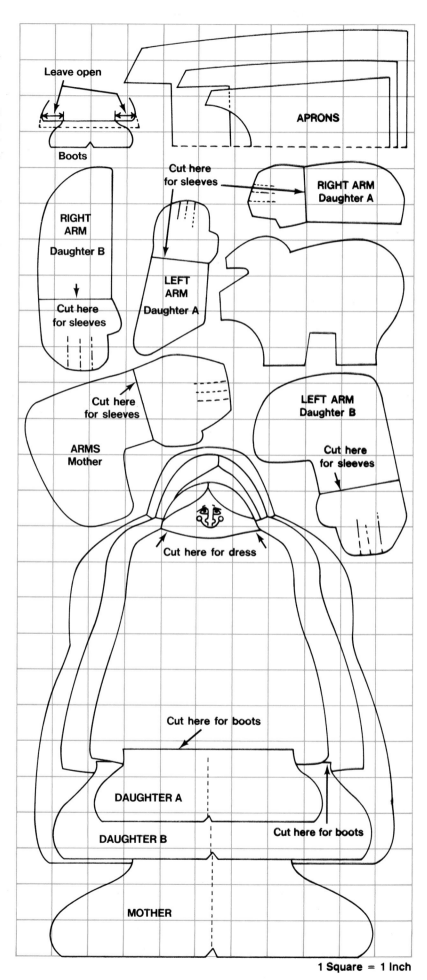

Leave open

Boots

APRONS

Cut here for sleeves

RIGHT ARM
Daughter A

RIGHT ARM
Daughter B

Cut here for sleeves

LEFT ARM
Daughter A

LEFT ARM
Daughter B

Cut here for sleeves

Cut here for sleeves

ARMS
Mother

Cut here for dress

Cut here for boots

DAUGHTER A

DAUGHTER B

Cut here for boots

MOTHER

1 Square = 1 Inch

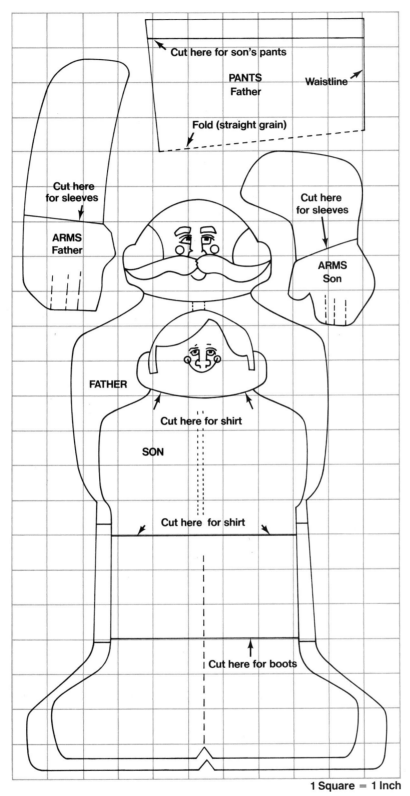

Cut here for son's pants

PANTS
Father

Waistline

Fold (straight grain)

Cut here
for sleeves

ARMS
Father

Cut here
for sleeves

ARMS
Son

FATHER

Cut here for shirt

SON

Cut here for shirt

Cut here for boots

1 Square = 1 Inch

For lower body, hem long sides and one short side of apron. Fold under raw edges of ties, fold ties in half lengthwise, then topstitch halves together. Place apron (raw edge at top) on skirt front center. Topstitch, tucking ties under apron at waist.

Sew bodice front and back to skirt front and back. Sew doll front to back, leaving bottom open. Turn; stuff half of doll firmly.

With right sides facing, sew half of skirt base to skirt front. Stuff rest of doll; sew skirt closed.

Sew hands to arms. Sew arm fronts to backs, leaving openings. Sew legs; leave tops open. Turn. Stuff, then blindstitch openings. Tack legs to skirt base. Tie shoelaces with ribbon. Sew fingers on hands; sew arms to shoulders at Xs.

Cut forty 25-inch pieces of string (hair); fasten at outer edges of head (see pattern). Braid string; fashion into bun at base of neck.

With right sides facing, sew hat circles; leave an opening. Turn; gather 1 inch from outer edge; sew hat to head.

continued

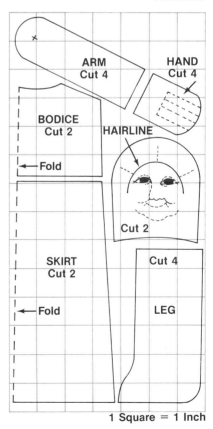

ARM
Cut 4

HAND
Cut 4

BODICE
Cut 2

HAIRLINE

Fold

SKIRT
Cut 2

Cut 2

Cut 4

Fold

LEG

1 Square = 1 Inch

INSTRUCTIONS: Enlarge patterns, *right* (patterns include ¼-inch seam margins). Cut pieces, except do not cut head until face is complete. Transfer face to head; sew features using black thread.

Cut 4⅞-inch-diameter circle (skirt base). Cut two 8-inch-diameter circles (hat). Cut a 3½x6-inch apron and two 1¼x14-inch ties. Sew head front to bodice front and head back to bodice back. Clip corners at neck.

Kentucky Rag Doll
Pictured on page 31

MATERIALS: ½ yard *each* linen (body) and green calico (dress); ⅓ yard red calico (pinafore); ¼ yard *each* light red calico (pinafore ruffles) and green striped fabric (bonnet); 4x16 inches velvet (boots); 8x24 inches muslin (pantaloons); 16 inches *each* lace trim and elastic; snaps; thread; green checked bias tape (dress); mohair (hair); green, pink, tan, brown embroidery floss; pink felt marker; ½ yard ribbon.

INSTRUCTIONS: Enlarge patterns, *right;* cut pieces. Also cut four 2¾x6-inch muslin legs, an 8½x28-inch pinafore, and a 1½x24-inch bonnet. (Patterns include ¼-inch seam margins.) Transfer face to muslin; embroider with two strands floss. Use tan stem stitches for nose, eye outline, and eyebrows; use pink satin stitches for lips. For eyes, use brown buttonhole stitches (iris) and green French knots (pupils).

Sew arms; leave tops open. Turn; stuff; blindstitch openings. Stitch finger divisions. Sew boots to bottoms of legs. (Reverse directions of feet.) Sew leg sections together; leave tops open. Turn. Stuff; blindstitch openings.

Sew center seam on head back. Sew head back to body back at neck (right sides facing). Sew face to body front. Sew arms to body front; position thumbs inward. Sew front to back; leave bottom open. Turn. Stuff; sew closed. Sew legs to doll.

For hair, sew 24-inch strands of mohair to center part. Braid.

For pantaloons, hem lower edges; trim with lace. Sew center front and back seams; sew inseams. Turn. Stitch waistband casing. Insert 10 inches of elastic; sew ends together.

For dress, sew front to back at shoulders. Sew center back seam; leave open top 3 inches. Turn under seam margin on opening; press. Gather neckline; bind with 10 inches of bias tape. Add snap.

Sew casing in sleeve. Insert 3 inches of elastic; sew elastic ends to seam edges. Sew sleeves into armholes; sew side seams. Hem dress.

For pinafore, sew bodice front to

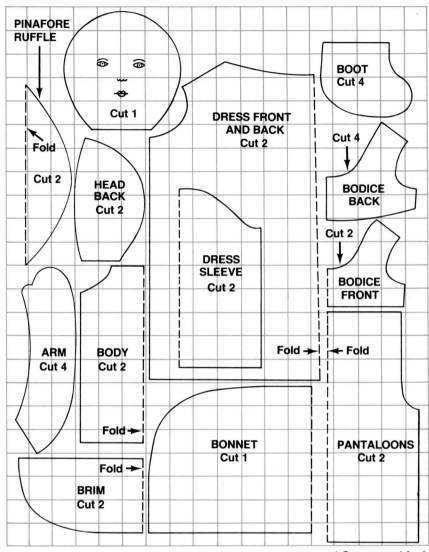

PINAFORE RUFFLE

Cut 1

Fold

Cut 2

HEAD BACK Cut 2

DRESS FRONT AND BACK Cut 2

BOOT Cut 4

Cut 4

BODICE BACK

Cut 2

DRESS SLEEVE Cut 2

BODICE FRONT

ARM Cut 4

BODY Cut 2

Fold → ← Fold

Fold →

Fold →

BRIM Cut 2

BONNET Cut 1

PANTALOONS Cut 2

1 Square = 1 Inch

back at shoulders. Repeat for lining.

Fold ruffles in half lengthwise (wrong sides facing); gather. Sew curved edges to armholes. Sew lining to bodice at neck. Turn. Sew sides of bodice and lining; sew lining to ruffle inside armholes.

Gather and stitch one long edge of pinafore skirt to bodice. Sew lining at waist. Hem remaining edges; sew snap to bodice back.

For bonnet, press under ¼ inch on straight edges of brim. With right sides facing, sew brims on curved edge; turn. Gather bonnet along straight edge. Sew right side of brim to wrong side of gathered edge. Topstitch brim edge over seam.

Gather curved edge of bonnet to 5 inches. Center on tie, then bind with tie, folding under raw edges.

Doll Chest
Pictured on page 31

MATERIALS: 48x48-inch piece of ½-inch particleboard; 12x18-inch piece of ⅛-inch hardboard; 8 feet of 1/16x½-inch trim; eight ½-inch-diameter drawer pulls; 5½-inch-diameter shaving mirror; dollhouse wallpapers; primer paint; off-white acrylic paint; acrylic gloss medium (available in art stores); paintbrushes; sandpaper; brads.

INSTRUCTIONS: Using pattern, *opposite,* cut particleboard chest pieces, except cut drawer bottoms from hardboard. Miter corners of drawer fronts, backs, and sides; cut rabbets on lower edges for drawer bottoms. Cut scallops on chest sides and around mirror; cut hole in chest back for mirror.

Glue and nail shelves between side panels. Nail small drawer divider in place; nail chest back to chest. Assemble drawers, fitting bottoms into rabbets. Nail and glue trim to chest front, mitering corners. Sand; coat with primer. Paint off-white.

With glue, cover chest with dollhouse wallpaper. When dry, sand excess paper edges. Coat outer surfaces with gloss medium. Attach drawer pulls, brackets, and mirror.

Nut-Head Dolls
Pictured on page 31

MATERIALS: Pecans; wire; batting; nylon stockings; scraps of fabric, lace, felt, and glove leather; thread; acrylic paints; clear acrylic spray; fine paintbrushes; white glue; plastic foam block; toothpicks.

INSTRUCTIONS: *Note: Wire armatures make these dolls unsuitable for young children.*

For the head, grip the nut in a wrench or vise; drill a hole in one end. Set heads on toothpicks; stand in foam block. Paint faces using acrylics. Coat with clear acrylic.

For body armatures, cut wire twice the height of doll. (Adults are 9 inches; boy is 6 inches.) Cut 6 inches of wire for arms and hands.

Bend longer wire in half (folded end will be inserted into head). Fold 1 inch of each end of wire at right angle; fold back again ½ inch (foot).

For the arms, wrap the second wire twice around body 2 inches below the neck. Wrap the joint with sewing thread to secure. Fold wire ends under for hands.

Cut quilt batting into 1-inch-wide strips; wrap the wires tightly, but do not wrap the neck. Secure batting with thread.

Drip glue into hole in head; insert body wire. Dry. Carefully wrap body with 1-inch-wide strips of stocking; sew in place.

Dress dolls in clothing made from fabric scraps (see photograph for ideas). Use ribbons, seed pearls, or small beads for trims; for shoes, use fingertips of leather gloves.

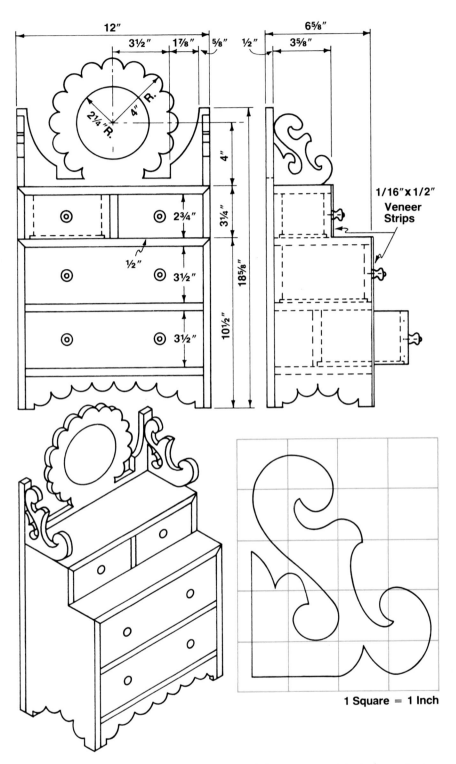

1 Square = 1 Inch

Rug Stocking and Duck
Pictured on pages 32-33

MATERIALS: Rag rugs; ¾ yard of denim; heavy duty sewing thread.

INSTRUCTIONS: On tissue paper, draw a stocking pattern to fit your rug. Cut one each from rug and denim. Cut a 6-inch-deep denim cuff. Sew stocking front to back. Turn. Hem one edge of cuff. Sew right side of cuff to wrong side of stocking. Turn cuff over stocking.

For the woven duck, use the pattern on *page 20.* Follow the instructions for the horse and goat, *page 38.*
continued

Country Cat
Pictured on page 32

MATERIALS: 15x18-inch towel; fiberfill; buttons (eyes); black embroidery floss; needle.

INSTRUCTIONS: Enlarge the pattern, *below*. Transfer outline to folded towel; stitch, leaving bottom open. Trim excess fabric, turn, stuff, and sew opening closed. Sew buttons at Xs for eyes; embroider nose and whiskers using floss.

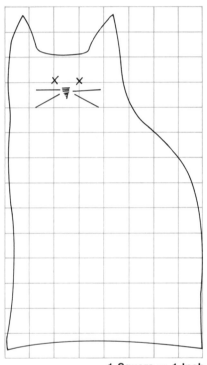

1 Square = 1 Inch

Horse and Goat
Pictured on page 32

MATERIALS: Handwoven napkins, place mats, or table runner; sewing thread to match fabric; polyester fiberfill.

INSTRUCTIONS: Enlarge the patterns, *right* and *far right*, adding ½-inch seam allowances all around each pattern piece. (Omit the rocker and instructions for the gusset on the horse.) Fold fabric in half, right sides together. Pin pattern pieces to doubled fabric. Stitch; leave openings for turning. Trim excess fabric; clip curves. Turn, stuff, sew closed. Stitch the horse's ears to the body.

Goose
Pictured on page 32

MATERIALS: ¾ yard brown velveteen (or pieced patchwork fabric); fiberfill; thread.

INSTRUCTIONS: Enlarge pattern, *below*. Add ½-inch seam allowances all around; cut pieces from fabric.

With right sides facing, sew wings together; leave open between Xs. Turn; blindstitch openings. Tack wings to body between Xs.

For legs, sew front seam on each leg (A to B). Sew legs to bottoms of feet, ending at D. Sew back seams (C to D). Turn, stuff, and attach to main body between Xs.

Sew body together; leave open between E and F. Stitch underside in place between E and F (legs tucked inside), leaving an opening for turning. Turn, stuff, and stitch closed.

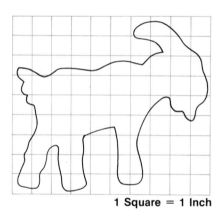

1 Square = 1 Inch

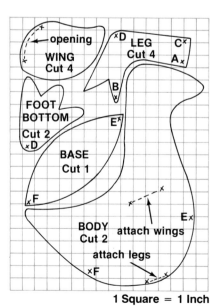

1 Square = 1 Inch

Rocking Horse
Pictured on page 33

MATERIALS: ½ yard of red, pink, and purple pieced fabric; small skein of purple yarn; 10x18-inch piece of ½-inch pine; brads; red fabric dye; white glue; fiberfill.

INSTRUCTIONS: Enlarge pattern, *below.* For rockers, cut two arcs from pine; also cut two 1¼x2-inch spacers. Nail spacers between rockers (horizontally) about 4 inches from ends. Dye rockers red (see cookie cutter ornament instructions on *page 20* for dyeing procedure).

For horse, cut 65 six-inch lengths of yarn for mane and 20 eight-inch lengths of yarn for tail.

Arranging patterns to take advantage of fabric design and adding ½-inch seam allowances, cut one horse and two ears from a *double* layer of pieced fabric; cut a gusset for under-

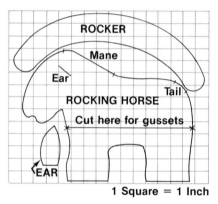

1 Square = 1 Inch

side (see area on pattern below Xs) from pieced fabric or yardage.

Sew mane and tail onto right side of one horse, fastening ends ½ inch from the raw edge. With right sides facing, sew upper halves of horse front and back between Xs. Turn.

Pin right side of gusset (inside leg) to right side of horse. Sew leg seams (around legs to Xs), leaving long edge of gusset open. Clip curves; turn legs right side out. Stuff horse firmly and stitch closed.

Stitch ear fronts to backs; leave an opening for turning. Turn, baste a small pleat at the base of each ear; tack ears to horse.

Secure horse to rockers with thread; slide glue between fabric and wood. Dry; remove threads.

BELOVED
CHRISTMAS
TRADITIONS

*Christmas customs in America are many
and varied. Every family celebrates
in their own way. Yet all who treasure
the traditions of Christmas
have a special appreciation for beautiful
handmade trims and delicious holiday
foods. Here are pages filled with treasures
inspired by the needlework
of America's past and festive dishes from
days gone by. Many of these projects
and recipes are lavish holiday specialties,
while others are quick and easy, yet
elegant. All are gifts, trims, and dishes
you'll be proud to make and enjoy
year after year.*

BELOVED CHRISTMAS TRADITIONS

A Season for Old-Fashioned Fancywork

Memories of holidays long ago will always hold a special place in our hearts. To help you recall those earlier times, here is a treasure trove of beautifully old-fashioned ornaments, lovely wreaths, and captivating gifts to make for those you love. Some of the projects are stitched with yesteryear's lace and linens, while others are based on timeless antique designs.

Elegant and enchanting is the mood and manner of this old-fashioned Christmas scene. A shower of crocheted snowflakes, worked in two different sizes, cascades over the tree. Each snowflake is made of two halves that are dyed, starched, and stitched together for a three-dimensional look. For the other trims, dye tiny flower baskets to match the snowflakes, and make French-inspired tuzzy-muzzies from dried flowers and paper doilies.

The graceful door wreath is made from a purchased doily that was dipped in dye and attached to a lightly stuffed base. You may use the same technique to add tinted doilies to pillow fronts.

The dolls that grace each end of the sofa are decked out in tinted muslin dresses trimmed with bits of antique laces.

Instructions begin on page 50.

42

With the lace and linens of a bygone era, why not create a keepsake stocking like the one *above?* Reminiscent of yesteryear's crazy quilts, this stocking is made from materials already on hand. (Or scour antique shops for timeworn linens.)

Laden with toys and other childish treats, the fanciful wreath, *opposite,* will appeal to all who are young at heart. The playful motifs are painted on dyed muslin, then the wreath is embellished with embroidery, appliqué, and beadwork.

44

A Season for Old-Fashioned Fancywork

Ornaments as captivating as these are sure to find a special place on your tree. The twelve Victorian-style motifs include a jolly Santa, winsome animals, treasured toys, and other trims. Combine various techniques—beadwork, embroidery, and appliqué—to create lavishly embellished trims like those on the tree, *opposite*. Or simply tint the ornaments with paint, crayons, or colored pencils. You can also use these designs to make package decorations, party favors, sweet-smelling sachets, or appliqués for children's clothing.

Gifts made by hand often grow in meaning with each passing year. What family member wouldn't love to receive this elegant lady or dashing toy soldier, *opposite?*

Fashioned in the same manner as the keepsake fabric ornaments on the previous pages, this handsome pair stands 15 inches tall when complete. Embellish the lady with pretty rosettes, silk flowers, dainty bows, and ribbon stripes. To give the soldier military flair, add colorful plumes, shiny medals, and gilded epaulets.

Our sentimental duo are ideal playthings for kids or charming sachets for adults. Simply add potpourri to the maiden and scented pine needles to the soldier.

Christmas stockings come in all shapes and sizes, but few are as distinctive as the high-buttoned shoes, *above*. To make these stunning muslin stockings, paint the designs using old-fashioned tones like antique red and soft moss green. Then, trim with polished buttons and dainty glass beads. Quilting gives added dimension, especially when worked with metallic thread.

Dyed Lace Projects
Pictured on pages 42-43

Many of the projects shown on these pages call for dyed lace. Below are the dye formulas (based on Rit dye colors) used on these projects. Test dyes on scrap material.

Desert Rose: Three parts old rose plus one part tan (*or a dash of brown*).

Evening Sand (purple): Three parts purple plus one part dark brown.

Smoky Sky (blue): One part royal blue plus one part gray.

Coral: One part scarlet plus one part tan; *or* mix one part coral, one part peach, plus a dash of brown.

Pine Green: One part aqua, one part light green, plus one part gray.

Crocheted Snowflakes
Pictured on page 42

MATERIALS: For large snowflakes: Coats & Clark Knit Cro-Sheen or Cronite Anchor thread in white; Size 7 crochet hook. For small snowflakes: J. P. Coats' No. 20 six-cord crochet cotton in white; Size 10 steel hook. For both sizes: sewing thread; starch.

Abbreviations: Page 310.

INSTRUCTIONS: *Note:* Large snowflakes are approximately 4½ inches high.

Ch 5, sl st to first to form ring.

Rnd 1: Ch 3 (counts as first dc), 11 dc in ring—12 sts.

Rnd 2: Ch 5, sc in next dc, ch 2, * dc in next dc, ch 2, sc in next dc, ch 2; rep from * 4 times, sl st last ch 2 to 3rd ch of ch-5.

Rnd 3: Ch 1, sc in same st as joining, ch 7, * sc in next dc, ch 7. Rep from * 4 times—6 lps made; end with sl st to first sc.

Rnd 4: Ch 1, in each loop around make 1 sc, 1 hdc, 7 dc, 1 hdc, 1 sc. Sl st to first sc.

Rnd 5: Ch 1, sc in same st, * sc in each of next 10 sts, ch 18, sc in next st, rep from * 4 times, sl st last ch-18 to first sc.

Rnd 6: Sl st in each of next 2 sts, ch 1, sc in next st, ch 6, skip 4, sc in next st, in next loop (loop is ch-18 of previous rnd) make 7 dc, ch 5, 7 dc, ch 5, 7 dc, ch 5, 7 dc, * skip 2 sts in next section, sc in next st, ch 6, sk 4 sts, sc in next st, in next loop make 7 dc, ch 5, 7 dc, ch 5, 7 dc, ch 5, 7 dc, rep from * 4 times. Sl st last dc to first sc. Fasten off. This makes half the snowflake. Rep for second half.

Dye two rounds for each snowflake in colors of your choice. Crochet cotton takes dye quickly and thoroughly so simply dip rounds into hot dye for a minute or two, then remove and rinse. Dry rounds; press, using hot iron.

Sew motifs tog into completed ornament by placing one motif atop another, aligning loops, and placing long lps at top and bottom. Sew pieces tog by stitching down the center (top to bottom) and around the inside of two opposite loops.

To stiffen ornaments, dissolve 2 tablespoons starch in ¼ cup cold water; add 1¾ cups boiling water. Saturate ornament; squeeze out excess starch. Lay ornament flat on a board covered with waxed paper. Stretch and pin points. When ornaments are dry, peel sides of snowflake apart and press again with hot iron to form four-sided snowflake.

Tuzzy-Muzzy Ornaments
Pictured on page 42

Make dried-flower nosegays from statice, baby's breath, yarrow, strawflowers, bachelor's buttons, and other blossoms of your choice. Trim with paper doilies and gold cord.

Dyed Baskets
Pictured on page 42

MATERIALS: Small natural-colored baskets (from variety or crafts stores); gold ribbon; paper lace edging; dried flowers; baby's breath.

INSTRUCTIONS: Dip the baskets into diluted dyes for a few minutes, then dry; do not rinse. Line the edge of each basket with gold cord or paper lace; fill with flowers.

Lace Wreath
Pictured on page 42

MATERIALS: Large lace doily with fabric center (to be cut out); foam-core board (from an art supply shop) 2 inches larger than doily; batting; muslin; tape; ribbon.

INSTRUCTIONS: Dye doily the color desired, using dye formulas, *above;* starch. Trace outline on foam-core board. Using a razor blade, cut board ¼ inch outside traced lines. Carefully cut away fabric center of doily.

Cover the board with two layers of batting and two layers of muslin (taped to the back). Using small whipstitches and fine sewing thread, appliqué lace to front of board. Embellish wreath with ribbon bow.

Lace Pillows
Pictured on page 43

MATERIALS: Lace doilies; muslin pillows; embroidery thread.

INSTRUCTIONS: Hand-appliqué dyed lace doilies to fronts of muslin pillows. Add welting made from dyed fabric, if desired. Embellish fronts with embroidery stitches.

Dolls
Pictured on page 43

MATERIALS: ⅓ yard of muslin for body (for each doll); assorted fabrics and laces for clothing; No. 5 pearl cotton in peach (or old rose), beige, and light and dark brown; sport-weight wool yarn for hair; fiberfill; embroidery needle.

INSTRUCTIONS: To duplicate the old-fashioned quality of these dolls, select subtle, natural-dyed-looking yarns and floss for hair and features, and rinse fabric and lace to be used for clothing in a dye bath to give them a coordinated tint.

Use the dye formulas, *above,* or strong tea or coffee to color fabrics and laces. You also may wish to overdye print fabrics with light backgrounds.

To begin, enlarge patterns, *below;* transfer to muslin. Embroider features before cutting out head. Work mouth in peach or old rose satin stitches, nostrils in dark brown French knots, pupils in dark brown satin stitches, irises (outer circles of eyes) in light brown satin stitches, eyebrows and lines beneath eyes in beige chain stitches, and eyelid (lash) line in dark brown chain stitches.

Cut out pattern pieces. Stitch and stuff head, arms, legs, and body. Whipstitch head to body at neck, and arms and legs to body as shown on pattern.

For hair, wind ¾ of a skein of yarn lengthwise around a 3x12-inch piece of cardboard. Remove (without clipping); machine-sew through center, making a part. (Bundle should be about 2½x12 inches.) Fold eight 6-inch pieces of yarn in half; tack to forehead at seam line for bangs. Trim at eyebrow level.

For brown-haired doll: Tack wig along center of head, using yarn to cover machine stitching. Spread loops of yarn down to base of head along sides and back; tack carefully and evenly to head with matching yarn, using a backstitch.

For "sausage curls," cut 30 strands of yarn, each 36 inches long. Bind both ends of this bundle, then twist the strands tightly until bundle begins to curl on itself. Make four or five loops of this twisted bundle; tack to side of doll's wig at cheek level, concealing raw ends under strands of the wig. Repeat curls on other side of head.

To dress dolls, make simple clothing from squares, rectangles, and strips of fabric and lace.

For example, for the sandy-haired doll, whipstitch beige print fabric to front and back of body to form dress "bodice."

For sleeves, cut beige voile 3½x7 inches; seam short ends. Turn under raw edges; gather and tack one edge to shoulder. Gather and tack other edge at elbow; border with band of 1-inch-wide lace.

For pinafore top, tack 1½-inch-wide lace across bodice; gather 2 pieces of 2¼x9-inch lace; tack over shoulder to form ruffled sleeves of pinafore.

Make slip from 7x14-inch piece of fabric, adding lace to bottom. For skirt, gather 8½x21 inches of fabric; for overskirt, gather 5x21 inches of lace. Sew both to ribbon waistband.

Finally, add ribbons and lace to the neckline and waist to conceal all seams and raw edges, and tuck a few fake flowers into the neck of the doll's pinafore.

Antique Lace Stocking
Pictured on page 44

MATERIALS: ½ yard *each* of patterned satin (stocking), pink satin (lining), and polyester fleece; crocheted and other lace edgings; doilies; embroidered sections from worn tablecloths, runners, doilies; satin and brocade ribbons; washable fabric markers; tissue paper.

INSTRUCTIONS: Make your own stocking pattern or enlarge one of the patterns in this book and cut from tissue paper. Add ½-inch seam allowances. Trace outline of one stocking onto patterned satin, using washable fabric markers.

Lay doilies, edgings, laces, and embroidered pieces onto the stocking, arranging them in a pleasing pattern. Round doilies work well for the heel and toe section. Lay ribbons and laces in horizontal bands, if desired. Select a pretty embroidered motif for a central focus. (*Note:* Leave cuff area plain, because gathered lace will cover top of stocking.)

Next, pin pieces into place, covering raw edges with borders of lace or ribbon. Sew pieces in place.

Cut a backing, two linings, and two fleece pieces. Baste fleece to front and back of stocking. With right sides facing, sew stocking front to back. Repeat for lining. Slip lining into stocking.

Press under seam allowance at top edge of lining and stocking, slipping gathered lace edging in between. Slip-stitch lining and stocking together, catching cuff as you stitch.

Attach ribbon loop for hanging.

Painted Fabric Trims
Pictured on pages 45-49

These Christmas trims are designed to be painted on muslin, embellished in a variety of ways, and then made into projects. General instructions for decorating the designs and assembling them are included below. Materials lists and specific instructions for the wreath, ornaments, stockings, and dolls follow.

MATERIALS: Unbleached muslin; fine-point, permanent brown marker; acrylic paints (or a suitable substitute) in colors of your choice; paintbrushes; embroidery floss in colors of your choice; assorted trims; quilt batting (optional).

INSTRUCTIONS: Enlarge the design you intend to make by graphing it on a grid or taking it to a photoduplication service.

To transfer the design to fabric, place the enlarged pattern beneath the muslin, allowing adequate margins all around. Using a fine-point, brown permanent marker, lightly
continued

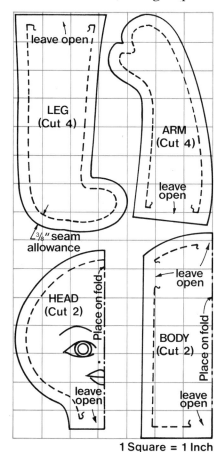

leave open

LEG
(Cut 4)

ARM
(Cut 4)

leave open

⅜" seam allowance

leave open

Place on fold

HEAD
(Cut 2)

Place on fold

BODY
(Cut 2)

leave open

leave open

1 Square = 1 Inch

trace the outlines of the design. Iron the fabric on the wrong side to heat-set the marker ink.

Embellish the designs with fabric dyes, paints, embroidery, appliqué, beading, or quilting *prior to cutting the pieces from fabric and assembling the projects.*

Fabric dye: To add background color, dip the fabric in a diluted dye-bath *before you transfer the design.* (Test the dye on a fabric scrap before dipping the entire piece.) The color should be light enough for design lines to be clearly visible. Tinted fabric may be used as it is or embellished with embroidery, beading, appliqué, or quilting.

Painting: Use high-quality acrylic or fabric paints and fine paintbrushes for small areas, larger brushes for larger areas.

To prepare paints, place a small amount on a glass plate and thin with a few drops of water until the paint is the consistency of light cream. The color should be transparent rather than opaque.

Lay the muslin atop several layers of newspaper or paper towels. Dip a brush into the paint; remove the excess by lightly dabbing the brush on a paper towel. Avoid overloading the brush with paint.

Beginning with the large design areas first, paint *up to but not over* the brown outlines. Leave a sliver of space between color areas to minimize bleeding. Allow the painted area to dry before working on adjacent areas of fabric.

When the fabric is dry, spray painted areas with a mixture of one part white vinegar to two parts water to set color and minimize fading. Dry fabric thoroughly, then gently press the wrong side with a warm iron to heat-set the paint.

Colored pencils, crayons, and fabric markers may be used to decorate fabric. Or choose fine-tip permanent marking pens that will not bleed on the fabric or cause the brown outlines to bleed. Test your pens by marking a piece of scrap fabric before beginning work on the fabric. For best results, use light pen colors since the ink often looks darker when applied to fabric.

Once the fabric is colored, heat-set it by pressing it on the wrong side with a warm iron.

Embroidery, worked by hand or machine, may be used alone or in combination with paint. Use simple stitches and a variety of cotton, silk, and metallic threads to embellish the designs. Or, use straight, zigzag, or decorative sewing machine embroidery stitches. (See photographs of projects for stitchery ideas.)

Appliqué and beading: Motifs may be enhanced with ribbon, lace, rickrack, buttons, fabric flowers and leaves (available at crafts and hobby stores), purchased appliqués, and lengths of rayon bias tape (see dolls, *page 49*).

Or accent design elements with purchased beads (see ornaments, *page 47*). To outline with beads, first thread them onto a single strand of quilting thread. With a second needle threaded with ecru, tack the strand between the already-strung beads along the design outline.

Quilting: Once decorated, the wreath, ornaments, stockings, and dolls may be quilted. Sandwich a layer of quilt batting between the decorated fabric and a lightweight backing fabric; machine- or hand-quilt along the design lines.

After decorating the fabric, assemble the trims as indicated in the specific instructions.

Painted Toy Wreath
Pictured on page 45

MATERIALS: Light green fabric dye; two pieces of muslin, each 26x26 inches (wreath and backing); 26x26 inches *each* of quilt batting and foam-core board (available in art supply stores); beads; tiny pearls; buttons; scraps of fabric, ribbon, lace, pompons, and other trims; 2½ yards *each* of ⅛-inch-wide scarlet ribbon, narrow gold cord, and ½-inch-wide ecru lace; 2 yards of 1-inch-wide ecru lace.

INSTRUCTIONS: Following manufacturer's instructions, dye one of the pieces of muslin pale green. Then, following general instruc-

tions for painted fabric trims, enlarge and transfer the pattern, *opposite,* to the center of the dyed muslin square.

Note: In the lower left corner of the pattern are pine needles to work as background behind the toys; these are optional. To include them, simply draw similar branches and needles freehand on the pattern after it has been enlarged.

Referring to the photograph for ideas, paint or color the wreath designs. Using a variety of embroidery stitches and colors, embellish the toys.

For example, the sailboat is trimmed with ribbons and a purchased star appliqué. The anchor is a child-size button. The clown has sequined dots on his shirt and voluminous appliquéd knickers; his barbell is made with gold buttons. Novelty buttons accent the elephant, cone, clown, doll, and ark.

In the background, work French knots, or outline-stitch pine needles in green. Accent portions of the design with decorative beads, buttons, appliqués, ribbons, and laces.

Cut out wreath, leaving a margin of 1½ inches all around. Stitch gathered lace around the inner and outer edges as shown in the photograph. Blindstitch narrow ribbon and gold cord atop the seam line.

To assemble the wreath, cut foam-core board slightly smaller than the outline of the wreath pattern. Cover it with a layer of quilt batting cut to fit. Stretch the decorated fabric over the wreath form, clipping curves and taping the excess to the back. Finally, blindstitch muslin backing (cut to size) onto the back of the wreath, hiding all raw edges.

Ornaments
Pictured on pages 46-47

MATERIALS: Unbleached muslin; acrylic paints and paintbrushes (optional); embroidery floss; metallic thread; glass beads; novelty sequins, such as stars; narrow metallic ribbons; narrow lace trims; fiberfill.

INSTRUCTIONS; Enlarge patterns, *page 54;* transfer to muslin, allowing 2 inches between designs. Trace two of each design onto fabric (for ornament front and back). Color and embellish designs following general instructions for painted trims, *page 52*, and referring to the photographs for ideas.

Some suggestions: After embroidering portions of the designs, sew tiny round glass beads atop small dots on the patterns—in Santa's eyes, the center of the heart, or on the peacock feathers, for example. Couch gold thread or strings of bugle beads along design lines, as on the Christmas tree and stocking. Accent the bugle with heart-shape sequins; braid embroidery floss and tack over the cord.

In other words, be as creative and adventurous as you wish, making the most of every last scrap of embroidery floss, ribbon, lace, and other trims that you have in your sewing and craft baskets.

To assemble, cut out decorated fabric 1 inch beyond outlines. Pin fronts to backs, right sides facing. Stitch ⅛ inch beyond outlines, leaving openings for turning. Then clip curves, turn, stuff lightly with fiberfill, and blindstitch openings closed.
continued

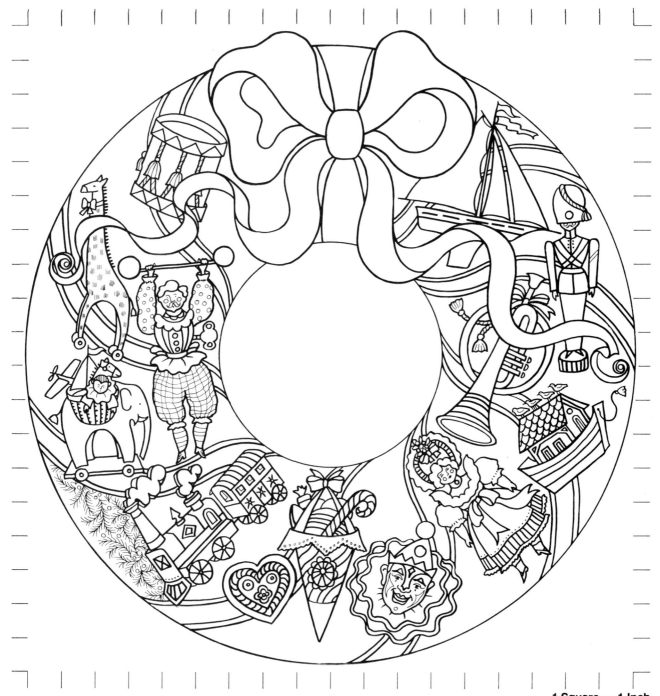

1 Square = 1 Inch

1 Square = 1 Inch

Stockings
Pictured on page 48

MATERIALS: Two pieces of un- bleached muslin, each 14x18 inch- es; 14x18 inches of polyester fleece; 14x18 inches of backing fabric; ½ yard of lining fabric; acrylic paints and paintbrushes; embroidery floss; metallic thread; 11 small ball-shape buttons in color of your choice; glass beads; ½-inch-wide ribbon.

INSTRUCTIONS: Enlarge pat- tern, *below,* and transfer it to one piece of muslin, then paint and dec- orate following general instructions for painted trims, *page 52.* (See pho- tograph for color, stitch, and trim ideas.)

Note: Small squares on stocking may be painted two shades of the same color (for example, scarlet or green) to highlight the design. Sew tiny beads along the base of the shoe as shown in the photograph.

Before assembling the stocking, hand- or machine-quilt the front by sandwiching a layer of polyester fleece between the painted front and plain muslin backing.

Baste, then quilt along design lines of small squares using pearl cotton or metallic thread. Embroi- der the outline of the ribbon using stem stitches. Or, couch down me- tallic thread using matching sewing thread and stitching through all lay- ers. Stitch shoe buttons in place.

Stitch metallic thread atop seam line; trim excess fabric, allowing ½- inch seam margin.

Cut backing fabric to match front. With right sides facing, sew back to front just outside the stocking out- line; leave the top open. Trim seams, clip curves, and turn.

For lining, cut two stocking shapes from lining fabric. With right sides facing, stitch them together as for the decorated stockings, *above,* but do not turn. Slip lining into stocking, turning raw edges under at top; blindstitch lining in place. At- tach a ribbon for hanging.

Soldier and Lady Dolls
Pictured on page 49

MATERIALS: Two 12x18-inch pieces of muslin (doll fronts); back- ing fabric; quilt batting (optional); fiberfill; acrylic paints and paint- brushes; embroidery floss; buttons, ribbons, and other trims.

INSTRUCTIONS: Enlarge pat- terns, *page 56;* transfer designs to centers of muslin. Referring to the photograph for color, stitch, and trim ideas, paint and embellish the doll fronts according to general in- structions, *page 52.*

Note: The soldier's hat is artificial fur; his medals and hat trim are an- tique buttons, earrings, and military medals. Three feathers are tacked to his hat. Gold embroidery thread is worked into the shoulder detail. His jacket is trimmed with small gold beads and narrow upholstery braid threaded with red embroidery floss. Narrow (⅛-inch-wide) red ribbon outlines the vest and trousers.

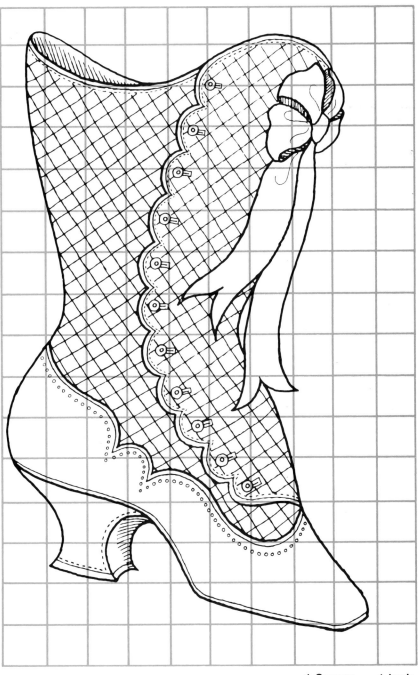

1 Square = 1 Inch

continued

The lady's hat is edged with pleated ⅛-inch-wide scarlet ribbon; gathered ½-inch-wide lace surrounds her hair.

To approximate the flowers on the lady's bonnet and basket, embroider a bouquet of blossoms in lazy daisy stitches. Or, add tiny silk leaves and flowers and purchased floral appliqués. You can make larger flowers by gathering one long edge of rayon seam binding, forming it into a circle, and tacking it in place. Embellish flower centers with gold glass beads, antique buttons, or old-fashioned earrings.

Trim the bodice and skirt with snippets of lace cut from handkerchiefs or other hand- or machine-made lace edgings. Embellish the hem with 2-inch-wide gathered taffeta ribbon; top with a length of ⅜-inch-wide ribbon.

To finish the dolls, trim excess fabric from around dolls, leaving a 1-inch margin.

From backing fabric, cut doll back to match front. With right sides facing, pin back to front. Stitch ⅜ inch beyond the outline of the doll, leaving an opening in the side or bottom for turning. Clip curves, trim seams, and turn right side out. Stuff carefully with fiberfill. Blindstitch the opening closed.

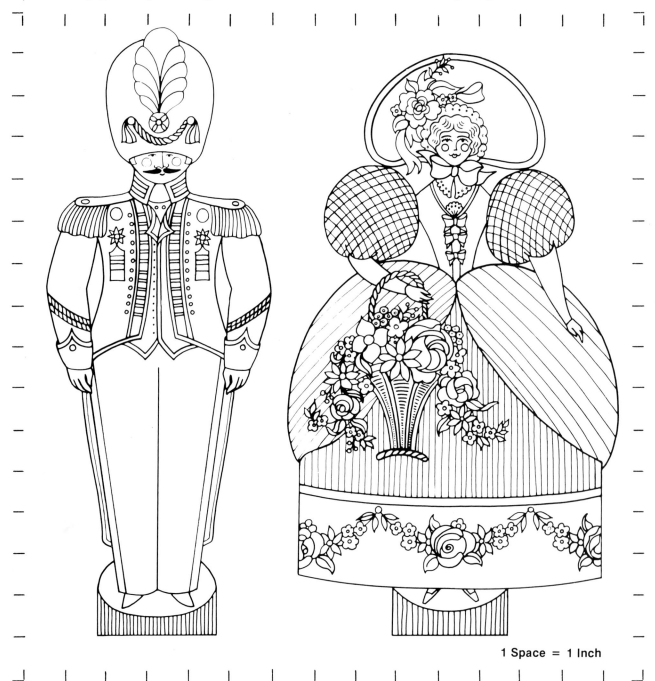

1 Space = 1 Inch

Enlarging and Transferring Designs

Successful completion of a craft project often begins with accurately enlarging a pattern—a relatively easy job when you use a grid. Once you've mastered the grid technique, the design possibilities are endless. Besides enlarging scaled-down designs from books and magazines, you can transfer designs from any source and scale them up or down by using a grid.

Here are tips and techniques for enlarging and transferring designs with grids.

Enlarging Designs

Most of the patterns in this book appear on grids—small squares laid over the design. Enlarge these patterns by marking off a grid on graph paper, using the scale indicated on the pattern. For example, if the scale is "one square equals 1 inch," mark off a series of 1-inch squares on your graph paper to enlarge the drawing to the recommended size.

• Graph paper is available in many grid sizes ranging from 1 square to 14 squares per inch. Graph paper that has heavy line divisions every 5 or 10 squares makes transferring and enlarging a design easier. If the paper has no divisions, mark off every fifth line with a ruler. And, to avoid confusion, use heavy lines to mark off the paper in squares that correspond to the scale called for in the original design.

You can purchase graph paper in sheets from office supply and art stores. Because the paper must be large enough to accommodate the enlarged pattern, you can tape together several small sheets, if necessary. Or, purchase large graph paper sold by the yard at many art stores and engineering supply companies. Some fabric shops also carry pattern-enlarging tissue marked with small dots at 1-inch intervals.

• To form a working grid, first count the number of horizontal and vertical rows of squares on the original pattern. With a ruler, mark the exact same number of horizontal and vertical rows of larger squares on the graph paper.

• Number horizontal and vertical rows of squares in the margin of the original pattern. Then transfer these numbers to corresponding rows that appear on your pattern.

• Begin by finding a square on your grid that corresponds with a square on the original. Mark your grid with a dot wherever a design line intersects a line on the original. (Visually divide every line into fourths to gauge whether the design line cuts the grid line halfway or somewhere in between.)

Working one square at a time, mark each grid line where it is intersected by the design. After marking several squares, connect the dots, following the contours of the original, as shown in the diagrams, *right.* Work in pencil so you can erase any errors easily.

Transferring Designs

• *Dressmaker's carbon paper:* Use dressmaker's carbon (not typist's carbon paper) as close as possible to the color of the fabric you intend to mark, yet dark enough that it will still be visible. Place it face down between the fabric and the pattern. Trace the design lines, using a tracing wheel or pencil and just enough pressure to transfer the design lines to the fabric.

• *Hot transfer pencil:* Available at craft and fabric stores, this pencil transfers designs to fabric with the aid of an iron. Keep the transfer pencil sharp so the design lines do not blur. Lightly trace the outlines of the design onto the *back* of the pattern. Then, following manufacturer's instructions, iron the transfer in place, being careful not to scorch the fabric.

It's a good idea to test your transfer pencil on scrap fabric before you begin because the color deposited on the fabric does not always fade when the article is washed or dry-cleaned. Practice drawing on paper, varying the pressure on the pencil and the sharpness of its point. Also practice ironing the transfer onto your fabric until you have marked a design line that is dark enough to see while you work the project but faint enough not to show when the project is completed.

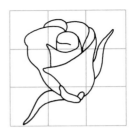

THE ORIGINAL DESIGN

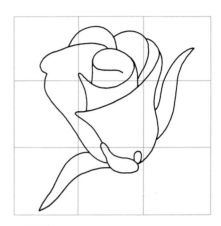

THE ENLARGED DESIGN

• *Blue lead pencil:* A colored pencil is effective on light-colored, light-weight fabrics. Tape the pattern to a window; then tape the fabric over it (centering the design beneath the fabric). Trace the pattern using the pencil, making dotted lines instead of solid ones.

• *Washable marking pen:* This is a blue felt tip marker especially designed for needlework and craft projects. Using a light touch, draw or trace directly onto light-colored fabric, work the design, and when you are finished, simply dampen the fabric and the blue lines will disappear. Look for this pen in needlework, fabric, and quilt shops.

• *Basting:* This is an efficient way to transfer design lines to dark, soft, highly textured, stretchy, or sheer fabrics. Use this method whenever other methods suggested above will not work.

Draw the pattern on tissue paper and pin it to the fabric. Hand- or machine-baste around design lines, using a thread that contrasts slightly with your fabric. Tear away tissue paper and proceed with the project. Remove basting stitches when you have finished working.

BELOVED CHRISTMAS TRADITIONS

An Elegant Tribute to Christmas

For many families, Christmas is a sentimental sampler of past celebrations. Ornaments and trims, lovingly collected and treasured for years, call to mind cherished memories of Christmases past. Each year, newly crafted trims take their places among the family favorites, adding their own special flavor to the holiday festivities.

In this section is a dazzling array of Christmas delights—festive trims, enchanting gifts, and elegant ideas for entertaining. You're sure to find just the right project to add to your own family's Christmas this year.

A joyous celebration of color and pattern is at the heart of this spectacular Christmas scene. The tree is enhanced with an elegant assortment of handcrafted trims, which are shown again on the following pages.

A lovely Christmas keepsake like the star doily crocheted with wool (pictured beneath the candlesticks) will enchant anyone on your gift list. Or stitch a vibrant heart-shape pillow (in the chair).

Holiday dress-ups include a purchased pullover adorned with an antique lace collar that has been dyed and a child's lavender-tinted doily dress.

Instructions for projects in this section begin on page 66.

On special days, little girls love to dress up. And what could be more fitting inspiration for a pretty party frock than the beautiful embroidery of days gone by? The delicate child's dress, *right,* combines a collection of yesteryear's embroidered doilies, dresser scarves, and table runners that can be found easily at secondhand stores. Assemble the dress using a commercial sewing pattern with simple lines, then dye it the color of your choice.

Fancy French fabrics were used to create the charming doll set, *below,* but you can use any unusual fabrics you have on hand. To make the quaint country dolls (another doll is shown on the preceding page), pick the liveliest prints from your scrap bag of fabrics, and sketch facial features on muslin with watercolor pens. Stitch the soft eyelet-edged cradle from similar fabrics. A tiny comforter and petite pillow complete the set.

Fancy up a country basket with a fresh coat of paint and a brilliant embroidered border. To make the beruffled basket, *above,* cut the decorative edge from a damaged table-cloth or other embroidered piece, gather it on a length of elastic, and attach the ruffle to the rim of the basket.

The subtle patternings of damask dinner napkins add tex-ture and dimension to the easy-to-assemble stockings shown *at left* and on the preceding pages. Lay out the stocking pattern to make the most of the napkin's design. Quilt the stocking along design lines and embellish with lace, ribbon, and novelty trims.

Vibrant floral motifs embla-zon the dazzling display of embroidered Christmas orna-ments, *right.* Worked on wool with vivid shades of crewel yarn, the teardrop trims imitate the shape of traditional orna-ments. The folk art trims—rocking horse, tree, and candle—are fashioned from felt and stitched with pearl cotton. All of these softly stuffed orna-ments are enhanced with an edging of gold thread.

An Elegant Tribute to Christmas

What a generous feeling of welcome fills homes at holiday time! Candles and firelight lend luster and majesty to even the simplest things, and small touches such as fresh flowers, a fancy tablecloth, or a starched doily add elegance. You can capture this mood of easy elegance for your holiday festivities by making these beautiful accessories.

A basket filled with greenery and sachets is a lovely way to dress up a window, *top right.* The painted hearts are easy to make from scrap lumber. Suspend these pastel trims from satin ribbons to decorate everything from packages to the traditional tree.

All it takes to make the sumptuous hostess apron, *bottom right,* is a fancy lace curtain and a ribbon for the waistband. You also can use lace and ribbons to transform ordinary towels into designer-look linens, *below.* To create coordinating bath accessories, paint unfinished Shaker-style boxes and embellish with floral decals.

Set a stylish table for Christmas—or any special occasion—with tabletop accessories and ideas as enchanting as those shown *above and right*. The pretty heart-shape place mats are fashioned from off-white wool fabric and embellished with floral motifs embroidered in jewel-bright colors. The glitter of gold metallic thread outlines each place mat. To add a shimmering touch to this festive table setting, craft a cluster of wooden heart candle holders in a variety of sizes, then paint them in several pastel shades. Other delightful decorating ideas include a lamp draped with lacy doilies and a wicker basket painted a soft blue and filled with prettily wrapped packages and petite treats.

Christmas is a special time for children. So why not treat your little ones to a tree of their own? The kid-size Christmas tree, *left,* is trimmed with simple stars and hearts stitched from dinner napkins or dish towels. Checked toweling also was used to stitch the whimsical bistro bears beneath the tree and *below.*

Kids love to help in the kitchen, especially when the "chores" include the making

and baking of Christmas goodies. Your littlest helper is sure to delight in the bunny apron, *opposite.* Create this charming cover-up from muslin and embellish it with embroidery and a dab of fabric paints.

The enchanting stuffed animals, *opposite,* are actually two toys in one. To make this reversible toy, paint and embroider the dog for one side and the rabbit for the other.

Lace-Trimmed Sweater
Pictured on page 58

MATERIALS: Antique lace collar; purchased sweater; fabric dye in a color to complement sweater; starch; sewing thread.

INSTRUCTIONS: Before dyeing the collar, examine the lace for tears. Mend it carefully if necessary, then wash and rinse it thoroughly. Mix fabric dye according to manufacturer's instructions. Dye the lace, starch it lightly, and allow to dry.

Using thread to match, pin and then hand-sew the collar in place; avoid distorting the shape of the lace or the sweater as you stitch. Lace must be securely anchored to the sweater at the neckline, along outer edges, and in the center to prevent unsightly wrinkles when it is worn.

Heart Pillow
Pictured on page 58

MATERIALS: ½ yard of red wool (front and back); ecru 3-ply Persian wool; scraps of blue and ecru felt; ecru piping; fiberfill; dressmaker's carbon paper; fabric glue.

INSTRUCTIONS: Enlarge the pattern, *below;* add ½-inch seam allowances. Using dressmaker's carbon, transfer pattern to wool.

Shaded portions of the pattern indicate felt appliqués. Without adding seam allowances, cut four blue leaves, six blue dots, and four ecru hearts from felt. Glue in position.

Couch the design, using one ply of yarn as a tacking thread and two plies as base (couched) threads. Lay base threads along design lines; tack in place at ¼-inch intervals.

After stitching, cut out the heart. Cut back to match front. Baste ecru piping to front, then stitch front to back, leaving an opening.

Turn, stuff with fiberfill, and hand-stitch the opening closed.

Child's Frock
Pictured on page 60

MATERIALS: Embroidered table runners, dresser scarves, and small fabric doilies; purchased pattern for child's dress; fabric dye.

INSTRUCTIONS: Use embroidered pieces in place of yardage for this dress. Begin by laying out pattern pieces. Position table runners, doilies, and other pieces from your collection atop patterns until you are satisfied with the arrangement. Pin patterns in place, cut them out, and stitch the dress according to pattern directions. When the dress is assembled, dip the dress in fabric dye, following manufacturer's instructions.

Woolen Star Doily
Pictured on page 58

MATERIALS: Five 1.6-ounce skeins of Unger Shetland-Type Britania No. 541 blue yarn (or a suitable substitute); Size D aluminum crochet hook.

Abbreviations: Page 310.

INSTRUCTIONS: Finished size is 32 inches in diameter. Ch 6, join to form ring.

Rnd 1: Work 16 sc in ring; join with sl st to first sc. *Rnd 2:* Ch 1, sc in same st as sl st; * 2 sc in next sc, sc in next sc. Rep from * around; join to first sc—24 sc. *Rnd 3:* Ch 1, sc in same st as sl st and in next sc; * 2 sc in next sc, sc in next 2 sc. Rep from * around; join—32 sc. *Rnd 4:* Ch 1, sc in same st as sl st and in next 2 sc; * 2 sc in next sc, sc in next 3 sc. Rep from * around; join—40 sc.

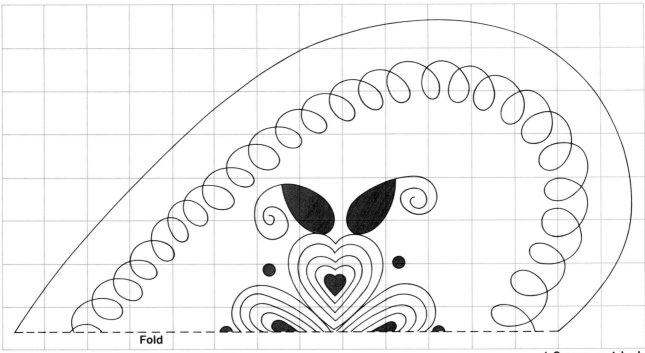

Fold

1 Square = 1 Inch

Rnd 5: Ch 1, sc in same st as sl st and in next 8 sc; * 2 sc in next sc, sc in next 9 sc. Rep from * around; join—44 sc. *Rnd 6:* Ch 1, sc in same st as sl st and in next 9 sc; * 2 sc in next sc, sc in next 10 sc. Rep from * around; join—48 sc.

Rnd 7: Ch 1, sc in same st as sl st and in next 10 sc; * 2 sc in next sc, sc in next 11 sc. Rep from * around; join—52 sc. *Rnd 8:* Ch 1, sc in same st as sl st and in next 11 sc; * 2 sc in next sc, sc in next 12 sc. Rep from * around; join—56 sc.

Rnd 9: Ch 1, sc in same st as sl st and in next 12 sc; * 2 sc in next sc, sc in next 13 sc. Rep from * around; join—60 sc. *Rnd 10:* Ch 1, sc in same st as sl st and in next 4 sc; * 2 sc in next sc, sc in next 5 sc. Rep from * around; join—70 sc.

Rnd 11: Ch 1, sc in same st as sl st and in next 5 sc; * 2 sc in next sc, sc in next 6 dc. Rep from * around; join—80 sc. *Rnd 12:* Ch 3, in same st as sl st work dc, ch 1, 2 dc; ch 1, * sk 3 sc, in next sc work a *shell of 2 dc, ch 1, 2 dc,* ch 1. Rep from * around; join last ch-1 to 3rd ch of ch-3 at beg of row—20 shells.

Rnd 13: Sl st in next dc and in ch-1 sp; ch 3, in same sp work dc, ch 1, 2 dc; * ch 2, sc in ch-1 sp bet shells, ch 2 work a shell in ch-1 sp of shell. Rep from * around, ending with ch 2, sc in ch-1 sp bet shells, ch 2, join to third ch of ch-3 at beg of row.

Rnd 14: Sl st in next dc and in ch-1 sp; ch 3, in same sp work dc, ch 1, 2 dc; ch 3, * work shell in ch-1 sp of next shell, ch 3. Rep from * around; join last ch-3 to 3rd ch of ch-3 at beg of row. *Rnd 15:* Ch 4, * dc in ch-1 sp of shell, ch 1, sk dc, dc in next dc, ch 1, dc in second ch of next ch-3 grp, ch 1, dc in next dc, ch 1. Rep from * around; join last ch-1 to 3rd ch of ch-4 at beg of row—80 ch-1 sp.

Rnd 16: Ch 1, sc in same st as sl st and in each st around; join to first sc—160 sc. *Rnds 17-18:* Rep Rnd 16. *Rnd 19:* Ch 4, * sk next sc, dc in next sc, ch 1. Rep from * around; join last ch-1 to 3rd ch of ch-4 at beg of row.

Rnd 20: Ch 4, * dc in next dc, ch 1. Rep from * around; join as in Rnd 19. *Rnd 21:* Ch 3, in same st work dc, ch 1, 2 dc; ch 1, * sk dc; work shell in next dc, ch 1. Rep from *

around; join last ch-1 to top of ch-3.

Rnd 22: Rep Rnd 13. *Rnd 23:* Rep Rnd 14. *Rnd 24:* Rep Rnd 15.

Rnd 25: Sl st in next ch-1 sp; ch 3, in same sp work 2 dc; ch 4, * sk 3 dc, sc in next dc, (2 sc in next ch-1 sp, sc in next dc) 9 times—28 sc; ch 4, sk next 3 ch-1 sps; 3 dc in next ch-1 sp, ch 4. Rep from * around; join last ch-4 to top of ch-3 at beg of row.

Rnd 26: Ch 3, * work 2 dc in each of next 2 dc, ch 4, sk first sc, sc in next 26 sc; ch 4, dc in next dc. Rep from * around; join as Rnd 25.

Rnd 27: Ch 3, dc in next dc, 2 dc in next dc, dc in next 2 dc; ch 4, sk sc, sc in 24 sc, ch 4; * dc in next 2 dc, 2 dc in next dc, dc in next 2 dc, ch 4, sk sc, sc in 24 sc, ch 4. Rep from * around; join as before.

Rnd 28. Ch 3, dc in next 2 dc, ch 3, dc in next 3 dc, ch 4, sk sc, sc in next 22 sc, ch 4; * dc in 3 dc, ch 3, dc in 3 dc, ch 4, sk sc, sc in 22 sc, ch 4. Rep from * around; join as above.

Rnd 29: Ch 3, dc in next 2 dc, (ch 3, dc in same lp) twice; ch 3, dc in next 3 dc; ch 4, sk sc, sc in next 20 sc, ch 4; * dc in next 3 dc, (ch 3, dc in same lp) twice; ch 3, sk sc, sc in next 20 sc, ch 4. Rep from * around; join. *Rnd 30:* Ch 3, dc in next 2 dc, ch 3, dc in next dc; (ch 3, dc in same lp) twice; ch 3, dc in next dc; ch 3, dc in next 3 dc; ch 4, sk sc, sc in 18 sc, ch 4; * dc in next 3 dc, ch 3, dc in next dc; (ch 3, dc in same lp) twice; ch 3, dc in dc, ch 3, dc in 3 dc; ch 4, sk sc, sc in 18 sc, ch 4. Rep from * around; join.

Rnd 31: Ch 3, dc in next 2 dc; (ch 3, dc in next dc) twice; (ch 3, dc in same ch-3 lp) twice; (ch 3, dc in next dc) twice; ch 3, dc in next dc; ch 4, sk sc, sc in 16 sc, ch 4; * dc in 3 dc; (ch 3, dc in next dc) twice; (ch 3, dc in same ch-3 lp) twice; (ch 3, dc in next dc) twice; ch 3, dc in next dc; ch 4, sk sc, sc in 16 sc, ch 4. Rep from * around; join—7 ch-3 lps in point.

Row 32: Continue as established; there will be 14 sc in grp and 9 ch-3 lps. *Row 33:* 12 sc in grp, 11 ch-3 lps.

Row 34: 10 sc in grp, 13 ch-3 lps.
Row 35: 8 sc in grp, 15 ch-3 lps.
Row 36: 6 sc in grp, 17 ch-3 lps.
Row 37: 4 sc in grp, 19 ch-3 lps.
Row 38: 2 sc in grp, 21 ch-3 lps.
Row 39: Sl st in next dc, overlap

the next dc over the 3rd dc at the end of the previous point and sl st the 2 dc too. ((Sl st in next ch-3 lp. * Ch 3, in next ch-3 lp work dc, *ch 3, sl st in third ch from hook*—picot and dc made; ch 3, sc in next ch-3 lp. Rep from * 3 times more. (Ch 3, in next ch-3 lp work dc, a picot, dc) 3 times; ch 3, sc in next ch-3 lp. Rep from * 4 times; sl st in next 2 dc. Overlap the first dc of the *next* point (place on top) with the next dc and sl st the 2 dc too. Sl st in next 2 dc.)) Rep bet (( )) 9 times more. End rnd with sl st in last 2 dc and in same st where first sl st made at beg of row. Fasten off. Block.

Elegant Country Dolls
Pictured on page 60

MATERIALS: Assorted cotton print scraps; muslin; watercolor marking pens; fine-point brown marking pen; lace, ribbon, buttons, and beads; fiberfill.

INSTRUCTIONS: Enlarge pattern, *below;* add ¼-inch seam allowances to all pieces. Cut head back, body, legs, and arms from prints; cut head front and hands from muslin.

Sketch face on head front with watercolor pens, using them sparingly for a faded, old-fashioned look. Use brown pen to make curls.

continued

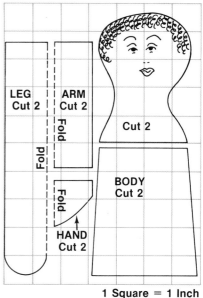

1 Square = 1 Inch

To make the body, sew front and back head pieces to front and back body pieces at neck. With right sides facing, sew body front to back; leave open at bottom. Turn, stuff, but do not close bottom of body. Set aside.

Fold legs in half lengthwise (right sides facing). Stitch, leaving tops open. Turn; stuff to within ½ inch of tops. Insert legs into body; whipstitch body closed, turning under raw edges and catching legs in seam.

For arms, sew one hand piece to each arm at wrist. Fold arms in half lengthwise, sew as for legs (leave shoulders open), turn, and stuff lightly. Turn under raw edges and whipstitch to body just above seam line between neck and body.

To complete the doll, join bands of print fabrics to form a 7x20-inch rectangle (skirt). Hem one long edge. Join short ends. Turn under remaining raw edge to make a drawstring casing, or gather skirt to fit doll and sew in place at waistline. (Conceal raw edges with a ribbon belt.) Trim bodice with buttons or beads. Hem a small triangular piece of print fabric for neckerchief.

Soft Cradle
Pictured on page 60

MATERIALS: ⅝ yard of print fabric (lining—A); ⅝ yard of contrasting fabric (outside of cradle—B); assorted prints equal to ⅓ yard (pillow, blanket); 1 yard of 1½-inch-wide ruffled eyelet lace (cradle trim); ¾ yard of ruffled eyelet (pillow and blanket trim); 2 yards of ¼-inch-wide satin ribbon; fiberfill.

INSTRUCTIONS: Enlarge patterns, *above*. Patterns include ¼-inch seam allowances.
• **To make the cradle,** fold fabric A in quarters. Position the pattern along the folds; cut out the lining. Unfold the fabric; trim the footboard end to match the pattern. Repeat these steps for fabric B. Mark the position of the rockers on fabric B with tailor's tacks.

With right sides facing, pin and stitch the cradle lining to the outer fabric. Leave openings for turning.

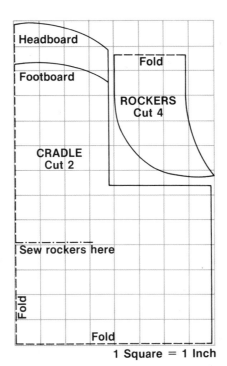

1 Square = 1 Inch

Trim seams, clip corners and curves, turn right side out, and press.

Fold sides and ends of the cradle toward center; press to make crease lines. Sew on crease lines, leaving a 3-inch-wide opening along one long side of center section for stuffing.

Stuff center section firmly; sew opening closed. Next, stuff headboard, footboard, and both sides of cradle. Slip-stitch openings. Bring sides up to meet head- and footboards; whipstitch corners together.

Mark dots on rockers with tailor's tacks. Sew two rocker pieces, leaving an opening. Turn, stuff firmly. Slip-stitch the opening closed. Repeat for second rocker.

Stitch rockers to cradle, matching tailor's tacks.

To trim cradle, blindstitch eyelet-edged, ruffled lace along sides and footboard. Thread eyelet with narrow satin ribbon. Fold lace down, toward outside of cradle; tack ribbon bows in corners.
• **For blanket,** join two 10x12-inch pieces of contrasting print around three sides. Turn and insert 1-inch-wide ruffled lace in opening; close.
• **For pillow,** cut two 5½x4½-inch pieces from contrasting prints. Edge one piece with 1-inch-wide ruffled lace. Sew pillow back to front; turn, stuff, and sew opening closed.

Damask Stocking
Pictured on page 61

MATERIALS: Purchased 16-inch-square cotton or linen damask napkin; ⅓ yard of muslin (back); assorted lace trims and edgings; assorted medium-wide ribbons; quilt batting (for quilted stocking).

INSTRUCTIONS: Enlarge pattern, *below*; add ½-inch seam allowances. Cut stocking front from napkin; cut back from muslin.

Referring to the photograph for inspiration, decorate the front of the stocking with lace, ribbons, or other trims. Or, baste quilt batting behind the stocking front and quilt along design lines on napkin using matching or contrasting thread.

Sew stocking front to back using ½-inch seam. Leave top open. Line stocking top with muslin. Add hanging loop.

Basket Ruffle
Pictured on page 61

MATERIALS: Purchased woven basket with handle; embroidered fabric that is as wide as the basket is deep and 1½ to 2 times as long as the circumference of the basket; narrow ribbon; elastic; twill tape.

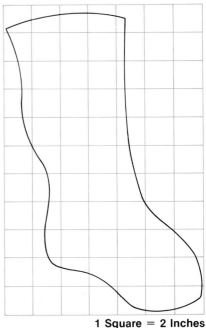

1 Square = 2 Inches

INSTRUCTIONS: Stitch embroidered fabric into a ruffle to fit basket. Make casing for elastic using twill tape. Embellish top and bottom of ruffle with narrow ribbon.

Folk Art Horse, Candle, and Tree Ornaments
Pictured on page 61

MATERIALS: For one of each of the designs—¼ yard of white felt; scraps of yellow, purple, and royal blue felt; 2 yards of thin gold braid; matching threads; assorted DMC pearl cotton thread; fiberfill; embroidery hoop and needle; dressmaker's carbon paper.

INSTRUCTIONS: Enlarge patterns, *below* and *right*. Using dressmaker's carbon, transfer patterns to white felt, leaving 3 inches between designs. Mount felt in an embroi-

dery hoop, if desired. Embroider designs in colors of your choice. Use stem stitches for lines and satin stitches for filling shapes. Press finished embroidery on wrong side.

Cut out ornaments along outer

1 Square = 1 Inch

solid lines. Cut ornament backs from felt scraps, making them ½ inch larger all around than fronts. Sew fronts to backs along dotted lines; leave openings for stuffing. (For horse, leave openings at top *and* bottom.)

Stuff ornaments lightly; sew openings closed.

Couch gold braid over machine stitching line; poke braid ends inside ornament with point of seam ripper. Trim backing, leaving a ¼-inch edge around embroidered front. Attach braid for hanging.

Teardrop Trims
Pictured on page 61

MATERIALS: Smooth, evenly woven white wool (fronts and backs); assorted crewel yarns; gold crewel thread; thread; embroidery hoop and needle; fiberfill; dressmaker's carbon paper.

continued

1 Square = 1 Inch

1 Square = 1 Inch

1 Square = 1 Inch

69

INSTRUCTIONS: Enlarge patterns, *page 69.* Using dressmaker's carbon, transfer designs to wool; leave 2 inches between shapes.

Referring to the photograph for colors, embroider ornaments. Fill shapes with satin stitches using single strands of yarn. Couch borders with metallic thread. Press finished embroidery on wrong sides. Cut out ½ inch from outlines. Cut backs to match fronts. Sew fronts to backs ¼ inch from raw edges; leave openings for turning. Turn, stuff lightly with fiberfill, and sew openings.

Elegant Guest Towels
Pictured on page 62

MATERIALS: Purchased fingertip towels; ribbon and lace trims.

INSTRUCTIONS: Preshrink all trims. Then, embellish ends of towels with satin, taffeta, or grosgrain ribbon and delicate lace edgings. For example, gather lace and sew to both sides of ribbon. Or, thread narrow ribbon through openings along top of lace trim; stitch to towel. (See photograph for additional ideas.)

Easy Decaled Boxes
Pictured on page 62

MATERIALS: Unfinished boxes; water-applied decals (available in craft and hobby shops); ecru or pink latex enamel.

INSTRUCTIONS: Paint boxes, using enamel. When dry, apply decals to box tops and sides.

Lace Curtain Apron
Pictured on page 62

MATERIALS: ¾ yard of a 30-inch-long lace curtain panel; 2 yards of 1-inch-wide ecru ribbon; thread.

INSTRUCTIONS: Stitch a rolled hem along the raw edges of the lace panel. Thread ribbon (waistband and ties) through curtain-rod channel at top of panel.

Wooden Heart Trims and Candle Holders
Pictured on pages 62-63

MATERIALS: 1¼-inch-thick pine (candle holders); ½-inch-thick pine (stands, ornaments); sandpaper; ¼-inch-diameter doweling; wood glue; enamel paint.

INSTRUCTIONS: Enlarge pattern, *below;* cut a cardboard template for each heart.
- *For ornaments:* Draw around smallest template on ½-inch-thick pine. Cut out with jigsaw. Drill holes for hanging. Sand; paint.
- *For candle holders:* Draw around large and medium-size templates onto 1¼-inch-thick pine. *Before cutting out the heart shapes,* drill ¾-inch-diameter candle holes in heart tops. Holes should be deep enough to hold candles securely.

For candle-holder stands, cut 1x2-inch pieces from ½-inch pine; angle ends slightly for a trim look.

To stabilize hearts on stands, drill ¼-inch-diameter holes ½ inch deep into bottoms of hearts; drill corresponding holes in centers of stands. Drop glue into holes and insert 1-inch lengths of dowel in holes, connecting stands to hearts. Allow to dry. Sand all wood surfaces and paint in desired colors.

1 Square = 1 Inch

Heart Place Mats
Pictured on page 63

MATERIALS: White wool (1 yard, 60 inches wide, makes three mats); crewel yarn; gold thread.

INSTRUCTIONS: Enlarge pattern, *below,* onto 14x18-inch piece of paper folded in half widthwise. Draw pattern so the heart is 18 inches wide and 12 inches deep from top of center fold to point. Draw cutting line 1 inch beyond line for gold cord. Transfer designs to wool.

Referring to the photograph for color suggestions, embroider fronts. Fill shapes with satin stitches in single strands of yarn. Use stem stitches for outlines. Couch borders with metallic thread.

Press finished embroidery on wrong sides; cut out ½ inch from gold outlines. Cut matching backs. Sew fronts to backs ¼ inch from raw edges; leave openings for turning. Turn right side out; sew openings closed. Press on backs.

Rabbit and Dog Toy
Pictured on page 64

MATERIALS: ½ yard of white fabric; fiberfill; black embroidery floss; thread; dressmaker's carbon paper; fabric paints; paintbrushes.

Gold cord →

Top of placemat

Fold

1 Square = 1 Inch

INSTRUCTIONS: Enlarge patterns, *below*; transfer to white fabric with dressmaker's carbon. Paint shaded areas blue (vests), red (pants, rabbit tie and eyes, dog tongue and eye) and brown (dog face, rabbit lower lip).

With three strands of floss, embroider outlines. Cut out designs 1 inch from black outlined edge.

To assemble, stitch pieces together (right sides facing and matching all edges) ½ inch from embroidered outline; leave an opening for turning. Turn, stuff, and sew closed.

1 Square = 1 Inch

1 Square = 1 Inch

Bunny Apron
Pictured on page 64

MATERIALS: ¾ yard of 45-inch-wide unbleached muslin; acrylic or fabric paints; paintbrushes; 3 yards of tan single-fold bias tape; assorted embroidery flosses; two ½-inch-diameter buttons (eyes); dressmaker's carbon paper.

INSTRUCTIONS: Enlarge pattern, *below*. Preshrink muslin; transfer design onto muslin using dressmaker's carbon. Cut out; join ties to apron front at ears. Bind all raw edges with bias tape.

To paint apron, see photograph for color suggestions. Thin paint with water to lighten color. Place fabric atop several layers of paper toweling; paint shaded areas (see pattern). Use just a small amount of paint on the brush at a time to prevent bleeding; daub loaded brush on paper towels to remove excess paint. Paint *up to but not over* lines.

When paint is dry, press the apron on wrong side to set colors.

Finish the apron with touches of embroidery. Use satin stitches for pupils and button, and French knots for the polka dots on the bunny's tie. Using stem stitches, outline the pants and facial details in black; the shirt in light blue; the collar, cuffs, and carrot in gold; and the face and paws in light brown.

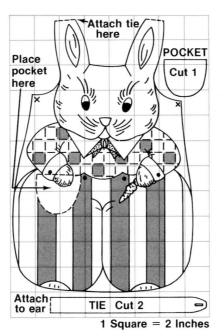

1 Square = 2 Inches

Damask Ornaments
Pictured on pages 59 and 65

MATERIALS: Cotton or linen damask napkins and towels in colors of your choice; narrow lace trims; fiberfill; narrow ribbons.

INSTRUCTIONS: Allowing for seam margins, cut simple star and heart shapes from napkins and towels; cut matching backs.

Baste narrow lace edgings to fronts, if desired. With right sides facing, sew fronts to backs; leave openings for turning. Clip seams, turn, stuff with fiberfill, and sew closed. Add hanging loops made with narrow ribbons.

Bistro Bear
Pictured on page 65

MATERIALS: ⅓ yard of blue and white checked tablecloth fabric; polyester fiberfill; four sets of Size 4 snaps; two round or heart-shape buttons (eyes); heart-shape button (optional nose or heart); white carpet thread; long needle; assorted ribbons and laces.

INSTRUCTIONS: For patterns and basic how-to instructions, see the directions for the Tyrolean bears, *pages 278-280*.

Before cutting, fold fabrics in half so that checks on top and bottom layers of fabric match *exactly*. Cut pattern pieces on the straight grain of the fabric; checks on the right and left or front and back of each pattern piece should match.

Assemble the bear (or bears) following construction techniques for Tyrolean bears, except, if you are making a baby bear, use a button for his nose. Omit nose on adult bears. Omit embroidered mouths; instead, position patterns on fabric so the checked design suggests a mouth.

Add ribbon bows around the bear's neck; sew a button heart to the bear's breast, if desired. Gather a 4-inch-wide strip of scalloped lace on a length of ribbon to form an apron, or embellish the bear's ears with narrow strips of lace slip-stitched along the seam line of each ear, if desired.

BELOVED CHRISTMAS TRADITIONS

In Praise of American Patchwork

Carefully pieced and lovingly hand-stitched, patchwork quilts call to mind a spirit of family tradition and homey simplicity. It was just these lovely sentiments that inspired this quilt-patterned Christmas. Colonial quilters created countless patchwork patterns still cherished by today's crafters. In this section, you'll see how easily these time-honored designs can be adapted to a variety of craft techniques to make delightful gifts and trims for your home and family.

The patchwork quilts of America's past provided the patterns for this keepsake collection of holiday handmades. Only the sawtooth star quilt is an authentic, pieced design, but the crazy-quilt bull and rooster are stitched from remnants salvaged from an old quilt.

Schoolhouse motifs have been favorites with quilters since pioneer days. Here, this ever-popular pattern appears on a hardy hooked rug worked in rich tones of wool fabric.

For more information on patchwork-patterned projects, please see the following pages.

Instructions for projects in this section begin on page 80.

In Praise of American Patchwork

On the American frontier, quilting bees were festive times full of laughter, sharing, and exchanging bits of gossip. Many a happy occasion was commemorated with a quilt lovingly stitched by family and friends. Why not celebrate this spirit of fellowship at Christmastime by making quilt-patterned gifts for those you love?

An old-time saying, *below,* is beautifully "written" in counted cross-stitches and framed with simple patchwork patterns. A scrap from an antique quilt makes the rooster. And nine different quilt designs pattern a needlepoint pillow, *opposite.*

To welcome family and friends with heartfelt hospitality, craft a homespun wreath from corn husks and patchwork, *right.*

The lively designs of traditional quilts make splendid motifs for Christmas ornaments crafted in a myriad of techniques, *opposite*.
Paint patchwork patterns on scrap pieces of pine to create the wooden ornaments. Or stitch and stuff a menagerie of wondrous animals from a timeworn quilt. The needlepoint trims repeat the patterns of the pillow shown on page 74. Petite pillowlike trims are simply made with rubber stamps bearing quilt patterns. To create the needlepoint pillow in the foreground, *opposite*, work a series of schoolhouse designs bordered by a quaint alphabet.

Holiday handmades as simple to stitch as the appliquéd apron and tea cozy, *above*, are sure to appeal to any down-home hostess.

Hand-painted floorcloths, much like this one, *right,* were sturdy stand-ins for carpet during colonial times. The one shown here is crafted from artist's canvas, painted with acrylics, and varnished.

Crafty kids can lend a hand when it comes to making package wraps. These, *below,* are paper bags embellished with stenciled quilt motifs.

Familiar farmyard animals, *below* and *opposite,* are easy to make from old or new patchwork. The Christmas cupboard, *opposite,* is filled with a selection of the homemade goodies shown on pages 76-77.

Schoolhouse Rug
Pictured on pages 72-73

MATERIALS: 33x48 inches of burlap; No. 5 or No. 6 crochet hook; 1 yard of medium gray wool (background); ¾ yard of dark gray wool (border); ½ yard *each* of blue, dark yellow, yellow, and maroon wool; 1 yard (total) of a variety of gray wools; ⅜ yard *each* of brown, celery green, avocado, and light red wool; 4¼ yards of gray rug binding; embroidery hoop or rug frame; butcher paper; permanent markers; masking tape; heavy-duty thread; liquid latex; paintbrush.

INSTRUCTIONS: Enlarge pattern, *below*, onto butcher paper. With dark permanent marker, transfer design to burlap. Color areas with permanent markers, if desired. Tape raw edges of burlap. Machine-sew the burlap 1 inch beyond outer edge of pattern to prevent raveling.

• *To prepare wool:* Tear wool yardage into 3-inch-wide strips. Cut strips into narrow widths about ⅛ inch wide, cutting carefully along the weave of the wool. (The average length for a strip is about 12 inches.)

• *To hook wool:* Practice hooking on a burlap scrap before beginning the rug. Stretch burlap tautly (pattern side up) in a hoop or on a frame. Hold hoop in left hand with wool strip underneath.

With right hand (reverse positions if you're left-handed), push crochet hook through one mesh of burlap; pull end of wool strip up through hole to a height of 1 inch. (Strip ends will be trimmed later.)

Reinsert hook in next mesh and pull up a *loop* of wool to a height of ⅛ inch. The wool strip should be smooth on the underside of the burlap. Continue this hooking procedure, spacing loops evenly, until strip is used up. Then pull the end of the strip to the top side.

Continue working strips, changing colors as needed. Space loops farther apart when the pile of the rug strains the burlap or when it is packed too tightly. Trim the ends of the strips flush with the rug pile; do not cut loops.

• *To hook rug:* Outline the shapes first. Then fill them in with colors indicated in the color key. Outline basic house shapes (see photograph) with celery green; outline doors, windows, and chimneys with brown. Outline medium gray center of rug with a row of gold and a row of maroon.

When hooking is finished, hand-sew rug binding tape as close to the loops as possible using heavy-duty thread. Then cut off excess burlap and fold back; hem.

To minimize slipping and stabilize the back of the rug, paint the underside with liquid latex, if desired.

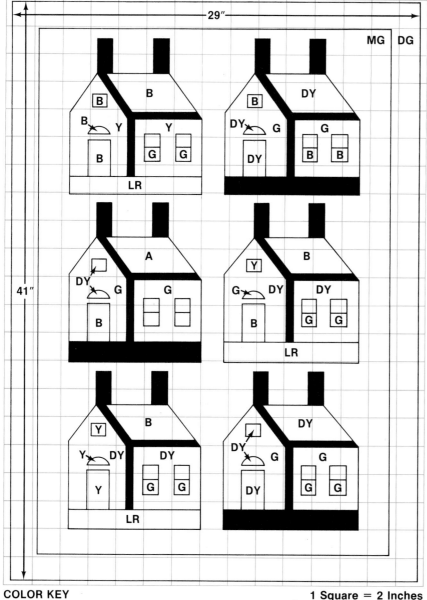

29"

41"

MG | DG

COLOR KEY

B = Blue	G = Gray
Y = Yellow	DG = Dark Gray
DY = Dark Yellow	A = Avocado Green
LR = Light Red	■ = Maroon
MG = Medium Gray	

1 Square = 2 Inches

Crazy-Quilt Bull
Pictured on page 73

MATERIALS: 12x28 inches of old patchwork, or substitute newly pieced and quilted patchwork; 12x28 inches of muslin; two buttons; white glue; fiberfill; scrap of narrow rope.

INSTRUCTIONS: Enlarge pattern, *below.* Pin patchwork and muslin rectangles together, right sides facing. Then pin pattern pieces atop fabrics; trace around shapes. Cut out ¼ inch beyond outlines. With right sides facing, sew body front to back and head front to back along traced lines, leaving openings for turning. Trim seams, clip curves, turn, and stuff with fiberfill. Sew openings closed. Sew buttons on head for eyes and glue head to body.

For the tail, fold a 1½x5-inch strip of patchwork in half lengthwise; sew ¼ inch from long edge and across one end. Turn; insert rope so that it extends 2 inches out of casement. Tack in place; unravel rope ends.

Quilt Pattern Needlepoint Pillow
Pictured on pages 72 and 74

MATERIALS: 18x18 inches of No. 12 needlepoint canvas; 18x18 inches of backing fabric; Size 20 tapestry needle; three-ply Persian yarn (We used Paternayan yarn.) in the following colors and amounts (in strands): blue (20); green (25); light gold (20); dark gold (15); red (125); white (80); masking tape.

INSTRUCTIONS: Finished pillow is 14 inches square.

Tape raw edges of canvas. Using basket-weave stitches and two or three plies of yarn (whichever covers canvas best), work from center of design, *page 82,* toward edges. Stitch background last. Block, if necessary, and assemble into pillow.

Sawtooth Star Quilt
Pictured on pages 72 and 74

MATERIALS: 44-inch-wide fabrics in the following colors and amounts: 2 yards of green; ½ yard of red; 8½ yards of white; quilt batting; quilting thread; needle.

INSTRUCTIONS: Finished size is approximately 78x94 inches. Each pieced block is 11x11 inches.

Enlarge pattern, *below;* trace each pattern piece onto a separate sheet of paper.

To make templates, trace pattern pieces onto sturdy cardboard or plastic lids. Make a template for each of the six shapes in the square and add ¼-inch seam allowances to all pieces.

continued

Quilt Diagram

Quilt Block

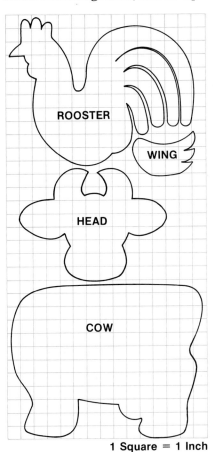

1 Square = 1 Inch

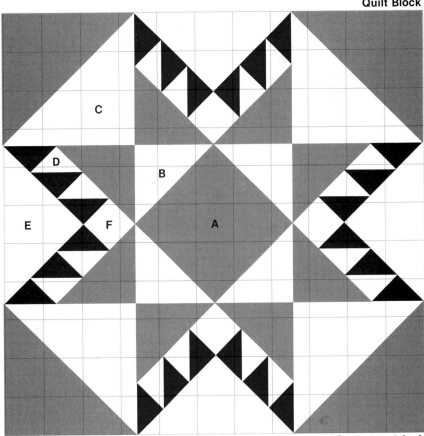

1 Square = 1 Inch

Trace around the templates onto the wrong side of the fabric. For each quilt block, cut the following pieces: from green fabric: 1-A, 8-B, and 4-C; from red fabric: 24-D; from white fabric: 4-B, 4-C, 16-D, 4-E, and 4-F.

From white fabric, cut twenty 11½-inch squares.

For the 18 triangles that border the quilt, draw an 11-inch square

pattern; cut it in half diagonally. Use one side for the triangle pattern, adding ¼-inch seam allowances.

For the four corner triangles of the quilt, cut the remaining triangular pattern in half again. Add ¼-inch seam allowances to all sides; cut four from white fabric.

• *To piece each quilt block,* treat the block as a nine-patch square, and piece each portion of the nine-patch separately, then join together. Be-

gin with the upper left-hand corner patch: Stitch a green C to a white C (¼-inch seams) along the base of the triangles. Repeat this procedure for all four corners of the block.

• *To piece the four star patches* of the block (the center patch on the top, bottom, and at each side of the block): Piece small red and white D triangles; add white square F and white triangle E. Finish by adding two green B triangles.

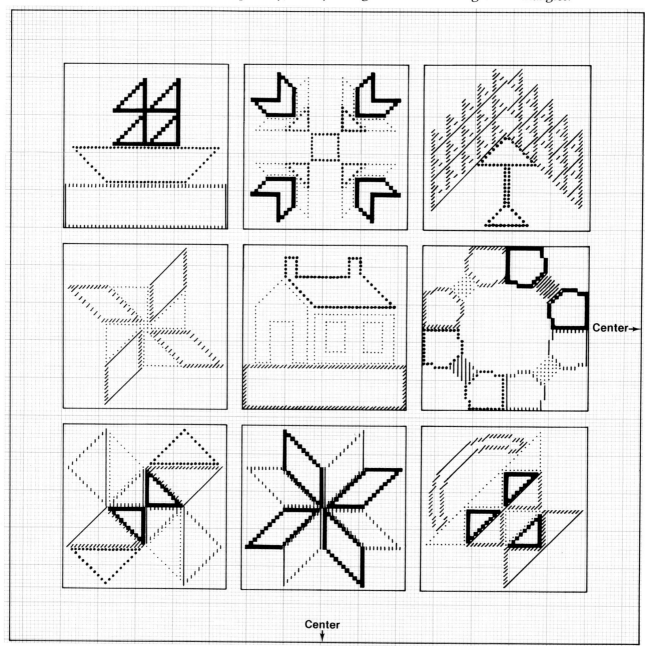

COLOR KEY
☐ Blue
◪ Green
■ Light Gold
● Dark Gold

⊡ Red
☐ White-background of
   each square design

1 Square = 1 Stitch

Center

To piece the center patch, add white B triangles to each side of square A.

Arrange all nine patches into a block, stitch, and press seams toward the outer edges of the block. Make 30 pieced blocks.

• *To join blocks into quilt top,* arrange alternating blocks of pieced and white squares in diagonal strips, beginning with the center strip of the quilt running from upper left-hand corner to lower right-hand corner of quilt top. Add appropriate white triangles at ends of each diagonal strip. (See diagram, *page 81.*)

Join diagonal rows to make the complete quilt top.

• *To finish,* piece white backing to size. Lay backing on floor or table, wrong side up; cover with batting, then the pieced top, right side up. Baste all layers together, and quilt along seams between each block. Quilt interiors of blocks in the quilting pattern of your choice. When quilting is finished, bind the edges with bias-cut strips of green fabric.

Corn Husk Heart Wreath
Pictured on page 75

MATERIALS: Wire coat hanger; 10 corn husks; narrow red rickrack; two 7-inch-square quilt blocks; 7-inch-square quilt batting; ¼-inch-diameter button; white glue.

INSTRUCTIONS: Enlarge the pattern, *above right.* Cut two hearts from quilt blocks and one from batting. With right sides facing, pin quilted hearts together; pin batting behind fabric. Using ¼-inch seam allowances, sew around heart; leave an opening for turning. Trim seams, clip curves, turn, and press. Sew opening closed. Glue rickrack around edge of heart.

• *To make the wreath,* soak corn husks in water for 10 minutes. Bend a coat hanger into a heart shape, placing the hook in the center. Tear husks into ½-inch-wide strips. Fold a strip in half; lay folded end of strip over wreath wire. Slip ends of strip around wire and through the loop (making a lark's head knot). Pull the

HEART

Fold

1 Square = 1 Inch

ends of the strip until the strip is wrapped tightly around the hanger. Repeat until wire is covered. Set wreath on flat surface to dry.

To assemble the wreath, glue rickrack over covered wire. Hang heart ornament from wreath center with rickrack. Tie and glue a rickrack bow to the heart ornament. Glue a button over the bow.

"East-West" Sampler
Pictured on page 75

MATERIALS: 18-inch square of white or ecru hardanger fabric; blue, red, and green embroidery floss; embroidery hoop or frame; small tapestry needle; graph paper; colored pencils or felt pens.

INSTRUCTIONS: The finished sampler is approximately 15 inches square.

To begin, make a master chart of the design: With blue, red, and green felt pens or colored pencils, transfer the diagram, *page 84,* to graph paper. (To transfer the design, begin in the lower left corner and work toward the center, copying the design from the chart.)

Complete the right side of the design by repeating the column of houses and hearts from the left side, *except* stitch a heart in the top square

and alternate down the column (see photograph). Chart the appropriate date in the middle of the design.

Before you begin to stitch, stay-stitch edges of the fabric and mount fabric in a hoop or frame. Then, using three strands of floss, work each cross-stitch over two threads of fabric. Follow your master pattern or the chart and color key, *page 84.*

Work the first stitch 1½ inches from the edge and in the middle of one side of the fabric. Work the blue border all the way around. Continue working the design from the edges toward the center.

Stretch and frame the completed design as desired.

Crazy-Quilt Rooster
Pictured on page 75

MATERIALS: 13x20 inches of old patchwork, or substitute newly pieced and quilted patchwork; 13x20 inches of muslin; fiberfill; button; white glue; wooden dowel; 1x2x3-inch wood block (base).

INSTRUCTIONS: Enlarge pattern on *page 81.* Pin quilted and muslin rectangles together, right sides facing, then pin patterns on top. Trace around shapes. Cut out pieces ¼ inch beyond traced lines.

With right sides facing, sew quilted fronts and muslin backs together along lines, leaving openings for turning. Turn, stuff with fiberfill, and sew openings closed. Stitch or glue wing to rooster body. Sew button on for eye.

Clip a few threads from bottom seam and insert sharpened dowel into body. Drill a hole in wood base and glue other end into base.

Schoolhouse Tea Cozy
Pictured on page 76

MATERIALS: ⅜ yard of pre-quilted muslin; 1¾ yards of ⅝-inch-wide eyelet lace; ⅓ yard of blue calico; ⅓ yard of fusible interfacing; ecru seam binding; ecru and blue thread; glue stick.

continued

INSTRUCTIONS: Enlarge the pattern, *opposite*. Fuse interfacing to the calico. From muslin, cut out the tea cozy front, back, and center panel. From calico, cut out the schoolhouse appliqué.

Secure appliqué to tea cozy front with glue stick. Machine satin-stitch the appliqué in place, using matching thread. Baste lace ¼ inch from curved edges on tea cozy front and back. With right sides facing, sew front to center panel. Repeat for back. Bind bottom edge with seam binding; add muslin loop at top.

Schoolhouse Apron
Pictured on page 76

MATERIALS: Purchased apron pattern; muslin yardage for apron; 12x12 inches of prequilted muslin (pocket); 8x8 inches *each* of blue calico and fusible interfacing; 1¼ yards of blue calico piping; 3½ yards of blue calico bias tape; 2 yards of red ribbon (apron straps); 1 yard of ⅝-inch-wide lace (pocket edge); scrap of red fabric (hearts); glue stick.

INSTRUCTIONS: Enlarge pattern, *opposite*. Fuse interfacing to calico; cut out schoolhouse. Cut three hearts, apron pieces, and pocket.

⊟ Blue ⧄ Red ⊡ Green

1 Square = 1 Stitch

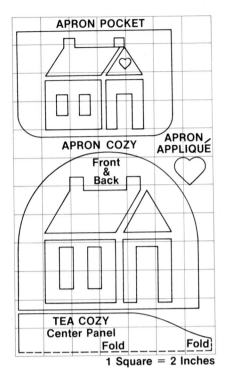

APRON POCKET

APRON COZY
Front & Back

APRON APPLIQUÉ

TEA COZY
Center Panel
Fold   Fold

1 Square = 2 Inches

Glue schoolhouse appliqué on pocket; glue hearts to apron bib. With a machine, satin-stitch all appliqués in place. Baste piping ¼ inch from raw edge around pocket. Sew lace next to piping on sides and bottom of pocket. Turn raw edges under and sew pocket to apron, stitching close to piping. Trim apron with bias tape. Stitch ribbon straps to neck and sides of apron.

Schoolhouse Pillow
Pictured on page 77

MATERIALS: Needlepoint yarn in the following colors and amounts (We used Paternayan yarns.): ½ skein of blue, 45 strands of red, 1 skein of off-white, and 50 strands of green; 15-inch square of 12-mesh interlock needlepoint canvas; tapestry needle; pillow form; 15-inch square of backing fabric; cording (optional); zipper (optional).

INSTRUCTIONS: Beginning in centers of canvas and design, work needlepoint according to the chart, *page 86*. Use two plies of yarn for stitching. Work motifs in continental stitches; fill background with white basket-weave stitches.

Finish the pillow in block or knife-edge form, adding piping or zipper on back, if desired.

Floorcloth and Pillows
Pictured on page 78

MATERIALS: 2x3-foot piece of artist's canvas (floorcloth); two 13-inch squares of artist's canvas (pillows); gesso; acrylic paints in colors of your choice; acrylic varnish; 2⅔ yards of blue upholstery piping (pillows); fiberfill (pillows); backing fabric (pillows).

INSTRUCTIONS: For the floorcloth, enlarge the pattern, *below*. Lay artist's canvas atop newspaper; brush gesso onto canvas (some shrinkage will occur).

When dry, transfer the quilt design to the canvas with pencil, repeating the pattern to fill in the sides and corners. Paint the design and background of the floorcloth with acrylics, using colors of your choice. Varnish when dry.

• *For pillows,* enlarge one star pattern to measure 9 inches across from point to point. Place star diagonally on a 9¼-inch background square (see photograph). Using gesso, paint 13-inch squares of artist's canvas for pillow fronts. Transfer design to centers of canvas squares and paint in colors of your choice.

Baste piping ½ inch from raw edges. With right sides facing, sew pillow backs (cut to size) to painted fronts, using ½-inch seams. Leave openings for turning. Turn, stuff with fiberfill, and sew openings.

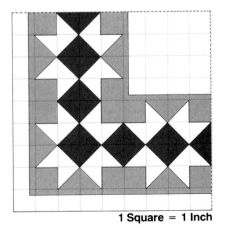

1 Square = 1 Inch

Stenciled Gift Bags
Pictured on page 78

MATERIALS: Stencil paper; stencil brush; craft knife; acrylic paints in colors of your choice; brown paper bags; masking tape.

INSTRUCTIONS: Draw designs of your choice onto paper, filling in with pencil those areas to be cut out. Place drawing under stencil paper and tape to a firm cutting surface. Cut out darkened areas with knife. Using masking tape, tape the stencil to the front of a paper bag.

To stencil, dip stencil brush into paint, remove excess paint by daubing paper towels, then daub through openings on stencil. Remove stencil and allow paint to dry.

To make two- or three-color stencils, cut one stencil plate for each color. Stencil the first color; let dry. Then line up each successive stencil plate and stencil patterns.

Wooden Quilt-Pattern Ornaments
Pictured on page 79

MATERIALS: Scraps of 1-inch-thick clear pine; sandpaper; acrylic or oil paints in colors of your choice; Sizes 5 and 10 sable brushes; clear acrylic spray; nylon thread.

INSTRUCTIONS: Enlarge patterns, *page 87,* or make your own from favorite quilt designs.

Transfer designs to pine. Using a jigsaw, cut out around quilt pattern shapes; sand all surfaces. Paint designs using acrylics or oils in the colors of your choice; see photograph for color ideas. When completely dry, coat the ornaments with clear spray. Drill holes as shown for nylon thread hanging loops.

Stamped Quilt-Pattern Ornaments
Pictured on page 79

MATERIALS: Assorted quilt-pattern rubber stamps (available in gift shops or by mail); red, green, or *continued* blue stamp pads; muslin; calico scraps; thread; fiberfill; quilt batting.

INSTRUCTIONS: Before cutting muslin, stamp quilt patterns in checkerboard or solid arrangements (see photograph). Make stamped areas 2 to 4 inches square. Sandwich batting between stamped muslin and muslin backing. Quilt around the designs. Cut out the quilted fronts, adding ¼-inch seam allowances all around.

Add calico borders to muslin squares. Sew calico backs to fronts, leaving openings. Turn, stuff with fiberfill, and sew openings. Attach thread loops for hanging.

Quilted Animal Trims
Pictured on page 79

MATERIALS: Quilt remnants or newly pieced and quilted patchwork; unbleached muslin; fiberfill; ¼-inch-diameter buttons; ribbon scraps; embroidery thread (cat whiskers); toothpicks and yellow acrylic paint (rooster); yarn scraps (horse).

INSTRUCTIONS: Enlarge patterns, *opposite*. For horse or cow, make a simple outline drawing (or use pattern, *page 38*). Pin animal patterns to quilt remnants or new patchwork; trace outlines. Cut out, adding ¼-inch seam allowances.

Cut muslin backs to match fronts.

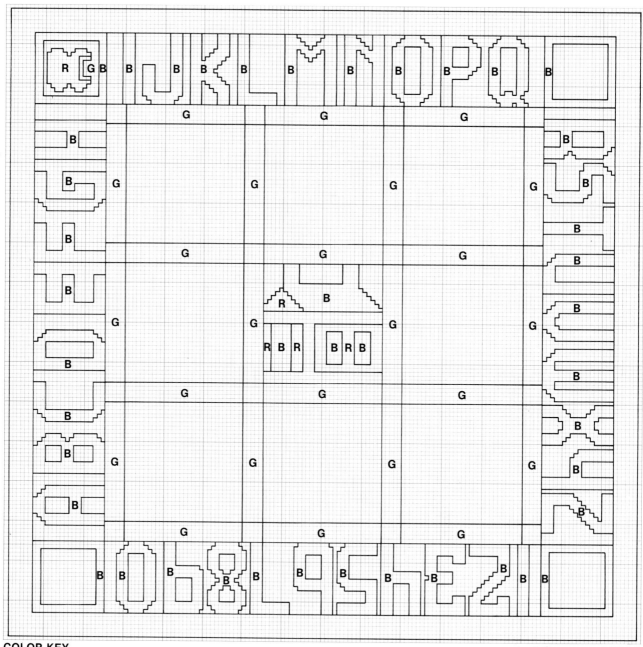

COLOR KEY
B = Blue   G = Green   R = Red

1 Square = 1 Stitch

Sew fronts to backs; leave open between Xs. Clip seams, turn, stuff with fiberfill, and sew openings.

Using the same procedure, make hen combs, wings, tail feathers, wattles, and cat's tails. Sew to animals between slash marks on patterns. Paint toothpicks yellow and insert in rooster for beak and legs. Embellish trims with ribbon ties, button eyes, yarn tails, manes, and whiskers. Add ribbon hanging loops.

Needlepoint Trims
Pictured on page 79

MATERIALS: 5-inch squares of No. 12 interlock canvas; Size 20 tapestry needle; scraps of felt; ribbon; masking tape; white glue; 32-inch strands of three-ply Persian yarn in the following colors and amounts:

Sailing ship—4 blue, 3 dark gold, 3 light gold, 8 white. *Goose tracks*—3 red, 2 dark gold, 5 light gold, 10 white. *Tree of Life*—6 green, 2 dark gold, 10 white. *Shooting star*—4 red, 5 green, 10 white. *House on a hill*—4 red, 4 green, 3 dark gold, 8 white. *Bow tie*—3 green, 3 blue, 1 red, 2 light gold, 2 dark gold, 6 white. *Whirligig*—4 blue, 2 red, 2 green, 2 light gold, 2 dark gold, 8 white. *Eight-pointed star*—6 blue, 6 light gold, 10 white. *Basket*—3 red, 2 light gold, 4 green, 10 white.

INSTRUCTIONS: Ornaments are 3½ inches square. For designs, use needlepoint pillow chart, *page 82.* Bind canvas edges with masking tape. Find center of canvas and center of design to begin stitching. Use basket-weave stitches. Stitch one row of continental stitches around finished design on all sides.

Block ornament, if necessary, and trim canvas to within ⅛ inch of stitches. Glue a ribbon loop (hanger) at top. Glue felt square, cut to size, to back of canvas; glue ribbon border around ornament on front to cover raw edges of canvas.

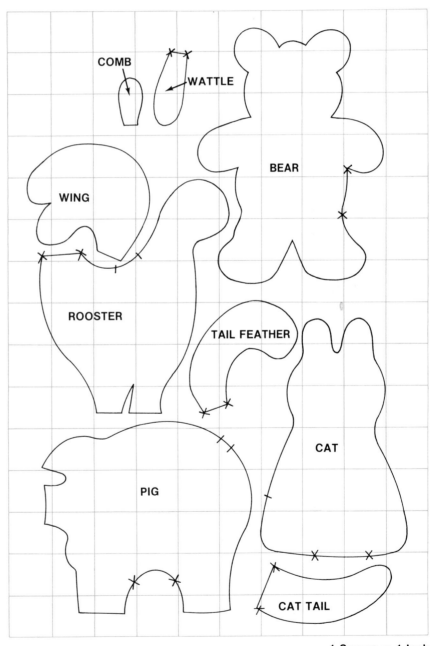

1 Square = 1 Inch

1 Square = 1 Inch

CHRISTMAS FOODS FROM AMERICA'S PAST

When our forefathers first set foot in the New World, they found a host of unusual foods awaiting them. They learned how to steam clams on the ocean shore, to tap maple trees for sticky syrup, and to harvest from bogs a small red berry that has become the most typical American holiday food of all, the cranberry.

The settlers combined these strange new delicacies with familiar ingredients of the Old World to create American dishes, deserving of any special occasion or holy day.

To this day, many of these foods that once meant a fresh start to our ancestors still are served on that very special holiday—Christmas.

Kentucky Bourbon Cake (see recipe, page 99), Brandy-Eggnog Deluxe (see recipe, page 103), and Sweet Potato Pie (see recipe, page 102)

ROAST BEEF BÉARNAISE

1 6-pound beef rib eye roast
⅓ cup wine vinegar
2 teaspoons finely chopped shallots *or* green onion
8 whole black peppercorns, crushed
¼ teaspoon dried tarragon, crushed
¼ teaspoon dried chervil, crushed
2 teaspoons cold water
8 egg yolks
1 cup butter *or* margarine, softened

Place beef, fat side up, onto a rack in a shallow roasting pan. Sprinkle with salt and pepper. Insert meat thermometer. Roast in a 350° oven for 1½ to 1¾ hours or till thermometer registers 140° for rare. Let stand 15 minutes before carving.

For sauce, in small saucepan combine wine vinegar, shallots, peppercorns, tarragon, and chervil. Bring to boiling; reduce heat. Simmer, uncovered, till the liquid is reduced by half (¼ cup). Add the cold water.

Beat egg yolks in top of double boiler (not over water). Slowly add herb liquid. Add *2 tablespoons* butter; place over, but not touching, boiling water. Cook and stir till butter melts and sauce starts to thicken. Continue adding remaining butter, 2 tablespoons at a time, stirring constantly. Cook and stir to the consistency of thick cream. Serve over sliced beef. Makes 14 to 16 servings.

Crown Roast of Pork, Potato-Stuffed Artichoke Bottoms (see recipe, page 94), and Citrus Cider (see recipe, page 103)

CROWN ROAST OF PORK

1½ cups cranberries
8 ounces bulk pork sausage
2 tablespoons finely chopped onion
1 small clove garlic, minced
4 cups firm-textured bread cubes (5½ slices)
1 cup chopped walnuts
¼ teaspoon dried sage, crushed
¾ to 1 cup chicken broth
1 7- to 7½-pound pork rib crown roast (14 to 16 ribs)
  Lettuce leaves (optional)

For stuffing, chop the cranberries; set aside. In a large saucepan or Dutch oven cook the sausage, onion, and garlic till meat is brown and onion is tender. Stir in cranberries, bread cubes, walnuts, and sage. Add enough chicken broth to moisten; toss gently to mix.

Place the pork roast, bone side up, onto foil on a rack in a shallow roasting pan. Spoon about *3 cups* of the stuffing into the center of the roast. Insert a meat thermometer into thickest portion of meat, away from fat or bone. Cover top loosely with additional foil. Roast pork in a 325° oven for 3½ to 4 hours or till the thermometer registers 170°.

Spoon remaining stuffing into a 1-quart casserole. Bake, covered, the last 30 to 45 minutes of roasting time. Uncover the stuffed pork roast the last 15 minutes. If desired, garnish with paper ruffles and serve on a lettuce-lined platter. Let stand for 15 minutes before carving. Makes 14 to 16 servings.

PLANKED HAM DINNER

8 slices fully cooked boneless ham, cut ⅜ inch thick (2 pounds)
2 17-ounce cans sweet potatoes, drained
1 egg
2 tablespoons butter *or* margarine, melted
1 cup currant jelly
3 tablespoons crème de cassis *or* pineapple juice
¼ teaspoon dry mustard
¼ teaspoon prepared horseradish
1 10-ounce package frozen peas
8 pineapple slices
2 tablespoons butter *or* margarine, melted

Arrange ham slices on a large oven-proof platter or board, overlapping slices slightly. In a mixer bowl combine sweet potatoes, egg, and 2 tablespoons melted butter or margarine. Beat with electric mixer till smooth and fluffy. Arrange the mixture into eight mounds around the ham. Using the back of a spoon, shape mounds into eight "nests." Cover; bake in a 375° oven for 35 to 45 minutes or till warm.

Meanwhile, in a saucepan combine the jelly, crème de cassis or pineapple juice, dry mustard, and horseradish. Cook and stir till jelly is melted. Cook peas according to package directions; keep warm.

Arrange the pineapple slices between the sweet potato nests. Brush some jelly mixture over the ham and pineapple. Spoon peas into sweet potato nests; drizzle with 2 tablespoons butter. Bake, uncovered, for 10 to 15 minutes more or till heated through. Pass remaining jelly mixture. Makes 8 servings.

ROAST TURKEY WITH OYSTER STUFFING

  1 10- to 12-pound turkey
  1 pint shucked oysters
  ½ cup chopped celery
  ½ cup chopped onion
  1 bay leaf
  ¼ cup butter *or* margarine
  6 cups dry bread crumbs
      (about 24 slices)
  2 beaten eggs
  1 tablespoon snipped
      parsley
  1 teaspoon poultry
      seasoning
  ½ teaspoon salt
      Dash pepper
      Cooking oil

Rinse turkey; pat dry with paper toweling. Sprinkle cavities with salt. Drain oysters, reserving liquid. Cut up oysters.

For stuffing, cook celery, onion, and bay leaf in hot butter or margarine till tender but not brown. Discard bay leaf. Stir in oysters, bread crumbs, eggs, parsley, poultry seasoning, salt, and pepper. Add enough reserved oyster liquid to moisten; toss gently to mix.

To stuff, spoon *some* of the stuffing loosely into the neck cavity. Pull neck skin to back; skewer closed. Loosely spoon remaining stuffing into body cavity. Tie legs to tail. Twist wing tips under back.

Place bird, breast side up, onto a rack in a shallow roasting pan. Brush with oil. Insert a meat thermometer into the center of the inside thigh muscle, making sure bulb does not touch bone. Roast in a 325° oven for 4 to 5 hours or till the thermometer registers 180° to 185° and drumstick twists easily in socket. Garnish turkey with spiced crab apples and parsley, if desired. Makes 12 servings.

PLYMOUTH SUCCOTASH

  1 pound dry navy beans
  1 2½- to 3-pound broiler-
      fryer chicken, cut up
  1 2½-pound corned beef
      brisket
  4 ounces salt pork
  3 cups sliced potatoes
  1 cup chopped turnips
  1 cup chopped carrots
  1 medium onion, sliced
  ½ teaspoon dried thyme,
      crushed
  2 16-ounce cans yellow
      hominy, drained
      Dash pepper (optional)

Rinse beans. In a Dutch oven or large kettle combine beans and 3 cups *water*. Bring to boiling. Reduce heat; simmer for 2 minutes. Remove from heat. Cover; let stand 1 hour. (Or, soak beans in water overnight in a covered pan.) Drain beans and rinse. In the same Dutch oven or kettle combine rinsed beans and 3 cups more *water*.

Meanwhile, in a covered saucepan cook chicken in 4 cups *water* over low heat for 35 to 40 minutes or till tender. Drain chicken, reserving broth. When chicken is cool enough to handle, remove meat, discarding skin and bones; chill.

Add reserved chicken broth, corned beef, and salt pork to beans. Cover and simmer for 1 hour. Add potatoes, turnips, carrots, onion, and thyme. Cover and simmer for 1 hour more. Remove corned beef and salt pork. Discard salt pork. Skim fat from broth. Mash beans slightly. Dice beef; return to bean mixture. Stir in chicken and hominy. Season with pepper, if desired. Cook about 15 minutes more or till heated through. Serves 16.

CODFISH BALLS

  8 ounces salt cod
  3 cups diced potatoes
  ¼ cup chopped onion
  1 egg
  ¼ cup snipped parsley
  2 tablespoons butter *or*
      margarine
  ½ teaspoon Worcestershire
      sauce
  ¼ teaspoon pepper
      Shortening *or* cooking oil
      for deep-fat frying

Soak cod in water for several hours, changing the water frequently. Drain the fish; cut into small pieces. In a large saucepan cook cod pieces, diced potatoes, and chopped onion in boiling water about 10 minutes or till tender; drain.

Turn the mixture into a mixer bowl. Beat on medium speed of electric mixer till smooth. Add the egg, parsley, butter or margarine, Worcestershire sauce, and pepper; beat till smooth.

In a saucepan or deep-fat fryer heat about 2 inches of shortening or cooking oil to 375°. Carefully drop cod mixture from a tablespoon into deep hot fat. Fry codfish balls, a few at a time, for 2 to 3 minutes or till golden, turning once. Drain on paper toweling. Keep warm in a 325° oven while frying remaining balls. Makes 30.

Roast Turkey with Oyster Stuffing, whipped mashed potatoes, Codfish Balls, Rye and Indian Bread (see recipe, page 96), Fruit Juice Jelly (see recipe, page 103), Cranberry Tarts (see recipe, page 102), Indian Pudding (see recipe, page 99), Steamed Clams (see recipe, page 94), and Plymouth Succotash

STEAMED CLAMS

Pictured on page 93—

24 soft-shell clams in shells
3 gallons cold water
1 cup salt
1 cup hot water
   Butter *or* margarine,
      melted

Wash clams. In a kettle combine *1 gallon* of the cold water and *⅓ cup* of the salt. Add clams; let stand for 15 minutes. Rinse well. Repeat soaking and rinsing clams twice more. Place clams onto a rack over the hot water in a kettle. Cover tightly; steam about 5 minutes or till shells open. Discard any clams that do not open. Loosen clams from shells. Serve with butter or margarine. Serves 2 to 4.

CRANBERRY SWEET POTATOES

3 large sweet potatoes
½ cup cranberry-orange
   relish
¼ cup raisins
2 tablespoons butter *or*
   margarine
¼ cup packed brown sugar
¼ cup broken walnuts

Cook sweet potatoes in boiling salted water for 25 to 35 minutes or till tender. Cut in half lengthwise. Scoop out centers, leaving ¼-inch-thick shells; set aside. Mash centers; add relish. Beat till fluffy. Stir in raisins. Spoon into shells. Place into a 12x7½x2-inch baking dish. Cut butter into brown sugar; stir in nuts. Sprinkle over sweet potatoes. Bake in a 350° oven for 30 minutes. Makes 6 servings.

TURNIP-BACON PUFF

1 pound turnips, peeled and
   shredded (3 cups)
4 slices bacon
4 egg yolks
¼ cup mayonnaise *or* salad
   dressing
¼ cup milk
1 teaspoon lemon juice
2 tablespoons all-purpose
   flour
¼ teaspoon salt
   Dash pepper
2 tablespoons snipped
   parsley
4 egg whites

Cook shredded turnips, covered, in a small amount of boiling salted water about 15 minutes or till tender; drain. In a skillet cook bacon till crisp; drain on paper toweling. Crumble bacon. Set aside.

In a mixer bowl combine egg yolks, mayonnaise or salad dressing, milk, and lemon juice; beat on high speed of electric mixer about 5 minutes or till thick and lemon colored. Add flour, salt, and pepper; beat till smooth. Stir in cooked turnips, bacon pieces, and parsley. Using clean beaters, beat egg whites till stiff peaks form (tips stand straight). Gently fold the egg yolk mixture into the stiff-beaten egg whites.

Turn the mixture into a 2-quart soufflé dish. Bake in a 350° oven for 30 to 35 minutes or till a knife inserted near the center comes out clean. Makes 6 to 8 servings.

POTATO-STUFFED ARTICHOKE BOTTOMS

Pictured on page 90—

2 medium potatoes
1 tablespoon butter *or*
   margarine
1 egg yolk
¼ teaspoon dried basil,
   crushed
¼ cup butter *or* margarine
⅓ cup water
½ cup all-purpose flour
¼ teaspoon salt
2 eggs
1 14-ounce can artichoke
   bottoms, drained and
   rinsed
¼ cup shredded Swiss
   cheese (1 ounce)
   Paprika

In a saucepan cook the potatoes in boiling salted water for 25 to 30 minutes or till tender. Drain, peel, and mash (you should have ¾ cup mashed potato). Stir the 1 tablespoon butter or margarine, egg yolk, and basil into potato; set aside.

In a small saucepan melt the ¼ cup butter or margarine. Add the water; bring to boiling. Add flour and salt all at once; stir vigorously. Cook and stir till mixture forms a ball that doesn't separate. Remove from heat; cool slightly, about 5 minutes. Add whole eggs, one at a time, beating with a wooden spoon after each addition for 1 to 2 minutes or till smooth.

Fold the potato mixture into batter. Spoon about *¼ cup* of the mixture into *each* artichoke bottom, forming mounds. Sprinkle *each* with *some* of the shredded cheese; sprinkle paprika atop. Place the filled artichoke bottoms into a shallow baking pan. Bake in a 325° oven for 45 to 50 minutes or till brown. Makes 4 servings.

SPICED-PEACH SALAD MOLD

The peach halves sealed inside the gelatin are stuffed with tasty nuggets of cream cheese, walnuts, and spices—

2 3-ounce packages lemon-flavored gelatin
2 cups boiling water
1 29-ounce can peach halves
1 3-ounce package cream cheese, softened
¼ cup finely chopped celery
2 tablespoons finely chopped walnuts
⅛ teaspoon ground cinnamon
Dash ground cloves

In a mixing bowl dissolve gelatin in boiling water. Drain peach halves, reserving syrup; set the peach halves aside. Measure the syrup; add water, if necessary, to equal 2 cups liquid. Pour into gelatin. Pour *1 cup* of the gelatin mixture into a 10x6x2-inch baking dish. Chill in the refrigerator till almost firm. Let remaining gelatin stand at room temperature.

Meanwhile, in a mixing bowl combine the cream cheese, celery, walnuts, cinnamon, and cloves. Spoon the cream cheese mixture into peach-half cavities.

Arrange the filled peach halves atop the almost-firm gelatin layer in the baking dish. Spoon the remaining gelatin over the peaches. Chill in the refrigerator about 6 hours or till firm. Cut into squares to serve. Makes 6 to 8 servings.

CRANBERRY FROST SALAD

1 cup cranberries, finely chopped
⅓ cup sugar
2 medium oranges
1 8-ounce package cream cheese, softened
1 teaspoon vanilla
1 medium apple, cored and finely chopped
½ cup chopped pitted dates
1 cup whipping cream
Lettuce leaves
Orange sections *or* whole cranberries (optional)

In a mixing bowl combine cranberries and sugar; let stand for 10 minutes. Meanwhile, peel and section *1* of the oranges, reserving juice. Finely chop orange sections; set aside. Squeeze remaining orange; measure ⅓ cup juice.

In a mixer bowl combine the freshly squeezed orange juice, cream cheese, and vanilla; beat on medium speed of electric mixer till fluffy. Stir in the chopped orange sections, cranberries, apple, and dates.

Using clean beaters, beat whipping cream till soft peaks form. Fold the whipped cream into the cream cheese mixture.

Turn the mixture into a 5-cup mold, an 8x4x2-inch loaf pan, or 8 or 9 individual molds. Cover with moisture-vaporproof wrap; seal, label, and freeze for at least 3 hours (or up to 1 month).

Before serving, let the salad stand at room temperature for 10 to 15 minutes to soften slightly. Unmold onto a lettuce-lined platter or individual lettuce-lined salad plates. Garnish with additional orange sections or whole cranberries, if desired. Makes 8 or 9 servings.

Indians gave wild cranberries to the pilgrims as a sign of friendship. They taught the settlers not only to eat the berries, but also to use the dark red juice for a dye and the crushed berries for a poultice. Cranberries are harvested in the fall, so they are fresh and juicy for the Christmas feast.

MOLDED LETTUCE SALAD

2 3-ounce packages lime-flavored gelatin
2 cups boiling water
1½ cups cold water
2 tablespoons vinegar
3 cups coarsely chopped iceberg lettuce
¼ cup sliced green onion
Assorted relishes

Dissolve lime-flavored gelatin in boiling water. Stir in the cold water and vinegar. Chill in the refrigerator to the consistency of unbeaten egg whites (partially set).

Fold lettuce and green onion into the partially set gelatin. Pour into a 5-cup ring mold. Chill about 6 hours or till firm. Unmold onto a serving platter. Fill the center with assorted relishes. Makes 8 to 10 servings.

ASSORTED RELISHES: Use carrot curls, radish roses, ripe olives, celery sticks, cherry tomatoes, or green or red sweet pepper strips.

LOVE FEAST BUNS

1 large potato, peeled
¾ cup sugar
½ cup butter *or* margarine, cut up
5½ to 6 cups all-purpose flour
2 packages active dry yeast
2 eggs
1 teaspoon finely shredded orange peel
1 beaten egg

Cook potato in 1½ cups *boiling water* for 30 to 40 minutes or till tender. Do not drain. Mash potato in liquid; measure and add water, if necessary, to equal 1¾ cups. Add sugar, butter, and 1 teaspoon *salt.* Heat just till warm (115° to 120°).

In a mixer bowl combine *2 cups* of the flour and the yeast. Stir in the potato mixture; add the 2 eggs. Beat on low speed of electric mixer for ½ minute, scraping bowl. Beat for 3 minutes on high. Using a spoon, stir in as much remaining flour as you can. Stir in orange peel.

On a lightly floured surface knead in enough of the remaining flour to make a moderately stiff dough that is smooth and elastic (6 to 8 minutes total). Shape into a ball. Place into a lightly greased bowl; turn once. Cover; let rise in a warm place till double (about 1 hour).

Punch down; divide in half. Divide each half into six portions; shape into balls. Place onto a greased baking sheet. With a knife or kitchen shears, deeply cut an M atop each. Cover; let rise till nearly double (about 30 minutes). Mix the beaten egg and 1 tablespoon *water;* brush atop. Bake in a 375° oven for 17 to 20 minutes or till done. Makes 12.

MORAVIAN SUGAR CAKE

1 small potato, peeled
1 cup boiling water
1 package active dry yeast
⅓ cup sugar
⅓ cup lard *or* shortening, melted
1½ teaspoons salt
3 to 3½ cups all-purpose flour
2 tablespoons butter *or* margarine
½ cup packed brown sugar
½ teaspoon ground cinnamon

Cook potato in the boiling water about 25 minutes or till tender. Cool to lukewarm (110° to 115°). Pour ¼ *cup* of the potato water into a liquid measure; add yeast to soften. Mash potato in remaining water; measure and add water, if necessary, to equal 1 cup.

In a mixing bowl combine the potato mixture, yeast mixture, sugar, lard or shortening, and salt. Stir in *1 cup* of the flour. Let rise in a warm place till spongy (30 to 45 minutes).

Stir down; stir in as much remaining flour as you can. Turn out onto a floured surface; knead for 4 minutes. Shape into a ball. Place into a greased bowl; turn once. Cover; let rise till double (about 45 minutes).

Punch dough down; divide in half. Cover; let rest for 10 minutes. On a floured surface roll dough into two 8-inch squares; pat into two greased 8x8x2-inch pans. Cover; let rise till nearly double (45 minutes).

Make indentations at 1½-inch intervals. Dot with butter. Combine brown sugar and cinnamon; sprinkle atop. Bake in a 375° oven for 20 to 25 minutes or till done. Makes 2.

RYE AND INDIAN BREAD

Pictured on page 93—

2 to 2½ cups all-purpose flour
¾ cup cornmeal
1 package active dry yeast
1½ cups milk
¼ cup molasses
3 tablespoons lard *or* shortening
1 teaspoon salt
1 cup rye flour

In a large mixer bowl combine *1½ cups* of the all-purpose flour, the cornmeal, and the yeast. In a saucepan heat the milk, molasses, lard or shortening, and salt just till warm (115° to 120°) and shortening is almost melted; stir constantly.

Add warm mixture to flour mixture. Beat on low speed of electric mixer for ½ minute, scraping sides of bowl constantly. Beat for 3 minutes on high speed. Using a spoon, stir in the rye flour and as much of the remaining all-purpose flour as you can. Cover and let dough rise in a warm place till double (about 1 hour).

Stir dough down; divide in half. Place into two greased 1-quart casseroles. Cover and let rise in a warm place till nearly double (about 45 minutes). Bake in a 350° oven for 25 to 30 minutes or till bread tests done. Makes 2 loaves.

Moravian Sugar Cake, Love Feast Buns, and Café au Lait (see recipe, page 103)

CHOCOLATE ÉCLAIR CAKE

4 squares (4 ounces) unsweetened chocolate
1¾ cups sugar
2 cups all-purpose flour
1 tablespoon baking powder
½ cup cooking oil
7 egg yolks
1 teaspoon vanilla
7 egg whites
½ teaspoon cream of tartar
Custard Filling
Chocolate Icing
Vanilla Icing

Melt chocolate; stir in ¼ *cup* of the sugar and ½ cup *boiling water;* cool. Combine flour, remaining sugar, baking powder, and 1 teaspoon *salt.* Add oil, egg yolks, vanilla, and ¾ cup *cold water* all at once; beat till smooth. Stir in chocolate mixture. Combine egg whites and cream of tartar; beat till stiff peaks form. Pour chocolate mixture in a thin stream over entire surface of egg whites; fold in gently. Turn into a 10-inch tube pan; bake in a 325° oven for 65 minutes. Invert pan to cool; remove from pan.

Make Custard Filling. Split cake into 3 layers. Fill with filling. Prepare icings. Frost top with Chocolate Icing. Pipe 4 concentric circles of Vanilla Icing on top; draw spatula through icing for web. Chill. Makes 12 to 16 servings.

CUSTARD FILLING: Combine ¼ cup *cornstarch* and ¼ cup *sugar.* Stir in 3 cups *milk;* cook and stir till bubbly. Reduce heat; cook and stir for 2 minutes more. Add *1 cup* of the hot mixture to 2 beaten *eggs;* return

all to pan. Cook and stir till slightly thickened; reduce heat. Cook and stir for 1 to 2 minutes more but *do not boil.* Stir in 2 teaspoons *vanilla.* Cover surface with waxed paper; cool.

CHOCOLATE ICING: In a saucepan melt one 4-ounce package *German sweet cooking chocolate* and 3 tablespoons *butter or margarine* over low heat, stirring often. Remove from heat; stir in 1½ cups sifted *powdered sugar* and enough *hot water* (3 to 4 tablespoons) to make of drizzling consistency.

VANILLA ICING: Stir together 2 cups sifted *powdered sugar,* 1 teaspoon *vanilla,* and a dash *salt.* Stir in enough *milk* (2 to 3 tablespoons) to make of piping consistency.

KENTUCKY BOURBON CAKE

Pictured on pages 88-89—

1½ cups raisins
1¼ cups bourbon
4 cups all-purpose flour
2 teaspoons baking powder
1 teaspoon ground nutmeg
1 teaspoon ground mace
1½ cups butter *or* margarine
2¼ cups packed brown sugar
6 eggs
4½ cups chopped pecans (1 pound)
1 cup chopped candied cherries
1 cup chopped candied pineapple
1½ cups orange marmalade

Combine raisins and bourbon; let stand 1 hour. Drain raisins, reserving bourbon. Grease a 10-inch tube pan. Line with heavy brown paper; grease.

Combine flour, baking powder, nutmeg, and mace. In a mixer bowl beat butter with

electric mixer for 30 seconds. Add brown sugar; beat till fluffy. Add eggs, one at a time, beating well. Add dry ingredients and reserved bourbon alternately to beaten mixture, beating after each addition. Turn batter into a large mixing bowl. Combine raisins, pecans, cherries, and pineapple; fold into batter. Stir in marmalade.

Spoon batter into prepared pan. Bake in a 300° oven for 3 to 3¼ hours or till done. Cool 10 minutes. Remove from pan; cool. Wrap in a bourbon-moistened cheesecloth; overwrap with foil. Store in the refrigerator 3 to 4 weeks. Occasionally remoisten cheesecloth with bourbon; rewrap. To serve, unwrap; trim with additional candied cherries, if desired. Makes about 40 servings.

INDIAN PUDDING

Pictured on page 93—

3 cups milk
⅓ cup molasses
⅓ cup cornmeal
1 slightly beaten egg
¼ cup sugar
2 tablespoons butter *or* margarine
½ teaspoon ground ginger
½ teaspoon ground cinnamon

In a saucepan combine milk and molasses; stir in cornmeal. Cook and stir till bubbly; reduce heat. Cook and stir about 10 minutes more or till thickened. Remove from heat. Combine egg, sugar, butter, ginger, cinnamon, and ¼ teaspoon *salt.* Gradually stir in hot mixture. Turn into a 1-quart casserole. Bake, uncovered, in a 300° oven for 1½ hours. Serves 6.

Chocolate Éclair Cake

99

SYRUP-SOAKED CAKE

2 cups all-purpose flour
2 teaspoons baking powder
½ teaspoon baking soda
½ teaspoon salt
½ cup butter *or* margarine
¾ cup sugar
2 eggs
½ cup pure maple syrup *or* maple-flavored syrup
½ cup milk
Maple-Lemon Syrup

Grease and lightly flour a 7-cup fluted tube mold; set aside. Stir together flour, baking powder, baking soda, and salt.

In a mixer bowl beat butter or margarine on medium speed of electric mixer for 30 seconds. Add sugar and beat till fluffy. Add eggs, one at a time, beating well on medium speed. Stir in maple syrup. Add dry ingredients and milk alternately to beaten mixture, beating on low speed after each addition just till combined.

Turn the batter into the prepared pan. Bake in a 350° oven for 45 to 50 minutes or till done. Place cake onto a wire rack; cool for 10 minutes. Remove from pan; place cake onto rack over waxed paper.

Meanwhile, prepare Maple-Lemon Syrup. Prick warm cake with the tines of a fork. Slowly spoon Maple-Lemon Syrup over cake, allowing syrup to soak in. Makes 12 servings.

MAPLE-LEMON SYRUP: In a small mixing bowl combine ¼ cup *pure maple syrup or maple-flavored syrup* and 1 tablespoon *lemon juice.*

MAPLE DIVINITY

2 cups pure maple syrup
2 egg whites
¼ teaspoon salt
1 cup broken walnuts

In a heavy 3-quart saucepan bring maple syrup to boiling. Clip candy thermometer to side of pan. Cook, without stirring, over medium heat to 260° (hard-ball stage). Mixture should boil gently over entire surface. (At hard-ball stage, a few drops of syrup dropped into cold water form hard balls when removed from the water.) Remove from heat.

Immediately beat egg whites and salt on medium speed of electric mixer till stiff peaks form (tips stand straight).

Remove the candy thermometer. *Gradually* pour the hot syrup in a thin stream over egg whites, beating on high speed. (Add syrup *slowly* to ensure proper mixing. This should take about 3 minutes.) Continue beating for 5 to 6 minutes more or till the mixture holds its shape when beaters are lifted. (Candy falls in a ribbon, but mounds on itself and starts to lose its gloss.) When beaten enough, the mixture will stay mounded in a soft shape when a spoonful is dropped onto waxed paper. If it flattens out, beat for ½ to 1 minute more and check again. The candy is overbeaten if it is stiff to spoon and the surface is rough.

When the mixture holds its shape, stir in walnuts. *Quickly* drop by teaspoonfuls onto a baking sheet lined with waxed paper, swirling each candy to a peak. If the candy becomes too stiff to drop easily from a spoon, stir in a few drops *hot water.* Makes about 40 candies.

MAPLE LEAF CUTOUTS

1 cup butter *or* margarine
⅔ cup sugar
½ cup pure maple syrup *or* maple-flavored syrup
⅓ cup milk
3½ cups all-purpose flour
½ teaspoon baking soda
½ teaspoon ground ginger
Maple Glaze (optional)

In a medium saucepan combine butter or margarine, sugar, and maple syrup; bring to boiling. Remove from heat; cool to room temperature. Stir in milk.

In a mixing bowl stir together the flour, baking soda, and ginger. Stir in the cooled syrup mixture. Divide the dough in half; wrap in waxed paper or clear plastic wrap. Chill in the refrigerator for at least 2 hours.

On a lightly floured surface roll the dough, half at a time, to 3/16 to ¼-inch thickness. Cut with a maple-leaf-shape cookie cutter. Place onto an ungreased cookie sheet. Bake in a 375° oven for 8 to 10 minutes or till golden. Transfer to a wire rack over waxed paper.

Meanwhile, if desired, prepare Maple Glaze; immediately brush surface of cookies with glaze. Cool thoroughly. Makes about 42 cookies.

MAPLE GLAZE: In a mixing bowl combine ½ cup sifted *powdered sugar* and 3 tablespoons *pure maple syrup or maple-flavored syrup* to make a thin glaze.

Syrup-Soaked Cake, Maple Divinity, and Maple Leaf Cutouts

MORAVIAN CHRISTMAS COOKIES

These crispy, spicy cookies were first baked by the Moravians, a religious sect who settled in America in 1734—

1¾ cups all-purpose flour
1 teaspoon ground
    cinnamon
1 teaspoon ground ginger
½ teaspoon baking soda
¼ teaspoon salt
¼ teaspoon ground cloves
⅛ teaspoon ground nutmeg
¼ cup butter *or* margarine
¼ cup packed brown sugar
½ cup molasses

In a mixing bowl stir together flour, cinnamon, ginger, baking soda, salt, cloves, and nutmeg. In a mixer bowl beat butter or margarine on medium speed of electric mixer for 30 seconds. Add brown sugar and beat till fluffy. Add molasses; beat well. Add dry ingredients to beaten mixture and beat till combined. Cover and chill in the refrigerator for at least 2 hours.

On a well-floured surface roll the dough, half at a time, to 1/16-inch thickness. Cut with a 2-inch round cookie cutter. Place onto a greased cookie sheet. Bake in a 375° oven for 7 to 8 minutes or till cookies begin to brown. Transfer to a wire rack; cool thoroughly. Makes about 64 cookies.

SWEET POTATO PIE

Pictured on pages 88-89—

1 pound sweet potatoes *or* one 17-ounce can sweet potatoes
Pastry for Single-Crust Pie
¾ cup packed brown sugar
1 tablespoon butter *or* margarine, melted
1 teaspoon ground cinnamon
½ teaspoon salt
3 slightly beaten eggs
1¾ cups milk
Whipped cream (optional)

Cook fresh sweet potatoes, covered, in boiling water about 30 minutes or till tender; drain and peel. (*Or*, drain canned sweet potatoes.) Mash sweet potatoes (you should have 1½ cups). Prepare Pastry for Single-Crust Pie.

In a mixing bowl combine sweet potatoes, brown sugar, butter or margarine, cinnamon, and salt. Stir in eggs and milk; spoon into pastry shell. Bake in a 400° oven for 50 to 55 minutes or till a knife inserted near the center comes out clean. Cool. Garnish with whipped cream, if desired. Serves 8.

PASTRY FOR SINGLE-CRUST PIE: Stir together 1¼ cups *all-purpose flour* and ½ teaspoon *salt*. Cut in ⅓ cup *shortening or lard* till pieces are the size of small peas. Sprinkle 1 tablespoon *cold water* over part of the mixture; gently toss with a fork. Push to side of bowl. Repeat with 2 to 3 more tablespoons *cold water* till all is moistened. Form into a ball. On a lightly floured surface, roll into a 12-inch circle. Transfer to a 9-inch pie plate. Trim to ½ inch beyond edge of plate; flute edge.

CRANBERRY TARTS

Pictured on page 93—

Pastry for Tarts
3 cups cranberries
1 cup water
½ cup raisins
1½ cups sugar
2 tablespoons cornstarch
1 teaspoon vanilla
½ cup all-purpose flour
¼ cup sugar
¼ cup butter *or* margarine

Prepare Pastry for Tarts; set aside. For filling, in a saucepan combine cranberries, water, and raisins. Bring to boiling; reduce heat. Cover and simmer for 3 minutes. Stir together the 1½ cups sugar and the cornstarch; stir into the cranberries. Cook and stir till thickened and bubbly. Cook and stir for 2 minutes more. Remove from heat. Stir in the vanilla. Spoon the filling into tart shells.

For topping, stir together flour and the ¼ cup sugar. Cut in butter or margarine till mixture resembles coarse crumbs; sprinkle over tarts. Bake in a 400° oven about 30 minutes or till done. Makes 6 tarts.

PASTRY FOR TARTS: In a mixing bowl stir together 2 cups *all-purpose flour* and 1 teaspoon *salt*. Cut in ⅔ cup *shortening or lard* till pieces are the size of small peas. Sprinkle 1 tablespoon *cold water* over part of the mixture; gently toss with a fork. Push to side of bowl. Repeat with 5 to 6 more tablespoons *cold water* till all is moistened. Form dough into a ball. Roll the pastry to ⅛-inch thickness. Cut into six 7-inch circles. Fit the pastry into six 4½-inch tart pans; flute the edges high.

FRUIT JUICE JELLY

Pictured on page 93—

4 cups unsweetened grape, apple, orange, *or* pineapple juice *or* cranberry juice cocktail (not low-calorie)
¼ cup lemon juice
1 1¾-ounce package powdered fruit pectin
4½ cups sugar

In an 8- to 10-quart kettle combine the desired fruit juice, lemon juice, and pectin. Bring the mixture to a full rolling boil (a boil that cannot be stirred down). Stir in the sugar. Return to a full rolling boil. Boil hard for 1 minute, stirring constantly. Remove from heat; immediately skim off foam with a metal spoon.

Ladle into hot, sterilized jars, leaving a ¼-inch headspace. Seal, using metal lids or paraffin. Makes 6 half-pints.

CAFÉ AU LAIT

Pictured on page 97—

3 cups cold water
¾ cup chicory-blend ground coffee
3 cups light cream *or* milk
Sugar (optional)

Pour cold water into a percolator. Measure coffee into basket. Replace basket lid; cover pot. Bring water to boiling; reduce heat and perk gently for 6 to 8 minutes. Let stand for 1 to 2 minutes; remove basket. Keep coffee warm over very low heat till ready to serve.

Meanwhile, in a heavy saucepan heat the cream or milk over low heat. Beat with rotary beater till foamy. Pour equal amounts of the hot coffee and cream into serving cups. Stir in sugar to taste, if desired. Makes 10 (5-ounce) servings.

CITRUS CIDER

Pictured on page 90—

8 cups apple cider *or* apple juice
3 cups water
1 6-ounce can frozen pineapple-orange juice concentrate, thawed
½ cup light molasses
4 inches stick cinnamon
1 teaspoon whole cloves
Apple slices (optional)
Cinnamon stick stirrers (optional)

In a 4-quart Dutch oven combine the apple cider or juice, water, pineapple-orange juice concentrate, molasses, 4 inches cinnamon, and cloves. Bring to boiling; reduce heat. Cover and simmer for 10 minutes.

Pour the warm cider into a heat-proof punch bowl placed on a warming tray or into an electric slow crockery cooker turned to low-heat setting. If desired, float apple slices atop cider. To serve, ladle the cider into mugs; serve with cinnamon stick stirrers, if desired. Makes 24 (4-ounce) servings.

BRANDY-EGGNOG DELUXE

Pictured on pages 88-89—

6 egg yolks
¾ cup sugar
¾ cup brandy
¼ cup bourbon
½ teaspoon vanilla
¼ teaspoon ground nutmeg
3 cups whipping cream, chilled
2 cups cold milk
6 egg whites
⅓ cup sugar
Ground nutmeg (optional)

In a mixer bowl beat the egg yolks on high speed of electric mixer about 5 minutes or till thick and lemon colored. Gradually add the ¾ cup sugar, beating constantly. Stir in the brandy, bourbon, vanilla, and the ¼ teaspoon nutmeg. Cover and chill in the refrigerator about 2 hours or till cold.

Stir the whipping cream and milk into the chilled yolk mixture. Using clean beaters, beat egg whites on medium speed till soft peaks form (tips curl). Gradually add the ⅓ cup sugar, beating till stiff peaks form (tips stand straight).

Fold the yolk mixture into egg whites just till combined, leaving a few small fluffs of egg white. Serve immediately. Sprinkle with additional nutmeg, if desired. Makes 22 (4-ounce) servings.

FESTIVE FAMILY GATHERINGS

*W*hether you are out on a sleigh ride or a trip through the woods for the perfect tree, Christmas is a wonderful time for families to get together. To make your holiday outings memorable, create some of these easy-to-make warmers.

The woman's jacket, left, is a cozy wrap that takes on a fanciful look with floral appliqués. Chilly fingers warm up in a pair of knitted gauntlets.

For girls, there is a knitted prairie-style bonnet with flowers, left, or the charming Fair Isle motifs, opposite. Intricate folk-inspired embroidery adorns the scarf, opposite.

For how-to instructions, see page 112.

Ignore the cold and snow! Plan a spirited family reunion around a winter holiday.

*F*ew sweaters feel as warm as handmade ones. The festive pullovers, above, feature pretty knitted motifs and garter-stitch bands.

Bulky yarn is just right for the knitted caps, above and right. Both hats have extra-deep brims.

FESTIVE FAMILY GATHERINGS

*C*old, clear days are
just right for choosing
a Christmas tree and rid-
ing a pony among snow-
covered pines.

A teenager can bundle
up in a crocheted cap and
a purchased jacket embel-
lished with embroidery,
below left.

An oversize square collar
is the focal point of the
woman's knitted sweater,
below right. Trim collar
and cuffs with yarns in
contrasting colors.

A dapt a dress pattern to these festive designs. For example, enhance a child's smock with a collar and apron, or add a majestic yoke to a grown-up's dress.

FESTIVE FAMILY GATHERINGS

E legant clothes are especially appropriate for Christmas, when everyone is decked out in Sunday-best finery. Our collection of fool-the-eye lace collars, cuffs, and aprons begins with delicate outlines on any plain fabric background. The designs are embellished with embroidery, beading, and quilting.

One of these handcrafted heirlooms would make a stunning focal point for any family gathering. Each represents many symbols of the season and is sure to be cherished for years.

A circle of white poinsettias creates the elegant framed wreath, left. Stitched with Persian yarn, this beautiful needlepoint design measures 24 inches square when finished. The central greeting is outlined in glimmering gold thread.

FESTIVE FAMILY GATHERINGS

A lovely border of Christmas roses, poinsettias, and trees bedecked with candles frames the sampler, opposite. A cross-stitcher's delight, it includes a graceful alphabet and wonderful holiday motifs.

For the Christmas sign, right, make an oval tray of plywood and molding. Paint large shapes first, then stamp pine needles in place with painted cardboard turned on edge.

Appliquéd Jacket
Pictured on page 104

MATERIALS: *For the jacket*—twin-size blanket, or 1⅞ yards of 54-inch-wide wool; 6½ yards of satin binding or 1-inch-wide ribbon; cotton print (lining); three medium-size wooden toggle buttons; thread.

For the appliqué—⅛ yard of *each* of the following fabrics (for appliqués): dark aqua, light aqua, light gray, light pink, medium purple, maroon, and light yellow; ¼ yard of broadcloth (match the color to the jacket fabric); ½ yard of fusible webbing; assorted threads to match fabrics for the appliqués; dressmaker's carbon paper.

INSTRUCTIONS: Enlarge patterns, *below* and *right;* make a master pattern for the appliqué design.

• *To make the jacket,* cut pattern pieces from wool; cut pocket and collar linings from cotton (add ½-inch seam allowances to pocket).

Join right and left fronts to the back at the shoulders with ⅜-inch seams. Sew side and sleeve seams. Fit sleeves to jacket; pin and stitch. Baste cotton pocket (lining) to wool pocket, folding cotton seam allowance to back of wool pocket. Topstitch along top of pocket. Topstitch pocket to right front.

Baste cotton lining to collar. Bind top and side edges of collar with satin binding or ribbon. With cotton side to wrong side of jacket, baste collar in place. Machine-stitch. (Collar will fold in or stand up.)

Bind the neck and all raw edges of the jacket (including the sleeves) with satin binding or ribbon.

To make the jacket closures, cut six 6-inch-long strips of binding,

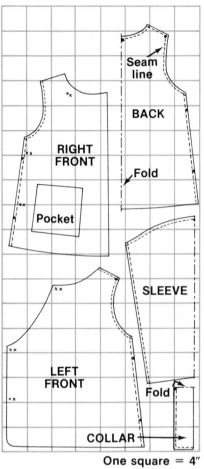

One square = 4″

fold the edges toward center, and stitch along the edge. Thread one button on each of three strips; stitch the strip in place on left front (see XXs indicated on pattern), trimming and tucking under raw edges at ends of strips. Make loops large enough to hold buttons snugly and attach at seam line between back and right front.

• *For appliqués,* trace over enlarged pattern for appliqués; cut out. Using master pattern, transfer design to broadcloth with dressmaker's carbon, creating a base upon which to appliqué colored pieces.

Pin appliqué patterns to corresponding colored fabrics (use color key); pin fusible webbing underneath. Cut around each pattern, colored fabric, and fusible webbing without adding seam allowances.

Place pieces just cut atop corresponding broadcloth shapes; fuse to broadcloth using an iron. (Place paper towels between iron and appliqué to blot stray wisps of webbing during fusing.) Appliqué pieces should fit together like a puzzle.

When pieces are fused to broadcloth, machine-satin-stitch around all shapes with matching thread. Embellish leaves, stems, and petals with additional stitching as desired.

Cut out the entire appliqué from broadcloth. Zigzag-stitch around outline again with a wider stitch to conceal any rough edges. Hand-sew the appliqué design to the jacket, using photograph as a guide.

COLOR KEY
1 Dark green
2 Light green
3 Light gray
4 Light pink
5 Medium purple
6 Maroon
7 Light yellow

1 Square = 1 Inch

Knitted Gauntlets
Pictured on page 104

Directions are for one size that will fit Sizes 6½, 7, and 7½.

MATERIALS: Coats & Clark Red Heart 4-ply hand-knitting yarn, or a suitable substitute—6 ounces of any color; Size 6 double-pointed needles, or size to obtain gauge given below.

Abbreviations: Page 310.

Gauge: Over st st, 5 sts = 1 inch; 7 rnds = 1 inch.

INSTRUCTIONS: *Left glove:* Beg at cuff, cast on 72 sts. Divide sts among 3 needles, with 24 sts on each. Join, being careful not to twist the sts.

Rnd 1: * K 1, p 1. Rep from * around. Change to st st (k each rnd) until total length is 3¼ inches.

Dec rnd 1: Dec 4 sts evenly spaced, k around—68 sts. Work even for 7 rnds.

Dec rnd 2: Being careful that decs are not in line with decs of previous dec rnd, k around, dec 4 sts evenly spaced. Work even for 7 rnds. Rep last 8 rnds twice more—56 sts.

Next dec rnd: * K 1, (k 2 tog) twice. Rep from * to last st, k 1—34 sts.

Next 4 rnds: Work in k 1, p 1 ribbing. Work in st st for 7 rnds. Mark end of rnd.

Thumb gore: Rnd 1: K 16, place a marker on needle, inc 1 st in each of next 2 sts for thumb gore, place another marker on needle, k 16.

Rnd 2: Sl markers, k around.

Rnd 3: K to first marker, sl marker, inc 1 st in next st, k to 1 st before next marker, inc 1 st in next st, sl marker, k rem sts.

Rep last 2 rnds alternately 3 times—12 sts bet markers.

Next rnd: K to the first marker, remove marker, sl next 12 thumb gore sts to holder, remove next marker, cast on 2 sts, k 16—34 sts. Continuing in st st, work until the length from the 2 cast-on sts is 2 inches, or until the glove, when tried on, reaches to the base of the little finger.

Index finger: Rnd 1: K 12, sl these sts to another holder and mark for palm section, k next 10 sts, cast on 2 sts, sl rem sts to another holder for back section, having point of holder

facing finger. Divide the 12 sts among 3 needles for index finger. Work in st st until length of finger is 2½ inches, or reaches to within ¼ inch of fingertip.

Last rnd: * K 2 tog. Rep from * around. Leaving a 6-inch tail, break off. Thread a needle with this length and draw through rem sts. Draw tog and secure.

Middle finger: Sl next 4 sts from back section onto needle, sl the 4 corresponding sts from palm section onto another needle.

Rnd 1: Pick up and k 2 sts along base of previous finger bet back and palm sections, k next 4 sts, with another needle cast on 2 sts, k next 4 sts. Divide the 12 sts evenly among 3 needles and work in st st until length of finger is 2¾ inches, or reaches to within ¼ inch of fingertip. Beg with last rnd, complete as for Index Finger.

Ring finger: Work as for Middle Finger until length is 2½ inches, or reaches to within ¼ inch of fingertip. Complete as for Middle Finger.

Little finger: Sl sts from holder onto needles as for Middle Finger.

Rnd 1: Pick up and k 3 sts along base of previous finger, k rem 8 sts. Work as for previous finger over the 11 sts until length is 2¼ inches, or reaches to within ¼ inch of fingertip. Complete as for previous finger.

Thumb: Sl sts from holder onto 3 needles, pick up and k 2 sts along the 2 cast-on sts at base—14 sts. Work as for previous finger until length is 2¼ inches, or reaches to within ¼ inch of fingertip. Complete as for previous finger.

Right glove: Work as for Left Glove until Index Finger has been completed. Beg each finger on palm instead of back, complete as for Left Glove.

Flowered Bonnet
Pictured on page 104

MATERIALS: Unger Britania (1.6-ounce skeins), or a suitable substitute: two skeins black (MC), one skein *each* of No. 789 tan (color A), No. 496 rose (color B), No. 530 grape (color C), No. 795 red (color

D), No. 1003 light blue (color E), No. 541 dark blue (color F), and No. 695 dark green (color G); small amount of knitting worsted-weight yarn in contrasting color for cast on; Size 6 circular knitting needle (16 inches long), or size to obtain gauge given below; Size 6 double-pointed needles.

Abbreviations: See page 310.

Gauge: With 2 strands yarn held tog, 9 sts = 2 inches.

INSTRUCTIONS: *Note on two-color knitting:* When changing colors of yarn, always twist the new color around the color in use to prevent making holes in work. Carry yarn loosely across the back of work.

All yarn is held double throughout except for cast on.

With circular needle and scrap of knitting worsted, cast on 66 sts. Break off knitting worsted.

Working back and forth in rows, and beg with Row 1 of chart, *page 114,* work pat in colors indicated. Beg with Row 3, inc 1 st at each end of every k row 6 times—78 sts.

Rep the pat as indicated for Rows 1-12.

At the end of each row, use successive MC sts when needed to avoid having to change colors in the middle of an inc and to avoid a partially completed motif.

Continue working pat until chart 1 is completed, work 1 row E, cast on 6 sts; join work—84 sts.

Crown: Place a marker on needle to indicate beg of rnd and work crown as follows (when using circular needle becomes too cumbersome, change to double-pointed needles):

Rnd 1: With E k 8, * k 2 tog, k 10. Rep from * around, ending with k 2 tog, k 2—77 sts.

Rnd 2: K 1 B, * 1 E, 3 B. Rep from * around.

Rnd 3: K 1 MC, 1 B, 3 MC, 1 B, 1 MC, k 2 tog MC, 1 B, 3 MC, 1 B, 3 MC, 1 B, k 2 tog MC, 1 MC, 1 B, 3 MC, 1 B, 3 MC, k 2 tog B, 2 MC, 1 B, 3 MC, 1 B, 2 MC, k 2 tog B, 3 MC, 1 B, 3 MC, 1 B, 1 MC, k 2 tog MC, 1 B, 3 MC, 1 B, k 2 tog MC, 1 MC, 1 B, 3 MC, 1 B, 3 MC, k 2 tog B, 2 MC—70 sts. Break off B.

Rnd 4: With MC work even.

continued

113

Rnd 5: K 6, * k 2 tog, k 8. Rep from * around, ending with k 2 tog, k 2—63 sts.

Rnd 6: * K 1 MC, 1 G. Rep from * around, ending with 1 MC. Break off G.

Rnd 7: With MC k 5, * k 2 tog, k 7. Rep from * around, ending with k 2 tog, k 2—56 sts.

Rnd 8: * K 1 C, 1 MC. Rep from * around. Break off C.

Rnd 9: With MC k 4, * k 2 tog, k 6. Rep from * around, ending with k 2 tog, k 2—49 sts.

Rnd 10: * K 1 MC, 1 F. Rep from * around, ending with 1 MC. Break off F.

Rnd 11: With MC k 3, * k 2 tog, k 5. Rep from * around, ending with k 2 tog, k 2—42 sts.

Rnd 12: * K 1 A, 1 MC. Rep from * around. Break off A.

Rnd 13: With MC k 2, * k 2 tog, k 4. Rep from * around, ending with k 2 tog, k 2—35 sts.

Rnd 14: K 2 MC, * k 1 F, 4 MC. Rep from * around, ending with 1 F, 2 MC.

Rnd 15: K 1 MC, * k 2 tog F, 1 F, 2 MC. Rep from * around, ending with 2 tog F, 1 F, 1 MC—28 sts.

Rnd 16: K 1 MC, 3 F. Rep from * around. Break off MC.

Rnd 17: With F k 2 tog, k 2 around—21 sts. Break off F.

Rnd 18: With E k 2 tog, k 1 around—14 sts.

Rnd 19: K 2 tog around—7 sts. Break off E, leaving a 6-inch tail; thread tail through rem sts, pull tight, and fasten. Weave in end.

Brim: Remove worsted-weight yarn from cast on and sl 66 sts to circular needle.

With right side facing and MC, pick up 23 sts along left edge. Continuing on, pick up 23 sts along right edge—112 sts.

Place marker to indicate beg of rnd. Work 2 rnds in MC, then 10 rnds from chart 2, *left.* Work 1 rnd in MC. *Next rnd:* K 2 MC, * 1 C, 3 MC. Rep from * around, ending with 1 C, 1 MC. Break off MC. *Following rnd:* With C * k 2 tog, yo. Rep from * around.

Brim facing: Work 11 rnds even.

Cord eyelet rnd: K 66, yo, k 2 tog, k 42, k 2 tog, yo. *Next rnd:* Work even. Fold facing to inside and sew with MC to rem sts, aligning sts.

Cord: With MC make a 50-inch-long twisted cord. Thread bet front brim and front facing, and through eyelets on Cord Eyelet Rnd.

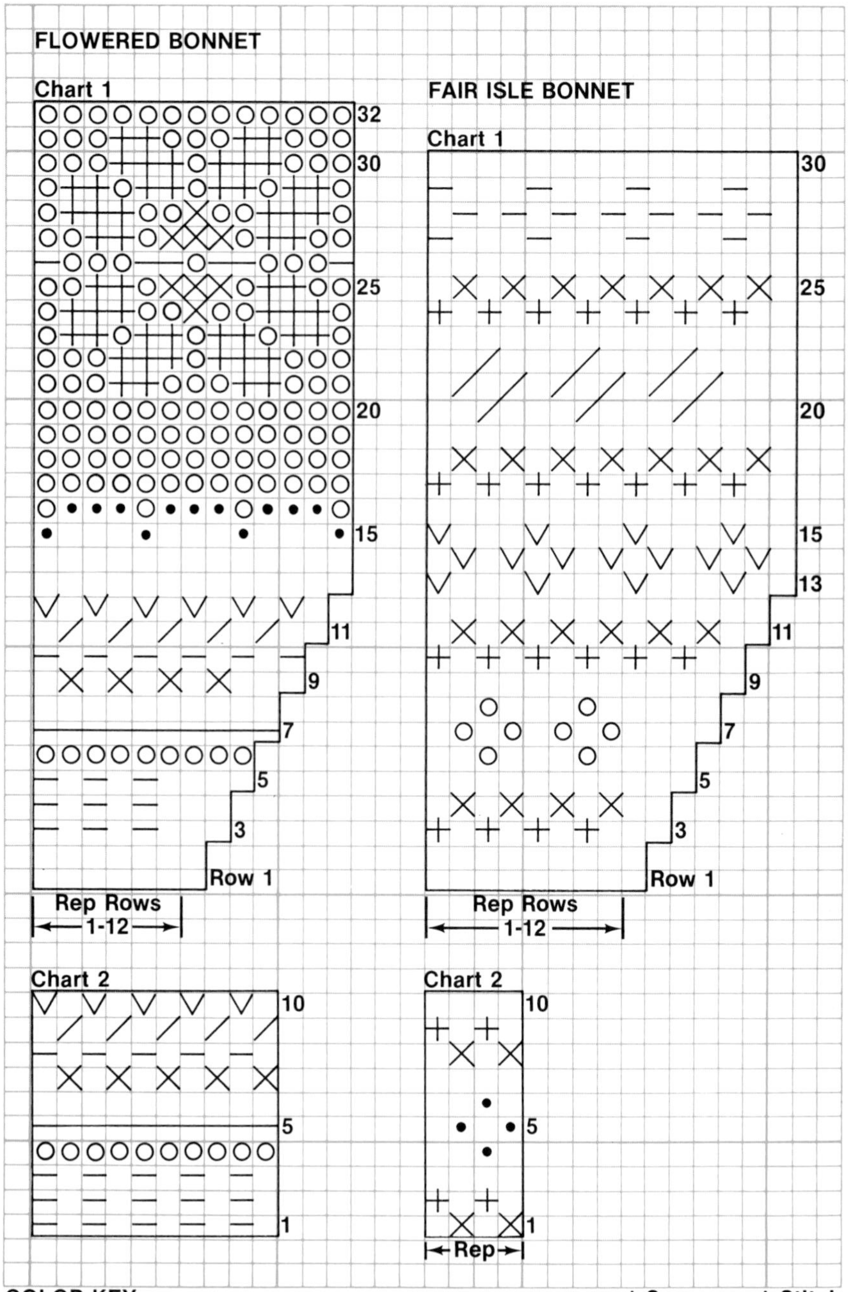

Knitted Fair Isle Bonnet
Pictured on page 105

MATERIALS: Unger Britania (1.6-ounce skeins), or a suitable substitute: two skeins of black (MC), one skein *each* of No. 789 tan (color A), No. 496 rose (color B), No. 530 grape (color C), No. 795 red (color D), No. 1003 light blue (color E), No. 541 dark blue (color F), and No. 695 dark green (color G); small amount of knitting worsted-weight yarn in contrasting color for

FLOWERED BONNET

Chart 1

FAIR ISLE BONNET

Chart 1

Chart 2

Chart 2

COLOR KEY
☐ Black (MC)   ☑ Grape (C)   ⊟ Dark Blue (F)
☒ Tan (A)   ⊞ Red (D)   ☑ Dark Green (G)
⊡ Rose (B)   ◯ Light Blue (E)

1 Square = 1 Stitch

cast on; Size 6 circular knitting needle (16 inches long), or size to obtain gauge given below; Size 6 double-pointed needles.

Abbreviations: Page 310.

Gauge: With 2 strands yarn held tog, 19 sts = 4 inches.

INSTRUCTIONS: *Note on two-color knitting*—when changing colors of yarn, always twist the new color around the color in use to prevent making holes in work. Carry yarn loosely across the back of work.

All yarn is held double throughout, except for cast on.

With circular needle and scrap of knitting worsted, cast on 66 sts. Break off knitting worsted.

Working back and forth in rows, and beg with Row 1 of chart, *opposite*, work pat in colors indicated. Beg with Row 3, inc 1 st at each end of every k row 6 times—78 sts. Rep pat as indicated for Rows 1-12. At end of each row, use successive MC sts when needed to avoid having to change colors in middle of an inc and to avoid partial motif.

Work even in colors indicated until chart 1 is completed.

Next row: * K 1 MC, 1 D. Rep from * across; cast on 6 sts with MC; join and change to circular knitting needle—84 sts.

Place a marker to indicate beg of rnd and work crown as follows (When using circular needle becomes too cumbersome, change to double-pointed needles):

Dec rnd 1: (K 1 MC, 1 A) 4 times; k 2 tog MC, * (k 1 MC, 1 A) 5 times; k 2 tog MC. Rep from * around, ending with 1 MC, k 1 A—77 sts. *Next rnd:* Work even in MC.

Dec rnd 2: K 7 MC, k 2 tog B, * k 9 MC, k 2 tog B. Rep from * around, ending with 2 MC—70 sts. *Next rnd:* K 7 MC, 2 B, * k 8 MC, 2 B. Rep from * around, ending with k 1 MC.

Dec rnd 3: * K 6 MC, k 2 tog B, 2 B. Rep from * around—63 sts. Continue as before, having 1 fewer MC and 1 more B on each rnd and dec every other rnd by k tog last MC st and first B st, using B.

When no more MC sts rem, continue to dec as above with B. Dec until 7 sts rem. Break off B, leaving 6-inch tail. Thread through last 7 sts, and weave in end.

Brim: Remove worsted-weight yarn from cast on and sl 66 sts to circular needle. With right side facing and MC, pick up 23 sts along left edge. Continuing on, pick up 23 sts along right edge—112 sts. Place marker to indicate beg of rnd. Work 2 rnds in MC, then 10 rnds from chart 2, *opposite.* Break off MC.

Brim facing: Work 11 rnds even.

Cord eyelet rnd: K 66, yo, k 2 tog, k 42, k 2 tog, yo. *Next rnd:* Work even. Fold facing to inside and sew with MC to rem sts, aligning sts.

Cord: With MC make a 50-inch-long twisted cord. Thread bet front brim and front facing, and through eyelets on Cord Eyelet Rnd.

Embroidered Scarf
Pictured on page 105

MATERIALS: 7¾x48-inch rust even-weave wool scarf or rust fabric; assorted wool yarns; dressmaker's carbon; butcher paper.

INSTRUCTIONS: *Note:* To make the scarf from wool fabric, cut yardage to the dimensions desired. Finish the long edges with a tiny rolled hem. Then fringe short ends, if desired, and stay-stitch above the fringe, using thread to match fabric.

Enlarge pattern, *above right,* onto paper. Transfer to wool scarf, using dressmaker's carbon and repeating the design over the entire length of the scarf. Embroider all lines in running stitches; press.

Child's Patterned Sweater
Pictured on page 106

Directions are for Size 2; changes for Sizes 4, 6, and 8 follow in parentheses. Finished chest size equals 24 (26, 28, 30) inches.

MATERIALS: Manos del Uruguay Strya 100 percent wool handspun yarn (3.5-ounce skeins), or a suitable substitute: 4 (5, 5, 5) skeins of fiery red, 1 skein *each* of magenta, grape, and cantaloupe, plus approximately 25 yards *each* of English green, persimmon, butane, and

1 Square = 1 Inch

spruce green; Sizes 7 and 9 knitting needles, or size to obtain gauge given below; Size 7 double-pointed needles; yarn bobbins.

Abbreviations: Page 310.

Gauge: With larger needles over st st, 15 sts = 4 inches; 18 rows = 4 inches.

INSTRUCTIONS: Before you begin, wind separate yarn bobbins for each color in each design repeat. Work each design repeat separately; do not carry yarn across the back of the work.

When changing colors while knitting, twist the new color around the color in use to prevent making holes in the work.

Front: With smaller needles and magenta, cast on 45 (49, 53, 57) sts. Work in k 1, p 1 ribbing for 1¾ inches. Change to larger needles, st st, and grape.

First charted band: Work 2 (4, 4, 6) rows. *Next row:* K 5 (7, 9, 11), beg 3 reps of chart C-1, *page 116,* as indicated, k 5 (7, 9, 11). Work chart C-1 for a total of 10 rows, then work 3 (3, 5, 5) rows even in st st.

First garter st band: With wrong side facing, k 1 row magenta, then 2 rows each of 4 (5, 5, 5) contrasting colors. K 1 row magenta.

continued

2nd charted band: With wrong side facing, k 1 row of cantaloupe. Change to st st; continuing with same color, work 2 (2, 4, 4) rows. *Next row:* K 4 (6, 8, 10), beg 4 reps of chart C-2 *(below)* as indicated, k 4 (6, 8, 10). Work chart C-2 for a total of 10 rows, then work 3 (3, 5, 5) rows even in st st.

2nd garter st band: With wrong side facing k 1 row magenta, then 2 rows with a contrasting color.

Armhole shaping: Change to another color, k next 2 rows, casting off 4 (6, 6, 8) sts at beg of each row—37 (37, 41, 41) sts. K 2 rows more each of 2 (4, 4, 4) colors. K 1 row magenta.

CHILD'S PATTERNED PULLOVER

Chart C-1

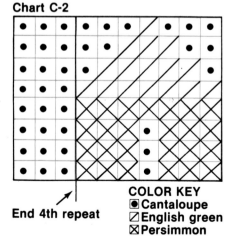

End 3rd repeat →

COLOR KEY
⊠ Fiery red   ● Grape

Chart C-2

End 4th repeat

COLOR KEY
● Cantaloupe
⊘ English green
⊠ Persimmon

Chart C-3

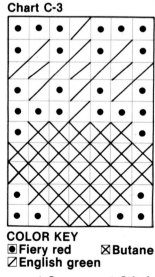

COLOR KEY
● Fiery red   ⊠ Butane
⊘ English green

1 Square = 1 Stitch

3rd charted band: With wrong side facing, k 1 row fiery red. Continuing with same color and changing to st st, work 2 (2, 2, 4) rows. *Next row:* K 4, work first row of chart C-3 once, k 15 (15, 19, 19), rep first row of chart C-3, k 4. Work chart C-3, *below,* for a total of 10 rows, slipping the center 11 sts to a holder for the neck.

Neck shaping: Continuing in st st, dec 1 st at neck edge every other row 5 times. Cast off rem 8 (8, 10, 10) sts. Rep for other side, joining yarn at neck edge and reversing neck shaping.

Back: Work same as for Front until ribbing has been completed. Change to fiery red and st st. Work even until total length to Armhole Shaping equals that of Front.

Armhole shaping: Cast off 4 (6, 6, 8) sts at beg of next 2 rows—37 (37, 41, 41) sts. Work even in st st until length past beg of armholes equals that of Front, ending with a p row. *Last row:* Cast off 8 (8, 10, 10) sts for shoulder, k 21 sts and sl to holder for back of neck, cast off rem 8 (8, 10, 10) sts.

Sleeves: With smaller needles and magenta, cast on 26 (28, 30, 32) sts. Work in k 1, p 1 ribbing for 1½ inches. Change to larger needles and fiery red and work even for 2 inches, ending with a p row. *Inc row:* K 1, inc in next st, k to the last 2 sts of row, inc in next st, k 1. Rep this inc on a k row every 2 inches 3 times more—34 (36, 38, 40) sts. Work even until the total length measures 14 (15, 16½, 18) inches. Cast off loosely.

Finishing: Sew shoulder and side seams. Sew sleeve seams, beg at cuff and leaving last 4 (7, 7, 9) rows free. Sew in sleeves, joining last open rows to the cast-off sts at underarm and cast off sleeve sts to armhole.

Neckband: With the right side facing, sl 21 sts from back neck to first double-pointed needle; with 2nd needle and fiery red, pick up 14 sts along left neck edge; sl 11 sts from front neck holder and k with 3rd needle and with same (3rd) needle pick up and k 14 sts along right neck edge—60 sts. With magenta, work k 1, p 1 ribbing for 4 rnds. Cast off very loosely in ribbing.

Adult's Patterned Pullover
Pictured on page 106

Instructions are for Size Small; changes for Sizes Medium and Large follow in parentheses. Bust-/chest measurement = 33¾ (36, 39½) inches.

MATERIALS: Manos del Uruguay Strya 100 percent wool yarn (3.5-ounce skeins): 7 (8, 8) skeins Main Color, 4 skeins contrasting colors (1 skein for ribbing color and 3 for background colors for charted designs), plus approximately 16 yards each of six contrasting colors for charted designs and garter st stripes; Sizes 7 and 9 knitting needles, or size to obtain gauge given below; Size 7 double-pointed needles; yarn bobbins.

Abbreviations: See page 310.

Gauge: With larger needles over st st, 14 sts = 4 inches; 20 rows = 4 inches.

INSTRUCTIONS: Wind separate yarn bobbins for each color in each design repeat. Work each design repeat separately; do not carry yarn across the back of the work. When changing colors while knitting, twist the new color around the color in use to prevent making holes in work.

Note on selecting colors: To make good use of scraps of yarn you might have on hand, and to create your own personal look for this sweater, select your own combination of yarn colors.

Begin with the Main Color, which is used predominantly for the Back and Sleeves (as well as background color for first charted band). Next select a color for the waist, cuff, and neckband ribbing. Then choose three coordinating colors to be used for background colors for the rows of repeat motifs.

From scraps, select six contrasting colors to be used for the motifs and garter-stitch stripes. See the list of materials for quantities.

Front: With smaller needles and ribbing color, cast on 59 (63, 69) sts. Work in k 1, p 1 ribbing for 3 inches. Change to larger needles and st st.

First charted band: With larger needles and background color for first charted band (Main Color), work 4 rows st st. *Next row:* Continuing in st st, k 3 (5, 8), beg 4 reps of chart A-1, *right,* as indicated, k 3 (5, 8). Work chart A-1 for a total of 11 rows, then work 4 (6, 6) rows more.

First garter st band: With wrong side facing, k 1 row ribbing color, 2 rows each of 6 contrasting colors. K 1 row ribbing color. With wrong side facing k 1 row of background color for chart A-2.

2nd charted band: Continuing with same color and changing to st st, work 2 rows. *Next row:* K 5 (7,

ADULT'S PATTERNED PULLOVER

Chart A-1

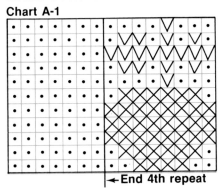

←**End 4th repeat**

Chart A-2

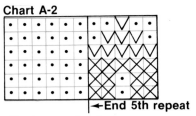

←**End 5th repeat**

•**Background color**

Chart A-3

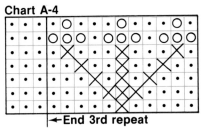

←**End 5th repeat**

Chart A-4

←**End 3rd repeat**

1 Square = 1 Stitch

10), beg 5 reps of chart A-2 as indicated, k 5 (7, 10). Work chart A-2 for a total of 6 rows, then work 3 rows more.

3rd charted band: With wrong side facing, k 1 row in background color of 3rd charted design. Change to st st and work 2 (2, 4) rows more. *Next row:* K 2 (4, 7), beg 5 reps of chart A-3, k 2 (4, 7). Work chart A-3 for a total of 8 rows, then work 3 (3, 5) rows more.

2nd garter st band: With wrong side facing k 1 row ribbing color, k 2 rows each of 4 colors, k 1 row ribbing color. With wrong side facing k 1 row background color of 4th charted design.

4th charted band and armhole shaping: Change to st st and with same color work 2 rows more. Cast off 6 (7, 9) sts at beg of next 2 rows. At the same time on the first cast-off row k 4 (5, 6) sts past cast-off, beg 3 reps of chart A-4, k 4 (5, 6). Work chart A-4 for a total of 7 rows, then work 4 rows more.

3rd garter st band: Next row: With wrong side facing, k 1 row ribbing color, k 2 rows each of 4 colors, k 1 row ribbing color. With wrong side facing k 1 row background color of chart A-1 (Main Color).

5th charted band: Change to st st and work 2 (4, 6) rows. *Next row:* K

3 (4, 4), work first row of chart A-1, k 25 (25, 27), rep first row of chart A-1, k 3 (4, 4). Continue to work from chart as established, stopping 1 row before chart is finished. *Next row:* Work 28 (29, 30) sts following last row of chart as established; slip last 9 sts worked to holder for neck; k 19 (20, 21).

Neck shaping: Dec 1 st every other row at neck edge 7 times. Work even until total length past beg of armholes measures 8½ (8¾, 8¾) inches. Cast off rem 12 (13, 14) sts. Join yarn at right neck edge and rep neck shaping, reversing shaping.

Back: Work same as for Front until ribbing has been completed. Change to larger needles and st st. With Main Color work even until length to Armhole Shaping equals that of Front.

Armhole shaping: Cast off 6 (7, 9) sts at beg of next 2 rows. Work even until total length to shoulder equals that of Front. Cast off 12 (13, 14) sts for shoulder, k 23 and sl sts to holder for back of neck, cast off rem 12 (13, 14) sts.

Sleeve: With smaller needles and ribbing color, cast on 45 (51, 53) sts. Work in k 1, p 1 ribbing for 3 inches. Change to larger needles, st st, and MC. Work even for 2 rows.

continued

Inc row: K 1, inc in next st, k to within last 2 sts, inc in next st, k 1. Work even for 2 inches, ending with a p row. Work inc row. Rep inc row every k row every 3 inches 3 times more—55 (61, 63) sts. Work even until total length measures 21 (22½, 23½) inches. Cast off loosely.

Finishing: Sew shoulder and side seams. Sew sleeve seams, beg at cuff and leaving the last 9 (11, 14) rows free. Sew in the sleeves, joining the last open rows to the cast-off sts at underarm and rem cast-off sleeve sts to armhole.

Neckband: With right side facing, sl 23 sts from back neck to the first double-pointed needle; with 2nd double-pointed needle and MC, pick up and k 19 sts along left neck edge; sl 9 sts from front holder to needle and k with 3rd needle; with same needle pick up and k 19 sts along right neck edge. With ribbing color work in k 1, p 1 ribbing for 7 rnds. Cast off loosely in ribbing.

Knitted Stocking Cap
Pictured on page 106

Directions are for Size Small; the changes for Size Large follow in parentheses.

MATERIALS: Manos del Uruguay Strya 100 percent wool yarn (3.5-ounce skeins), or a suitable substitute: one skein *each* of two contrasting colors for brim and crown; Sizes 7 and 9 knitting needles, or size to obtain gauge given below; buttons (optional).

Abbreviations: Page 310.

Gauge: With larger needles over st st, 4 sts = 1 inch.

INSTRUCTIONS: *Brim:* With smaller needles and 1 color, cast on 80 (84) sts. Work in k 2, p 2 ribbing for 10 (12) inches, dec 0 (4) sts evenly spaced across last row. Change to larger needle, contrasting brim color and st st. Work even for 2½ (3) inches.

Crown: Row 1: * K 6, k 2 tog. Rep from * across.

Row 2 and all even-numbered rows: P.

Row 3: * K 5, k 2 tog. Rep from * across.

Row 5: * K 4, k 2 tog. Rep from * across.

Row 7: * K 3, k 2 tog. Rep from * across.

Row 9: * K 2, k 2 tog. Rep from * across.

Row 11: * K 1, k 2 tog. Rep from * across.

Row 13: * K 2 tog. Rep from * across.

Break yarn, leaving a 15-inch tail. Thread tail through rem sts on needle; pull tight to form crown and secure. Sew side seam of crown with tail. Sew ribbing seam with matching yarn. Roll brim. Sew buttons to crown, if desired (see photograph, *page 106*).

Jacket with Embroidered Trim
Pictured on page 107

MATERIALS: Purchased Austrian-style, waist-length jacket (see note, below); small amounts of cranberry and gray-green 3-ply Persian yarn; crewel embroidery needle.

INSTRUCTIONS: *Note:* The jacket shown is made from white woven wool. The jacket features set-in knitted, cabled 1¼-inch-wide trim around the neckline, along the top of both pockets, and horizontally across the front and back yoke.

(Any purchased jacket with interesting styling is suitable for a project of this type. Or begin with a plain jacket and embellish it with purchased tapes or other trim.)

Plan position and type of embroidery. If your jacket features knitted panels, select stitches that will stretch with the fabric, such as loosely stitched backstitches or couching.

For the jacket shown, outline each cable twist with one strand of Persian yarn in couching. (To couch, thread an embroidery needle with required number of strands of yarn. Thread another needle with one or two strands of Persian yarn and tack down the first strand at intervals required to hold it in place. Move first strand to new position along underside of fabric as each shape is outlined in couching and bring needle to right side of work.)

After cables have been outlined, add couching to other structural elements of the jacket, such as over seams, along borders or trim, and along edges. Use colors desired.

Finally, add a small amount of stitching along yoke and along pocket tops. Couch yarn down in zigzags, or use featherstitches, French knots, or any other decorative stitching.

Crocheted Stocking Cap
Pictured on page 107

MATERIALS: Coats & Clark Red Heart hand-knitting yarn (3.5-ounce skein) or a suitable substitute: one skein in color desired; Size I aluminum crochet hook.

Abbreviations: Page 310.

INSTRUCTIONS: *Crown:* Ch 4, sl st to form ring. *Rnd 1:* 6 sc in ring; do not join, mark beg of rnd.

Rnd 2: Work 2 sc in each sc around.

Rnd 3: * 2 sc in next sc, sc in following sc. Rep from * around.

Rnd 4: * 2 sc in next sc, sc in each of following 2 sc.

Rnd 5: * 2 sc in next sc, sc in each of following 3 sc.

Rnds 6-10: Sc in each sc, inc 6 sc, evenly spaced, on each rnd—60 sc at end of Rnd 10.

Rnds 11-27: Work even.

Brim: At end of Rnd 27, ch 24; turn and sc in 2nd ch from hook and in each ch across; sl st in next sc on Crown; ch 1, turn.

Row 2: Working in back lps only, sc in each sc across; ch 1, turn.

Row 3: In back lps sc in each sc, sl st in next sc on Crown; ch 1, turn. Rep Rows 2-3 alternately around edge of Crown. Join first and last rows with sl st. Fasten off.

Knitted Black Cardigan
Pictured on page 107

Directions are for size Small (6-8); changes for size Medium (10-12) and size Large (14-16) follow in parentheses. Bust = 35 (39, 43) inches.

MATERIALS: Five skeins of black Bartlettyarns, or a suitable substitute; Sizes 6 and 9 knitting needles, or size to obtain gauge; contrasting yarn in similar weight (crocheted trim); five purchased buttons, or crocheted buttons (see instructions below); Size G aluminum crochet hook.

Abbreviations: See page 310.

Gauge: With larger needles over st st, 5 sts = 2 inches; 8 rows = 2 inches.

INSTRUCTIONS: The body of this sweater is worked in one piece from the lower edge of the Back to the lower edge of the Front. The collar is worked separately and then attached to the body.

Body: With smaller needles, cast on 40 (44, 48) sts. Work in k 1, p 1 ribbing for 5 inches, inc 10 (12, 12) sts evenly spaced across last row—50 (56, 60) sts. Change to larger needles and st st. Work even until total length measures 11 (12, 13) inches.

Back armhole shaping: Cast off 2 sts at beg of next 6 rows—38 (44, 48) sts. Work even until length past beg of armholes measures 7 (7, 7) inches.

Divide for neck: Work across first 13 (14, 16) sts and sl to holder; cast off center 12 (14, 16) sts for back of neck; work even over rem 13 (14, 16) sts for 2 inches.

Left front: *Next row:* Cast on 6 (7, 8) sts at center front. Work even until total length past beg of armholes measures 16 inches.

Front armhole shaping: Cast on 2 sts at armhole edge of every other row 3 (3, 3) times—25 (27, 30) sts. Work even in st st until length past last armhole cast on measures 6 (7, 8) inches, dec 5 (5, 6) sts evenly spaced across last row. Change to smaller needles and work k 1, p 1 ribbing for 5 inches. Cast off.

Right front: Sl rem sts from shoulder to larger needles, and complete to correspond to Left Front.

Sleeves: With smaller needles, cast on 28 (30, 32) sts. Work in k 1, p 1 ribbing for 5 inches, inc 9 (10, 10) sts evenly spaced across last row—37 (40, 42) sts. Change to larger needles and st st. Work even until total length is 16 (17, 18) inches.

Top shaping: Dec 1 st on each side every row until 5 sts rem. Cast off.

Collar: With larger needles, cast on 50 sts. Work even in seed st (k the p sts and p the k sts) for 8 inches. *Next row:* Work across first 17 sts and sl to holder; cast off center 16 sts; work over rem 17 sts for 3 inches. Then cast on 8 sts at center front. Continue in seed st for 7 inches more. Cast off. Sl sts from holder and complete as for first portion of the collar.

Neck and front bands: Row 1: With right side facing, and beg at the lower right corner of the center front, work a row of sc up along the front edge. Space sts to lie flat, and work through both the collar and body of sweater. Make 4 sc at the corner of the neck, continue sc along neck edge, making 4 sc at the other corner, and work down along the left front same as before to the lower edge; ch 1, turn.

Row 2: With pins, mark positions for 5 buttonholes evenly spaced along one front edge. Work around with sc in each sc, making 2 sc in each of 2 corner sc at neck edges. At buttonhole markings make ch 1, sk 1 sc, sc in next sc. At end of row, ch 1, turn.

Row 3: Sc in each sc around as for Row 2, inc at corners and making 1 sc over each buttonhole ch-1. Break off at end of row.

Row 4: With contrasting-color yarn, work 1 more row of sc around neck and front band. Break off.

Finishing: Sew the side seams. Sew sleeve seams; sew in sleeves, gathering sleeves slightly at top of shoulder. Sew collar to sweater body, aligning necklines of each, and sewing along front edges.

Crocheted buttons (optional): With crochet hook, ch 5, sl st to form ring. Work 1 sc in each ch. Rep for 4 rnds more to form small tube. Break off work, leaving a 10-inch tail. Stuff with yarn scraps, thread tail through sts and pull tight; thread tail through beg ch-5 circle and secure. Sew crocheted or purchased buttons to sweater.

Trim: With crochet hook and scrap of contrasting-color yarn, sc evenly along the edges of the collar and cuffs.

Fool-the-Eye Lace Collars, Cuffs, and Aprons
Pictured on page 108

MATERIALS: Unbleached muslin or other finely woven, lightweight fabric; fine-point permanent brown marking pen; acrylic or fabric paints, fabric dyes, crayons, or colored pencils; embroidery floss; appliquéd trims; lace trims; beads; quilt batting or polyester fleece.

INSTRUCTIONS: Enlarge patterns, *below* and *on the following pages.*

Transfer designs to muslin with a *permanent* fine-point brown marker.

Decorate the collars, cuffs, and aprons with fabric crayons and markers, fabric dye, acrylic paints, embroidery, appliqué, beading, or quilting. (See page 52 for decorating tips and techniques.) Complete the decorating before assembling the pieces.

Note: You may use colored pencils for quick coloring, but washing or dry cleaning will eventually remove the color from the fabric. If you plan to wash *or* dry-clean the items, use coloring materials made specifically for application to fabric.

continued

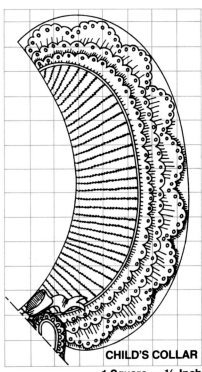

CHILD'S COLLAR

1 Square = ½ Inch

For background color, dip printed fabrics in a diluted dyebath, if desired. Mix a *weak* solution of fabric dye in the color of your choice and test a muslin scrap. The color should be light enough to allow design lines to show through. When dry, tinted pieces may be embellished with stichery.

Use embroidery, appliqué, and beading to enhance the collars, cuffs, and aprons. Use simple embroidery stitches and cotton, silk, or metallic threads to embellish lines and fill in motifs. Or appliqué cording, beads, and bits of lace and ribbon to the designs.

After all other decorating is completed, collars, cuffs, and aprons may be given added dimension with quilting. Sandwich a layer of thin batting or fleece between the decorated side and muslin backing fabric. Machine- or hand-quilt along design lines you wish to emphasize.

Assemble decorated collars, cuffs, and aprons, sewing lining fabrics to right sides; turn right side out and sew openings closed. Add hooks and eyes to fasten collars and cuffs.

Cross-Stitched Christmas Sampler
Pictured on page 110

MATERIALS: 25x29 inches of 22-count ecru hardanger fabric; embroidery floss in the following colors: burgundy, red, coral, dark and light blue, dark and light green, brown, and yellow; masking tape; embroidery hoop; needle; graph paper; felt-tip pens to match floss.

INSTRUCTIONS: The finished size is approximately 17x21 inches.

To begin, make a full-color pattern. Using marking pens, transfer the charts, *pages 122 and 126,* to graph paper, substituting colored Xs for the symbols. This is a portion of the pattern; you must "flop" (make mirror images of) some motifs in order to finish the pattern.

Flop the pattern to the left of the dashed line. (*Note:* The pear tree and all lettering are complete as shown on the charts. Do *not* flop the center vertical group of symbols. Repeat motifs A, B, and C as indicated in the border design.)

Add the alphabet, *page 122,* to the pattern using Xs at the bottom of the diagram as placement guides. Complete lower border by flopping motifs for upper border. The circled arrows on the diagram denote corresponding areas on the right-hand border design. To complete the lower right-hand corner, flop the symbols just above the arrow on the upper right-hand corner.

Tape the raw edges of the fabric to prevent threads from raveling. Work all cross-stitches with two strands of floss. Keep a record of the floss color numbers in case you need to purchase additional amounts.

Measure 4 inches down and 4 inches in from the upper left-hand corner of the fabric; mark this point with a water-erasable marking pen or a safety pin. Begin stitching here.

Work the cross-stitches over two threads of the hardanger. Begin with the light green border pattern.

Repeat this motif for ties

CHILD'S APRON

1 Square = ½ Inch

Complete the entire light green area before embellishing it with decorative motifs. Check your work periodically to make sure you've counted correctly and that the top stitch of every cross-stitch is worked in the same direction.

After stitching, remove tape. Block the piece by pressing carefully, using a damp press cloth and a medium-hot iron. Frame as desired.

Needlepoint Poinsettia Wreath

Pictured on page 111

MATERIALS: 30-inch square of 14-count needlepoint canvas; 3-ply Persian needlepoint yarn in peach and the colors listed in the color key, *page 125;* needlepoint frame or artist's stretcher strips; blunt-pointed needle; indelible marker.

INSTRUCTIONS: Bind edges of canvas with masking tape to prevent raveling. Using a ruler, measure both horizontally and vertically to determine the *exact* center of the canvas piece. Mark this point with an indelible marker.

From this point, count upward 60 stitches and mark this point. This represents the beginning stitch of the design, which is indicated by an arrow on the pattern, *page 125.*

Mount canvas on stretcher strips or a frame to avoid distortion and make blocking easier.

The wreath pattern, *pages 124* and *125,* is a repeat design and makes up one quarter of the total wreath. To complete the wreath, shift the quadrant three times to complete the circle. Follow the pattern to complete the first quadrant. Begin other quadrants by stitching from the end of each of the previous sections.

Work motifs in continental stitches using two plies of yarn. For background, use basket-weave stitches.

When flowers are complete, work "Joy," *page 123,* in the center and fill in the background color.

To block, dampen canvas and, with rustproof T-pins, mount it on a blocking board. Sprinkle with water; allow to dry at least 24 hours before removing from the board.

continued

ADULT'S COLLAR

1 Square = ½ Inch

121

To frame the needlepoint, mount the canvas on a plywood board the same size as the finished needlework. (Pad the board with one or more layers of quilt batting.) Stretch the needlepoint over the board, keeping corners square, and staple it securely to the back.

Or, mount the canvas on artist's stretcher bars cut to size, assembled, and stabilized with angle irons.

Cut and assemble the picture molding of your choice for a frame, or take the board to a local framer for professional finishing.

"Noel" Christmas Sign
Pictured on page 111

MATERIALS: 2x3 foot piece of ⅜-inch plywood; 8 feet of ⅞-inch quarter-round molding; 8 feet of ⅛x1¼-inch pine; small finishing nails or brads; sandpaper; brown

kraft paper; chalk; black semigloss enamel; acrylics in the following colors: green, red, brown, blue, black, and white; wood stain; polyurethane; wire.

INSTRUCTIONS: Enlarge the pattern, *opposite,* onto brown paper. Using the oval outline on pattern as a guide, cut the board for the sign from plywood. Cut pine trims to fit around the perimeter of the sign.

Soak the wood in water as long as necessary to make it pliable for bending to the oval shape.

Using small finishing nails or brads, nail boards for trim around the edge of the oval; also nail and glue quarter-round molding around the inside edge. Sand lightly.

Coat the sign with semigloss black enamel. When dry, transfer the design to the board by rubbing the

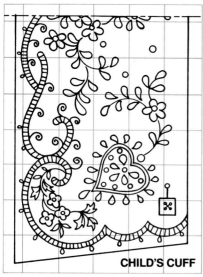

CHILD'S CUFF

1 Square = ½ Inch

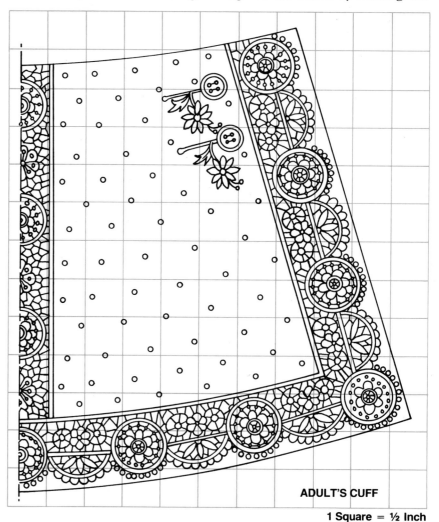

ADULT'S CUFF

1 Square = ½ Inch

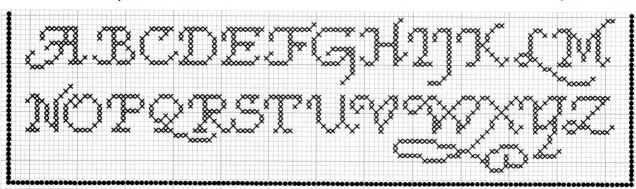

back of the pattern paper with light-colored chalk. Position the pattern atop the sign and go over the lines with a pencil.

Using the photograph as a guide, paint the design using shades of brown for the basket, pinecones, and pine branches. (On the pattern, one pinecone design is drawn in; use it as a guide to completing remaining pinecones.) Use two shades of green for the holly leaves.

For green needles, apply paint to the edge of a piece of cardboard; print stalks for needles using the edge of the cardboard. Print needles at random along the stalk (reapply paint to cardboard as needed).

Use reds for holly berries and blues for juniper berries (along needle stems). Add additional juniper berries to the design at random (see photograph). Highlight holly leaves and paint ribbon white. Use black for "Noel" and the berry centers.

When dry, sand sign very lightly and rub with wood stain for an antique effect. Finish with polyurethane and attach wire for hanging.

continued

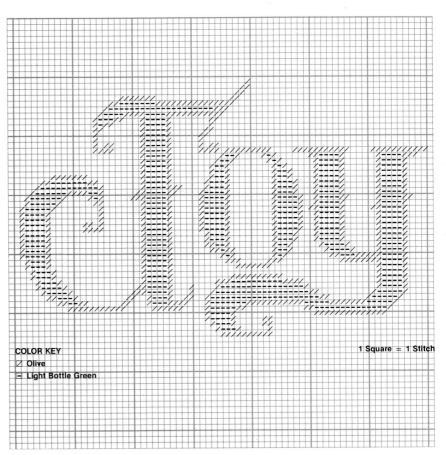

COLOR KEY
☑ Olive
⊟ Light Bottle Green

1 Square = 1 Stitch

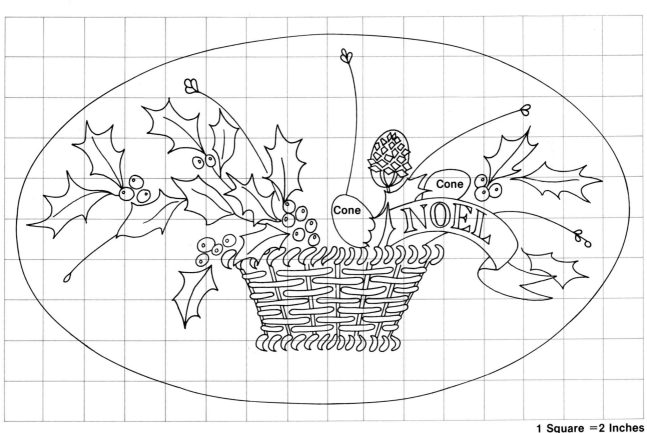

Cone

Cone

NOEL

1 Square = 2 Inches

123

124

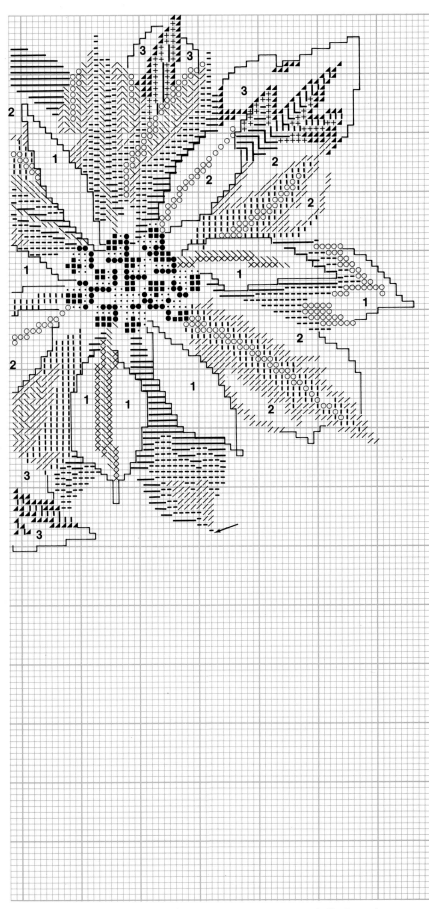

Tips for Working the Wreath Design

To translate the chart included here into a complete pattern, tape together enough pieces of 10-squares-to-the-inch graph paper to accommodate the entire design. Using markers or colored pencils, transfer the chart to your paper, substituting a color for each of the symbols on the chart and rotating the chart as indicated in the instructions.

When you have finished stitching the wreath and the word "JOY" in the center, outline the letters in gold metallic thread, if desired.

In this project, rich hues are achieved by using several shades of a limited number of colors. If you cannot locate all the shades listed in the color key, or do not wish to purchase an entire skein to obtain a small amount of yarn, you can use up small quantities of Persian yarn left over from previous projects.

When you make yarn substitutions, strive for overall color impact. A good test of color compatibility is to stand back and squint at the colors: If the "blur" looks good to you, any positioning of the colors in the groups will be successful.

COLOR KEY
- ▣ **Bright Red**
- ⊡ **Yellow Green**
- ◉ **Dark Yellow Green**
- ◨ **Off White (2)**
- ▨ **Yellow/White (Cream)**
- ⊡ **Pale Olive**
- ⊠ **Sea Green**
- ⊟ **Celery**
- ▭ **Medium Celery**
- ⊞ **Light Bottle Green**
- ◪ **Bottle Green**
- ◤ **Jade Green (3)**
- ❑ **Olive**
- ⊘ **White (1)**

COLOR KEY
- ■ Dark Green
- ⊙ Light Green
- ● Burgundy
- ⊠ Red
- ◻ Dark Blue
- ⊞ Light Blue
- ⊘ Brown
- ⊟ Coral
- ⊡ Yellow

Center

Center

Love and Joy at Christmas

1 Square = 1 Cross-stitch

CHRISTMAS MAGIC FROM EVERYDAY THINGS

It's Christmas—a time when even the simplest things are infused with a special magic. It's during these festive days that the spirit of giving transforms everyday events into occasions worth sharing. To inspire you to take an imaginative look at the familiar things around you, page after page is filled with gifts, ornaments, and other Christmas frills, including a section of tempting recipes to make with the most ordinary ingredients. Besides being thrifty, these are projects and good things to eat that the entire family can enjoy making together.

CHRISTMAS MAGIC FROM EVERYDAY THINGS

Prairie Christmas

The best-loved things are often those we live with every day. And what better way to celebrate the Christmas season than by creating wondrous gifts and trims inspired by and crafted from familiar items?

For example, the motifs and materials of the American prairie inspired this country Christmas. Crepe-paper prairie roses, stenciled schoolhouses, and tiny twig animals are just a few of the ornaments you can make using simple materials. You'll also find a delightful array of prairie-style trims and presents here and on the following pages.

Stenciled ornaments, calico hearts, and prairie roses transform this hardy evergreen tree into a crafter's beauty. A cardigan embellished with appliqués and an apron that bears a "home, sweet home" crocheted panel are prairie-style presents that are sure to please.

The Amish-inspired crib quilt is ablaze with color and pattern. And an old-fashioned prairie doll nestles into an easy-to-build doll cradle.

Directions for projects in this section begin on page 138.

Prairie Christmas

Glorious prairie roses, made of softly dyed crepe paper and dried flowers, grace the tabletop tree, *opposite*. These delicate "blooms," plus additional crepe paper leaves, also were used to adorn the 12-inch-diameter wreath.

An all-natural corn husk doll carrying a tiny pinecone wreath leads us down the wintry path of a simple-to-make wall hanging. This wooden mosaic is crafted from hardboard and fir lumber. The wooden candle holder, trimmed with painted trees and roses, is the perfect complement to the other prairie trappings

Popular with quilters since pioneer days, the primitive schoolhouse pattern has been adapted to a variety of craft techniques over the years. Here it provides a delightful design for the stenciled ornaments, *left.* These muslin trims are quick and easy to make with just a dab of paint and an edging of ecru lace.

Rejuvenate a cast-off cardigan by adding fabric appliqués and substituting brightly colored buttons for the originals. Its spirited style and frugal use of floral fabrics make this a sweater our pioneer ancestors would be proud of.

Prairie Christmas

The country life beckons all of us now and then. But even if you can't realize your dreams of rural living, you can still enjoy an old-time Christmas with these homespun trappings.

Soft-sculpture birds stitched from wool fabrics, pine shaving ornaments in a variety of shapes, and miniature wooden animals are the makings for a rustic tree like this one.

An ordinary apple is all you need to transform plain brown paper into charming gift wrap. Just dip halved apples into red acrylic paint and stamp onto wrapping paper. When the paint is dry, draw seeds and stems with a black marking pen.

Make pinecone baskets for decorative as well as functional use. Simply gather pinecones from your own backyard (or buy them at a florist's shop) and use florist's wire to bind them to a purchased wire basket. The baskets here are approximately eight and ten inches in diameter when completed.

134

Preserve the memories of Christmases past by recalling the holiday traditions that make Christmas such a meaningful celebration. If you step back in time, you can probably remember a revered adult teaching you an age-old game like checkers, *below.*

Our homespun checkers set looks just right on a woven board you can make on a simple rigid heddle loom using carpet warp and knitting yarn. The pieces are crafted from an old-time bread dough recipe and decorated with red and black hearts. Even tiny tots can help make this gift for a beloved family member.

Just-for-fun wagons, *above,* make delightful decorations for your holiday homestead. Construct them from pine and leave them plain, or wood-burn wildflower designs on the wagon's wheels and sides.

Ten muted shades of yarn are crocheted in rounds to create this unusual doily. Use wool yarns for subtler shades, or choose acrylics for a more striking effect.

The wooden doll is a relic from our prairie heritage and is bound to appeal to doll collectors and kids alike. This 12-inch-tall doll is crafted from pine and dressed in old-fashioned fabrics.

Youngsters will cherish the three-piece set of doll furniture, *below.* Made from wooden spools saved from the sewing baskets of long ago, this old-fashioned furniture is a keepsake gift to pass on from generation to generation. Open up your scrapbag to find plain and simple fabric remnants that can be stitched into a traditional patchwork quilt. With more snippets of fabrics and trims, you can piece a Log Cabin cushion for the spool chair and add touches of lace to dress up the pillows and canopy. The pig-tailed prairie doll (also shown on page 131) stands 14 inches tall and wears an authentic prairie-style frock and eyelet-trimmed pantaloons.

Schoolhouse Ornaments
Pictured on page 130

MATERIALS: Unbleached muslin; green, red, and blue acrylic paints; stencil paper or acetate; craft knife; stencil brushes; lace trim; fiberfill; narrow ribbon or cording.

INSTRUCTIONS: Transfer pattern, *right*, to stencil paper or acetate; cut out shaded areas using a sharp knife.

Place muslin on a hard, flat surface; tape pattern atop fabric. Using acrylics, stencil the design in desired colors, being careful not to let paint run under stencil edges. Remove stencil and let the paint dry.

To finish stenciled areas, paint a ¼-inch-wide strip across bottom of door and windows as follows: Place a 3-inch-long piece of tape on the muslin so it just touches bottom line of house; place another length of tape ¼ inch above the first piece. Paint the exposed area in matching colors using a stencil brush. Let paint dry; remove tape.

Cut out stenciled designs, adding ½-inch seam allowances. Cut muslin back to match front. Baste lace trim to front, then sew front to back, leaving an opening for turning.

Trim seams, turn, and stuff with fiberfill. Slip-stitch openings; add ribbon or cording for hanging.

Blue Calico Heart Ornaments
Pictured on pages 130 and 132

MATERIALS: Blue calicos; cardboard; fiberfill; narrow ribbon.

INSTRUCTIONS: From a folded 3½-inch-square piece of paper, cut heart pattern; trace around heart onto cardboard to make a template, and cut out. Draw around cardboard onto the back of various blue calicos. Cut out fabric hearts, adding ½-inch seam allowances.

With right sides facing, sew two hearts together, leaving an opening. Clip seams, turn, and press. Stuff lightly with fiberfill. Whipstitch the opening closed; add ribbon to the top center of each heart for hanging.

"Home Sweet Home" Apron
Pictured on page 130

MATERIALS: 1 yard (45-inch-wide) ecru cotton; 1 ball of ecru Coats & Clark "Big Ball" 3-cord mercerized cotton, Size 20; Size 9 steel crochet hook, or size to obtain gauge given below.

Abbreviations: Page 310.

Gauge: 4 sps or bls = 1 inch.

INSTRUCTIONS: For lace, ch 71 (12 ch sts per inch). Following chart, *opposite*, work as follows: *Row 1:* Dc in 8th ch from hook—starting sp made; * ch 2, sk next 2 ch, dc in next ch—sp made. Rep from * across— 22 sps, counting sp made at beg of row as 1 sp; ch 5, turn.

Row 2: Sk first sp, dc in next dc— starting sp over sp made; * ch 2, dc in next dc—sp over sp made. Rep from * to last sp; ch 2, dc in next ch—end sp over sp made; ch 5, turn. *Row 3:* Make starting sp, make 1 sp; * 2 dc in next sp, dc in next dc—bl over sp made. Rep from * to last 2 sps; make 1 sp, make 1 end sp; ch 5, turn.

Row 4: Make starting sp and sp; *dc in next 3 dc—bl over bl made; ch 2,

sk 2 dc, dc in next dc—sp over bl made; make 15 more sp over bls, 1 bl over bl, 2 sps; ch 5; turn.

Beg with Row 5, follow chart until Row 125 is completed; fasten off. (*Note:* Follow even-numbered rows on chart from left to right and odd-numbered rows from right to left.)

Starch work lightly and press.

• *For apron,* cut fabric 18x25 inches and 10x25 inches. Cut a 2½-inch-wide waistband that encircles waist, with excess for tying; set aside. Fold smaller rectangle in half lengthwise; sew to bottom of crochet, turning edges under. Hem sides. Hem short sides of larger rectangle; gather top. Fold waistband in half lengthwise and center apron in fold; finish edges. Sew panel to apron.

Appliquéd Sweater
Pictured on page 130

MATERIALS: Cardigan sweater; 30 to 40 two-inch squares of assorted fabrics; fabric for elbow patches and pockets; buttons.

INSTRUCTIONS: Press under edges of fabric squares ¼ inch. Pin

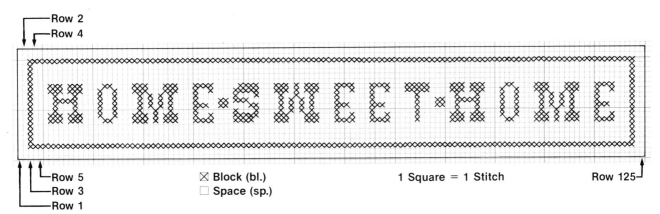

Row 2
Row 4
Row 5
Row 3
Row 1

⊠ **Block (bl.)**
☐ **Space (sp.)**

1 Square = 1 Stitch

Row 125

squares in place randomly around yoke of sweater, overlapping as desired. (Squares should fan out 6-7 inches below the neckline and 4-5 inches over the shoulders.)

Slip-stitch the squares in place. Do not sew too tightly; avoid stretching the sweater.

As you work, clip excess fabric where squares overlap. Make sure squares follow neckline and front plackets of sweater.

Cut two 5x7-inch ovals from extra fabric for elbow patches and two small hearts for pocket appliqués. Fold raw edges under ¼ inch; pin and sew pieces in place.

Prairie Doll
Pictured on page 131

MATERIALS: ⅓ yard of navy floral or calico fabric (dress); 5x18 inches of navy print fabric (dress trim); 6x6 inches of gray velveteen (shoes); ¼ yard of natural linen (body, arms, and legs); ⅓ yard of cotton eyelet (pantaloons); blue, black, tan, gray, and pink embroidery floss; fiberfill; 14 inches of narrow elastic; 12 inches of narrow satin ribbon (hair ribbons); mohair yarn (hair); pink felt-tip marking pen; three buttons; two snaps.

INSTRUCTIONS: Enlarge pattern, *right;* cut linen body, arms, and legs. Cut eyelet pantaloons, placing bottom of pantaloons along selvage. Cut gray velveteen shoes. Cut dress from navy floral or calico fabric.

With right sides facing, sew shoes to leg bottoms. (Use ¼-inch seams throughout.) Sew two leg pieces together, leaving top open. Repeat for

second leg. Clip curves, turn, and stuff. Baste tops closed.

Stitch legs to lower edge of front body. With right sides facing, sew the front and back body pieces together, leaving an opening along the bottom edge and at top of the head for turning. Clip curves, turn right side out, and stuff. Whipstitch openings.

With right sides facing, sew two arm pieces; leave top open. Clip curves, turn, and stuff. Repeat for second arm. Sew openings; tack arms to doll's body.

Embroider facial features, stitching through top layer of fabric only. For eyes, satin-stitch small blue circles. Work black French knots in centers. Outline-stitch gray eyelids and nostrils, tan eyebrows, and a

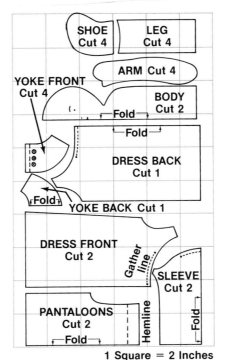

SHOE Cut 4
LEG Cut 4
YOKE FRONT Cut 4
ARM Cut 4
BODY Cut 2
Fold
Fold
DRESS BACK Cut 1
Fold
YOKE BACK Cut 1
DRESS FRONT Cut 2
Gather line
SLEEVE Cut 2
PANTALOONS Cut 2
Hemline
Fold
Fold

1 Square = 2 Inches

pink mouth. Lightly color cheeks with pink marking pen.

Sew pantaloons together along the front seam; clip curves. Turn under the top edge ½ inch (waistline casing); stitch. Thread 7 inches of narrow elastic through the casing; sew ends. Stitch pantaloons along back seam; clip curves. Stitch inside leg seam; clip curves.

To make the ruffle around the yoke of the dress (using contrasting navy print), cut a 1½x18-inch piece of fabric and fold it in half lengthwise. Fold short ends under; stitch together. Gather long raw edges. Repeat for ruffle around neckline.

With right sides facing, sew dress center front seam; leave 1¼ inches unstitched at top. Fold under seam allowance of top 1¼ inches; stitch.

Sew front and back yokes together at shoulders. Repeat for facings.

Gather the dress front and back at neckline. Sew front to back along shoulders. Baste ruffle to yoke. Sew yoke to dress pieces, matching shoulder seams and adjusting gathers. Baste neck ruffle in place. Sew yoke facing to yoke at neck edge and front opening. Turn; press under the raw edge of the yoke facing and slip-stitch closed.

Sew buttons to right side of yoke front; sew snaps to yoke front.

Cut sleeves to match dress; turn and stitch hems to form casings. Cut two 3-inch pieces of narrow elastic and thread the elastic through the casings. Stitch elastic ends together. Gather tops of sleeves between dots; stitch sleeves to dress. Sew underarm and side seams.

Cut a 1½x18-inch piece of contrasting navy print for hem band. *continued*

139

With right sides facing, stitch the band to the hem of the dress and stitch the ends of the band together. Turn hem band under and stitch.

Sew strands of mohair yarn to doll's head, making a center part. Braid each side; tie pigtails using 6-inch lengths of ribbon.

Heart Cradle
Pictured on page 131

MATERIALS: 4x4-foot piece of ³⁄₈-inch fir plywood; No. 7 brass roundheaded screws; sandpaper; Danish oil; wood glue; small nails.

INSTRUCTIONS: Enlarge the pattern, *below;* cut pieces from plywood. Cut two 5x16-inch sides and one 5¾x16-inch bottom. Glue and nail sides to bottom, beveling edges. Glue and nail ends in place. Add five screws at each end to help secure ends. Sand all surfaces smooth. Finish with Danish oil.

If desired, stitch a mattress and pillow for the cradle from fabric.

Crib Quilt
Pictured on page 131

MATERIALS: 1½ yards of blue cotton fabric for outside border and backing; small amounts of 12 solid-color cotton fabrics; quilt batting.

INSTRUCTIONS: Finished size is 39x52½ inches. Before cutting fabrics, plan the arrangement of colors using your fabric scraps and the

1 Square = 1 Stitch

pattern, *below*. Then, with colored pencils and graph paper, make a colored chart to use while you assemble the top. Key the squares on the graph paper to your fabrics.

Cut fabrics into 1¾-inch squares. Piece squares, referring to chart and working on the diagonal. End pieces on rows should be triangles (see pattern). As each row is finished, set it aside and piece the next row. Then, to assemble the top, join the rows. Use ¼-inch seams throughout.

Add a 3-inch-wide light blue border to the pieced top; finish with a 5½-inch-wide dark blue border.

Cut back to match top, sandwich batting between, baste, and quilt in the pattern of your choice. Finish edges by turning under raw edges and slip-stitching them together.

Prairie Rose Ornaments and Wreath
Pictured on pages 132 and 133

MATERIALS: Natural-color Super Crepe crepe paper (available at craft and hobby shops); pink and green liquid fabric dyes; dried flowers and stamens for flower centers; florist's tape; 19-gauge wire; white glue; 12-inch-diameter metal macrame hoop (for wreath); thread.

Amish-style Crib Quilt

INSTRUCTIONS: Mix dyes with hot water according to package instructions. (Combine dyes for various shades of pink and green.)

Cut each sheet of folded crepe paper into eight equal-size pieces; dip pieces into dye one at a time. Remove paper from dye and place it in a 350° oven until it dries and shrinks to about half its original size.

Cut 7-inch pieces of 19-gauge wire; bend one end of each wire into a small loop and wrap a piece of crepe paper through the loop and around the wire. Add dried flowers and stamens through the center of the loop, wrapping them around the wire. Secure flowers and stamens using a small amount of glue.

From paper, cut five to eight pink petals for each flower. Stretch each petal slightly in the center so it cups inward. Arrange petals around flowers and stamens; secure with thread. (Wrap thread around bottom of each petal and around wire.)

Cut leaves as desired from green paper. Begin wrapping the wire with florist's tape, starting at bottom of wire. Wrap leaves into the floral tape to secure them to stem. Wrap bottom of each flower to cover thread and bottom of petals.

• *For rosebuds,* cover a cotton ball with pink paper, using thread to secure bud to wire. Add small leaves as explained above; cover wire with florist's tape.

• *For the wreath,* secure flowers and buds to a hoop by wrapping stems around hoop; cover hoop and stems with tape.

Corn Husk Doll
Pictured on page 133

MATERIALS: Corn husks; glycerin (for brittle shucks); cotton balls; 1-inch-diameter foam ball (head); wire; lightweight poster board; straight pins; white glue.

INSTRUCTIONS: Make doll following instructions for crèche, *page 24*. Craft the head, arms, sleeves, torso, and bodice according to directions for Mary.

• *For the skirt,* cut a cardboard circle 15 inches in diameter; cut in half.

Wrap one half-circle into a cone 5 inches in diameter at the base. Top opening will be about 1 inch wide.

Make the bottom skirt layer by covering half of cone with corn husks, overlapping each strip slightly, pinning them *only* at base of cone. Trim husks toward top so they lie flat against cone. Wrap with thread to prevent buckling as husks dry. Repeat for remaining half of skirt. For top skirt, gather wide husks around cone top, using thread; wrap husks to cone until dry.

Insert bodice into cone. Secure bodice to skirt with a long needle, pushing it through skirt. Glue waist area from inside the cone; remove needle when glue is dry.

• *For apron,* cut curved edge along top of wide husk; this is the hem. Gather straight edge of husk to waistline. Wrap a narrow strip around waist, covering rough edges of skirt and apron husks. Tie in back.

• *For shawl,* drape a long husk over shoulders; tie ends in front.

• *For bonnet,* fold under 1 inch on a 3½-inch-wide husk. With folded edge next to face, wrap husk around head; secure with pins. Gather husk at back of head; wrap with thread. Tie a corn husk strip over thread; end of husk will look like a ponytail. Trim ends; pin in place.

Before husks dry, bend torso, arms, and head as pictured. When dry, trim base so doll stands easily; remove pins and cut threads.

• *For the wreath,* cut one 2½-inch-diameter circle from cardboard; cut a small circle from center. Apply linoleum paste to front of circle; press small cones and dried flowers into place. Glue into doll's hands.

Log Cabin Picture
Pictured on page 133

MATERIALS: 12x18-inch piece of ⅛-inch hardboard; scraps of ¾-inch fir lumber; 1x1-inch fir lumber (frame); wood glue; acrylic or watercolor paints; paintbrush; brads.

INSTRUCTIONS: Enlarge pattern, *below.* Rip ⅛-inch-wide strips from ¾-inch fir; cut pattern pieces. Glue pieces to hardboard, being careful not to get glue on front of wood. Paint with acrylics or watercolors. Rabbet 1x1-inch fir to make a frame with mitered corners; paint. Press picture into back of frame, using brads or small nails to hold the picture in place.

Candle Holder
Pictured on page 133

MATERIALS: ¾-inch pine lumber; 1½-inch fir; acrylic or watercolor paints; paintbrush; wood glue; ⅝-inch-long flathead screws; small nails or brads.

INSTRUCTIONS: Cut ¾-inch pine 4x15½ inches for base of candle holder. Rip ¾-inch pine into ⅛-inch-thick pieces; cut trees and roses from ⅛-inch pine, using patterns, *below.* Paint trees and flowers using diluted acrylics or watercolors.

continued

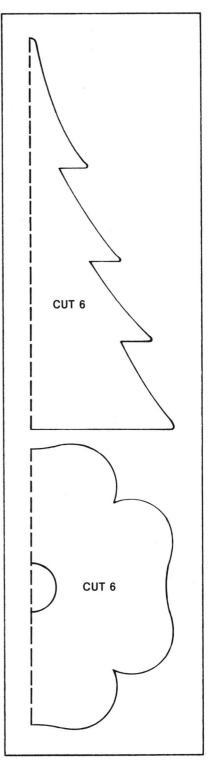

CUT 6

CUT 6

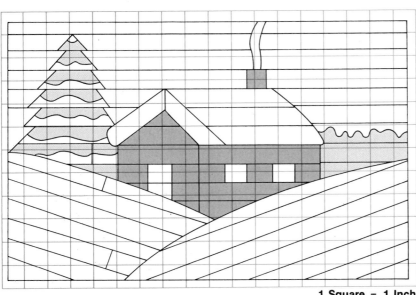

1 Square = 1 Inch

141

To make candle holders, pound four nails into 1½-inch fir; nip off nailheads with wire cutters. Attach fir to base using flathead screws.

Glue and nail trees and flowers to sides of base, alternating shapes and spacing evenly. Attach each shape so it is flush with the bottom. Place one shape at each end of the base.

Bird Ornaments
Pictured on page 134

MATERIALS: ¼ yard of wool fabric for three birds; pearl cotton thread; polyester fiberfill.

INSTRUCTIONS: Enlarge pattern, *below;* cut out pieces, adding ¼-inch seam allowances.

With right sides facing, sew body pieces; leave an opening. Turn and stuff. Stitch wings; turn and stuff. Quilt on dotted lines, using pearl cotton. Tack wings to body, stitching along bottom and each side.

Embroider eyes with pearl cotton.

To hang the ornament, determine balance point by holding bird between thumb and forefinger; attach hanging loop at balance point.

Pinecone Baskets
Pictured on pages 134-135

MATERIALS: 8- or 10-inch-diameter wire basket frames; pinecones (approximately 110 for small

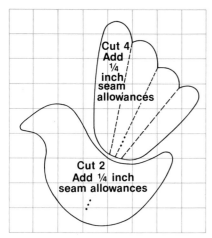

Cut 4
Add ¼ inch seam allowances

Cut 2
Add ¼ inch seam allowances

1 Square = 1 Inch

basket, 170 for large basket); heavy wire (handles); 20-gauge wire for securing cones; craft knife; dried sheet moss (optional); white glue; clear acrylic spray.

INSTRUCTIONS: Begin covering basket with pinecones by pushing cones from top of basket (where wires are far apart) to bottom (where wires are close together).

The bottom row of pinecone petals (scales) are held in place by basket wires. Work bottom rows first, covering wires with cones.

About two-thirds of the way up, cones will slip out of the frame unless they are wired in place. Twist a wire around each cone, then around the wire basket until cones are securely attached up to the rim.

For a handle, bend heavy-gauge wire into a half circle. Wire smallest cones to bent wire. Hook one end of the hanger to the basket; then hook and securely wire the other end to the other side of the basket.

If desired, trim sheet moss with a knife so it fits inside basket. Glue moss liner to inside of the basket, covering wires and rough edges.

Finish with clear acrylic spray.

Apple Wrapping Paper
Pictured on page 135

MATERIALS: Red acrylic paint; brown kraft paper; apples; black marking pen; artist's rubber brayer.

INSTRUCTIONS: Pour a small amount of paint into a pan and spread it evenly with a brayer.

Cut an apple in half and dip one of the halves into paint. Print the apple onto paper, making horizontal or vertical rows. Do not overlap apple designs when printing (leave a small space between each print) but cover paper completely with designs.

When paint is dry, draw seeds or stems on apples using a black pen.

Animal Ornaments
Pictured on page 135

MATERIALS: Scraps of ¼x1-inch pine lumber; coping saw; sand-

paper; wood stain; small wooden twigs; scraps of brown felt; No. 1 round reed; hemp twine; crochet cotton; small paintbrush; brown acrylic paint or brown marking pen; white acrylic paint; florist's wire; cotton ball; dried puffy weed.

INSTRUCTIONS: Transfer patterns, *opposite,* to pine; cut out with a coping saw. Sand edges, drill holes for legs, tails, and antlers; stain. Punch holes in top centers of ornaments; thread with hanging loops.

• *Reindeer:* Glue two twigs in place for antlers and hemp twine for tail. Use a dot of white paint or a brown marking pen to paint the eyes.

• *Mouse:* Insert a piece of reed for the tail. (To shape the reed without breaking it, soak it in water and bend it as desired; let dry.) Cut ears from brown felt; glue in place. Use wire cutters to cut two straight pins just below the pinheads; insert pinheads into the wood for eyes.

• *Sheep:* Use reed for legs, cotton string for tail, and felt for ears. Glue legs, tail, and ears in place; darken face slightly with a brown marking pen. Add "curls" to sheep's body using a brown pen. Paint and darken centers with a brown pen.

• *Pig:* Cut 1½ inches of florist's wire for the tail; bend it around a pencil. Insert tail as shown on pattern. Cut and glue brown felt ears in place.

• *Goat:* For horns, cut two 1½-inch pieces of reed; soak them in water, shape as desired, and let dry. Glue horns, hemp twine tail, and brown felt ears in place.

• *Rabbit:* Glue a small cotton ball in place for the tail. Cut ears from brown felt and glue them in place. Paint eyes.

• *Squirrel:* Glue a puffy dried weed (from a dried bouquet) in place for the tail; add brown felt ears.

Pine Shaving Ornaments
Pictured on page 135

MATERIALS: ½- and ¾-inch-wide pine plywood edging (available at lumberyards); white glue; paper clips; white sewing thread.

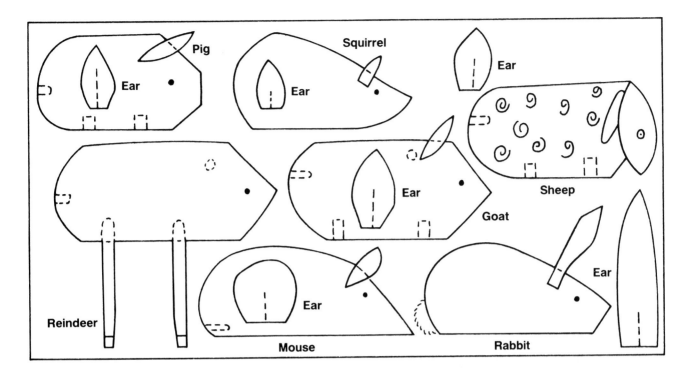

INSTRUCTIONS: For a heart, cut 28 inches of plywood edging; soften the strip in warm water (until flat), pat dry, and cut in half, making two 14-inch lengths. Apply glue to one end of one strip. Loop that end of the strip into a ¾-inch-diameter circle (rough side of wood should be inside). Apply glue on outside of this circle at point where circle is sealed; make another circle, leaving ¼ inch between circles at top.

Make three to five concentric circles, being sure pine edges are even. Use a paper clip to hold the thicknesses together until glue dries.

Repeat this procedure with the second strip, making sure circles are the same size so the two sides match.

Glue the two sides together where the circles are glued, keeping the two ends at the top; center a hanging loop inside the glued area. Hold the sides in place with a paper clip until the glue dries.

Shape outside of heart while shavings are damp; pull ends down and glue together. (If necessary, trim ends before gluing so sides are even.) Secure with paper clip until dry. Make adjustments while shavings are damp. Let dry for at least ½ hour before removing clips.

Craft variations of the heart for other ornaments.

Woodburned Wagons
Pictured on page 136

MATERIALS: ⅜-inch-thick pine (large wagon); ¼-inch-thick pine (small wagon); wood glue; nails; four brass roundheaded screws for each wagon; two 11½-inch-long, ⅜-inch-diameter dowels (large wagon); two 7¼-inch-long, ¼-inch-diameter dowels (small wagon); woodburning tool; acrylic paints; paintbrush; stain.

INSTRUCTIONS: Cut pieces from pine following the diagrams, *below.* (Dimensions of the larger wagon are in parentheses.) Glue

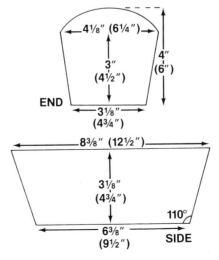

and nail the sides and ends to a bottom piece that is cut to size.

Cut four wheels for each wagon. The large wagon wheels are 5¾ inches in diameter; small wagon wheels are 3¾ inches in diameter.

Cut front and back axle blocks for each wagon from pine. Using wood glue, glue them to the underside of each wagon (across the front and back). Attach two wheels to each axle block using brass screws. Drill two holes in each front axle block to accommodate dowel "axles."

Finish the top edge of each sidepiece on the wagons by nailing a piece of narrow wood trim in place across top edges (see photograph).

Stain the wood as desired and let it dry thoroughly.

Enlarge the woodburning patterns, *page 144;* transfer them to the wagons, using a pencil. (Patterns are sized for the large wagon; reduce their size for the small wagon.) Refer to the photograph for design possibilities. Add designs to the wheels, if desired.

Woodburn over the pencil lines using a woodburning tool. (Practice on scrap wood first if you are inexperienced.) Paint the designs as desired using acrylic paints (thinned with water) or watercolor paints.

continued

143

1 Square = 1 Inch

Wooden Doll
Pictured on page 136

MATERIALS: Scraps of 2-inch-thick pine (body); scraps of ½-inch-diameter dowel (arms and legs); acrylic or enamel paints; scraps of fabrics, laces, and trims.

INSTRUCTIONS: To preserve the primitive charm of this doll, keep the design crude; do not refine its basic shape beyond sanding it to make it safe for children's play.

Cut a 5½-inch-long piece from 2-inch pine and shape head and torso on a lathe. Use dowels for 4-inch-long arms and 7-inch-long legs, or rip pieces of pine into ½-inch thicknesses and whittle rounded corners. Cut mortise-and-tenon-type joints for shoulders, elbows, hips, and knees; join with small wooden pins.

Whittle the ends of the arms to make hands; whittle the bottoms of the legs to make feet. Paint the head and face as desired using acrylic or enamel paints. Stitch doll clothes from scraps of old-fashioned fabrics.

Crocheted Wool Doily
Pictured on page 136

Doily is 15 inches in diameter.
MATERIALS: 1 ounce *each* of the following two-ply Coats & Clark Red Heart Sport Yarn: cranberry, mist green, bottle green, eggshell, camel, medium brown, pantile brown, vibrant orange, dark gold, amethyst; Size 0 steel crochet hook, or size to obtain gauge below.
Abbreviations: Page 310.
Gauge: 9 sts = 2 inches.
INSTRUCTIONS: Beg at center with cranberry, ch 4; join with sl st to form ring. *Rnd 1:* Ch 1, 6 sc in ring; join with sl st to first sc. Ch 1, *do not turn. Rnd 2:* 2 sc in joining, 2 sc in each sc around—12 sc; join with sl st to first sc. *Rnd 3:* 2 sc in joining, sc in next sc, * 2 sc in next sc, sc in next sc. Rep from * around—18 sc; join as before.

Rnd 4: Ch 1, inc 6 sts evenly spaced around making incs directly over incs of previous rnd, sc in each sc around—24 sc; join.

Rnd 5: Rep Rnd 4—30 sc. Cut yarn. *Rnd 6:* Attach eggshell, make lp on hook, sc in each sc around; join. *Rnd 7:* Ch 3 (counts as dirst dc), dc in joining, dc in next st, * 2 dc in next st, dc in next st. Rep from * around—45 dc; join with sl st to top of ch-3. Cut yarn.

Rnd 8: Attach amethyst, make lp on hook, sc in joining, * 2 sc in next dc, sc in next sc. Rep from * around—67 sc; join. *Rnd 9:* Ch 3, dc in each sc around, inc 3 dc evenly spaced around—70 dc; join. Cut yarn. *Rnd 10:* Attach cranberry, make lp on hook, sc in joining, sc in each st around; join.

Rnd 11: Ch 1, sc in joining, sc in each of next 3 sc, * 2 sc in next sc, sc in each of next 4 sc. Rep from * around—84 sc; join. Cut yarn.

Rnd 12: Attach orange, make lp on hook, sc in joining, sc in each st around; join. Cut yarn. *Rnd 13:* Attach new camel, make lp on hook, dc in joining, dc in each of next 4 sts, 2 dc in next st, * dc in each of next 5 sts, 2 dc in next st. Rep from * around—98 dc; join. Cut yarn.

Rnd 14: Attach mist green, make lp on hook, sc in joining and in each st around; join.

Rnd 15: Ch 1, sc in joining and in each st around, inc 2 sc evenly spaced—100 sc; join. Cut yarn.

Rnd 16: Attach bottle green, make lp on hook, 2 dc in joining, dc in each of next 3 sts, * 2 dc in next st, dc in each of next 4 sts. Rep from * around—120 dc; join. Cut yarn.

Rnd 17: Attach new camel, make lp on hook, sc in joining, sc in each st around; join. *Rnd 18:* Ch 3, dc in joining, dc in each of next 4 sts, * 2 dc in next st, dc in each of next 5 sts. Rep from * around—140 sts; join. Cut yarn.

Rnd 19: Attach cranberry, make lp on hook, sc in joining and in each sc around; join. *Rnd 20:* Ch 3, dc in joining, dc in each of next 5 sts, * 2 dc in next st, dc in each of next 6 sts. Rep from * around—160 sts; join. Cut yarn.

Rnd 21: Attach pantile brown, make lp on hook, sc in joining, sc in each st around; join. *Rnd 22:* Ch 1, sc in each st around; join. Cut yarn.

Rnd 23: Attach amethyst, make lp on hook, dc in joining and in each st around; join. *Rnd 24:* Ch 1, sc in joining and in each st around; join. Cut yarn.

Rnd 25: Attach medium brown, make lp on hook, 2 dc in joining, dc in each of next 2 sts, * 2 dc in next st, dc in each of next 3 sts. Rep from * around—200 dc; join.

Rnd 26: Ch 1, sc in each st around; join. Cut yarn. *Rnd 27:* Attach new camel, make lp on hook, sc in joining, sc in each st around; join.

Rnd 28: Ch 1, sc in each st around; join. Cut yarn; turn. *Rnd 29:* Attach dark gold, make lp on hook, sc in joining and in each sc around; join.

Rnd 30 (shell rnd): Ch 1, * sc in sc, sk next sc, shell of 5 dc in next sc, sk next sc, sc in next sc. Rep from * around; join. Cut yarn. Weave yarn ends on wrong side; block.

Checkers and Checkerboard
Pictured on page 136

MATERIALS: *Checkers*—Flour; salt; aluminum foil; red, black, and green acrylic paints; small paintbrush; clear satin finish varnish.

Checkerboard—Black and red carpet warp; 1 skein black rug yarn; simple rigid heddle loom.

INSTRUCTIONS: Mix 1 cup flour, ¼ cup salt, and ½ cup water. This is enough dough for one set of checkers (24). On a floured surface, knead dough with your hands until it is smooth. If dough feels sticky, add a small amount of flour.

Form 24 balls of dough (about ½ inch in diameter); place dough on aluminum foil. (To make small heart design on checkers use a ceramic cookie press.) Shape pieces into designs of your choice.

Place the dough on a cookie sheet and bake for 2½ to 3 hours in a 275° to 300° oven. Let the dough cool completely before painting.

Paint heart designs with acrylic paints, making 12 red and 12 black checkers. Varnish when dry.

• *Checkerboard:* The secret to this project is in threading the loom. Warp the loom with 12 threads per inch: Begin with a 1½-inch *border* (on each side eventually) using black carpet warp thread.

After warping one border, start with the red thread. Continue alternating black and red thread until there are 16 threads. (Each *series* is made up of 16 threads.) Begin each new series with the same color that ends the preceding series. (See the sequence below for threading the warp.) This repeat pattern creates a red/black checkerboard effect.

Continue until eight series are repeated. End with another 1½-inch border of black thread.

Sequence for threading warp:
(1) Border 18 black.
(2) Rb rb rb rb rb rb rb rb.
(3) Br br br br br br br br.
(4) Continue repeat pattern.
(5) Border 18 black threads.

Weaving: Use black carpet warp for a lightweight thread and black rug yarn for a heavy-weight thread.

Begin with two shuttles—one filled with thread, the other with yarn. Raise the heddle so half of the warp threads are raised. Pass shuttle with carpet warp between threads.

Alternate heavy and light thread until you have woven a 3-inch-wide border. End the weaving with a lightweight thread.

For the checkerboard squares, begin weaving with thread, then use yarn; alternate thread and yarn until a square is formed. Finish with thread. Begin next square with thread. Weave a series of eight squares. Finish with a 3-inch border (at top and bottom).

Wooden Spool Doll Furniture
Pictured on page 137

MATERIALS: Use spools of almost any size and shape, but match the size, shape, and height of spools for bed posts, table legs, and so forth. Spools for each row should be the same height so finished pieces are square and symmetrical. Materials lists and instructions are for spools approximately ⅞ to 1 inch in diameter and 1⅛ to 1¼ inches tall.

• *For all pieces:* Stain; paintbrush; wood glue; wood putty; sandpaper; electric drill with ¼-inch bit.

• *Bed:* 68 spools; 6 feet of ¼-inch-diameter dowel; 12x15-inch piece of ¼-inch plywood (bed platform); two 1x15-inch lath or plywood strips (crosspieces to hold canopy); two 12x15-inch pieces of 1-inch foam rubber (box spring, mattress); scraps of calico fabrics, white fabric, fiberfill, and eyelet (bed linens).

• *Chair:* 16 spools; 4¼-inch plywood square; ¼-inch-diameter dowels—eight 4¼ inches long, one 36 inches long; two small wooden buttons (optional); cardboard; fabric scraps; fiberfill (cushion).

• *Table:* 16 spools; 7-inch plywood square; ¼-inch-diameter dowels.

INSTRUCTIONS: Sand edges of plywood. Stain plywood, spools, and dowels.

• *Bed:* Glue two spools together (one atop another), making four legs. To align spools insert a dowel through centers. Glue eleven spools together for each of four bedposts. Glue eight spools together for each of two horizontal dividers at head and foot of bed.

When glue is dry, count up four spools from bottom of the two posts for head of bed. Drill a ¼-inch hole in center side of each spool. Count

up five spools from bottom of two posts for foot of bed. Drill a ¼-inch hole in center side of each spool.

Cut two 9¾-inch dowels to fit between posts at head and foot of bed. Slip one set of eight spools onto each dowel; fit dowel ends into drilled holes.

Place bedposts in corners of plywood platform; mark position of each post. Drill holes in corners of plywood; slip a dowel through each bedpost, plywood base, and leg. Trim dowels flush with top of bedposts. Glue together in each corner. (If dowels are loose inside posts, secure with glue and wood putty.)

Trim the canopy crosspieces from 1 inch wide in the center down to ⅛ inch wide at the ends. Glue and nail in place (from head to foot of bed) to top of bedposts.

Cut 1-inch squares from corners of foam rubber pieces so box spring and mattress fit around bedposts. Sew dust ruffle, bedspread, and pillow from fabric and lace scraps.

Cut and gather a rectangle of white fabric to fit over the top of the bed for a canopy. Add an eyelet ruffle around the edges and tack the canopy in place to the crosspieces.

• *Chair:* Glue three spools together for each leg; make four. Center and drill two ¼-inch holes in middle spool of each leg, drilling in two sides so holes are at 90° angles. Fit dowels into holes, making four chair rails between legs. Insert dowels through center of each leg for extra strength; cut dowels flush with top and bottom of legs.

Mark position of legs on chair seat; glue legs in place.

Drill ¼-inch holes in centers of eight spools; fit spools on ends of four dowels. Glue the two sets together to make two chair posts. Add another spool to bottom of each post so posts are five spools tall. Insert dowels through centers of posts (for added strength), trim dowels flush, and glue posts to top of chair seat.

Glue a small wooden button to the top of each chair post if desired. Sew cushion from fabric scraps.

• *Table:* Glue four spools together for legs, insert dowels in legs, and trim flush with spools. Glue legs to tabletop.

CHRISTMAS MAGIC FROM EVERYDAY THINGS

Holiday Trims from Simple Materials

Christmas is a time for conjuring up wonderful things. And all it takes to create a houseful of holiday magic is a little seasonal sleight of hand.

In this section, you'll find a bevy of ways to transform everyday materials into enchanting decorations and gifts. All of the projects can be made with inexpensive, easy-to-find materials, some of which you may already have. Many projects are so simple you can make them in a twinkling, while others are a bit more time-consuming but worth the wondrous results.

Sprightly calicos and colorful felt provide the makings for the festive array of projects pictured here. The tree, bell, and star ornaments, *opposite,* are embellished with clusters of wooden beads, as is the easy-sew quilted tree skirt. The tree-top angel with eyelet wings and curly yarn hair is fashioned around a wooden dowel. The oversized stocking, *below,* is lightly quilted and accented with appliquéd felt stars.

How-to instructions for all of the projects in this section begin on page 154.

147

Holiday Trims from Simple Materials

Scraps of Christmasy plaids form the stately trees that embellish the quilted place mats, *below*. A trio of candle dolls crafted from wood turnings also brightens this holiday nook, along with packages topped with marking-pen-graphed geometrics.

An advent calender makes waiting for Christmas a lot more fun. The felt-and-fabric banner, *right,* is decorated with cooking-crystal ornaments that tuck into numbered pockets.

The patchwork picture, *opposite,* is machine-stitched in felt and calico fabrics and makes a delightful country Christmas decoration or gift.

Holiday Trims from Simple Materials

If you have any doubts about the magical properties of muslin, feast your eyes on the imaginative array of projects pictured here and on the next two pages. Muslin is the basis for each one of these captivating trims and gifts—even the Christmas trees.

The elegant coverlet and pillows are made from squares of muslin, appliquéd with doilies and lace.

Muslin—painted and plain—also was used to stitch the soft baskets placed around this enchanting holiday scene.

A veritable garden of painted flowers covers a ribbon-trellis stocking of magnificent proportions. These pretty floral motifs appear again on the diamond-shape trims that decorate a muslin tree along with lace-inset teardrop trims. To crown a mantel with holiday cheer, fashion a fan of muslin and shimmering ribbons.

For details on other muslin projects, please turn the page.

150

Make a Christmas package as festive as the gift inside by covering the box in muslin and adding a flowing embroidered bow, *above.* To create a classy clutch purse for holiday evenings, line a flea-market dresser scarf with muslin, fold in thirds, and stitch to form a rectangular pocket.

Use peach-colored cotton or unbleached muslin painted a soft shade of apricot to create the teardrop trims that appear, *below,* and on the previous page. Accent them with lace insets, seed pearls, and shiny satin ribbon bows.

With just two yards of muslin and a few simple trims, you can craft a pair of prim-and-proper dolls, *above,* that are sure to become a little girl's Christmas dream come true. The "fancy" doll on the left is dressed in tiers of ecru lace and has tiny silk flowers tucked into her elegant pearl cotton braids. She's about two feet tall, and her "plain" sister is 19 inches tall.

Transform ordinary muslin into a plump fabric tree to showcase all manner of fanciful trims. The tabletop tree, *left,* is machine-quilted and topped with a three-dimensional star also made of muslin.

Delicate nosegays crafted from dried flowers and paper lace doilies trim the "boughs" of this whimsical tree. Around the base, muslin candles cast a continuous glow throughout the holiday season. These festive stitch-and-stuff ornaments stand on a floral motif base. The bright flames are painted with fabric paints.

Though humble in origin, simple muslin can be fashioned beautifully into such graceful symbols of the Christmas season as the Madonna and Child, *right.* You can make this elegantly stylized Nativity with a single yard of muslin plus a few scraps of colored cotton. (The Madonna is approximately 15 inches tall.)

The simple figures are machine-appliquéd and accented with gray embroidery floss that's been machine-couched along the outlines of the design. Petite pillows stitched from the same fabrics complete this Christmas scene.

Tree, Bell, and Star Ornaments
Pictured on page 146

MATERIALS: Yellow, red, and green felt; yellow, red, and green calico fabrics (or use colors of your choice); small (5-mm) wooden beads to contrast with fabrics; embroidery floss to match or contrast with fabrics; polyester fiberfill; cardboard or plastic lids.

INSTRUCTIONS: Enlarge the patterns, *below,* onto tissue paper. Make templates for cutting ornament shapes by transferring pattern outlines to cardboard or plastic lids. Cut out templates.

With a sharp pencil, trace around templates onto felt or the wrong side of the calico fabric.

For felt ornaments, cut a double layer of fabric (for front and back) along pencil lines; for calico ornaments, add ¼-inch seam allowances, then cut out.

Mark dots for placement of beads as indicated on patterns. Sew beads in place using three strands of embroidery floss.

To assemble felt ornaments, pin fronts to backs, wrong sides facing. Using three strands of floss and running stitches positioned ⅛ inch from raw edges, sew fronts to backs. Leave an opening. Tuck fiberfill into ornament, then close opening.

To assemble calico ornaments, machine-sew backs to fronts, right sides facing, in a ¼-inch seam. Leave an opening. Clip curves, turn ornaments right side out, and press. Stuff lightly with fiberfill and sew opening closed. For hanging, sew thread loops to tops of ornaments.

Easy Tree Skirt
Pictured on page 146

MATERIALS: 45x45 inches *each* of calico (skirt), green polka dot fabric (appliqué), quilt batting, and white cotton (backing); 4 yards green polka dot bias binding; 9x12 inches gold felt; 48 small (5-mm) green wooden beads; thread to match fabrics.

INSTRUCTIONS: For the calico background, cut a circle 44 inches in diameter. Fold the circle into quarters, then into eighths. Press sharp creases along folds, clearly marking eight divisions in the circle. Cut a 40-inch-diameter circle from polka dot fabric; press creases into place the same as for calico circle.

Enlarge the tree pattern, *right,* and cut from folded polka dot fabric. *Do not cut sides* of trees along folds. The piece should form a ring of trees when opened up.

Unfold both pieces and center the tree piece atop the circle, matching folds in both pieces. Pin trees into place. Baste trees to circle, placing stitches ¼ to ⅜ inch from raw edge of trees. (Do not fold under raw edges yet.) Finally, press the basted fabric, *except* leave one fold *on the straight grain of the fabric* unpressed. This fold will be your guide to cutting the slit in the tree skirt.

Using thread to match, appliqué the trees in place. Turn under the raw edges as you work. Leave an inch of appliqué unsewn on each side of the remaining fold (2 inches total). Sew this after the slit has been cut in the fabric.

Using the pattern, *above right,* cut eight stars from yellow felt; stitch green beads to the centers. Appli-

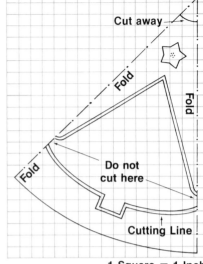

qué the stars to the tops of the trees as shown in the photograph.

Sandwich batting between the appliquéd top and backing fabric. Carefully baste the layers together. Mount the basted fabrics in a quilting frame, if desired; then outline-quilt around trees and stars. Trim excess batting and backing fabric when quilting is complete.

Slit the circle along the fold line, then cut a 3½-inch-diameter circle in the exact center of the larger circle for the tree trunk. Bind the raw edges of the tree skirt with polka dot binding.

Calico Angel
Pictured on page 146

MATERIALS: ¼ yard *each* calico print, white eyelet, white broadcloth, and heavy nonwoven interfacing; ½ yard of 1-inch-wide eyelet trim; scraps of green polka dot fabric and white- and flesh-colored felt; 4 yards of bulky white yarn; quilt batting; narrow ribbon; 10 small (5-mm) green wooden beads; embroidery floss; craft stick or small dowel 4 inches long; 2x2 inches of 1-inch-thick plastic foam.

INSTRUCTIONS: Enlarge pattern, *opposite, top;* cut pieces. Add ¼-inch seam margins to all pieces except those cut from felt, nonwoven interfacing, and dotted fabric.

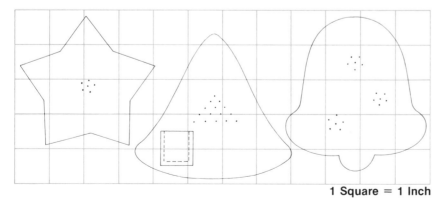

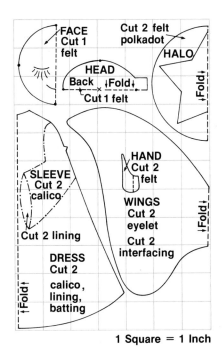

1 Square = 1 Inch

Using floss, embroider facial features with simple stitches.

Gather the edge of the face slightly, and whipstitch it to the head back, matching dots. Leave a small opening, stuff lightly, then sew the opening closed. Attach a craft stick or dowel to the head back (at the X marked on the diagram) by sewing over and around the stick.

Beginning at the center back of the head and working in a spiral, couch bulky yarn "hair" in place with sewing thread. To simulate curls, keep the yarn loose and loopy while pulling thread tight. Cover the back of the head, then work at least two rows of loops around the angel's face.

For the body, baste eyelet trim to the hem of the dress front and back. Turn up a ¼-inch hem in the dress lining; trim ¼ inch from the hem edge of the batting pieces.

Turn under the seam allowance on the sleeves except along the notched edge. Pin felt wrist in place near the upper edge of the wrist opening. Position the sleeve on the sleeve lining (white), overlapping the edge of the lining ¼ inch. Blindstitch the sleeve to the lining, catching the hand in the seam.

Turn under the remaining raw edge of the sleeve lining. Appliqué the arm to the dress front, leaving

the notched edge open. Tuck a small amount of stuffing into the sleeve, then baste the notched area closed to hold stuffing in place.

Outline the sleeve with embroidered chain stitches. Sandwich batting between the dress front and lining; pin, then outline-quilt around the sleeve.

To assemble the body, layer the dress batting, lining, quilted front (right side up), and dress back (right side down). Stitch, beginning at the hemline and leaving 1 inch open at the neck. Do not sew across the hem edge. Turn right side out, then slipstitch the lining to the dress front and back along the hem edge.

For wings, sandwich interfacing between the front and back wings and stitch, leaving an opening. Clip curves, turn right side out, and slipstitch the opening closed.

For the halo, cut a star from the center of the circle; place the circle atop the polka dot lining.

Using two strands of green embroidery floss, sew around the star with small running stitches. Sew beads between star points. Repeat for the other side, then whipstitch the front and back together around the edges using white thread.

To assemble the angel, trim top corners of the plastic foam block (use a sharp knife) to fit into the shoulder area of the dress. Place foam inside the body; insert stick through opening in neck and plunge into foam.

Stitch the neck opening closed around the stick, catching stitches into the felt neck. Tack a small ribbon bow under chin. Tack the center of the halo to the head back. Tack the wings to the back of the dress, with the top of the wings about 1 inch below the neck.

Calico Stocking
Pictured on page 147

MATERIALS: ¾ yard of green and white polka dot fabric; ¾ yard of muslin; 14x24 inches of quilt batting; 9x12 inches of gold felt; 36 small (5-mm) green wooden beads; green and gold embroidery floss.

INSTRUCTIONS: Enlarge pattern, *below;* cut stocking front and back from polka dot fabric and muslin. Do not add seam allowances. Cut stars from felt *(see pattern, opposite)*. Also cut a 2x6-inch piece of polka dot fabric for the hanging tab.

Using a pencil, mark dots on stars for bead placement. Stitch beads to each star, using green floss.

Sew the stars to the stocking front using three strands of embroidery floss and running stitches positioned ⅛ inch from the edge of each star.

Sandwich quilt batting between the stocking top and a 14x24-inch piece of muslin. Baste layers together and outline-quilt around stars using yellow thread.

With right sides together, sew the stocking front to the back in a ½-inch seam. Trim the seam, turn the stocking right side out, and press.

Sew the lining front to the back, leaving open the bottom edge along the arch.

Turn in the long edges of the hanger tab, fold the tab in half lengthwise, and stitch along fold. Fold the tab in half crosswise and pin it in place atop the stocking front, with raw edges of tab and stocking even.

continued

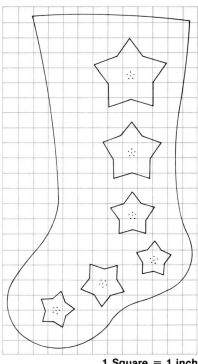

1 Square = 1 inch

155

Place stocking inside lining, right sides facing. Stitch stocking and lining together along top edge, catching hanger tab in seam. Pull the stocking through the opening in the lining. Slip-stitch lining seam, then tuck lining into the stocking.

Advent Calendar
Pictured on page 148

MATERIALS: 2 yards of red cotton; 18x24 inches *each* of green felt and polyester fleece; red bias tape; gold adhesive-backed numerals and 3-inch-diameter medallion; 20 inches of green ball fringe; ½ yard of ½-inch-wide gold trim; 5½ yards of narrow (¼-inch-wide) yellow ribbon; ¾ yard of 1½-inch-wide yellow ribbon; 19-inch-long dowel (hanging rod); red plastic cooking crystals; red Phunfelt; small safety pins.

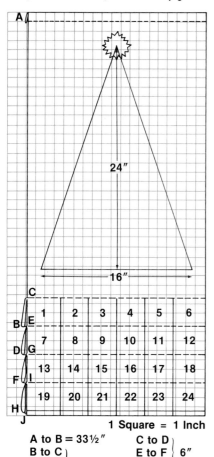

1 Square = 1 Inch

A to B = 33½″
B to C
D to E   } 3″
F to G
H to I

C to D
E to F   } 6″
G to H
I to J = 3½″

INSTRUCTIONS: Finished size is 19x46 inches.

Enlarge pattern, *below left.* Cut the tree shape from green felt and also from fleece. Cut the red fabric background to measure 19x68½ inches.

Place the fleece tree behind the green felt tree, then pin them to the red fabric with the top of the tree 5 inches below the top of the red fabric and centered between the left and right edges. Baste securely, then machine-zigzag-stitch the tree in place.

Fold down the top of the background fabric 1½ inches; turn under the raw edge and stitch, making a casing for the hanging rod.

Press folds in the fabric as indicated on the diagram for rows of pockets. Pin the folds in place.

Using red thread, machine-stitch five vertical rows between the pockets as shown, catching all layers of fabric in the stitching.

Sew gold trim along the lower edge of the tree. Bind the sides of the calendar with red bias tape. Sew green ball fringe along the bottom.

Add adhesive-backed numerals to the pockets and the gold medallion to the treetop. Cut narrow ribbon into 8-inch pieces; tie 24 small bows for the pockets. Pin a large bow to the top of the tree.

Make "ornaments" for the tree in clean or new muffin tins. Pour a spoonful of plastic cooking crystals into each segment of the muffin tins; add a layer of red Phunfelt cut to fit, then a second layer of crystals. Bake in a 375° oven for ½ hour or until smooth. If the ornaments bubble or the fabric is not completely covered, add more cooking crystals and carefully reheat.

Let the ornaments cool completely, then knock them out of the muffin tin using a wooden spoon.

File, grind, or sand down all the rough edges. Using an electric drill and a small drill bit, carefully drill a hole in the top of each disc, then reheat the ornaments on a foil-covered cookie sheet for 10 minutes or until they are smooth.

Thread ribbon or gold cord through the hole in each one, tie into a knot, and add safety pin. Tuck ornaments into pockets.

Candle Dolls
Pictured on page 148

MATERIALS: Three unfinished wooden spindles, such as table legs or balusters (available in lumberyards); gesso; acrylic paint; ribbon.

INSTRUCTIONS: Finished size is approximately 6½ inches tall.

The candle holders shown were cut from the lower portion of 14-inch table legs. The same design may be adapted for use on sections of other wooden spindles such as newel posts, post caps, or chair legs.

Enlarge the pattern, *opposite, top,* to use as a guide for cutting and painting your candle dolls.

Begin by cutting off the unwanted portion of the spindle. Be sure to leave a segment of spindle above the doll's "head" to hold the candle. Drill a hole (approximately ¾ inch in diameter and ¾ inch deep) in the top for the candle; sand.

Mold a small piece of wood putty into a "nose" approximately ⅛ inch in diameter. When putty dries, glue it to the "face."

To prepare the wood for painting, mix equal portions of gesso and water and apply three coats to the spindle, sanding lightly between each coat. Paint the candle doll with acrylics, then finish with varnish, if desired. Tie a ribbon around the doll's "neck."

Christmas Place Mats
Pictured on page 148

MATERIALS: ¾ yard of red prequilted fabric (for four place mats); assorted red and green plaid cotton fabrics; 7 yards *each* of red bias tape and 1-inch-wide ribbon.

INSTRUCTIONS: Cut prequilted fabric into 12x18-inch pieces.

Cut plaid scraps into a variety of triangular tree shapes (see the photograph for ideas). Machine-appliqué three "trees" (overlapped) onto each mat.

Baste ribbon around the edge of each place mat, carefully mitering the ribbon at the corners. Bind the edge with red bias tape, catching the ribbon in the seam.

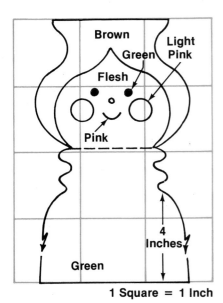

1 Square = 1 Inch

scraps, using the photograph as a guide. Do not add seam allowances.

Back each cutout shape with interfacing, then baste fabric and felt shapes to the background in the sequence noted on the pattern. Tuck the edges of some pieces underneath other pieces as indicated by broken lines.

When all pieces except the windows and tree trunks are basted to the background, machine-appliqué them in place using loosely spaced zigzag stitches. Use matching or contrasting thread for appliqué. Finally, glue windows and tree trunks in place. Embroider the tree.

To finish, mount the picture on cardboard (pad with quilt batting, if desired), mat, and frame.

Geometric-Pattern Gift Boxes
Pictured on page 148

MATERIALS: Graph paper (8 or 10 squares per linear inch); gift wrap; boxes; felt pens in a variety of colors; rubber cement.

INSTRUCTIONS: Wrap the boxes with gift wrap, except leave the tops plain. Cut a piece of graph paper to fit the top of each box. Color the graph paper squares with felt pens using your favorite quilt patterns or other geometric designs as a guide. Glue paper to box tops with rubber cement.

Patchwork Picture
Pictured on page 149

MATERIALS: ½ yard of nonwoven interfacing; felt, calico, and solid-color fabric scraps in variety of complementary colors and patterns; embroidery floss; picture frame.

INSTRUCTIONS: Before framing, the appliquéd picture measures 8x11 inches.

Enlarge the pattern, *right,* and transfer the outlines, centered, onto a 12x15-inch piece of interfacing. This will be the background to which pieces are sewn.

Trace individual pattern elements onto interfacing and cut out. Also cut out shapes from felt and fabric

Fabric Gift Basket
Pictured on page 150

MATERIALS: Prequilted muslin; green fabric scraps; assorted double-fold bias tape and lace trims; thread.

INSTRUCTIONS: Enlarge pattern, *page 158.* From quilted fabrics, cut front and back, handle, a 3½x4½-inch piece (bottom), and two 3x7½-inch pieces (sides).

Decorate the basket front with lace trim stitched 1¾ inches from the top edge. Appliqué leaves to the front. Pin a fabric-painted flower to the basket front. (To assemble flowers, see candle ornament how-to instructions, *page 158.*)

continued

1 Square = 1 Inch

With *wrong* sides facing, sew the front, sides, bottom, and back of the basket together using ½-inch seams. Topstitch bias tape over all raw edges. Attach handle.

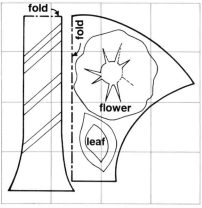

fold

fold

flower

leaf

1 Square = 2 Inches

Ribbon-Trellis Stocking
Pictured on page 150

MATERIALS: 1½ yards of 45-inch-wide muslin; 1 yard of 36-inch-wide polyester fleece; 4½ yards of ½-inch-wide picot-edged taffeta ribbon; liquid embroidery pens.

INSTRUCTIONS: Enlarge pattern for stocking, *right,* adding ½-inch seam allowances. Cut four stocking shapes from muslin and two from fleece.

Transfer lattice lines to one stocking (front). Using flower designs from *Historic Floral and Animal Designs for Embroiderers and Craftsmen* by Suzanne Chapman (Dover Publications), or floral designs of your own, draw flowers inside the lattice lines. Color the motifs with liquid embroidery pens. Let dry, then sew ribbons atop the lattice lines.

Baste fleece backing to the wrong sides of the stocking front and back. With right sides facing, sew the stocking front to the back, leaving the top open. Trim the seams and turn the stocking right side out.

Sew the two remaining stocking pieces together for the lining, and slip them inside the decorated stocking. Turn the raw edges to the inside and whipstitch the lining to the stocking.

Muslin Coverlet and Pillows
Pictured on page 150

MATERIALS: 6⅔ yards of 36-inch-wide muslin; 1 yard *each* of off-white and tan fabrics; ¾ yard of peach fabric; 72 yards of assorted old laces and 20 lace or crocheted medallions (cut apart and collected from antique tablecloths, bedspreads, or other inexpensive lace sources); 62x72-inch piece of quilt batting; polyester fiberfill; 2¼ yards of peach printed fabric (ruffle); 7 yards of 1-inch-wide peach ribbon; 7 yards of 2-inch-wide ruffled lace.

INSTRUCTIONS: Finished size of the coverlet is 55x66 inches, excluding the ruffle.
* *For the coverlet,* cut thirty 12-inch squares from muslin (save the remainder of the muslin for the backing). Referring to the photograph for design ideas, trim the squares with medallions, lace pieces, and strips of peach and tan fabrics. Assemble the coverlet top using ½-inch seams, sewing squares together in five rows of six squares each.

To make the ruffle, cut peach printed fabric in 8x45-inch strips. Seam strips together end to end. Fold the strip in half lengthwise (wrong sides facing) and gather along the raw edges until the strip fits the perimeter of the coverlet (about 7 yards).

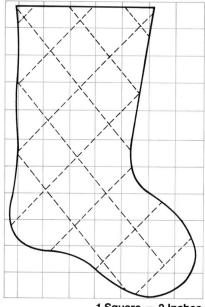

1 Square = 2 Inches

Pin 2-inch-wide lace ruffling atop the peach ruffle and peach ribbon atop the lace. Sew all layers together ½ inch from the raw edges. Pin the ruffle to the coverlet edge. Sew the layers together along the previous stitching line.

Cut and piece remaining muslin for coverlet backing. With right sides facing, stitch back to front, leaving an opening for turning. Turn right side out, then slip-stitch the opening closed. Secure coverlet top to bottom by tying or quilting through all layers.
* *For pillows,* trim 12-inch muslin squares as for coverlet. Cut pillow backs from muslin.

With right sides facing, sew backs to pillow fronts ½ inch from raw edges, leaving opening for turning. Turn pillows right side out, fill with fiberfill; sew closed.

Candle, Diamond, and Quilted Lace Ornaments
Pictured on pages 150-153

MATERIALS: Scraps of muslin; prequilted peach fabric; dark green fabric; green felt; fleece; fiberfill; assorted 2-inch-wide lace trims; assorted ribbons; adhesive-backed foam (available at drug counters); wood scrap; bead trims; thread; fabric paints; liquid embroidery pens.

INSTRUCTIONS: Make candlestick bases using the flower pattern from the basket project, *above left,* a printing block, and fabric paints. For a printing block, cut the flower shape from adhesive-backed foam, remove the paper backing, and adhere the foam to a wood scrap. Brush fabric paint on printing block; press onto muslin. Print one flower for each ornament, leaving 2 inches between. Dry.
* *For candle bases,* sew flowers to muslin backing (right sides facing) ½ inch beyond edges of printed flowers. Leave openings in seams. Turn right side out, then sew openings closed. Cut leaves from felt; glue them to undersides of flowers.
* *For a candle,* cut a piece of muslin 2½x6 inches; sew the long edges together, shaping a flame at the top.

158

Leave bottoms open. Turn candles right side out. Paint flames, stuff them, and sew them to flower bases.

Tie ribbons at bases; fasten ornaments to tree branches with T-pins or wires sewn to bases.

• **For diamond trims,** enlarge pattern, *below*. For each ornament, cut two muslin diamonds and one of polyester fleece. Decorate the fronts with flowers as for the muslin stocking, *opposite.* Sew ribbon along lines indicated on pattern.

Using ¼-inch seams, sew fleece, plain muslin, and a decorated front together. Leave an opening. Turn right side out, sew the opening closed, and trim the edges with picot ribbon. Finish with a bow and hanger at the top of the ornament.

• **For quilted lace ornaments,** enlarge the teardrop pattern, *below*. For the ball-shape ornament, draw a 5-inch-diameter circle; adapt the top of the circle to a teardrop.

For each ornament, cut one shape from prequilted peach fabric (front) and one from muslin (back). Cut 2-inch-wide strips of dark green fabric. Appliqué green strips and lace across the ornament front, using the photograph as a guide. (Or design your own simple motifs to adorn the ornaments.)

Sew the front to the back ¼ inch from the raw edges, leaving an opening. Turn right side out, stuff lightly, and sew closed. Add bows and ribbon hangers at tops. Add beads across fronts, if desired.

Fireplace Fan
Pictured on page 151

MATERIALS: 1⅓ yards of 45-inch-wide muslin; 18x36 inches of fleece padding; 2 yards of 1½-inch-wide peach satin ribbon; 4⅔ yards of 1½-inch-wide green satin ribbon; 4 yards of ⅜-inch-wide ruffled eyelet; ⅔ yard of lace trim; green topstitching thread; white glue; 20x40 inches of cardboard.

INSTRUCTIONS: Enlarge pattern, *below,* adding ½-inch seam allowances. Cut two fans from muslin and one from fleece. With muslin pieces together and fleece on top, stitch layers together; leave an opening. Turn right side out and stitch opening closed.

To decorate the front of the fan, use green thread to topstitch along the lines indicated on the pattern; sew green and peach 1½-inch-wide ribbons between lines. Add two rows of ruffled eyelet along scalloped edges; trim the eyelet seam with narrow green ribbon and small bows tacked at scallop points.

Ease-stitch two rows of 1½-inch-wide green ribbon along half-circle lines at the center of the fan, top-stitching them in place. Trim this ribbon section with lace.

Glue a half-circle of cardboard, cut slightly smaller than the fan, to the fan back. Cut a 2x20-inch strip of cardboard for a stand. Score the strip 2 inches from one end, bend the end back, and glue the short end to the fan back near the top.

Plain and Fancy Dolls
Pictured on pages 150, 152

MATERIALS: 1 yard of 45-inch-wide muslin; 2 yards of 1-inch-wide ecru lace; 1 yard of ½-inch-wide ecru lace; assorted ecru lace scraps; 3½ yards of narrow ecru satin ribbon; 4 skeins of ecru No. 5 pearl cotton; buttons; snaps; ecru thread; pink felt marker; fine-point black *permanent* marker; fiberfill; pink and red felt scraps.

INSTRUCTIONS: Before you begin, see doll-making tips, *pages 281-282.* Enlarge patterns, *page 160.* Cut pieces out of paper.

On double layers of muslin, draw with pencil around all pattern pieces *except* the fancy doll's head. Join layers by sewing along drawn lines; leave openings for turning. Cut out doll parts ¼ inch beyond seams. Clip curves and turn pieces right side out.

For the fancy doll's head, draw one front and two backs. Cut out, adding ¼-inch seam allowances.

Sew the back sections together along the broken lines, leaving an opening for turning. With right sides facing, sew the head front to the back ¼ inch from the raw edges. (Position the head-back seam *horizontally,* not vertically.) Clip curves carefully; turn the doll's head right side out.

Stuff each doll firmly through openings; sew the openings closed. Stitch across the tops of the legs on the plain doll. Attach legs to the bottom of the fancy doll; sew the head to the neck, matching the center back seam to the neck top.

continued

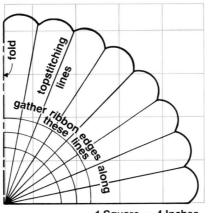

1 Square = 1 Inch

1 Square = 4 Inches

159

Add facial details with felt markers; glue felt mouths in place.

For hair on the plain doll, embroider along the hair lines using pearl cotton and outline stitches. For the fancy doll, cut a ½x5-inch strip of muslin. Untwist three skeins of pearl cotton. Center them along the strip, spreading the strands to cover the strip. Machine-stitch in place, making a center "part." Sew the strip to the head from nape to forehead. Twist skein ends into curls; sew curls to the head. Attach a fourth skein from ear to ear around the face.

• *To dress the plain doll,* cut bodice pieces from muslin (two backs, one front on fold); join bodice at waist. With right sides facing, sew skirt to bodice. Trim bodice sleeves and neck with lace. Slip dress on doll; hand-sew back opening closed. Sew buttons on front.

• *For the fancy doll,* sew lace scraps to doll body to resemble a blouse. Decorate a 7½x9-inch rectangle (skirt) with rows of lace. Seam the center back of the skirt; slip it onto the doll. Gather the waist to fit; sew in place. Circle the waist with lace and ribbon trim. Circle ankles and wrists with lace trims; tie bows, flowers, and ribbons on feet.

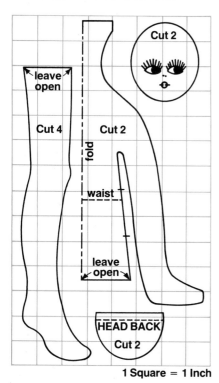

1 Square = 1 Inch

Muslin-Covered Boxes
Pictured on pages 150, 152

MATERIALS: Muslin to cover boxes; polyester fleece; topstitching thread; white glue.

INSTRUCTIONS: Enlarge bow pattern *at right* and transfer to tissue paper to make patterns for each box.

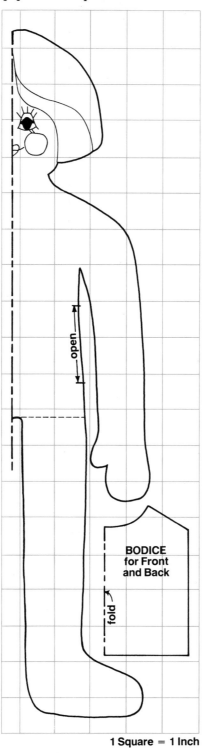

1 Square = 1 Inch

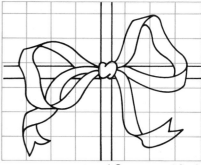

1 Square = 1 Inch

Cut muslin pieces large enough to cover box tops and sides, plus an extra inch all around. Cut fleece to fit *tops* of lids.

Center fleece under muslin rectangle (this will be the top of the box). Next, center paper bow design atop muslin and fleece; pin.

Stitch through bow pattern. After stitching, tear away paper. Extend stitched "ribbon" lines to the edges of the fabric.

Glue center bow motif on box lid. Wrap the remaining fabric around sides, gluing raw edges inside.

Clutch Purse
Pictured on page 152

MATERIALS: Place mat or embroidered doily; lining fabric; antique button (closure) or snaps.

INSTRUCTIONS: Cut lining fabric to match size of doily. With right sides facing, stitch doily to lining, leaving an opening for turning. Turn right side out, press, and blindstitch the opening closed. Fold the doily in thirds to form a pocket with flap; sew sides together. Fold remaining third over bag (flap). Add snaps or an antique button closure.

Muslin Tree and Star
Pictured on page 153

MATERIALS: 2 yards of 44-inch-wide muslin (tree); quilt batting; 3 pounds of fiberfill; thread.
• *For star:* Muslin scraps; 3 yards of gold cording; batting scraps.

160

INSTRUCTIONS: Enlarge patterns, *below.* Cut twelve tree shapes from muslin and six from batting.

Sandwich a batting tree between two muslin trees; machine-quilt layers, with the first quilting line 1½ inches inside raw edges, the second and third lines 1 inch from previous stitching lines. Make five more.

Using ½-inch seam allowances, sew two quilted trees together; leave an opening between Xs. Make two more tree sections; turn.

Lay trees atop each other; sew through all layers from top to bottom along center. Stuff fiberfill through openings, filling until tree stands firmly; sew openings closed.

• *For star,* cut six stars from muslin and three from batting. Using ¼-inch seams, sew together one batting star and two muslin stars; leave an opening. Turn star right side out; sew opening closed.

Topstitch the stars ½ inch from the edges. Stack all the stars atop each other, then sew through all layers along the center. Hand-sew gold cord around edges.

Madonna and Child
Pictured on page 153

MATERIALS: 1 yard of 45-inch-wide muslin; ¼ yard of 18-inch-wide fusible webbing; ⅛ yard *each* of peach, light orange, fuchsia, tan, and blue broadcloth or other lightweight fabrics; fiberfill; gray embroidery floss; gray thread.

INSTRUCTIONS: Enlarge the pattern, *below.* On a 2-inch square of paper, draw a stylized tulip, using the photo for reference.

• *For the Madonna,* cut two body shapes and two 5-inch-diameter circles for the halo. With gray thread, appliqué the hair, face, and robe shapes onto the front of the figure. (See the pattern for colors—O is orange; B is blue; T is tan; and P is peach.) Use strips of fusible webbing to position and secure appliqués before stitching.

With narrow zigzag stitches, machine-couch six-strand embroidery floss along dotted lines.

To make the halo, appliqué three tulips onto the muslin circle (see photograph). Alternate colors and overlap flower petals to fit neatly inside the circle.

Using ¼-inch seam allowances, sew the figure front to the back, leaving the bottom open. Sew the halo front to the back, leaving an opening. Turn both pieces right side out; stuff the figure firmly and stuff the halo lightly. Sew the halo closed; fasten to the Madonna's head.

To make the figure stand, cut a cardboard oval and a muslin oval (plus seam allowances) to fit the base of the Madonna. Turn under all raw edges on the oval and the bottom of the figure and slip-stitch the oval to the base.

• *For the Child,* cut two oval body shapes and two 5-inch-diameter circles from muslin. Sew the Child's halo same as Madonna's.

Appliqué colored fabrics to the body front (see pattern). Sew front to back, leaving an opening. Turn right side out; sew halo behind head of Child.

For Child's pillows, decorate three 5x7-inch pieces of muslin and three 4-inch squares of muslin with tulip appliqués. Cut backs to match fronts, then sew fronts to muslin backs. Turn, stuff, and sew closed.

1 Square = ½ Inch

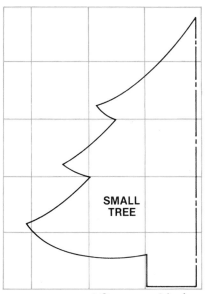

SMALL TREE

1 Square = 4 Inches

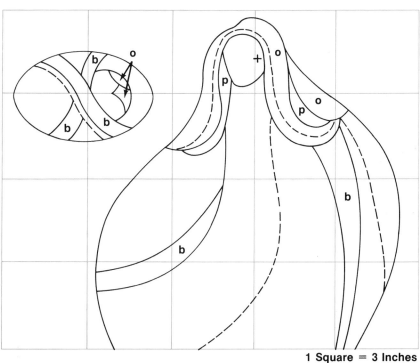

1 Square = 3 Inches

FESTIVE FOODS FROM EVERYDAY INGREDIENTS

If you're like most people, you don't have time to run to specialty shops for exotic ingredients during the Christmas season. With this in mind, all of the recipes in this chapter have been created for extra-special holiday foods that you can make from common ingredients, many of which you probably already have on your kitchen shelves. When the Christmas cooking spirit strikes at your house, take a quick check of the ingredients in your cupboards, freezer, and refrigerator. Then choose the recipe in this chapter that contains the ingredients you have on hand.

Cinnamon Whirl, Bubble Wreath, Swedish Tea Wreath, and Sugar Plum Loaf (see recipes, pages 168 and 169)

HAM-SPINACH STUFFING

  6 cups sliced fresh
     mushrooms
  1 cup chopped onion
  ½ cup butter *or* margarine
  1 16-ounce package herb-
     seasoned stuffing mix
  2 10-ounce packages frozen
     chopped spinach,
     cooked and well
     drained
  3 beaten eggs
  3 cups finely chopped,
     fully cooked ham
  2 cups ricotta cheese
  1 cup grated Parmesan
     cheese
  ½ cup snipped parsley
  ½ cup chicken broth

Cook mushrooms and onion in butter till tender. Pour mushroom mixture over stuffing mix; toss to coat. Squeeze spinach to remove excess water. Fold into the stuffing mixture. Stir together eggs, ham, ricotta cheese, Parmesan, parsley, ¼ teaspoon *salt*, and ⅛ teaspoon *pepper*. Stir into stuffing mixture. Use about *8 cups* of the stuffing mixture to stuff Skip-the-Bones Turkey (see recipe, page 166) or a whole turkey.

  Stir the chicken broth into the remaining stuffing mixture. Spoon into a 2½-quart casserole. Cover; bake in a 325° oven for the last 1 hour of the turkey roasting time. Makes about 15 cups stuffing.

Skip-the-Bones Turkey filled with Ham-Spinach Stuffing, Speedy Pickled Peaches, Green Beans with Parsley Butter, Mom's Sweet Potatoes with Marshmallows, Creamed Onions, and Squash-Carrot Casserole (see Index for recipe pages)

*C*hances are, your kitchen is the most popular gathering place at Christmastime, so share the fun of cooking

with a family member or a friend. It doesn't matter if you work together on one recipe or separate recipes. You'll both enjoy the companionship and sharing of the warm Christmas spirit.

GREEN BEANS WITH PARSLEY BUTTER

Pictured on pages 164-165—

> 3 9-ounce packages frozen whole green beans
> ½ cup butter *or* margarine, softened
> ¼ cup snipped Italian parsley *or* regular parsley

Cook the green beans according to the package directions; drain well. Stir together the butter or margarine and the Italian or regular parsley. Toss with the hot green beans. Makes 10 to 12 servings.

SKIP-THE-BONES TURKEY

Pictured on pages 164-165—

> 1 10- to 12-pound turkey
>   Ham-Spinach Stuffing
>   (see recipe, page 166)
>   Cotton twine

To bone the turkey,* start at neck with turkey on its back; make two horizontal cuts (one on each side of bird) to expose bones that attach wings to back. Break or sever joints (leave wings intact). Use fingers to loosen meat from wishbone, cutting ligaments as necessary; remove wishbone. (It may be necessary to cut wishbone away from the breastbone.)

Next, work your index finger down along each side of breastbone, freeing the meat from the bone as you go. Cut skin from cartilage, if necessary, to release breastbone. Work your hands around rib cage and as far along backbone as you can, loosening meat and cutting cartilage, if necessary. When you reach the backbone, turn bird around. With fingers, break ribs; remove breastbone and attached ribs. Loosen remaining meat from backbone, cutting as necessary. Cut tail from backbone, leaving tail attached to back skin, if desired. Cut joint that connects the lower backbone to the thighbone by pulling meat away and cutting the ligament. Remove the remaining portion of the rib cage and backbone from bird.

Break joints between legs and thighs. Use fingers to loosen meat from thighbones, cutting ligaments as necessary; remove thighbone. If some meat comes out along with bones, remove it from bones and return it to cavity.

Using a 20-inch piece of thread, sew back closed, if necessary. Lay bird breast side up. With a 40-inch piece of thread, sew neck closed. Do not cut thread. Spoon about *8 cups* of the Ham-Spinach Stuffing lightly into breast cavity. Continuing thread from neck, sew breast and bottom opening closed. Insert a long skewer through wings and breast to hold wings in place. Insert a second skewer through thighs and cavity to hold legs in place. Using kitchen twine, secure skewers together to hold bird in its natural shape as it roasts.

Place bird on a rack in a shallow roasting pan. Use your hands to plump bird to resemble turkey shape. Insert meat thermometer in breast to reach center of stuffing. Cover with foil. Roast in a 325° oven for 4 to 4½ hours or till meat thermometer registers 165°. Baste occasionally with drippings during the last half of roasting. Remove foil during last 45 minutes of roasting. Remove to platter. Remove threads and twine; remove skewers. Garnish with orange shells filled with cranberry sauce, if desired. Let turkey stand 10 to 15 minutes before slicing. Makes 12 servings.

*NOTE: If you do not want to bone the turkey, you can use the Ham-Spinach Stuffing to stuff a 10- to 12-pound turkey, leaving the bones in the turkey. Then roast in a 325° oven for 4 to 4½ hours.

MOM'S SWEET POTATOES WITH MARSHMALLOWS

Pictured on pages 164-165—

2 pounds sweet potatoes *or* yams, cooked, drained, and peeled
¼ cup butter *or* margarine
¼ cup packed brown sugar
½ teaspoon salt
Dash ground cinnamon
⅓ cup light cream *or* milk
8 marshmallows, halved

Mash potatoes; stir in butter, brown sugar, salt, and cinnamon. Add cream, beating till fluffy. Turn into a shallow 1½-quart casserole. Bake in a 350° oven for 20 to 25 minutes. Top with marshmallows; broil 1 to 2 minutes or till marshmallows are browned. Makes 8 servings.

NUTMEG SCONES

2⅓ cups packaged biscuit mix
¼ cup sugar
¼ teaspoon ground nutmeg
1 egg
¼ cup milk
2 tablespoons butter *or* margarine, melted
Sugar

Combine biscuit mix, ¼ cup sugar, and nutmeg. Stir together egg, milk, and melted butter; stir into dry mixture just till dough clings together. Knead gently on floured surface for 8 strokes. Pat into a 6-inch circle. Cut into 10 wedges. Sprinkle with sugar. Place on ungreased baking sheet. Bake in a 425° oven for 10 to 12 minutes. Serve warm. Makes 10.

SPEEDY PICKLED PEACHES

Pictured on pages 164-165—

1 29-ounce can peach halves
Whole cloves
½ cup vinegar
½ cup sugar
3 inches stick cinnamon, broken

Drain peaches, reserving 1 cup syrup. Stud each peach half with 3 or 4 cloves. In a saucepan combine reserved syrup, vinegar, sugar, and cinnamon. Add peaches. Bring to boiling. Simmer, uncovered, for 3 to 4 minutes. Cool. Cover; refrigerate. Before serving, drain and remove broken cinnamon sticks. Makes 4 servings.

SQUASH-CARROT CASSEROLE

Pictured on pages 164-165—

7 cups sliced crookneck squash *or* zucchini
½ cup chopped onion
1 10½-ounce can condensed cream of chicken soup
1 cup shredded carrot
1 cup dairy sour cream
½ of an 8-ounce package (2 cups) herb-seasoned stuffing mix
¼ cup butter *or* margarine, melted

In a Dutch oven cook crookneck squash or zucchini and onion, uncovered, in boiling salted water for 5 minutes. Drain well. Stir together the cream of chicken soup, carrot,

and sour cream. Fold in drained vegetables.

Stir together stuffing mix and butter or margarine. Sprinkle *two-thirds* of the stuffing mixture into a 12-inch quiche dish or a 12x7½x2-inch baking dish. Spoon vegetable mixture atop. Sprinkle remaining stuffing mixture around edges of dish. Bake, uncovered, in a 350° oven till warm through. (Allow 25 to 30 minutes for the quiche dish and 30 to 35 minutes for the baking dish.) Makes 6 to 8 servings.

CREAMED ONIONS

Pictured on pages 164-165

1 cup salted peanuts
3 tablespoons butter *or* margarine
¼ cup all-purpose flour
1 teaspoon salt
3 cups milk
3 16-ounce cans stewed onions, drained
1 cup soft bread crumbs
2 tablespoons butter *or* margarine, melted

Coarsely chop *half* of the peanuts; set both portions aside. In a large saucepan melt 3 tablespoons butter or margarine. Stir in flour and salt. Add milk; cook and stir till thickened and bubbly. Cook and stir 1 minute more. Stir in onions and whole peanuts. Turn into an ungreased 12x7½x2-inch baking dish. Toss together bread crumbs and 2 tablespoons melted butter or margarine. Sprinkle around edges of baking dish. Top with chopped peanuts. Bake, uncovered, in a 375° oven for 25 minutes. Makes 10 to 12 servings.

BASIC SWEET DOUGH

The Cinnamon Whirl, Swedish Tea Wreath, and Bubble Wreath, which are pictured on pages 162-163, all start with this versatile recipe—

3½ to 4 cups all-purpose flour
  1 package active dry yeast
1¼ cups milk
  ¼ cup sugar
  ¼ cup shortening
  1 teaspoon salt
  1 egg

In a large mixer bowl combine *2 cups* of the flour and the yeast. In a saucepan heat milk, sugar, shortening, and salt just till warm (115° to 120°) and shortening is almost melted; stir constantly. Add milk mixture and egg to flour mixture. Beat on low speed of an electric mixer for ½ minute, scraping sides of bowl constantly. Beat 3 minutes on high speed. Stir in as much of the remaining flour as you can mix in with a spoon.

Turn out onto a lightly floured surface. Knead in enough of the remaining flour to make a moderately soft dough that is smooth and elastic (3 to 5 minutes total). Shape into a ball. Place in a lightly greased bowl; turn once to grease surface.

Cover and let rise in a warm place till double (about 1½ hours). Punch down, cover; let rest 10 minutes. Use for Cinnamon Whirl, Swedish Tea Wreath, or Bubble Wreath.

BUBBLE WREATH

Pictured on pages 162-163—

  ½ cup packed brown sugar
  3 tablespoons butter *or* margarine, melted
  2 tablespoons light corn syrup, honey, *or* maple-flavored syrup
  ½ cup candied cherry halves, chopped; diced mixed candied fruits and peels; *or* raisins
  ¼ cup chopped *or* sliced nuts
  ½ cup sugar
  1 teaspoon ground cinnamon
    Basic Sweet Dough
  ¼ cup butter or margarine, melted

Stir together the brown sugar; 2 tablespoons melted butter or margarine; and corn syrup, honey, or maple-flavored syrup. Spread in the bottom of a greased 10-inch tube pan. Place candied cherries, candied fruits and peels, or raisins atop the brown sugar mixure. Sprinkle with the nuts. Set aside.

Stir together sugar and cinnamon. Set aside. Prepare Basic Sweet Dough. Shape into 48 small balls; roll balls in ¼ cup melted butter or margarine, then in sugar-cinnamon mixture. Place coated balls in layers in the prepared pan. Let rise in a warm place till nearly double (about 30 minutes). Bake in a 400° oven about 35 minutes or till done; cover loosely with foil the last 10 minutes of baking time. Let cool 1 minute; loosen from pan. Quickly turn out onto a wire rack. Cool. Makes 1 loaf.

SWEDISH TEA WREATH

Pictured on pages 162-163—

    Basic Sweet Dough
  2 tablespoons butter *or* margarine, melted
1¼ cups diced mixed candied fruits and peels, raisins, *or* candied cherries, chopped
    Confectioners' Icing
    Candied cherries *or* raisins (optional)
    Nuts (optional)

Prepare Basic Sweet Dough. Roll the dough into a 13x9-inch rectangle. Brush with the melted butter or margarine. Sprinkle with the 1¼ cups diced mixed candied fruits and peels, raisins, or candied cherries. Roll up jelly-roll style, starting at the long end. Seal seams. Shape roll into a circle, sealing ends together. Transfer to a greased baking sheet.

Using kitchen shears, snip two-thirds of the way through the roll at 1-inch intervals. Turn cut sections one at a time to alternate sides. Let roll rise in a warm place till nearly double (about 30 minutes). Bake roll in a 350° oven about 25 minutes or till done.

Transfer bread to a wire rack. Cool. Drizzle with Confectioners' Icing. Garnish with candied cherries or raisins and nuts, if desired. Makes 1 loaf.

CINNAMON WHIRL

Pictured on pages 162-163—

¼ cup sugar
1½ teaspoons ground
    cinnamon
    Basic Sweet Dough
1½ teaspoons water
    Confectioners' Icing

Stir together sugar and ground cinnamon; set aside. Prepare Basic Sweet Dough. Roll into a 15x7-inch rectangle; spread with sugar mixture. Sprinkle with water. Roll up jelly-roll style, starting at the narrow end. Seal seam. Place in a greased 9x5x3-inch loaf pan. Cover; let rise in a warm place till nearly double (about 30 minutes). Bake in a 375° oven about 30 minutes or till done. Transfer from pan to a wire rack. Cool. Drizzle with Confectioners' Icing. Makes 1 loaf.

CONFECTIONERS' ICING

1 cup sifted powdered
    sugar
½ teaspoon vanilla
    Dash salt
    Light cream *or* milk

In a small bowl combine powdered sugar, vanilla, and salt. Stir in enough light cream or milk to make an icing of drizzling consistency.

SUGAR PLUM LOAF

Pictured on pages 162-163—

3¾ to 4¼ cups all-purpose
    flour
  2 packages active dry yeast
  1 cup milk
  ¼ cup sugar
  ¼ cup shortening
1½ teaspoons salt
  2 eggs
  1 cup chopped nuts
  ¾ cup raisins
  ¼ cup candied cherries *or*
    raisins
  ¼ cup diced candied citron
    or raisins
  1 tablespoon diced candied
    orange peel *or* raisins
  1 tablespoon ground
    cardamom *or* ground
    cinnamon

In a large mixer bowl combine *2 cups* of the flour and the yeast. In a saucepan heat milk, sugar, shortening, and salt just till warm (115° to 120°) and shortening is almost melted; stir constantly. Add to flour mixture. Add eggs. Beat on low speed of electric mixer for ½ minute, scraping sides of bowl constantly. Beat 3 minutes at high speed. Stir in nuts, raisins, candied cherries or raisins, candied citron or raisins, candied orange peel or raisins, and cardamom or cinnamon. Stir in as much of the remaining flour as you can mix in with a spoon.

Turn out onto a lightly floured surface. Knead in enough of the remaining flour to make a moderately soft dough that is smooth and elastic (3 to 5 minutes total). Place in lightly greased bowl; turn once. Cover; let rise in warm place till double (about *2 hours*). Punch down; divide dough in half. Let rest 10 minutes. Shape into 2 round

loaves. Place on a greased baking sheet. Cover; let rise till nearly double (about 30 minutes). Bake in a 350° oven about 1 hour or till done. Makes 2 loaves.

MOCHA-YOGURT COFFEE CAKE

¼ cup packed brown sugar
¼ cup chopped nuts
1 tablespoon unsweetened
    cocoa powder
1½ teaspoons ground
    cinnamon
1 teaspoon instant coffee
    crystals
⅓ cup butter *or* margarine
¾ cup sugar
1 teaspoon vanilla
2 eggs
1½ cups packaged biscuit
    mix
¾ cup plain yogurt
    Sifted powdered sugar

In a small bowl combine brown sugar, nuts, cocoa powder, cinnamon, and coffee crystals; set aside. In a mixer bowl beat butter or margarine on medium speed of an electric mixer for 30 seconds. Add the sugar and vanilla; beat till fluffy. Add eggs, one at a time, beating well after each addition. Add biscuit mix and yogurt alternately to beaten mixture, stirring just till combined.

Spoon about *half* of the batter into a greased 8x8x2-inch baking pan. Sprinkle nut mixture atop. Spoon remaining batter over all. With a narrow spatula, swirl to marble. Bake in a 350° oven for 35 to 40 minutes or till done. Cool slightly on a wire rack. Sprinkle lightly with powdered sugar. Makes 1 coffee cake.

CHOCOLATE MERINGUES

3 egg whites
¾ teaspoon vanilla
¾ cup sugar
¼ cup unsweetened cocoa
    powder
    Chocolate Glaze

Let egg whites stand in a large mixer bowl about 1 hour or till they come to room temperature. Meanwhile, cover cookie sheets with brown paper. Beat egg whites and vanilla on medium speed of an electric mixer about 1 minute or till soft peaks form (tips curl over). Gradually add sugar, beating on high speed for 7 to 9 minutes or till stiff peaks form (tips stand straight).

Sift cocoa powder over egg white mixture; gently fold cocoa powder into egg white mixture. To make individual star-shape cookies, pipe meringue through a pastry bag fitted with a large star tip onto prepared cookie sheets. Bake in a 300° oven for 35 to 45 minutes. Peel meringues off of the paper; cool on a wire rack.

Dip one-half of each meringue in Chocolate Glaze (or dip bottoms); place the meringues on a cookie sheet lined with waxed paper till the chocolate hardens. Makes about 36.

CHOCOLATE GLAZE: In a small heavy saucepan, over low heat, melt together ½ cup *semisweet chocolate pieces or* three squares (3 ounces) *semisweet chocolate* and 1 tablespoon *shortening.*

Chocolate Meringues, Sacher Bites, and Brownie Tassies

BROWNIE TASSIES

¾ cup all-purpose flour
⅓ cup sugar
¼ cup unsweetened cocoa
    powder
⅛ teaspoon salt
⅓ cup butter *or* margarine,
    softened
2 to 3 tablespoons water
½ cup semisweet chocolate
    pieces
2 tablespoons butter *or*
    margarine
⅓ cup sugar
1 egg
1 teaspoon vanilla
½ teaspoon ground
    cinnamon
    Semisweet chocolate
    pieces (optional)

In a small bowl stir together flour, ⅓ cup sugar, cocoa powder, and salt. Cut in ⅓ cup butter or margarine till pieces are the size of small peas. Sprinkle *1 tablespoon* of the water over part of the mixture; gently toss with a fork. Push to side of bowl. Repeat till all is moistened. Form dough into a ball. Divide into 24 balls. Place balls in ungreased 1¾-inch muffin cups. Press dough onto the bottom and sides of cups.

In a small saucepan melt ½ cup semisweet chocolate pieces and 2 tablespoons butter or margarine. Remove from heat.

Stir in sugar, egg, vanilla, and cinnamon. Divide chocolate mixture evenly among muffin cups. Bake in a 325° oven for 25 to 30 minutes or till filling is nearly set. Top each with a semisweet chocolate piece, if desired. Return to oven for 1 minute or till chocolate is melted. Cool slightly; loosen and carefully remove tassies from the pan with a narrow metal spatula. Makes 24.

SACHER BITES

Change the flavor of these cookies by substituting any flavor of preserves for the raspberry preserves—

¾ cup butter *or* margarine
3 squares (3 ounces)
    unsweetened chocolate
1½ cups sugar
3 eggs
1½ teaspoons vanilla
1¼ cups all-purpose flour
¾ cup raspberry preserves
1 6-ounce package (1 cup)
    semisweet chocolate
    pieces

In a heavy medium saucepan melt butter or margarine and unsweetened chocolate over low heat. Remove from heat; stir in sugar. Add eggs, one at a time, mixing well after each. Stir in vanilla. Add flour; mix well. Spread in a greased 15x10x1-inch baking pan. Bake in a 325° oven for 15 to 20 minutes or till done. Cool.

Spread the preserves over the top of cookies in baking pan. Cut in half lengthwise, then crosswise to make four rectangles. Loosen edges; remove from pan. Stack two rectangles, preserves side up. Trim off edges, if necessary.

Cut into 2x1-inch bars and place on a wire rack covered with waxed paper. Repeat with remaining stacked rectangles. In a small heavy saucepan melt semisweet chocolate pieces over low heat. Drizzle some chocolate over top of each bar; chill to harden chocolate. Makes 40.

ORANGE EGGNOG FRAPPÉ

2 cups dairy eggnog
⅓ cup orange liqueur
3 tablespoons orange juice concentrate, thawed
1 pint vanilla ice cream
Ground nutmeg

Combine the eggnog, orange liqueur, and orange juice concentrate. Scoop vanilla ice cream into 3 tall glasses; pour eggnog mixture over ice cream. Muddle mixture slightly with spoon. Sprinkle a little nutmeg over each serving. Makes about 3 (10-ounce) servings.

PORTOFINO FROST

2 cups white grape juice
½ cup cherry brandy *or* brandy
⅓ cup ruby port
Fresh mint

Combine grape juice, brandy, and port. Pour into a freezer tray or an 8x8x2-inch baking pan. Cover; freeze at least 6 hours or overnight. Place glasses in the freezer to frost. Break grape mixture into chunks; place in a blender container. Cover and blend just till slushy. Spoon mixture into frosted glasses. Garnish with a mint sprig, if desired. Makes about 4 (6-ounce) servings.

Orange Eggnog Frappé, Portofino Frost, Bananas Foster Cup, Hot Pineapple Punch, and Cherry Burgundy Jubilation

BANANAS FOSTER CUP

3 cups milk
3 medium bananas, cut up
1 cup banana liqueur
¼ cup packed brown sugar
¼ teaspoon ground cinnamon
Dash ground nutmeg
Whipped cream

In a blender container combine milk and bananas. Cover; blend about 1 minute or till smooth. In a saucepan combine milk mixture, banana liqueur, brown sugar, cinnamon, and nutmeg. Heat through, but *do not* boil; stir till sugar dissolves. Ladle into mugs. Top with whipped cream. Sprinkle with additional brown sugar and cinnamon, if desired. Makes about 6 (6-ounce) servings.

HOT PINEAPPLE PUNCH

3 cups unsweetened pineapple juice
¼ cup sugar
2 tablespoons lime juice
⅛ teaspoon ground nutmeg
1¾ cups dry white wine
Cinnamon sticks
Fresh pineapple

In a large saucepan combine pineapple juice, sugar, lime juice, and nutmeg. Bring to boiling, stirring till sugar dissolves. Reduce heat; stir in wine. Heat through, but *do not* boil. Pour into heat-proof glasses or mugs. Garnish each serving with cinnamon stick stirrer and pineapple wedge. Makes about 5 (8-ounce) servings.

CHERRY BURGUNDY JUBILATION

1 cup frozen dark sweet cherries
½ cup cherry brandy *or* Kirsch
1 teaspoon whole allspice
1 teaspoon whole cloves
3¼ cups burgundy
¼ cup sugar
½ cup cherry brandy *or* Kirsch
1 pint vanilla ice cream

Combine cherries and ½ cup brandy or Kirsch; set aside. Tie allspice and cloves in cheesecloth. Combine spice bag, burgundy, and sugar. Simmer, uncovered, for 10 minutes. Remove spices. Stir in cherry mixture; heat through. Pour into heat-proof bowl. Warm ½ cup cherry brandy or Kirsch. Ignite and pour into punch. When flame subsides, pour into mugs. Top with small scoop of vanilla ice cream. Serve with demitasse spoons or cocktail picks for cherries. Makes about 6 (8-ounce) servings.

CHERRY FIZZ

⅓ cup cherry preserves
2 teaspoons water
1 pint vanilla ice cream
1 10-ounce bottle (1¼ cups) lemon-lime carbonated beverage

Combine preserves and water. Pour into 2 tall glasses. Add scoops of ice cream. Slowly pour carbonated beverage down sides of glasses. Makes about 2 (10-ounce) servings.

THE HOLIDAY BAZAAR

A Christmas bazaar is a surefire fund-raising activity and a great opportunity for fun and fellowship. To prepare for it, organize a presale workshop for the participating crafters; it will make creating the items you plan to sell as enjoyable as the bazaar itself.

Whether you schedule a bazaar during the holidays or use a Christmas theme during other times of the year, the seasonal decorations and trims here and on the next four pages are sure to be best sellers.

The ribbon-trimmed tree ornament, left, is quick and easy to stitch. Using bits of ribbon and muslin, you can make dozens of trims from this simple design.

The needlepoint Santa, right, and the felt-appliquéd quilt, opposite, are ideal raffle prizes for a bazaar. Santa is a sampler of interesting canvas-work stitches, and the quilt is a collection of floral wreath designs. Single quilt blocks make charming wall hangings to sell or give as prizes.

Instructions begin on page 180.

*C*hristmas-bright colors and trims of painted thread enhance the papier-mâché heart ornaments, *left*, and the Santa, snowman, stocking, and train engine ornaments, *below*.

The other trims in the photo, *below*, include a clown formed around a foam ball, tatted candy canes and wreaths, needlepoint snowflakes worked on plastic canvas, and felt medallion ornaments accented with embroidery.

THE HOLIDAY BAZAAR

*E*veryone loves a beautifully wrapped gift! Appliqué a fabric bow and ribbon onto fabric "paper" for the easy throw pillows, *above*. Quilting adds the detail, and the pillows are stuffed with foam slabs to simulate boxes.

*T*he whimsical Santa and reindeer puppets, above left, inspired an array of matching cards and a card holder.

To make the holiday log carrier, above, simply embellish a canvas rectangle with a calico tree.

Make greeting cards, like those below, with Christmas lace, a photocopier, and the help of a fast printing service.

THE HOLIDAY BAZAAR

*O*rnaments like the needlepoint candle, left, are
beautiful on a tree. And because each takes only a
small amount of yarn or thread, they're profitable, too.

   If you have a collection of woolens and other fancy
fabrics, laces, and trims, you can make the soft-
sculpture Nativity, below. Stitch only Mary, Joseph, and
the baby, or add the three kings and a shepherd.

   To make the festive ribbon ornaments, opposite, glue
and pin bows and streamers to plain satin balls. The
unusual and colorful ceramic plate and tiles are easily
created with glaze pencils and a little help from a local
ceramics studio.

Ribbon Ornament
Pictured on page 174

MATERIALS: Muslin; ribbons; trims; fabric glue; polyester fiberfill.

INSTRUCTIONS: Draw a tree shape; trace onto muslin and sew along line. Mark tree center; glue trims and ribbons to tree *diagonally*, starting at center and extending beyond outline. Sew tree to muslin back along stitched line; leave opening. Turn, stuff, and sew closed.

Needlepoint Santa
Pictured on page 174

MATERIALS: 18x18 inches of 10-count mono canvas; 3-ply Per-sian wool yarn: 3½ ounces red, ½ ounce *each* of white and black, six strands pink, and three strands peach; gold pearl cotton (belt); 12x12 inches of red felt; two small bells; fiberfill; water-erasable mark-ing pen; acrylic paints; glue; thread.

INSTRUCTIONS: Work all the tent stitches in 2-ply strands and the decorative stitches in 1-ply strands.

Enlarge pattern, *below;* transfer to canvas with marking pen. (Draw two arms and two legs.) Paint can-vas with acrylics. Work designs ac-cording to patterns. Trim canvas to within ¼ inch of designs; apply a thin glue line to outer edges to pre-vent raveling; dry.

Turn under one raw edge of the body piece and overcast-stitch the edge to the wrong side of the can-vas. Repeat for arms and legs.

Cut one red felt backing piece for each arm and leg; whipstitch to back of each piece. Sew arms to body. Wrap body pieces into cone shape, leaving bottom open. Sew the two edges together, overlapping the overcast-stitched edge slightly. At-tach legs. Stuff. Cut a red felt circle to fit bottom of Santa; sew in place. Add pompon and bells.

Felt-Wreath Quilt and Wall Hangings
Pictured on page 175

MATERIALS: *For the quilt*—72-inch-wide felt: 2 yards of green, 1½ yards of white, ½ yard of chartreuse; 9x12-inch pieces of felt in red, pink, fuchsia, rose, and light orange; 1

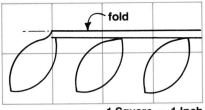

1 Square = 1 Inch

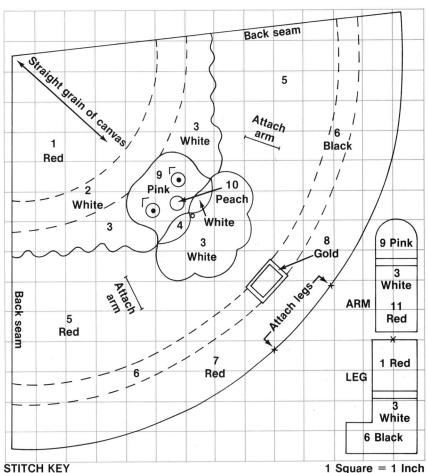

1 Square = 1 Inch

STITCH KEY
1. Diamond eyelet
2. Turkey work — ½-inch uncut loops
3. Turkey work — ¼-inch uncut loops
4. Turkey work — ½-inch cut loops
5. Star in diamond
6. Straight horizontal Gobelin
7. Bargello
8. Straight vertical Gobelin
9. Tent stitch
10. Diagonal stitch
11. Upright cross-stitch in diamond

1 Square = 1 Inch

yard fusible webbing; thread. *For wall hangings*—12-inch squares of green felt; 8-inch squares of white felt; scrap of felt; 10-inch artist's stretching frames.

INSTRUCTIONS: Enlarge patterns, *below* and *opposite.*

1 Square = 1 Inch

1 Square = 1 Inch

• *For quilt:* From white felt, cut twenty 8-inch square blocks, two 4½x59-inch strips and two 4½x49-inch strips for borders. From green, cut four border vines with 11 pairs of leaves and four with 13 pairs. Cut four sets of each wreath from scraps.

1 Square = 1 Inch

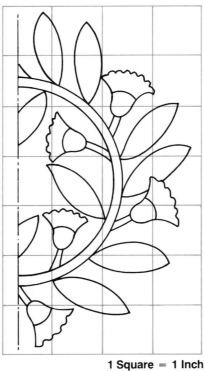

1 Square = 1 Inch

Cut fusible webbing into small pieces. Slip them between the appliqué shapes and white background squares; iron in place. Zigzag-stitch appliqués in place. Press, then trim squares to 7¾x7¾ inches. Fuse and appliqué short vines to short border strips and long vines to long strips.

Cut green felt background 56x66 inches. In the center, arrange appliquéd squares in four rows of five squares each; leave 1¾ inches between squares. Sew squares in place. Fuse, then sew border strips 1¾ inches from outer edge of white squares. Miter corners; hem.

• *For wall hangings (finished size is 10 inches square):* Cut enlarged designs from scrap felt; apply to white squares as for quilt. Mount on green squares; stretch over frames.

Papier-Mâché Trims
Pictured on page 176

MATERIALS: Cardboard; white glue; flour; newspaper; brown paper; cotton string; acrylic paints; gold paint; high-gloss plastic glaze; paper clips; graphite paper; black felt marker; paintbrushes.

INSTRUCTIONS: Enlarge the patterns, *below* and *on page 182.* For
continued

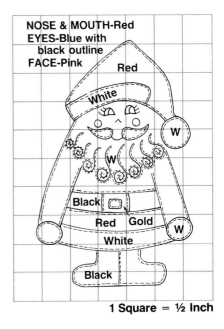

NOSE & MOUTH-Red
EYES-Blue with black outline
FACE-Pink

1 Square = ½ Inch

181

the heart-shaped ornaments, draw heart patterns in desired sizes.

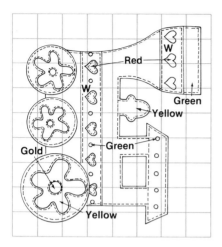

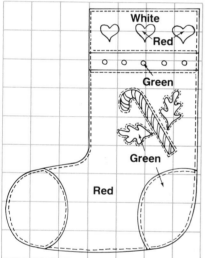

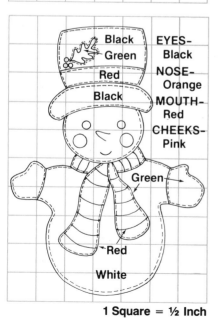

1 Square = ½ Inch

Transfer outlines to cardboard; cut out. Place clips (hangers) at tops of cardboard shapes. For paste, cook 2 cups water and 6 tablespoons flour until thick. Cool; mix with 3 tablespoons white glue.

Cut newspaper and brown paper into ¼-inch-wide strips. Dip newspaper strips in paste; smooth them onto cardboard shapes, rounding all edges. Cover clips, securing them to cardboard. Repeat with brown paper strips. When dry, paint ornaments with two coats of white acrylic; dry. Transfer designs to both sides of ornament.

Glue string around ornament edges and design elements. Paint designs; paint string gold. Lacquer.

Package Pillows
Pictured on page 176

MATERIALS: Several 22x34-inch pieces of thin quilt batting and calico; 4x12x12-inch foam rubber; ⅓ yard of red or green felt; thread.

INSTRUCTIONS: Place batting on wrong side of calico. Wrap foam rubber like a package, folding ends in. Pin under raw edges; whipstitch.

For bow, enlarge pattern, *below.* Cut two bows from felt; topstitch together ⅛ inch from edges, padding as you sew. Topstitch. Sew felt ribbon to package and add bow.

Santa Card Holder and Cards
Pictured on page 177

MATERIALS: *For card holder—* ⅜ yard dark blue fabric; ⅝ yard red

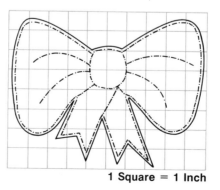

1 Square = 1 Inch

print fabric; 9x12-inch squares of chartreuse, red, pink, and white felt; scraps of green and red cotton, green calico; red baby rickrack; ¾x15-inch dowel; 1 yard ¾-inch-wide red ribbon; embroidery floss. *For cards*—purchased note cards; envelopes; adhesive-backed papers; black felt-tip pen.

INSTRUCTIONS: Enlarge pattern, *below.*

• *For card holder,* cut blue background (12x29 inches) and pocket (9x12 inches). Cut out pieces; add ¼-inch seam allowances to woven fabric shapes. *Do not* add seam allowances to felt. Appliqué Santa, sled, and "ho ho ho" onto background; embroider details. For pocket, turn down raw edge of 12-inch side ⅜ inch; sew edge of red ribbon along fold line. Stitch along remaining edge of ribbon, hiding raw edge. Appliqué and embroider pocket front; sew to banner.

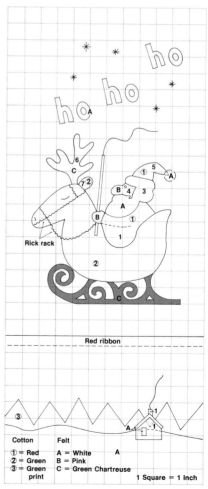

1 Square = 1 Inch

Trim banner with 2-inch-wide red print borders. Finish back with red print, sewing a dowel casing at top.
• *For cards:* From adhesive-backed papers, cut motifs; adhere to cards.

Clown Ornament
Pictured on page 177

MATERIALS: 3-inch-diameter plastic foam ball; 12 large and 48 small red pompons (hair); 6x9 inches red felt; 4x4 inches white felt; pink and blue felt scraps; ½ yard narrow blue ribbon; 1½x6 inches ruffled trim (collar); thread; embroidery floss; glue.

INSTRUCTIONS: From red felt, cut a 1x9-inch strip and a 3½-inch-diameter circle. Cut a 3½-inch circle from white felt. Pin red strip snugly around center of foam ball (ends should barely meet); sew ends together.

Pin red felt circle (head back) to ball on one side of center strip. Trim circle to fit, so edges of circle and center strip are about ⅛ inch apart before stitching. Whipstitch red circle snugly to center strip, pulling edges together.

Decorate white felt circle with simple clown face felt shapes; embroider details.

Whipstitch white circle around ball same as for red circle. Sew pompons around face and over head back; sew collar around neck.

Felt Medallion Trims
Pictured on page 177

MATERIALS: Red, white, and green felt; floss; fiberfill.

INSTRUCTIONS: Cut 3-inch and 2¼-inch circles of felt for each ornament, alternating red or green felt. Layer the circles, smallest on top, and tack securely. Using photograph for design ideas, embroider geometric designs in simple stitches, working through all layers.

Pin the ornament back to front, wrong sides facing. Work buttonhole stitches around edge, stuffing ornament with fiberfill as you sew.

Tatted Wreath and Candy Canes
Pictured on page 177

MATERIALS: Tatting shuttle; green, white No. 5 pearl cotton; 12 red beads for each ornament (holes in beads should be large enough to slip 2½ inches down the hook end of the crochet hook); Size 8 or 9 steel crochet hook; 6 inches of milliner's wire for each ornament; glue.

INSTRUCTIONS: *Wreath—* *Step 1:* Ring of 4, picot (closed picot should be as long as the length of the bead plus a bit more) 4, close ring, reverse work. *Step 2:* Chain of 12, slip bead over picot by placing the bead on crochet hook, then hooking the picot and sliding bead down hook and over picot. Put crochet hook through the tiny portion of the picot protruding through the bead and join to chain, reverse work. *Step 3:* Repeat Steps 1 and 2 alternately until 12 rings and 12 chains have been made. Two-thirds of the wreath will be complete. *Step 4:* Make a tiny picot after the join of the 12th bead and chain 11, join to base of 12th ring, chain 11 and join to base of 11th ring, etc., until 12 chains of 11 each have been completed to form final third of wreath. Cut threads. Slip all tails through the tiny picot at opposite end; tie; glue.
• *Candy cane curved to right:* Work as for wreath steps 1, 2, and 3. Do not make tiny picot after completing 12th chain. Chain final third of cane same as wreath step 4. Shape cane

by stiffening with milliner's wire.
• *Candy cane curved to left:* Reverse numbers of stitches in the two chain sides: Chains on side 1 (first ⅔)—11 stitches each; chains on final third (or chain side 2)—12 stitches.

Snowflake Trims
Pictured on page 177

MATERIALS: 7-count plastic needlepoint canvas; white 3-ply Persian yarn; tapestry needle.

INSTRUCTIONS: Cut canvas into patterns, *below;* make two sections for each. With a strand of yarn, overcast outer edges of canvas; wrap yarn twice around each side of square. Work two; place together, making eight arms; tack at center.

Santa and Reindeer Toys
Pictured on page 177

MATERIALS: 12x18 inches each red and green velveteen; felt scraps; fur scraps; white pompon.

INSTRUCTIONS: Enlarge patterns, *page 184.* Cut two basic body shapes from velveteen. Cut out remaining pieces. Sew facial details on fronts. Sew antler fronts to backs. Baste ears and antlers to reindeer front. Sew fronts to backs, catching mittens in Santa's sleeve and hooves in reindeer's seams. Turn; hem.

SNOWFLAKE TRIMS

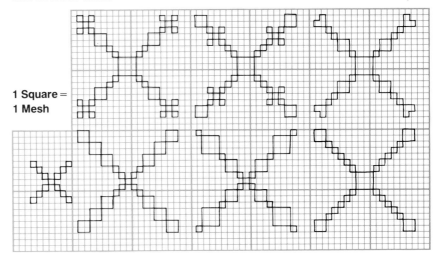

1 Square =
1 Mesh

Log Carrier
Pictured on page 177

MATERIALS: 22x32 inches of canvas; 96 inches of 1½-inch-wide heavy twill tape; green calico scrap.

INSTRUCTIONS: Hem edges of canvas. Sew tape 5 inches from edges of carrier; place tape ends at center and extra lengths at top (handles). Cut a tree appliqué from green calico and sew to carrier.

Lace Cards
Pictured on page 177

MATERIALS: Lace fabric medallion; photocopy of medallion.

INSTRUCTIONS: Take photocopy to a quick-print shop (see local listings in Yellow Pages) and have the design printed on colored paper.

Needlepoint Candle
Pictured on page 178

MATERIALS: Wool yarn in the colors listed in the color key, *except* pearl cotton in gold and dark copper; 13-count interlock canvas; needle; white felt; clear-drying glue.

INSTRUCTIONS: Using 2-ply strands of wool yarn and 1 strand of pearl cotton, stitch candle design according to pattern, *below right*. Maintain even tension throughout. (If you pull the yarn too tight, it will not cover the canvas completely; if stitches are too loose, the yarn will snag easily.) Apply glue around de-

---

sign; dry. Trim canvas at glue line. Glue felt shape to back of ornament. Add a hanger to the top.

Patchwork Fabric Crèche
Pictured on page 178

MATERIALS: Scraps of wool, velveteen, leather, crocheted doily, felt, cotton, upholstery fabric, metallic fabric, lace, and fleece; ribbon and rickrack; straw; two white pipe cleaners; twelve ¼-inch-diameter beads; assorted buttons and beads; miniature containers for the wise men; cardboard; bits of wool yarn; embroidery floss; polyester fiberfill; fabric glue.

INSTRUCTIONS: Enlarge pattern, *opposite.*

For figures, cut out all pieces from desired fabrics (use Mary's body front for Joseph). Appliqué body fronts; embroider faces. For sleeves, turn and stitch wrist edge under ¼ inch. With right sides facing, fold each sleeve in half lengthwise; stitch raw edges together, leaving shoulder edge open. Turn right side out; paste sleeves on body fronts. For hands, cover ¼-inch-diameter beads with fabric. Sew hands at sleeve ends. With right sides facing, sew

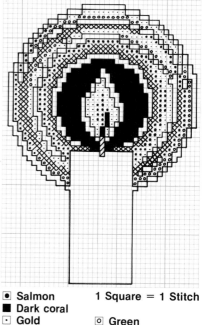

⊙ Salmon	1 Square = 1 Stitch
■ Dark coral	
· Gold	⊙ Green
⊠ Dark copper	□ White ⧄ Black

1 Square = 1 Inch (Lace Cards pattern)

1 Square = 1 Inch (Needlepoint Candle pattern)

Lace Cards pattern labels: White Felt; White; Dark Pink; Fur; Red Felt; Light Pink; Fur; MITTEN Cut two black; Place on Fold

Needlepoint Candle pattern labels: Antlers; Ears; White; Dark Pink; EAR Cut 2; ANTLER Cut 4 Chartreuse; HOOF Cut 2; Place on Fold

fronts and backs together, leaving bottoms open. Turn right side out; stuff firmly with fiberfill.

Cut cardboard bases; cut fabric circles ½ inch larger than bases. Sew to body bottoms, slipping cardboard bases inside. Sew crowns to wise men's heads and containers between hands. Bend a pipe cleaner into shape for the shepherd's crook.

For the crib, cut one pattern piece from fabric. With right sides facing, fold fabric in half lengthwise; sew raw edges together (leaving ends open). Turn; stuff and sew ends together to make a doughnut shape. Arrange straw along the top of the crib and place the baby on top of the straw, stitching the pieces together. (Baby's head should rest on the thickest part of the crib.)

For sheep, cut two body pieces from plain brown fabric; cut two body pieces from wool fleece (or pile), but do *not* cut the sheep's face (see pattern). Appliqué the fleece to the plain brown fabric. With right sides facing, stitch the body pieces together, leaving the bottom edge open. Clip curves, turn right side out, and stuff; slip-stitch the opening closed.

Embroider the sheep's facial features and cut ears from leather or felt, stitching the ears in place. Cut two 2½-inch pieces of pipe cleaner for legs. Bend each piece into a 3-sided square and stitch the legs to the bottom of the body—one piece along the front of the body and one piece along the back. Use wool yarn for the tail.

Ceramic Plate and Tiles
Pictured on page 179

MATERIALS: Greenware plate and tiles (available at ceramics studios); small sponge; assorted colors of underglaze; small pointed brush; compass, ruler, pencil, eraser; blue glaze pencil; ultraclear overglaze.

INSTRUCTIONS: Clean greenware with sponge, wiping away seam lines. Handle greenware *gently*. With compass, ruler, and pencil, draw a geometric design on plate and tiles. Mix water with underglaze

colors on foil, diluting it to the consistency of light cream. With brush, paint penciled lines. Add rows of dots; leave space for the plate caption and weblike lines.

Have plate or tiles fired for glaze.

With pencil, letter the caption and weblike lines. Go over these lines with blue glaze pencil, exerting enough pressure to ensure good coverage. Have plate or tiles fired for glaze.

Apply two coats of ultraclear overglaze (diluted with water to consistency of light cream) to plate and tiles. Be careful not to smear glaze pencil. Have plate or tiles refired for glaze.

Ribbon-Trimmed Ornaments
Pictured on page 179

MATERIALS: 2½- and 3-inch-diameter satin ball ornaments; assorted ribbons in ⅛-, ¼-, and ½-inch widths; silk pins.

INSTRUCTIONS: Wrap balls in assorted ribbons, using pins to fasten them in place. Gather extra lengths of ribbon together at the bottom for a tassel or add a ruffled ribbon at the top.

Add decorative loops of narrow ribbons at top or bottom. Finish ornaments with bows where desired; add loops of ribbon for hangers.

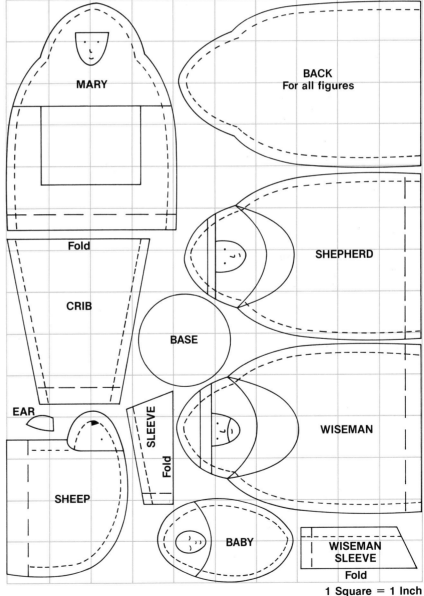

1 Square = 1 Inch

185

BAZAAR BEST SELLERS

At one time or another, we've all been asked to donate food to a food bazaar or bake sale. We've pondered over our recipe files looking for a special recipe that we hope will entice the shoppers. If in your cache of recipes you don't have just the right tartlet or cookie, look no further because you've come to the right place.

On the next few pages is an array of irresistible treats that are inexpensive to make and guaranteed to be best sellers. We've included recipes that will satisfy the gourmet food shopper, as well as the weary Christmas shopper who just happens to pass by for a quick snack.

From top center: Apple Giants, Baked Fruited Popcorn, Pear-Raspberry Jam, Rhubarb Cake Tarts, Lemony Jeweled Jelly, Pumpkin Cottage Cakes with Hard Sauce, Fruit-Filled Cheese Tartlets, Red-Paned Cookies, Quince Chutney, Lotsa Chip Bars, Date Tea Bread, Whole Grain Rounds (see Index for recipe pages)

WILD RICE PILAF MIX

    3 cups wild rice
    2 cups dry lentils
    2 cups light raisins
1½ cups dried mushrooms, chopped
    1 cup quick-cooking barley
    ½ cup shelled sunflower nuts
    3 tablespoons dried parsley flakes
    3 tablespoons instant beef bouillon granules
    2 tablespoons minced dried onion
    1 tablespoon dried basil, crushed
    2 teaspoons minced dried garlic
    ½ teaspoon ground cinnamon
    ¼ teaspoon pepper

Rinse the wild rice and lentils thoroughly in cold water; drain. Spread in a thin layer in a 15x10x1-inch baking pan. Heat in a 300° oven for 10 to 15 minutes or till rice is dry, stirring frequently. Remove from oven. Cool.

In a large bowl combine rice and lentils with raisins, dried mushrooms, barley, sunflower nuts, parsley flakes, bouillon granules, dried onion, basil, dried garlic, cinnamon, and pepper; mix well. Store in an airtight container. To take the pilaf mix to a bazaar or present as a gift, stir to distribute seasonings. Spoon ⅓- to 1-cup portions into plastic bags; secure bags with decorative ribbons. Place several portions in a sturdy decorative container. Makes 10 cups mix.

GIFT PREPARATION INSTRUCTIONS: Stir dry mix to distribute seasonings. In a saucepan combine ⅓ *cup* pilaf mix with 1 cup *water*. Bring to boiling; reduce heat. Cover and simmer 50 minutes or till rice and barley are tender. (If desired, add 1 cup *sliced carrots or chopped broccoli* to rice mixture after 30 minutes of cooking.) Makes 2 servings.

WHOLE GRAIN ROUNDS

Pictured on pages 186-187—

4¼ to 4¾ cups all-purpose flour
    2 packages active dry yeast
2¼ cups warm water (115° to 120°)
    ⅔ cup molasses
    ⅓ cup cooking oil
1½ teaspoons salt
2¼ cups whole wheat flour
    1 cup yellow cornmeal
       Yellow cornmeal

In a large mixer bowl combine *3 cups* of the all-purpose flour and the yeast. Add warm water, molasses, oil, and salt. Beat at low speed of an electric mixer ½ minute, scraping sides. Beat 3 minutes at high speed. Stir in whole wheat flour, cornmeal, and as much of the remaining all-purpose flour as you can mix in with a spoon. Turn out onto a lightly floured surface. Knead in enough of the remaining all-purpose flour to make a moderately soft dough that is smooth and elastic (3 to 5 minutes total). Shape into a ball; place in greased bowl. Turn once. Cover; let rise in a warm place till double (1 to 1¼ hours).

Punch down; turn out onto a lightly floured surface. Divide into thirds. Cover; let rest 10 minutes. Grease two baking sheets; sprinkle cornmeal lightly over each baking sheet. Shape dough into three round loaves. Place on baking sheets. Flatten each loaf slightly to a 6-inch diameter. Slash an X in the top of each loaf. Cover; let rise till nearly double (45 to 60 minutes). Sprinkle with additional cornmeal, if desired. Bake in a 375° oven for 30 to 35 minutes. If necessary, cover loaves with foil the last 5 to 10 minutes of baking to prevent overbrowning. Makes 3 loaves.

SWEET TARRAGON MUSTARD

    ¾ cup white wine vinegar
    2 1-ounce cans dry mustard (⅔ cup)
    ¼ cup dry white wine
    ½ cup butter *or* margarine
    ⅓ cup sugar
    1 teaspoon dried tarragon, crushed
    ½ teaspoon salt
    4 egg yolks

In the top of a double boiler combine vinegar, mustard, and wine. Cover and let stand at least 3 hours to mellow. Add butter or margarine, sugar, dried tarragon, and salt. Cook and stir over boiling water till the butter or margarine melts. Remove from heat; add egg yolks, one at a time, beating well after each. Cook and stir over boiling water till very thick (8 minutes). Transfer to jars. Cover; store mustard in the refrigerator. Makes 2¼ cups.

Wild Rice Pilaf Mix

HOMEMADE CURRIED SPICE MIX

Try substituting this homemade curry mixture for the curry powder in other recipes—

1 tablespoon finely shredded lemon peel
1 tablespoon curry powder
1 tablespoon ground allspice
1 tablespoon poultry seasoning
1 tablespoon sesame seed, toasted

Spread lemon peel on waxed paper; let stand, uncovered, 30 minutes or till dried. Mix peel with curry powder, allspice, poultry seasoning, and sesame seed. Store in an airtight container. Use mix in the Curried Cheese Spread below. Makes about ¼ cup.

CURRIED CHEESE SPREAD

1 8-ounce package cream cheese, softened
½ cup shredded Swiss cheese (2 ounces)
3 tablespoons milk
1 tablespoon Homemade Curried Spice Mix
1 teaspoon Worcestershire sauce
½ cup finely chopped walnuts
1 tablespoon snipped chives
   Unsalted crackers
   Celery sticks

Combine the softened cream cheese, shredded Swiss cheese, milk, Homemade Curried Spice Mix, and Worcestershire sauce. Mix till well blended. Stir in the finely chopped walnuts and snipped chives. Turn into a small bowl lined with plastic wrap. Cover and chill. Unmold; remove plastic wrap. Serve the spread with unsalted crackers or use to stuff celery sticks. Makes 1⅔ cups spread.

APPLE CHUTNEY

This apple and tomato combo will delight any chutney aficionado—

8 medium cooking apples, peeled and chopped (5 cups)
2 cups packed brown sugar
1 15-ounce can tomato sauce
1½ cups raisins
¾ cup vinegar
1 medium onion, chopped (½ cup)
½ cup lemon juice
1 tablespoon grated gingerroot
1 teaspoon salt

In a large Dutch oven combine chopped apples, brown sugar, tomato sauce, raisins, vinegar, chopped onion, lemon juice, gingerroot, and salt; mix well. Bring mixture to boiling, stirring to dissolve brown sugar. Reduce heat and simmer, uncovered, for 45 minutes or till thickened; stir occasionally.

Ladle chutney into hot, clean half-pint jars, leaving a ½-inch headspace. Wipe jar rims; adjust lids. Process in boiling water bath for 10 minutes (start timing when water boils). Makes 6 half-pints.

QUINCE CHUTNEY

Pictured on pages 186-187—

3 oranges
8 quinces, peeled, cored, and sliced (about 8 cups)
2 cups sugar
1½ cups vinegar
1½ cups water
1 cup light raisins
1 cup packed brown sugar
¾ cup finely chopped onion
¼ cup whole mustard seed, toasted
3 cloves garlic, minced
1 teaspoon ground ginger
½ teaspoon whole cloves
½ teaspoon ground cinnamon
¼ teaspoon crushed red pepper
2 tablespoons grated gingerroot

Remove the peel from one orange. Cut the peel into thin strips; set aside. Peel the remaining 2 oranges. Section all three oranges; reserve juice and discard peel and seeds.

In a large Dutch oven combine reserved strips of orange peel, reserved orange juice, orange sections, quinces, sugar, vinegar, water, light raisins, brown sugar, finely chopped onion, mustard seed, garlic, ground ginger, cloves, cinnamon, and red pepper. Bring to boiling. Cover; simmer for 30 minutes. Add the grated gingerroot and simmer, covered, for 5 minutes. Uncover; simmer for 45 minutes more.

Ladle chutney into hot, clean pint jars; leave a ½-inch headspace. Wipe jar rims; adjust lids. Process in boiling water bath for 10 to 15 minutes (start timing when water boils). Makes 4 pints.

LEMONY JEWELED JELLY

Pictured on pages 186-187—

- 1½ cups water
- 1 tablespoon finely shredded lemon peel
- ½ cup lemon juice
- 3½ cups sugar
- ¾ cup honey
- 1 6-ounce package liquid fruit pectin
- 5 strips candied orange peel *or* 5 red candied cherries

Combine the water, lemon peel, and lemon juice. Let stand 10 minutes. Strain the liquid; discard peel.

In a 5-quart Dutch oven heat and stir strained liquid and sugar till sugar dissolves. Stir in honey. Bring to a full rolling boil (a boil that cannot be stirred down), stirring constantly. Stir in the pectin and return to a full rolling boil; stir constantly. Boil hard, without stirring, for 1 minute. Remove from heat. Quickly skim off the foam with a metal spoon.

Ladle the jelly into hot, clean half-pint jars, leaving ¼-inch headspace. Cool about 5 minutes or till jelly is partially set. Using clean tongs, insert *one* candied orange peel strip or *one* candied cherry into center of *each* jar. Wipe jar rims; adjust lids. Process in a boiling water bath for 10 minutes (start timing when water boils). Makes 5 half-pints.

BANANA-BERRY JAM

- 12 ounces fresh cranberries, chopped (3 cups)
- 1½ cups water
- 7 cups sugar
- 2 cups mashed banana
- ½ of a 6-ounce package (1 foil pouch) liquid fruit pectin

In a 5-quart Dutch oven combine cranberries and water. Simmer, covered, 10 minutes. Stir in the sugar and mashed banana. Bring to a full rolling boil (a boil that cannot be stirred down). Boil hard, uncovered, for 1 minute, stirring constantly. Remove from heat. Stir in pectin. Quickly skim off foam with a metal spoon. Ladle jam at once into hot, clean half-pint jars, leaving a ¼-inch headspace. Wipe jar rims; adjust lids. Process in boiling water bath for 15 minutes (start timing when water boils). Makes 8 half-pints.

PEAR-RASPBERRY JAM

Pictured on pages 186-187—

- 2½ pounds ripe pears
- 2 cups fresh *or* frozen loose-pack red raspberries, thawed
- 1 1¾-ounce package powdered fruit pectin
- 2 tablespoons lemon juice
- ¼ teaspoon ground mace *or* ground nutmeg
- 5 cups sugar

Peel, core, and coarsely grind the pears; measure 3 cups. Crush red raspberries; measure 1 cup. In an 8-quart Dutch oven combine ground pears, crushed berries, pectin, lemon juice, and ground mace or ground nutmeg. Bring the mixture to a full rolling boil (a boil that cannot be stirred down). Stir in sugar. Boil hard, uncovered, for 1 minute, stirring constantly. Remove from heat; quickly skim off the foam with a metal spoon.

Ladle jam at once into hot, clean half-pint jars, leaving ¼-inch headspace. Wipe jar rims; adjust lids. Process in boiling water bath for 15 minutes (start timing when water boils). Makes 6 to 7 half-pints.

SPICY SHERRIED WALNUTS

- 1½ cups packed brown sugar
- ¼ cup dry sherry
- 2 tablespoons light corn syrup
- 1 teaspoon pumpkin pie spice
- ¼ teaspoon salt
- 5 cups walnut halves

In a saucepan combine brown sugar, dry sherry, corn syrup, pumpkin pie spice, and salt. Heat and stir till brown sugar is dissolved. Add walnut halves and stir till well coated. Turn the walnut halves out onto a baking sheet. Let stand till dry. Store in a loosely covered container. Makes 2 pounds.

PUMPKIN COTTAGE CAKES WITH HARD SAUCE

Pictured on pages 186-187—

2¼ cups all-purpose flour
 2 teaspoons baking powder
 2 teaspoons finely shredded
     orange peel
 1 teaspoon baking soda
 1 teaspoon ground
     cinnamon
 ¼ teaspoon salt
 ¼ teaspoon ground nutmeg
 3 eggs
 1 16-ounce can pumpkin
 1 cup sugar
 ¾ cup cooking oil
 ¼ cup buttermilk
 1 cup raisins
     Hard Sauce (optional)

Stir together the flour, baking powder, orange peel, soda, cinnamon, salt, and nutmeg. In a large mixer bowl combine eggs, pumpkin, sugar, oil, and buttermilk; beat well. Add dry ingredients; beat till well blended. Fold in the raisins.

Spoon the mixture into 20 greased 3¾-inch fluted tart pans or muffin pans. Bake in a 350° oven about 25 minutes or till done. Immediately remove cakes from pans; cool on wire racks. Reheat to serve, if desired. To reheat, wrap cakes in foil. Bake in a 350° oven about 15 minutes or till heated through. Serve cakes with Hard Sauce, if desired. Makes 20.

HARD SAUCE: Beat together 6 tablespoons *butter or margarine*, softened; 1½ cups sifted *powdered sugar*; and ⅛ teaspoon *ground cinnamon*. Stir in ¾ teaspoon *vanilla*. Pipe or spoon sauce into twenty 1½-inch paper cups. Cover and chill. Makes 1 cup.

JAVA WALNUT SAUCE

 2 cups sugar
 3 tablespoons instant coffee
     crystals
 3 cups hot water
 ½ cup cold water
 ¼ cup cornstarch
 1 cup broken walnuts
 ¼ cup butter *or* margarine,
     softened

In a heavy 10-inch skillet melt sugar slowly over low heat till golden brown, stirring constantly. Remove from heat. Dissolve coffee crystals in hot water; carefully stir into melted sugar. Heat and stir over low heat till the sugar redissolves. Combine cold water and cornstarch; stir into sugar mixture. Cook and stir till mixture is thickened and bubbly. Cook and stir 2 minutes more. Stir in walnuts and butter or margarine. Pour into three 1-cup heat-proof glass jars. Store, covered, in the refrigerator for up to 2 weeks. Serve chilled or slowly reheat in a saucepan. Serve over ice cream or cake. Makes 3 cups.

DATE TEA BREAD

Pictured on pages 186-187—

1¾ cups all-purpose flour
 2 teaspoons baking powder
 ½ teaspoon salt
 ⅓ cup shortening
 ⅔ cup sugar
 2 eggs
 ¼ cup frozen tangerine *or*
     grapefruit juice
     concentrate, thawed
 1 teaspoon vanilla
 ⅔ cup milk
 ⅔ cup pitted whole dates,
     finely snipped

Stir together the flour, baking powder, and salt. In a large mixer bowl beat shortening on medium speed of an electric mixer for 30 seconds. Add the sugar and beat till fluffy. Add eggs, one at a time, beating well on medium speed. Beat in the tangerine or grapefruit juice concentrate and vanilla. Add the dry ingredients and milk alternately to the beaten mixture, beating on low speed after each addition till just combined. Stir in the snipped dates.

Turn mixture into one greased and floured 8x4x2-inch loaf pan or three 6x3x2-inch loaf pans. Bake in a 350° oven for 60 to 65 minutes for a large pan (35 minutes for smaller pans) or till a wooden pick inserted near center comes out clean. Cool bread 10 minutes in pan. Remove from pan; cool thoroughly on wire rack. Wrap in foil and store overnight for easier slicing. Makes 1 large or 3 small loaves.

FRUIT-FILLED CHEESE TARTLETS

Pictured on pages 186-187—

⅓ cup butter *or* margarine
1 3-ounce package cream cheese
1½ cups all-purpose flour
4 to 5 tablespoons water
1 11-ounce can mandarin orange sections, drained
1 8¼-ounce can crushed pineapple
¼ cup sugar
5 teaspoons cornstarch
⅛ teaspoon salt
½ cup orange juice
1 tablespoon lemon juice
¼ cup toasted, chopped almonds
  Several drops almond extract

For pastry, in a mixing bowl cut butter or margarine and cream cheese into flour; gradually add water, tossing till moistened. Form dough into a ball. On a lightly floured surface roll pastry to ⅛-inch thickness; cut into thirty-two 2½-inch rounds. Press pastry into 1¾-inch muffin pans. Bake in a 400° oven for 12 to 15 minutes. Cool tartlets thoroughly in pans on wire racks. Remove from pans before filling.

For fruit filling, reserve 16 orange sections; chop remaining. Drain pineapple, reserving juice. In a small saucepan combine sugar, cornstarch, and salt. Stir in reserved pineapple juice, the orange juice, and lemon juice. Cook and stir till mixture is thickened and bubbly. Cook and stir 2 minutes more. Remove from heat. Cool. Stir in chopped orange sections, pineapple, almonds, and almond extract. Spoon fruit mixture into cooled tartlets. Halve the 16 reserved orange sections; place one orange section half atop each tartlet. Makes 32.

RHUBARB CAKE TARTS

Pictured on pages 186-187—

2 cups all-purpose flour
½ teaspoon salt
¾ cup shortening
5 to 6 tablespoons cold water
1 16-ounce package frozen rhubarb
3 tablespoons butter *or* margarine
⅔ cup sugar
¼ cup light corn syrup
½ cup all-purpose flour
¾ teaspoon baking powder
¼ teaspoon salt
¼ cup butter *or* margarine
⅓ cup sugar
½ teaspoon vanilla
1 egg
¼ cup milk

For pastry, stir together the 2 cups flour and the ½ teaspoon salt; cut in shortening with a pastry blender till pieces are the size of small peas. Sprinkle *2 tablespoons* of the cold water over part of the mixture; gently toss with a fork. Push to side of bowl. Repeat till all is moistened. Divide dough in half; form dough into 2 balls. On a lightly floured surface roll *each* ball to ⅛-inch thickness. Cut *each* half into three 6½- or 7-inch circles. Reroll as necessary. Line six 4-inch foil tart pans with pastry. Flute edges high; do not prick pastry. Line pastry with heavy foil and fill with dry beans or pie weights. Bake in a 450° oven for 10 to 12 minutes. Remove the dry beans and foil. Cool the tart shells on wire rack.

For rhubarb filling, thaw frozen rhubarb. Drain, reserving liquid. If necessary, add water to reserved liquid to equal ⅔ cup. In small saucepan combine the 3 tablespoons butter or margarine, the ⅔ cup sugar, corn syrup, and the reserved rhubarb liquid. Cook and stir over medium heat till mixture comes to boiling. Reduce heat; simmer, uncovered, for 3 minutes. Remove from heat. Stir in rhubarb (mixture will be thin). Cool to lukewarm.

For cake batter, stir together the ½ cup flour, baking powder, and the ¼ teaspoon salt. In a small mixer bowl beat the ¼ cup butter or margarine on medium speed of an electric mixer about 30 seconds. Add the ⅓ cup sugar and vanilla; beat till fluffy. Add egg; beat on medium speed for 1 minute. Add the dry ingredients and milk alternately to beaten mixture, beating well after each addition; set aside. (Mixture may appear curdled.)

Pour about ⅓ cup rhubarb mixture into each cooled baked pastry shell. Spoon a scant ¼ cup cake batter atop each, spreading carefully to edge. Bake in a 375° oven about 30 minutes or till cakes test done. Makes 6 tarts.

*W*hile the recipes on these pages are ideal for taking to food bazaars, they also are great gifts to give that person on your Christmas list who has everything. You soon will discover that homemade food gifts are as much fun to make as they are to receive.

BASIC ROLLED COOKIE DOUGH

Pictured on pages 186-187—

2 cups all-purpose flour
1 teaspoon baking soda
¼ teaspoon salt
¾ cup butter *or* margarine
¾ cup packed brown sugar
½ cup sugar
1 egg
1½ teaspoons vanilla

Stir together flour, baking soda, and salt; set aside. In a large mixer bowl beat butter or margarine on medium speed of an electric mixer for 30 seconds. Add brown sugar and sugar and beat till fluffy. Add egg and vanilla; beat well. Add the dry ingredients to beaten mixture and beat till well blended. Divide dough into quarters; cover and chill about 2 hours for easier handling.

Continue as directed in Red-Paned Cookies, Apple Giants, and Lotsa Chip Bars recipes. *Or,* on a lightly floured surface, roll *each* portion of the basic dough to ⅛-inch thickness; cut the dough with a 2½-inch cookie cutter. Place on an ungreased cookie sheet. Bake in a 375° oven for 6 to 7 minutes. Makes about 60 cookies.

RED-PANED COOKIES: Prepare Basic Rolled Cookie Dough as above. On a lightly floured surface, roll *each* portion of the dough to ⅛-inch thickness. Cut into desired shapes such as circles, triangles, diamonds, or hearts with a 3½-inch cookie cutter; place on a foil-lined cookie sheet. Cut out a small heart, star, circle, or diamond (1 to 1¼ inches) in center of each. Set aside.

Meanwhile, crush 3 to 4 ounces *hard red candy*; place about ½ teaspoon crushed candy in cutout center of each cookie. Bake in a 375° oven for 6 to 7 minutes or till candy melts and cookies are golden. Cool thoroughly; remove from foil. Makes about 36 cookies.

APPLE GIANTS: Prepare Basic Rolled Cookie Dough as above, *except* add an additional ½ cup *sugar* and beat till well combined. Add 1 additional *egg*; beat well. Stir in 1 cup finely chopped unpeeled *apple*, ¾ cup *granola*, ½ teaspoon *ground cinnamon*, and ⅛ teaspoon *ground nutmeg*. For each cookie, spoon about ¼ cup dough onto a greased cookie sheet, placing cookies 3 inches apart; flatten slightly with fingers. Bake in a 375° oven for 12 to 14 minutes or till done. Cool 1 minute before removing to wire rack; cool completely. Sprinkle with sifted *powdered sugar*, if desired. Makes 18 cookies.

LOTSA CHIP BARS: Prepare Basic Rolled Cookie Dough as above, *except* decrease the flour to *1 cup* and omit the sugar and salt (use the brown sugar). Stir in ¾ cup quick-cooking *rolled oats* and ½ cup chopped *unsalted peanuts*. Spread mixture into a greased 13x9x3-inch baking pan. Sprinkle one 6-ounce package *semisweet chocolate pieces* over. Bake in a 350° oven for 4 minutes. Remove from oven; cut through dough with a knife to marble. Bake 15 minutes more. Cut into bars while warm. Makes 24.

CRÈME DE MENTHE SQUARES

½ cup butter *or* margarine
½ cup unsweetened cocoa powder
½ cup sifted powdered sugar
1 beaten egg
1 teaspoon vanilla
2 cups graham cracker crumbs
½ cup butter *or* margarine
⅓ cup green crème de menthe
3 cups sifted powdered sugar
¼ cup butter *or* margarine
1½ cups semisweet chocolate pieces

For the bottom layer, combine ½ cup butter or margarine and the cocoa powder. Heat and stir till well blended. Remove from heat; add the ½ cup powdered sugar, the egg, and the vanilla. Stir in the graham cracker crumbs; mix till well combined. Press into the bottom of an ungreased 13x9x2-inch baking pan.

For the middle layer, melt ½ cup butter or margarine. In a small mixer bowl combine the melted butter or margarine and the crème de menthe. Beat in the 3 cups powdered sugar; beat till smooth. Spread over the bottom layer. Chill 1 hour.

For the top layer, combine the ¼ cup butter or margarine and the chocolate pieces. Cook and stir over low heat till melted. Spread over middle layer. Chill 1 to 2 hours. Cut into small squares. Store in refrigerator. Makes 96 squares.

PLUM PUDDING CANDY

1¼ cups chopped peanuts
1 8-ounce package pitted whole dates, finely snipped
1 cup dried figs, finely chopped
¾ cup dried apricots, chopped
½ cup flaked coconut, toasted
3 cups sugar
1 cup milk
1 tablespoon light corn syrup
1 tablespoon butter *or* margarine
1 teaspoon vanilla

Combine the peanuts, dates, figs, apricots, and coconut; mix well. Set aside.

Butter the sides of a heavy 3-quart saucepan. In it combine the sugar, milk, and corn syrup. Cook and stir over medium heat till the sugar is dissolved. Continue cooking till the mixture reaches 234° (soft-ball stage). Remove mixture from heat. Stir in butter or margarine and vanilla. Cool, without stirring, to 110°.

Beat candy for 3 to 4 minutes or till mixture starts to lose its gloss and becomes very creamy in appearance. Quickly stir in the fruit mixture. Immediately turn the mixture out onto a buttered baking sheet. Knead with buttered hands till gloss is gone. Divide mixture in half. Roll each half into a 12-inch-long log. Wrap each roll in clear plastic wrap. Cover securely to keep candy fresh. To serve, cut each roll into ¼-inch slices. Makes 3 pounds candy.

BAKED FRUITED POPCORN

Pictured on pages 186-187—

7 cups popped popcorn (⅓ cup unpopped)
1 cup broken pecans
¾ cup red candied cherries, cut up
¾ cup packed brown sugar
6 tablespoons butter *or* margarine
3 tablespoons light corn syrup
¼ teaspoon baking soda
¼ teaspoon vanilla

Remove all the unpopped kernels from popcorn. In a 17x12x2-inch baking pan combine popped popcorn, broken pecans, and candied cherries. Set aside.

In a 1½-quart saucepan combine brown sugar, butter or margarine, and corn syrup. Cook and stir over medium heat till butter or margarine melts and mixture comes to boiling. Reduce heat; cook over low heat for 5 minutes more. Remove from heat. Stir in baking soda and vanilla. Pour mixture over popcorn-nut mixture; gently stir to coat mixture evenly. Bake in a 300° oven for 15 minutes; stir. Bake 5 to 10 minutes more. Cool mixture; turn into a large bowl. Makes 8 cups.

BASIC DIVINITY

For best results, use a freestanding electric mixer when preparing this recipe—

2½ cups sugar
½ cup light corn syrup
½ cup water
2 egg whites
1 teaspoon vanilla
1 or 2 drops food coloring (optional)
½ cup chopped candied fruit *or* dried fruit (optional)
½ cup chopped nuts (optional)

In a heavy 2-quart saucepan stir together sugar, corn syrup, and water. Clip candy thermometer to side of pan. Cook and stir over medium-high heat till sugar dissolves and mixture boils (5 to 7 minutes). Avoid splashing syrup on sides of pan.

Reduce heat; cook, without stirring, over medium heat to 260° (hard-ball stage). Mixture should boil gently over entire surface. (At hard-ball stage, a few drops of syrup dropped into cold water form a hard ball when removed from the water.) Remove saucepan from heat. Immediately begin to beat egg whites in a large mixer bowl on medium speed of electric mixer till stiff peaks form (tips stand straight).

Remove the candy thermometer from the side of the saucepan. *Gradually* pour hot syrup in a thin stream (slightly less than ⅛-inch diameter) over egg whites, beating constantly on high speed of electric mixer. (Add syrup *slowly* to ensure proper blending. This should take about 3 minutes.) Add vanilla and a few drops food coloring, if desired. Continue to beat on high speed of electric mixer till candy holds its shape when beaters are lifted. This should take about 5 to 6 minutes. (Mixture falls in a ribbon, but mounds on itself and starts to lose its gloss.)

When candy is beaten enough, mixture will stay mounded in a soft shape when a spoonful is dropped onto waxed paper. If mixture flattens out, beat ½ to 1 minute more and check again. The mixture is overbeaten if it is stiff to spoon and the surface is rough. If mixture is too stiff, beat in *hot water,* a few drops at a time, till candy is a softer consistency.

When candy holds its shape, stir in fruits and nuts, if desired; *quickly* drop candy by teaspoonfuls onto waxed paper, or follow one of the shaping variations below. Cool; store tightly covered. Makes about 40 pieces.

BONBONS: Drop by spoonfuls into bonbon cups.

CUTOUTS: Spread candy in a buttered 9x9x2-inch dish or 12x7½x2-inch dish; cool and cut into squares or diamonds, or cut into shapes with small cookie or canape cutters.

LOGS: With lightly buttered fingers, shape candy mixture into two 12-inch-long rolls. Roll the logs in finely chopped nuts, coconut, or crushed peppermint candy. Slice crosswise about ⅜ inch thick.

BLACK-BOTTOM DIVINITY

2 8-ounce bars milk chocolate
Basic Divinity*
Small decorative chocolate candies (optional)

Prepare a 9x9x2-inch pan by lining it with foil, overlapping pan edges. Place chocolate bars side by side in bottom of pan.

Quickly spread the divinity over the chocolate bar layer in the prepared pan. Sprinkle with small decorative chocolate candies, if desired, pressing in lightly with hands. Cool. Remove candy from pan by lifting out foil. Cut candy into 1-inch squares. Store tightly covered. Makes about 80 pieces.

*Prepare BASIC DIVINITY, *except* substitute ½ teaspoon coconut extract or peppermint extract for vanilla. Omit fruit options and nuts.

EASY FUDGE

½ cup butter *or* margarine
⅓ cup water
1 16-ounce package powdered sugar
½ cup nonfat dry milk powder
½ cup unsweetened cocoa powder
Dash salt
½ cup chopped nuts

In a small saucepan heat together butter or margarine and water just to boiling, stirring to melt butter or margarine. Sift together powdered sugar, dry milk powder, cocoa powder, and salt into a large mixing bowl. (If powdered sugar mixture seems lumpy, sift again.) Add melted butter mixture. Stir till well blended; stir in chopped nuts. Turn into a buttered 8x8x2-inch pan. Chill several hours. Cut into squares. Makes about 1½ pounds.

197

CHOCOLATE-DIPPED ORANGE PEEL

  4 large oranges
1½ cups sugar
  ¾ cup water
  3 tablespoons light corn
      syrup
  ¼ teaspoon salt
  4 squares (4 ounces)
      semisweet chocolate
  1 tablespoon shortening

Score the orange peel lengthwise into 4 sections. Loosen the peel from the pulp using the bowl of a spoon; save the orange for another use. Place the orange peel into a large saucepan; add enough cold water to cover. Bring to boiling; reduce heat. Cover and simmer for 20 minutes. Drain well. Repeat cooking and draining twice. Cool slightly. Carefully scrape excess pulp from the peel. Cut peel into ¼-inch-wide strips.

For the syrup, in a heavy 2-quart saucepan combine the sugar, the ¾ cup water, corn syrup, and salt. Clip a candy thermometer to the side of the pan. Cook and stir over medium heat till sugar dissolves and mixture boils. Reduce heat and continue cooking, without stirring, to 236° on the candy thermometer (soft-ball stage).

Add the orange peel; simmer gently for 30 to 35 minutes or till peel is translucent, stirring frequently. Remove peel from syrup; drain well. Dry on a wire rack for several hours.

In a small heavy saucepan melt the chocolate and shortening over low heat, stirring often. Dip one end of each strip of orange peel into the melted chocolate; drain off excess chocolate. Place on a tray lined with waxed paper. Cool. Cover and chill. Makes 5 cups.

LIQUEUR CANDY CUTOUTS

Offer a taste of these liqueur-flavored candies to browsers, and they'll sell as fast as fir trees on Christmas Eve—

  ½ cup butter *or* margarine,
      softened
  ½ cup ground *or* finely
      chopped nuts
  ¼ cup unsweetened cocoa
      powder
  2 tablespoons orange,
      raspberry, coffee,
      cherry, *or* coconut
      liqueur
  1 pound powdered sugar,
      sifted (4¾ cups)

In a large mixer bowl combine the softened butter or margarine, ground or chopped nuts, cocoa powder, and desired liqueur; beat on medium speed of electric mixer till mixed. Gradually add the powdered sugar, beating on medium speed till combined. (The mixture will be stiff. If it is too dry, beat in enough additional liqueur, a teaspoon at a time, to make of rolling consistency.)

Place the mixture between 2 sheets of waxed paper; roll to ½-inch thickness. Using small cookie cutters, cut the dough into desired shapes. (Roll the trimmings into 1-inch balls and top each with a piece of nut, if desired.) Cover and chill the candies in the refrigerator till ready to serve or package. Makes about 1½ pounds.

*W*hen you're ready to sell your homemade Christmas treats, remember it's the packaging that catches a customer's eye. To make festive containers, look around for small boxes, cookie tins, jars, and bags, then decorate them with gaily colored gift wrap, ribbons, bows, stickers, and sequins.

EUROPEAN-STYLE MARZIPAN

Use small cutters, molds, your fingers, and your imagination to shape the marzipan, as European children do—

  1 cup blanched whole
      almonds *or* 1⅓ cups
      slivered almonds
1⅓ cups sifted powdered
      sugar
  ½ teaspoon almond extract
2¼ cups sifted powdered
      sugar
  1 slightly beaten egg white

Place almonds in a blender container or food processor bowl. Cover and blend or process till ground. In a mixer bowl combine the ground almonds, the 1⅓ cups powdered sugar, almond extract, and 2 tablespoons *water;* beat with electric mixer till the mixture forms a ball. Gradually add the 2¼ cups powdered sugar, beating till combined. Stir in enough egg white (about 1 tablespoon) to form a claylike mixture. Tint with food coloring, if desired. Mold or shape the marzipan as desired, using about *2 teaspoons* marzipan for each shape. Makes 2 cups mixture.

CHRISTMAS JOYS
FOR
CHILDREN

*Children are the heart of the holidays,
for it's through a child's vivid
imagination and breathless anticipation
that we truly appreciate the joy
and vitality of this most special season. On
the following pages, we focus on the things
kids love about Christmas. There are
fanciful ornaments, colorful
Christmas wraps, recipes for holiday
cookies especially for kids, and other child-
pleasing projects. Or let a child
lend a hand. There's no better way
to teach the joy of sharing at Christmas
and the simple pleasure of making
things by hand.*

CHRISTMAS JOYS
FOR CHILDREN

Enchanting Gifts and Trims

Few things can make your Christmas merrier than the sparkling warmth of children during this festive season. And there is no nicer way to add to your own enjoyment of the holidays than by crafting gifts and decorations with and for the youngsters you love best.

One of the most inviting places to delight in the pleasures of children is the kitchen. Making cookies brings light into the eyes of any child. And cookies make tasty trims for a tiny tree, *below,* or thoughtful gifts for loved ones and friends.

For an extra-special treat, let the kids help you make cookie molds like these, *opposite*. Press the molds onto dough and cut around the shapes. After baking and decorating the cookies, the kids can package their best efforts for gift-giving.

The little girl's embroidered T-shirt also is a gift you can make. Instructions for projects in this section begin on page 212.

For more gift-wrapping fun, give the kids large sheets of finger-painting paper. Dip their tiny hands into finger paint and stand back to watch them create artistic wraps like these, *left.* Older children can cut geometric stamps to print organized patterns on shelf paper, *below.*

Two more happy ideas are a tree trimmed with pastel pinwheels, *left,* and a child's rocking horse, *above,* lovingly painted with flowers.

Christmas is child's play when you include tree trims, wrappings, and gifts like these. The tree, *opposite,* is bedecked with colorful woven fabric ornaments. If you prepare the fabric strips beforehand, the youngsters can weave them in and out.

The easy string-printed gift wrap is perfect for preschoolers or teens to make. Just ask your helpers to dip household string into paint and trail it in swirling movements across shelf paper.

Stenciled T-shirts, *opposite, above,* and *right,* herald the holidays and set the mood for the festivities.

Enchanting Gifts and Trims

A bustling Christmas workshop, staffed by pint-size sculptors, can turn out dozens of diminutive trims—and the "elves" will have the time of their lives. Supply the kids with clay, or dough that resembles clay, and start the assembly line rolling.

Youngsters can make simple oval and round body shapes for the spool-size dolls, *below.* After you have baked the clay in the oven, paint the doll parts with bright colors. Then assemble the bodies with string and add yarn hair.

For the nutshell ornaments, *opposite,* gather a bagful of walnuts, split them in half, and carefully remove the nuts. Mix up a batch of salt dough and set eager little hands to rolling basic shapes to make special character ornaments. If you call children's imaginations into play, you will have all sorts of one-of-a-kind trims in no time at all. Bake the dough characters in their nutshells and finish with colorful paints.

Enchanting Gifts and Trims

Nativity scenes bring the Christmas story to life in homes and churches every year. By crafting your own crèche, you can celebrate this age-old story and share it with those you love.

The muslin Nativity figures, *below,* are simple designs, but elegant trims give them a dressy look. Why not ask your youngsters to help you collect pretty ribbons, delicate laces, floral cutwork bands, satiny drapery cords, and shiny embroidery flosses to make a crèche this year?

If your little angel is lucky enough to play a part in the annual Christmas Nativity pageant, surprise her with this delightful costume. Pretty enough for any pageant (or party), this embroidered charmer is really a basic full-length dress. The fanciful apron and satin wings transform this otherwise plain dress into finery fit for a member of the heavenly host!

For embroidery ideas, look through the patterns in this book to find designs that suit your skills. Decorate a ready-made apron with rich satin stitches in bright colors. Add lace trims and gold cording to cherubic wings cut from soft white satin. Then purchase a golden halo for the crowning touch.

Enchanting Gifts and Trims

Every child loves a Christmas dream, and here is an imaginative dream come true for the holiday season. Whether you are a youngster or just plain young-at-heart, you are sure to be smitten by this happy collection of playtime pals.

The charming quilt, *opposite,* features small fry on fabric-painted muslin blocks. Pieced together with a coordinating print, the blocks compose a cozy coverlet recalling happy childhood days.

Fabric appliqué was used to make the special-pal dolls, *above.* You also can adapt the paint-and-embroider technique used for the quilt. Or get the kids involved in making this project by having them color the designs with crayons. Then just stitch the dolls together and stuff them firmly.

Don't be surprised if not-so-small youngsters request these dolls for their own rooms, too. There are eight adorable designs to choose from—and chances are you'll soon populate your block with the entire lovable gang!

Ornament Cookies
Pictured on page 202

INSTRUCTIONS: Cream 1½ cups butter and 2 cups packed brown sugar; add 1 egg. Beat until light. Mix 4 cups all-purpose flour, 2 teaspoons ground cinnamon, 1 teaspoon ground nutmeg, ½ teaspoon ground cloves, and ¼ teaspoon baking soda. Stir into egg mixture. Cover; chill 2 hours.

On floured surface, roll dough to ⅛-inch thickness. Cut into desired shapes with cookie cutters. Place on ungreased cookie sheet. Cut paper drinking straw into 1-inch pieces. Push one piece into top of each ornament. Bake at 350° for 8 to 10 minutes. Remove straw pieces. Cool 1 minute; remove to rack. Hang with ribbon or yarn.

Wooden Cookie Molds
Pictured on page 203

MATERIALS: 3 feet of 1x12-inch pine board; 3 feet of ¼x12-inch plywood; 2 inches of ⁵⁄₃₂-inch dowel; sandpaper; wood glue; razor blade; jigsaw; ⁵⁄₁₆-, ⁵⁄₃₂-, ⁷⁄₃₂-, and ½-inch drill bits; ¾-inch countersink bit; rattail file; basting brush; olive oil; glass dishes.

INSTRUCTIONS: Enlarge patterns, *below* and *right;* trace onto pine board, spacing designs 1 inch apart and away from knots. Dark areas on pattern indicate areas to be drilled and cut through; shaded areas indicate countersunk shapes. Drill holes and countersink shapes on pine

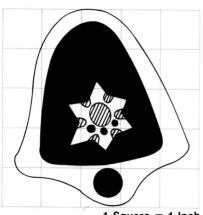

1 Square = 1 Inch

board. In bear eyes, glue 1-inch dowels; cut bear's mouth line with razor. Drill holes in large black areas for jigsaw blade; cut away black shapes with jigsaw. Clean rough areas with rattail file.

Coat back of pine board evenly with glue. Set back side on plywood; place heavy object on boards to weight the molds while drying; dry overnight. With jigsaw, cut outer lines of cookie molds, separating them. File rough spots and sand the face and back of each mold.

To seal the molds, use a basting brush to coat all surfaces with olive oil. Place the molds in glass baking dishes and place dishes in a warm, dry place for two days. Coat again; place in same place for three days.

Hand-wash molds after each use and coat with olive oil to reseal them when necessary.

Embroidered T-Shirt
Pictured on page 203

MATERIALS: White cotton T-shirt; interfacing; needlecrafter's transfer pen; green variegated embroidery floss; red floss; ⅓ yard lace; white thread.

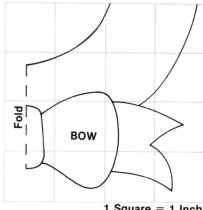

1 Square = 1 Inch

1 Square = 1 Inch

INSTRUCTIONS: Enlarge pattern, *opposite,* onto paper. To stabilize embroidery areas, iron the shirt and baste a 3-inch-wide strip of interfacing inside the neck of shirt; baste a rectangle of interfacing behind bow area. Using transfer pen, trace design onto shirt.

With three strands of green floss, fill bow and ribbon shape around neck using split stitches. Add red French knots on bow. Trim excess interfacing when stitching is finished. If shirt has a pocket, baste lace trim in handkerchief shape over pocket. Trim edges of lace with green floss.

Soft-Sculpture "Woven" Ornaments
Pictured on page 204

MATERIALS (for 8 to 10 ornaments): ½ yard green and white polka dot fabric; ½ yard red and white polka dot fabric; ½ yard muslin; ½ yard quilt batting; red and green pearl cotton; transparent tape.

INSTRUCTIONS: Enlarge patterns, *right.*

• *Tree:* Cut pieces from fabric. Cut two 1¼x12-inch strips of fabric (one of muslin and one of polka dot); fold and press raw edges so each strip is ⅝ inch wide. Cut each strip into three smaller strips that measure 4½ inches (1), 4 inches (2), and 3½ inches (3).

Clip corners along inside edge of each front piece; fold and press the two inner edges to the seam line.

On the wrong side, lay strips along the lower folded back edge (shown as 1, 2, and 3 on pattern), following the direction of the arrow. Hold strips in place with transparent tape. With the right side up, stitch strips in place along the folded edge. Remove tape.

Overlap tops of tree fronts and pin the two pieces together. Weave together the strips on the two front pieces, using the back piece to determine the finished size.

With right sides facing, fold the trunk in half along the dotted line and sew the two sides together. Turn the trunk right side out and

fold it in half again to make a small square. Baste the tree trunk to the right side of the tree front, making raw edges even.

Baste two layers of quilt batting to wrong side of tree back; trim batting to tree shape. With right sides facing, sew front to back tree piece, leaving a small opening in trunk for turning. Trim seams, turn; sew closed. Tie muslin bows at top; add hanger behind bows.

• *Bell:* Cut pattern pieces from fabric. Cut two 1¼x10-inch strips of fabric (1 muslin and 1 polka dot); fold and press raw edges so each strip is ⅝ inch wide. Cut each strip into 3 smaller strips that measure 3 inches (1), 3½ inches (2), and 3½ inches (3).

Clip corners along inside edge of each front piece; fold and press the

two inner edges to the seam line. With right sides facing, stitch the two front pieces together at the bell top; press seam open.

On wrong side, lay strips (1, 2, and 3) along the top folded edge of the front pieces, following the direction of the arrow. Hold pieces in place with tape. Sew along fold, catching the strips in seam.

Overlap and pin the lower center sections of front pieces. Weave the strips together. (Treat the bottom "flare" part of the bell as a strip and weave it also.) Use the back piece to determine finished size.

Baste two layers of batting to wrong side of back; trim to bell shape. With right sides facing, sew front to back; leave opening along top. Trim seams, turn; sew closed.
continued

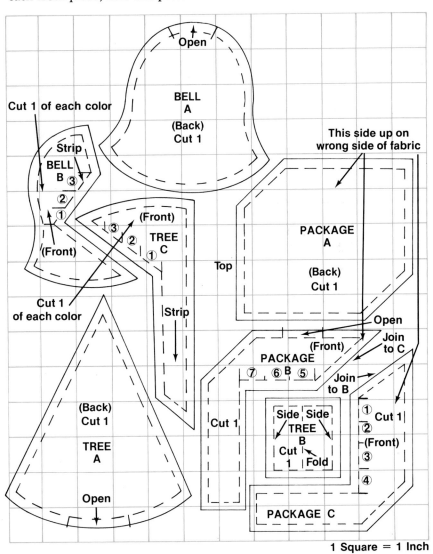

1 Square = 1 Inch

213

Tie polka dot bows at top of bell. Add pearl cotton hanger behind ornament bow.

• *Package:* Cut out pattern pieces from fabric. Cut a 1¼x14-inch strip of fabric to match front B; cut the strip into four 3½-inch strips (1, 2, 3, and 4). Cut a 1¼x12-inch strip of fabric to match front C; cut the strip into three 4-inch strips (5, 6, and 7). Remember to turn and press raw edges so each strip measures ⅝ inch wide *before* cutting the strips into smaller lengths.

Clip corners along inside edge of each front piece; fold and press the two inner edges to seam line.

With right sides facing, stitch the two front pieces together; press the seam open.

On the wrong side, lay the strips along the folded edge of the front pieces, holding the strips in place with tape. With the right side up, stitch the strips in place along the folded edge. Remove tape.

Overlap and pin the two strips on the front pieces. Weave strips together, using back piece to determine the finished shape.

Baste two layers of quilt batting to the wrong side of the back piece and trim batting to package shape.

Cut and stitch strips of contrasting fabric in place to the front of the package to make "ribbon" ties. With right sides facing, stitch front and back pieces together, leaving a small opening for turning. Trim seams, turn; sew closed.

Tie a fabric bow at top; add hanger behind bow.

String-Design Gift Wrap
Pictured on page 204

MATERIALS: Rolls of white craft paper; string; red and green acrylic paints.

INSTRUCTIONS: Cover working surface with newspapers, then layer with craft paper; pour paint into shallow aluminum pie plates. Cut different size lengths of string and dip the string into the paint. Drag the string along the craft paper

to make abstract designs. Allow the paint to dry thoroughly, then repeat the above procedure on the next section of paper.

Stenciled T-Shirts
Pictured on pages 204-205

MATERIALS: White cotton T-shirts; acrylic paints in assorted colors; precut letter stencils in various sizes; stencil paper; stencil brushes; craft or utility knife; heavy cardboard; masking tape or straight pins.

INSTRUCTIONS: Draw a straight line across the stencil paper. Align the stenciled letters for each word or phrase (such as "Joy," "Noel," "Bah Humbug," "Happy Ho Ho," or "Merry Kissmas") on the straight line and draw the outline of each letter onto the stencil paper. Place the stencil paper on a piece of heavy cardboard and cut each letter from stencil paper using a sharp utility knife.

Place heavy cardboard under the area of the T-shirt to be stenciled. Making sure fabric is smooth and taut, pin or tape the stencil in place using straight pins or masking tape.

Dip a stencil brush into acrylic paint; tap the brush on several layers of newspapers to remove excess paint. Begin stenciling, painting the outside, then the inside of each letter. Apply a light first coat, then reapply a second light coat to deepen the color. (Too much paint at once will run under the stencil edges.)

Wash paintbrushes immediately after every use.

Remove pins or tape and lift the stencil after the paint has dried for 5 to 10 minutes. Lay the T-shirt flat to dry an additional 8 hours. If desired, press the fabric to set the colors.

Finger-Painted Gift Wrap
Pictured on page 205

MATERIALS: Sheets of finger-paint paper; finger paints in a variety of colors; water; wooden ice cream sticks; paper towels.

INSTRUCTIONS: To minimize clean-up chores, cover your work surface with newspapers. You also might wish to tie aprons over children's clothes (or dress them in old shirts).

Place sheets of finger-paint paper atop newspapers and place jars of finger paint and a small bowl of water for adding to paint nearby.

Apply paint to paper using a wooden ice cream stick.

Wet your fingers (or your child's fingers) with water and work the paint with your fingers, covering the entire sheet of paper with paint. Make patterns in the paint with your fingers as desired (see photograph); dry. Use paper towels to remove excess paint from fingers.

Pinwheel Ornaments
Pictured on page 205

MATERIALS: *For one ornament—* 5½-inch square of unbleached muslin; 5½-inch square of calico print fabric; 5-inch square of fusible webbing; 1 yard of ¼-inch-wide satin ribbon in color to complement the printed fabric; small dried or silk flowers (optional).

INSTRUCTIONS: Place a layer of fusible webbing between the muslin and print fabric and press the layers together using a warm iron. Using pinking shears, trim the edges to make a 5-inch square.

Make four 2½-inch diagonal cuts from the corners into the center of the square. Fold every other corner piece (four pieces in all) into the center of the square and tack them in place. Leave the other four corner pieces flat.

Tie a double or triple bow from a 12-inch length of satin ribbon and tack the bow to the center of the pinwheel.

Fold a 24-inch length of ribbon in half and tie an overhand knot in the ribbon 4½ inches from the folded end. Tack the ribbon to the center back of the pinwheel, using the looped end for hanging.

Glue a small cluster of dried or silk flowers to the center of each bow, if desired.

Printed Gift Wrap
Pictured on page 205

MATERIALS: White, 18-inch-wide shelf paper; plastic foam meat trays; red and orange water-soluble ink; green felt-tip pen; waterproof glue (for plastics); paint brayer; scraps of wood; craft knife; straight-edge; glass palette.

INSTRUCTIONS: Cut 1-inch squares, triangles, and diamonds from the flat area of plastic foam meat trays. Glue the plastic foam pieces to wood blocks and let dry.

Cover a hard, flat surface with a thick layer of newspapers. Pour a small amount of ink onto a piece of glass and spread it evenly with a brayer. Dip printing block into ink and press block onto white shelf paper. Continue inking and printing, changing colors and blocks as desired. Print designs across the paper, leaving a narrow space between design rows.

Let the ink dry thoroughly and draw green stripes between the printed designs with a felt pen and straightedge.

Painted Rocking Horse
Pictured on page 205

MATERIALS: 1x8x9-inch pine; 14-inch length of 2x4 pine; 2x4-foot piece of ½-inch-thick particleboard; ¾x6¾-inch dowel; finishing nails; 2¼-inch screws; wood glue, putty; red enamel; acrylic paints; brushes; graphite paper; pecan ink; varnish.

INSTRUCTIONS: Enlarge patterns, *right*. The body of the horse is a shaped 2x4, clad on top and sides with particleboard. Cut the 2x4 according to the seat top and end view patterns. Cant sides at 13°; cant in the ends ½ inch from bottom to top.

Cut the particleboard seat top. From one end, cut a ¾-inch-wide notch 4⅝ inches long to accept the head. Glue and nail the top onto the 2x4. Cant edges flush. Cut head from 1x8-inch pine; position it in seat notch. Drill holes up through the 2x4 into head; set head aside.

Cut two particleboard sides to shape; round edges with router.

Glue and nail rockers to sides of seat. Sand edges smooth. Drill hole in head for dowel as indicated on pattern. Glue head into notch; secure with screws. Insert dowel; glue.

Sand horse smooth and paint red. Let dry, sand, and repaint.

Transfer designs with graphite paper. Paint rocker edges; fill in shapes with desired colors. Double-load paintbrush for shading; add details with fine brush. Antique horse with pecan ink. Let dry; varnish.

continued

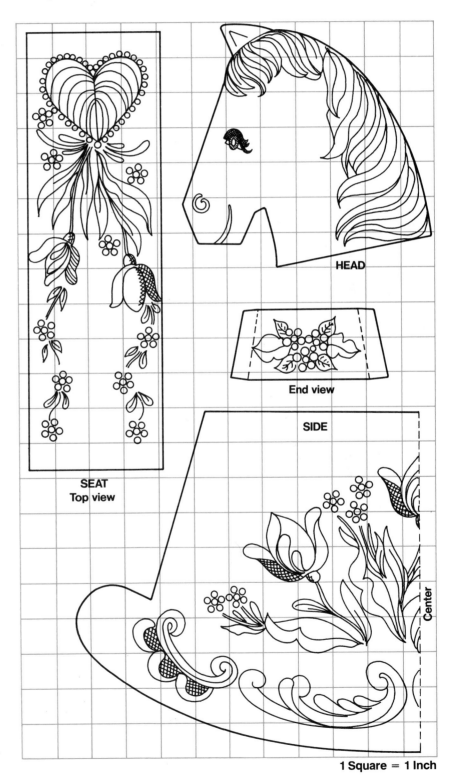

HEAD

End view

SIDE

SEAT
Top view

Center

1 Square = 1 Inch

Sculptured Dolls
Pictured on page 206

MATERIALS: Sculpey clay; clear nail polish; acrylic paints; fine-point permanent marker; sturdy string; Size 1 steel crochet hook; mohair yarn (hair).

INSTRUCTIONS: Form a 1-inch-diameter ball of clay for the head, rolling it in your hands until surface is smooth. Set aside.

Work a golf-ball-size piece of clay until smooth, then form it into oval shape (body) 1¾x1 inches. Pinch in top and bottom slightly for arms and legs. With crochet hook, push a hole through body at shoulders and at body base. Place head on body; push gently to secure in place.

For arms, roll 1½x⅜-inch cylinders of clay; form thumb and fingers with needle on one end of each arm. Gently push crochet hook through shoulder. Repeat for legs, rolling 3x½-inch cylinders and bending ¾-inch forward at bottom for foot.

Bake clay parts on aluminum-foil-lined cookie sheet for 20 to 30 minutes in a 325° oven. Dolls should be golden brown. Allow to cool; paint doll parts with acrylic paints; add details with marker. See photograph for design and color ideas. Dry; coat all parts with clear nail polish.

Run string through body and arms, tying arms to body at ends with knots. Cut excess string and secure knots with nail polish. Repeat for the legs.

For hair, cut 26 strands of yarn 9 inches long. Place in a bundle about 1 inch wide and sew center part by hand or machine. Cut a few ½-inch strands for bangs. Paint forehead with nail polish and set bangs in place. Fasten hair bundle across head, pulling it down into place. Dry five minutes; braid; tie off braids with yarn bows.

Nutshell Ornaments
Pictured on page 207

MATERIALS: Flour; salt; walnuts; acrylic paints; brushes; 4 ounces of plastic polymer resin.

INSTRUCTIONS: To make dough for 12 to 18 ornaments, mix one cup of flour with ¼ cup salt. Add ⅓ cup of water, stirring the dough thoroughly.

Knead the mixture for five minutes until dough has smooth consistency. Add flour if dough is sticky; add a few drops of water if it is dry. To prevent drying, wrap dough in plastic when not in use.

Halve walnuts and hollow out shells. Starting with a piece of dough the size of the walnut shell's cavity, roll dough in hands until smooth ball is formed. (Be sure each ball of dough is smooth and free of cracks.) Position dough evenly in the walnut shell until it has a slightly rounded surface.

Roll a smaller piece of dough for the head. Form facial features, sculpting details with a toothpick. (See photograph for character ideas.) Use a drop of water to secure one piece of dough to another. For blanket, place a thin circle of dough across top of shell and tuck in edges. Insert small hairpin or wire loop into top of head for hanging.

Place each shell in a piece of aluminum foil and crumple the edges of the foil to create a baking cradle. Bake in a 225° oven for 4 to 5 hours. Ornaments are done if there is no "give" when the top is gently pushed with a thumb.

Cool completely and paint with acrylics. See photograph on page 207 for color ideas. Let dry for at least 24 hours before sealing.

Apply resin to surfaces with brush to seal; dry eight hours. Store in a moisture-proof container.

Muslin Crèche
Pictured on page 208

MATERIALS: 1 yard 45-inch-wide muslin; ¼ yard each of ecru fabric, ivory and black striped fabric, and ivory and black dotted fabric; fusible webbing; 1¼ yards of 1-inch-wide ecru gathered lace; ½ yard *each* tan and bone single-fold bias tape; ⅓ yard of 1½-inch-wide rose appliqué ivory trim; ½ yard brown and tan piping (2-color combination); ¾ yard of ¼-inch-wide ecru braided satin trim; ½ yard of ⅛-inch-wide ivory ribbon; polyester fiberfill; ecru embroidery floss, thread; excelsior or straw; ¼-inch-diameter dowel; cardboard.

INSTRUCTIONS: Enlarge patterns, *opposite,* onto paper. Use ¼-inch seam allowances throughout.

• *Baby:* Cut one face from ecru fabric and one from fusible webbing; cut two body pieces from muslin. Use an iron to fuse the face to the front body, and machine-appliqué around outside edges. Embroider the facial features and hair as shown on the pattern, using three strands of ecru floss.

With right sides facing, sew front and back together, leaving open between Xs. Turn right side out, stuff; sew closed. Sew purchased rose appliqué to baby's front.

• *Manger:* Cut four manger pieces from muslin. With right sides facing, sew two of the pieces together, leaving open between Xs. Turn right side out, stuff firmly, and insert ¼-inch-diameter dowels through the manger legs; sew closed. Repeat for other set of legs.

Tack front and back manger together at two top ends. Sew a 2-inch strip of fabric to manger bottom to hold excelsior in place.

• *Mary:* Cut two body pieces from muslin. Cut one face from ecru fabric and one from fusible webbing; cut two cheeks from muslin and two from fusible webbing. Fuse the cheeks to the face and fuse the face to the front; machine-appliqué around edges of the cheeks and face. Embroider the facial features using three strands of embroidery floss.

Stitch fabric overlays to the front body piece as indicated on the pattern, trimming the edges with lace. Stitch purchased rose appliqués in place on the front dress panel.

With right sides facing, stitch the front and back body pieces together, leaving the bottom edge open. Turn right side out and stuff.

Cut a cardboard oval to fit the bottom opening; cut a muslin oval slightly larger than the cardboard. Place the cardboard inside the opening, covering the cardboard with muslin. Turn raw edges under and stitch the pieces together along the bottom edge. Stitch a piece of tan single-fold bias tape around top of head; trim with lace and bow.

• *Joseph:* Follow instructions for Mary (above), using two-color piping for trims instead of ecru. Cut beard from muslin. Stitch a piece of bone single-fold bias tape to the top of the head and tie ecru cording around the head.

• *Star:* Cut two stars from muslin. With right sides facing, sew together, leaving open between the Xs. Turn right side out, stuff lightly, and sew closed. Add hanger.

• *Donkey:* Cut two body pieces and two underside pieces from muslin. Cut two ear pieces and two nostrils from ecru fabric; cut two nostrils from fusible webbing.

With right sides facing, stitch the two ear pieces together, leaving open between the Xs. Turn right

side out, press lightly, and slip-stitch the opening closed. Fuse nostrils in place on body front. Embroider and machine-appliqué facial features.

With right sides facing, sew front and back together, leaving open at bottom edge between Xs. Turn.

With right sides facing, stitch the two underside pieces together along the short distance between the Xs. Press seam open. With right sides facing, stitch the underside piece to the donkey's body, making four legs and leaving a small opening. Turn; stuff; sew closed. Add floss mane, tail, and ears.

Angel Costume
Pictured on page 209

MATERIALS: Purchased dress pattern; red velveteen yardage;

white apron; embroidery flosses; gold cording; foam-core board; ½ yard of satin; ½ yard of white cotton; 12x12 inches of quilt batting; masking tape.

INSTRUCTIONS: Cut and sew red velveteen dress following pattern instructions. Trim dress with gold cording. For apron, embroider bib with design (see photograph for ideas). For wings, draw a wing about 10x12 inches. Add detail lines, using photograph as guide.

Transfer wing to satin, reversing pattern for other wing. Cut out, leaving 2 inches of fabric around edges. Place a layer of quilt batting behind satin wing; couch gold cording along all lines.

From foam-core board, cut out wings. Fit satin wings firmly around board edges, slashing raw edges of satin where necessary. Fasten raw edges at wing back with masking tape. Cut cotton lining for wing backs as for wing fronts. Tucking all the raw edges inside, sew the satin front to the cotton back along edges of wings. Glue lace trim around wing edges.

Playtime Pals Quilt
Pictured on page 211

MATERIALS: 10 yards (45-inch-wide) muslin; 3½ yards printed fabric for decorative strips, ruffle; 1⅓ yards (45-inch-wide) prequilted fabric (to match printed fabric); quilt batting; fabric paints; 8 skeins red, 3 skeins brown embroidery floss; quilting thread; brown *permanent* felt-tip pen; butcher paper.

INSTRUCTIONS: The finished quilt is 72x90 inches, excluding the printed fabric ruffle.

Cut top blocks (see diagram, *page 218* for sizes). Add ½-inch seam allowances to blocks. Cut plain blocks from muslin. Cut shaded blocks from prequilted fabric. From batting and remaining muslin, cut matching padding and quilt block backs. Set batting and backing aside.

Enlarge patterns, *pages 218, 219,* onto butcher paper. Transfer the doll designs to muslin quilt blocks.
continued

EARS
Cut 2
(Ecru fabric)

MARY
FRONT/BACK
Cut 2 entire shapes
(Muslin)

Cut 1
(Polka dot ivory fabric)

Cut 1
(Striped ivory fabric)

DONKEY
Cut 2
(Muslin)

JOSEPH
Cut 2 entire shapes
(Muslin)

Ecru fabric

Cut 1
(Striped ivory fabric)

Cut 1
(Polka dot ivory fabric)

Cut 2
(Muslin)

Cut 1
(Polka dot ivory fabric)

DONKEY
UNDERSIDE

MANGER
Cut 4
(Ecru fabric)

BABY
Cut 2
(Muslin)

STAR
Cut 2
(Muslin)

1 Square = 2 Inches

Lay muslin pieces atop drawings; trace all lines onto the muslin with a brown permanent marker.

Paint the dolls. (Refer to the photograph for color ideas.) Place a small amount of paint on a glass plate and thin with a few drops of water until the paint is of light-cream consistency.

Fill in an area, painting *close to, but not up to or over* the lines. Leave a sliver of unpainted fabric between colors to minimize bleeding. Dry each area before painting adjoining areas. Work light colors first; work darker colors last. For a light wash of color, first thin the paint with water and apply with relatively dry brush.

When paint is dry, heat-set colors on the wrong side using a warm iron. Clean brush with water after making each color change.

Embroider all design lines with outline stitches, using two strands of red embroidery floss to define all but the eyes and nose. Use one strand of brown embroidery floss on facial features.

To quilt the squares, sandwich batting between decorated blocks and the muslin backing. With ecru quilting thread and running stitches, quilt the layers together along embroidered lines.

To assemble the quilt, sew blocks into four horizontal strips, inserting the purchased prequilted fabric blocks; use ½-inch seam allowances. *Do not include muslin backs in the seams.* Pin their edges away from the seams until blocks are joined.

On fronts of the horizontal strips, add 3-inch-wide vertical decorative strips cut from printed fabrics long enough to cover the 5 seams that are not adjacent to prequilted blocks. Sew strips in place over seams, lining them up with each other.

Next join horizontal strips into quilt top, pinning the muslin backing *away* from the seams.

Cut printed fabric to make 18 yards of 6-inch-wide (unfinished

17"x21"	17"x21"	21"x13"	21"x9"	21"x16"
17"x9"				
17"x20"	39"x29"			29"x16"
23"x3"	34"x23"		26"x23"	23"x9"
18"x17"	35"x17"		19"x17"	

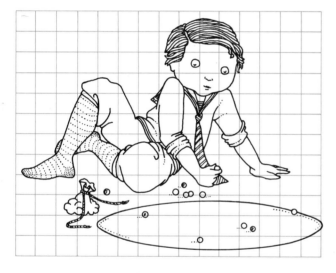

1 Square = 1 Inch

width) strips for ruffle. Join strips end to end, roll hem along outside edge, and gather remaining raw edge. With right sides facing, line up raw edge and sew ruffle to quilt edges, remembering to leave muslin backing free.

To finish quilt back, press under all raw edges of backing, butting block edges. Blindstitch along all folded edges and along ruffle.

Playtime Pals Dolls
Pictured on page 210

MATERIALS (for each 24-inch doll): ⅔ yard black cotton fabric for background and backing; assorted fabric scraps and trims for appliqués; ½ yard fusible webbing, 18 inches wide; muslin scrap for face and hands; kraft paper; tissue paper; sewing thread to match appliqués; polyester fiberfill.

INSTRUCTIONS: Doll fronts are constructed from machine-appliquéd fabric. Appliqués, cut without seam allowances and fused onto a black fabric background, fit together like jigsaw puzzle pieces. After edges are machine-appliquéd with zigzag satin stitches, doll fronts and plain fabric backs are stitched together, stuffed, and finished with three-dimensional details such as shoelaces, hair, and bows.

Enlarge doll patterns, *right* and *opposite,* onto kraft paper to make master patterns. Use a scale of 1 square = 1½ inches for the small dolls and 1 square = 2½ inches for the large dolls. Place tissue paper on top of master patterns and trace to form individual patterns.

Add a 3-inch margin to master pattern outline. For one doll, cut two black fabric pieces (front and back) to match doll outline.

For each doll front, cut appliqué pieces using tissue paper patterns, beginning with pieces at the doll base and working toward the head.

Cut matching pieces from fusible webbing. Lay fabric appliqués and fusible webbing in place on front background piece. Fuse in place.

Cut face shape from muslin; lightly sketch nose and mouth onto mus-

lin using a pencil. Fuse in place. Next, machine-appliqué all raw edges, using machine satin stitches and threads to match the fabrics. Machine-embroider facial details with close, short zigzag stitches.

With right sides facing, pin appliquéd doll front to backing fabric; sew them together 1 inch from raw

edges, leaving an opening along a straight edge for turning. Trim seams, clip curves, and turn; stuff firmly with fiberfill and slip-stitch closed. Add hair bows, yarn pompons, shoelaces, buttons, ribbons, lace, or yarn hair where appropriate. (*Note:* Girl's broom is made from a whisk broom attached to a dowel.)

1 Square = 1 Inch

CHRISTMAS TREATS FOR KIDS

To a child (and to most adults), Christmas just wouldn't be Christmas without a mind-boggling array of cookies and candies to choose from. This year, let the youngsters at your house help make some of those tasty goodies. Once you stage a kids' cookie- or candy-making party, it just might become a tradition.

Of course, you'll want to select easy recipes, so we've chosen some ideal candidates that are child's play to make. To get your party off to a fast start, make some of the cookie doughs ahead of time and have decorating tidbits and frostings waiting for your creative, young cookie makers.

Santa Claus Cookies, Cherry-Chocolate Cups, Easy Pull Taffy, and Crunchy Marshmallow Balls (see Index for recipe pages)

SANTA CLAUS COOKIES

Pictured on page 220—

  3 cups all-purpose flour
  1 teaspoon baking powder
  1 teaspoon salt
  ¾ cup butter *or* margarine
  1 cup sugar
  2 eggs
  1 teaspoon vanilla
    Cherry-flavored round
      hard candies
    Green gumdrops, sliced
    Pearl sugar *or*
      crushed sugar cubes

Grease a cookie sheet. Stir together flour, baking powder, and salt. In a mixer bowl beat butter or margarine on medium speed of electric mixer for 30 seconds. Add the 1 cup sugar and beat till fluffy. Add eggs and vanilla; beat well. Add dry ingredients to the beaten mixture. Cover and chill about 1 hour or till easily handled. Divide dough into quarters. On a lightly floured surface, roll each portion into a 9½-inch circle. Invert a 9x1½-inch round baking pan atop dough; trim edges. With a sharp knife, cut the circle into 8 wedges. Transfer the wedges to cookie sheet. Lift the tip of each wedge and fold over to the left about 1 inch from the top to form Santa's hat. Place one cherry-flavored candy near the center of the wedge to form a mouth. Use sliced gumdrops for the eyes. Brush the bottom edge of triangle, the edge of the hat, and the tip of the hat lightly with water. Sprinkle with pearl sugar or crushed sugar cubes to form fur on the hat and beard. Bake in a 375° oven for 8 to 10 minutes. Cool 1 minute; remove to wire rack. Cool completely. Makes 32 cookies.

CHERRY-CHOCOLATE CUPS

Pictured on page 220—

 1¾ cups all-purpose flour
 1¼ teaspoons baking powder
  ½ teaspoon salt
  ¾ cup butter *or* margarine
  1 cup sugar
  1 egg
  1 teaspoon vanilla
  ¼ cup chopped walnuts
  1 square (1 ounce)
    unsweetened chocolate,
    melted
 32 maraschino cherries,
    drained and halved

Stir together the flour, baking powder, and salt. In a mixer bowl beat the butter or margarine on medium speed of electric mixer for 30 seconds. Add the sugar and beat till fluffy. Add the egg and vanilla; beat well. Add the dry ingredients to the beaten mixture and beat till well combined. Divide the dough in half.

Stir the chopped walnuts and the melted chocolate into *half* of the dough. Press *1 teaspoon* of the chocolate dough into the bottom and up the sides of ungreased 1¾-inch-diameter muffin pans just to rims. Place a maraschino cherry half in the center of each pan. Place *1 teaspoon* of the white dough atop each. Top with another maraschino cherry half. Bake in a 375° oven for 15 to 20 minutes or till done. Cool 10 minutes. Remove from muffin pans to a wire rack; cool completely. Makes 32 cookies.

*C*hristmastime magically lures children of all ages to the kitchen. The aroma of cakes baking in the oven, the lively fun of candy makers, and the sight of colorfully decorated cookies are impossible to resist and bring smiles to all who pass by. Cook up some Christmas magic in your kitchen this year and make your holiday a special one.*

EASY PULL TAFFY

Pictured on page 220—

1 cup sugar
¾ cup light corn syrup
½ cup water
½ teaspoon salt
2 tablespoons butter *or* margarine
½ teaspoon peppermint extract
　Few drops red *or* green food coloring

Butter the sides of a heavy 2-quart saucepan. In it combine sugar, corn syrup, water, and salt. Cook over medium heat, stirring constantly, till sugar is dissolved. Continue cooking to 248° (firm-ball stage), without stirring (mixture should boil gently over entire surface).

　Remove from heat. Stir in butter or margarine, peppermint extract, and food coloring. Pour into a buttered 8x8x2-inch baking pan. Cool till easily handled. Butter hands and shape candy into a ball. Return to baking pan, allowing the ball to flatten naturally. When it is cold, wrap in clear plastic wrap. Store overnight or up to 2 weeks at room temperature. Unwrap taffy and place in a well-buttered 8x8x2-inch baking pan. Bake in a 300° oven about 4 minutes or till just heated. Remove and let stand 5 minutes or till easily handled. Butter hands and pull candy till light in color. Pull into long strips. With buttered scissors snip taffy into bite-size pieces. Wrap each in clear plastic wrap. Makes ¾ pound.

ORANGE-WALNUT FUDGE

3 cups sugar
½ cup orange juice
1 12-ounce package (2 cups) semisweet chocolate pieces
1 tablespoon finely shredded orange peel
4 cups coarsely chopped walnuts

Line a 13x9x2-inch baking pan with foil; set aside. Butter the sides of a heavy 3-quart saucepan. In it combine sugar, orange juice, and ½ cup *water*. Cook and stir over medium heat till sugar dissolves and mixture comes to boiling. Continue cooking to 234° (soft-ball stage), stirring only as necessary to prevent sticking (mixture should boil gently over entire surface). Remove from heat. Add the chocolate pieces and orange peel, stirring till chocolate is melted. Stir in the walnuts. Spread mixture in the prepared pan. Chill till firm. Cut into squares. Store in refrigerator. Makes 3 pounds.

BUTTERSCOTCH-PEANUT FUDGE

1 12-ounce package (2 cups) butterscotch pieces
1 14-ounce can (1¼ cups) Eagle Brand sweetened condensed milk
1½ cups tiny marshmallows
⅔ cup chunk-style peanut butter
1 teaspoon vanilla
1 cup chopped peanuts

Butter a 9x9x2-inch baking pan. In a saucepan combine the butterscotch pieces, sweetened condensed milk, and marshmallows. Cook and stir over medium heat till the marshmallows melt. Remove from heat; beat in peanut butter and vanilla. Stir in the chopped peanuts. Turn into the prepared pan. Cover; chill till firm. Cut into squares. Store in the refrigerator. Makes about 2½ pounds.

CHRISTMAS JELLY CANDY

5 envelopes unflavored gelatin
½ cup sugar
2 cups desired fruit juice, fruit nectar, *or* fruit drink (such as cranberry, grape, orange, or apricot)
2 tablespoons lemon juice

In a medium saucepan combine the unflavored gelatin and sugar. Add the fruit juice, fruit nectar, or fruit drink; let stand for 5 minutes. Bring mixture to boiling; reduce heat. Cook and stir till gelatin dissolves. Add lemon juice. Pour into shallow baking pans or paper bake cups. Chill till firm. (If desired, loosen sides. Carefully turn out of pans, using a wide spatula. Cut with cookie cutters. Place on a wire rack to dry.) Cover pans or store cutouts in single layers between waxed paper in airtight containers up to 5 days. Makes 24 (1½-inch) pieces.

CHURCH-WINDOW CANDY

1 6-ounce package
    (1 cup) semisweet
    chocolate pieces
¼ cup butter *or* margarine
3 cups assorted-flavored
    tiny marshmallows
¾ cup chopped pecans *or*
    walnuts

In a saucepan combine the chocolate pieces and the butter or margarine. Cook and stir over low heat till melted. Remove from heat; cool. Stir in marshmallows and ¼ *cup* of the pecans or walnuts. Divide the mixture in half. Shape each half into a 6-inch-long roll; roll each in the remaining pecans or walnuts. Wrap in waxed paper or clear plastic wrap; chill thoroughly. Cut into ½-inch-thick slices. Store, covered, in the refrigerator. Makes 24 pieces.

PEANUT BUTTER-DATE COOKIES

These cookies need no flour—

1 slightly beaten egg
½ cup sugar
½ cup packed brown sugar
1 cup peanut butter
½ cup pitted whole dates,
    snipped

Combine egg, sugar, and brown sugar. Add peanut butter, stirring well. Stir in dates. Shape into 1-inch balls. Place 2 inches apart on an ungreased cookie sheet. Make crisscross markings with a fork. Bake in a 350° oven for 10 to 12 minutes. Cool 2 minutes; remove to wire rack. Makes 24 cookies.

PUDDIN' HEAD GINGERBREAD MEN

1½ cups all-purpose flour
½ teaspoon baking soda
1½ teaspoons ground ginger
½ teaspoon ground
    cinnamon
½ cup butter *or* margarine
½ cup packed brown sugar
1 package 4-serving-size
    regular butterscotch
    pudding mix
1 egg
2 cups sifted powdered
    sugar
3 tablespoons milk
    Decorative candies

Stir together the flour, baking soda, ginger, and cinnamon. In a mixer bowl beat the butter or margarine on medium speed of electric mixer for 30 seconds. Add the brown sugar and beat till fluffy. Add the butterscotch pudding mix and egg; beat well. Add the dry ingredients to the beaten mixture; beat till well combined. Cover and chill thoroughly.

Divide the dough in half. Working with half of the dough at a time, on a lightly floured surface, roll to ⅛-inch thickness. Cut with a 4-inch-long gingerbread man cutter. Place 2 inches apart on an ungreased cookie sheet. Bake in a 350° oven for 8 to 10 minutes or till done. Remove to a wire rack; cool completely.

For the frosting, combine the powdered sugar, milk, and enough water to make of spreading consistency (about 1 tablespoon). Frost the gingerbread men or use a pastry tube to pipe on the frosting. Decorate with decorative candies. Makes about 30 cookies.

NO-COOK MINT PATTIES

⅓ cup light corn syrup
¼ cup butter *or* margarine,
    softened
1 teaspoon peppermint
    extract
4 cups sifted powdered
    sugar
2 drops red food coloring
2 drops green food coloring

In a small mixer bowl combine the light corn syrup, butter or margarine, and peppermint extract; beat till well combined.

Gradually add *2 cups* of the powdered sugar, beating well. Stir in as much of the remaining powdered sugar as you can mix in with a spoon. Turn out onto a surface lightly coated with a little powdered sugar. Knead in enough of the remaining powdered sugar to make a stiff dough that is smooth.

Divide dough into thirds. Using one-third of the dough, knead in the red food coloring till evenly distributed. Knead the green food coloring into another third of the dough. (Leave the remaining dough white.) Shape the dough into ¾-inch balls; place 2 inches apart on baking sheets lined with waxed paper. Press with tines of a fork. If necessary, dip the fork in powdered sugar to prevent sticking. Let dry several hours. Makes about 75 mints.

No-Cook Mint Patties, Puddin' Head Gingerbread Men, and Church-Window Candy

COCOA KISSES

2 teaspoons instant coffee
  crystals (optional)
1 teaspoon hot water
  (optional)
1 cup sugar
¼ cup unsweetened cocoa
  powder
2 tablespoons all-purpose
  flour
4 egg whites
¼ teaspoon cream of tartar
1 21-ounce can cherry pie
  filling

Grease a cookie sheet; set
aside. If using the instant coffee
crystals, dissolve in the hot water. In a small bowl stir together *¼ cup* of the sugar, the
unsweetened cocoa powder,
and flour; set mixture aside.

In a small mixer bowl combine the egg whites, cream of
tartar, and the coffee-water
mixture, if desired. Beat on
high speed of electric mixer till
soft peaks form (tips curl over).
Gradually beat in the remaining sugar, beating till stiff peaks
form (tips stand straight). Fold
in the cocoa mixture.

Spoon mixture into a pastry
bag fitted with a large star tip.
Pipe the mixture into rosettes
or desired shapes, about 1½
inches in diameter, onto
greased cookie sheet. With the
back of a small spoon, make an
indentation in the center of
each. Bake in a 325° oven for
15 to 20 minutes or till done.
Remove cookies to a wire rack;
cool completely.

To serve, place a cherry from
the cherry pie filling in the indentation of each cookie.
Makes about 48 cookies.

HONEY FRUITCAKE COOKIES

1½ cups whole wheat flour
1 cup all-purpose flour
1 teaspoon baking powder
1½ teaspoons ground
  cinnamon
½ teaspoon ground ginger
½ teaspoon ground nutmeg
¼ teaspoon baking soda
¼ teaspoon salt
½ cup butter *or* margarine
½ cup sugar
½ cup honey
2 eggs
1 teaspoon vanilla
¼ cup milk
1 8-ounce package
  pitted whole
  dates, quartered
1 cup candied cherries,
  halved
1 cup broken pecans
  Pecan halves *or* candied
  cherries (optional)

Stir together the whole wheat
flour, all-purpose flour, baking
powder, cinnamon, ginger, nutmeg, baking soda, and salt.

In a mixer bowl beat butter
or margarine on medium speed
of electric mixer for 30 seconds. Add the sugar and honey; beat till well combined.
Add the eggs and vanilla; beat
well. Add the dry ingredients
and milk alternately to the beat-
en mixture; beat well. Fold in
the dates, 1 cup candied cherries, and 1 cup pecans.

Drop from a teaspoon 2
inches apart onto an ungreased
cookie sheet. Top each cookie
with a pecan half or candied
cherry, if desired. Bake in a
375° oven for 8 to 10 minutes
or till done. Remove from
cookie sheet to wire rack; cool
completely. Makes 48 cookies.

GINGERBREAD DOUGH

*Use this spicy dough, Vanilla Dough,
or Chocolate Dough to make Teddy
Bears, Funny Faces, and Angels—*

1 cup butter *or* margarine
⅔ cup packed brown sugar
⅔ cup dark corn syrup
  or molasses
1½ teaspoons vanilla
1 beaten egg
4 cups all-purpose flour
¾ teaspoon baking soda
1½ teaspoons ground
  cinnamon
1 teaspoon ground ginger
½ teaspoon ground cloves

In a saucepan combine the butter or margarine, brown sugar,
and dark corn syrup or molasses. Cook and stir over medium
heat till butter or margarine is
melted and sugar dissolves. Remove from heat; pour the butter mixture into a mixing bowl.
Stir in the vanilla. Cool for 5
minutes. Add the egg; beat
well. Stir together the flour,
soda, cinnamon, ginger, and
cloves; add to the beaten mixture; mix well. Divide the
dough in half. Cover and chill
for 2 hours or overnight.

VANILLA DOUGH: Pre-
pare Gingerbread Dough as
above *except* for the brown sugar substitute ⅔ cup *granulated
sugar* and for the dark corn syrup or molasses substitute ⅔ cup
light corn syrup. Omit cinnamon,
ginger, and cloves. Continue as
directed.

CHOCOLATE DOUGH:
Prepare Gingerbread Dough as
above *except* for the brown sugar substitute ⅔ cup *granulated
sugar;* reduce butter or margarine to ⅔ *cup;* and melt 2
squares (2 ounces) *unsweetened
chocolate* with the butter mixture.
Omit cinnamon, ginger, and
cloves. Continue as directed.

TEDDY BEARS, FUNNY FACES, AND ANGELS

Gingerbread Dough,
Vanilla Dough, *or*
Chocolate Dough
(see recipes at left)
1 beaten egg yolk
1 tablespoon water
Several drops red food
coloring
Sifted powdered sugar
Milk *or* light cream
Blue food coloring

Prepare the desired dough; chill for 2 hours or overnight. Working with half of the dough at a time, on a lightly floured surface roll to ⅛-inch thickness. Cut and trim as directed for Teddy Bears, Funny Faces, and Angels. Place 2 inches apart on ungreased cookie sheets. (Make a small hole at top of cookies if they are to be used as tree ornaments.) Brush the facial or body features of cookies with a mixture of egg yolk mixed with the water and red food coloring, using a fine paintbrush. Bake in a 350° oven for 8 to 10 minutes or till light brown. (Thick cookies such as Teddy Bears may require longer baking time.) Remove from cookie sheet; cool on a wire rack.

For the icing, combine powdered sugar and enough milk or light cream to make of piping consistency. Tint *half* the icing with blue food coloring. Use blue and white icing in pastry bags fitted with decorative tips to decorate cookies.

To shape Teddy Bears: For each of the cookies, shape dough into 1 large ball (body), 5 medium-size balls (head, arms, and legs), 3 small balls (nose and ears), and 4 tiny balls (paws). On an ungreased cookie sheet flatten the large ball slightly for body. Attach the medium-size balls for the head, arms, and legs. Place the small balls on the head for nose and ears. With a wooden pick, draw eyes and a mouth. Arrange the tiny balls atop the ends of legs and arms for paws; trace a circle around each.

To shape Funny Faces: Cut dough with 2½- or 3-inch-round cookie cutter. For nose, cheeks, mouth, and hair, use scraps of dough. For the nose, shape a narrow strip of dough into a ½-inch-long nose; place dough in center of cookie. For the eyes, with tip of finger make indentations on both sides of nose. For the cheeks, roll small pieces of dough into balls and place below eyes. For the mouth, roll a thin strip of dough; arrange dough under nose to form a smile or frown. For the hair, fill a garlic press with dough. Squeeze out the dough; cut off with a sharp knife. Starting at top of cookie, press dough strands onto outer edge. Repeat pressing and cutting till desired amount of hair is obtained.

To shape Angels: Roll dough to ⅛-inch thickness. For each cookie, cut a 2½-inch rectangle; place each on an ungreased cookie sheet. For wings, cut out a 2-inch circle; cut the circle in half and attach to long sides of rectangle as wings. For head, attach a ¾-inch ball. Use a garlic press, as directed for Funny Faces, to create hair. Attach strands of dough to head for hair. Place 2 small balls of dough to bottom of body for feet. Place one small ball of dough in center of body for button. For eyes and nose, make an indentation with finger. Place tiny balls of dough on face for cheeks.

*B*aking cookies is a sure-fire way to boost your holiday spirit. This year, make a colorful assortment of fun-shaped cookies like Teddy Bears, Funny Faces, and Angels. You don't have to use special cookie cutters. Simply let the creative little fingers at your house shape and decorate these adorable creatures.

227

FOUR-GRAIN COOKIES

½ cup whole bran cereal
½ cup milk
½ cup all-purpose flour
½ cup whole wheat flour
½ cup quick-cooking
    rolled oats
½ cup Grape Nuts cereal
1 teaspoon baking powder
¼ teaspoon baking soda
¼ teaspoon salt
½ cup packed brown sugar
½ cup cooking oil
2 tablespoons molasses
½ teaspoon vanilla
1 egg
¼ cup peanut butter
½ cup raisins

In a mixing bowl combine the bran cereal and the milk; let stand for 5 minutes. Stir together the all-purpose flour, whole wheat flour, oats, Grape Nuts cereal, baking powder, soda, and salt.

In a large mixing bowl combine the brown sugar, cooking oil, molasses, and vanilla; beat well. Add the bran-milk mixture, the egg, and the peanut butter; beat till smooth. Add the dry ingredients to the beaten mixture and beat till well combined. Stir in the raisins. Drop from a tablespoon 2 inches apart onto an ungreased cookie sheet.

Bake in a 350° oven about 10 minutes or till done. Remove from cookie sheet to wire rack; cool completely. Makes 42 cookies.

ALMOND PINECONES

1 cup butter *or* margarine
2 3-ounce packages cream
    cheese, softened
½ cup sugar
1 egg
1 teaspoon finely shredded
    lemon peel
½ teaspoon almond extract
2 cups all-purpose flour
    Sliced almonds *or*
    blanched whole
    almonds
    Light corn syrup
    Sugar

In a large mixer bowl combine the butter or margarine and cream cheese; beat on medium speed of electric mixer for 30 seconds. Add the ½ cup sugar; beat till fluffy. Add the egg, finely shredded lemon peel, and almond extract; beat well. Add the flour; mix well. Cover and chill about 3 hours.

Divide dough in half. On a well-floured surface, roll *each* portion to ⅛-inch thickness. Cut with a 2½- to 3½-inch oval or round cookie cutter with fluted edge; place 2 inches apart on an ungreased cookie sheet. Arrange the sliced almonds or blanched whole almonds atop the cookies, overlapping them to resemble pinecones and lightly brushing the almonds with light corn syrup as each is placed. Brush the almonds with additional light corn syrup. Sprinkle lightly with sugar.

Bake in a 325° oven for 13 to 15 minutes or till done. Remove from cookie sheet to wire rack; cool completely. Makes 48 cookies.

CHEWY RAISIN-APRICOT COOKIES

¾ cup whole wheat flour
¼ cup wheat germ
¼ cup nonfat dry milk
    powder
¾ teaspoon salt
¼ teaspoon baking powder
¼ teaspoon baking soda
¾ cup honey
½ cup butter *or* margarine
½ cup peanut butter
1 egg
1 teaspoon vanilla
1 cup raisins
1 cup dried apricots,
    snipped
¾ cup quick-cooking rolled
    oats
½ cup chopped walnuts
⅓ cup sunflower nuts
⅓ cup coconut

In a bowl stir together the flour, wheat germ, nonfat dry milk powder, salt, baking powder, and baking soda.

In a large mixer bowl combine honey, butter or margarine, and peanut butter; beat on medium speed of electric mixer for 30 seconds. Add egg and vanilla; beat well. Add the dry ingredients to the beaten mixture and beat till well combined. Add the raisins, apricots, oats, chopped walnuts, sunflower nuts, and coconut; mix well. Drop dough from a teaspoon 2 inches apart onto an ungreased cookie sheet.

Bake in a 350° oven for 10 to 11 minutes or till done. Cool about 1 minute; remove to a wire rack. Cool completely. Makes about 60 cookies.

BROWN SUGAR-ALMOND BARS

½ cup butter *or* margarine
½ cup sifted powdered
   sugar
1 cup all-purpose flour
3 tablespoons butter *or*
   margarine
½ cup packed brown sugar
1 tablespoon water
1 teaspoon lemon juice
¾ cup sliced almonds
½ teaspoon vanilla

In a small mixer bowl beat the
½ cup butter or margarine on
medium speed of electric mixer
for 30 seconds. Add the sifted
powdered sugar and beat till
fluffy. Add the flour and beat
well. Press the beaten mixture
evenly in an ungreased 9x9x2-
inch baking pan. Bake in a
350° oven for 12 to 15 minutes
or till light brown.

In a small saucepan melt the
3 tablespoons butter or margarine. Add the brown sugar, the
water, and the lemon juice;
bring mixture to boiling, stirring constantly. Remove from
heat and stir in the sliced almonds and the vanilla. Spread
the almond mixture over the
baked layer.

Bake in a 350° oven for 15
to 20 minutes or till done. Cut
into bars while warm. Cool
completely in pan on a wire
rack. Makes 24 bars.

OATMEAL CHRISTMAS ROUNDS

*Chilling the cookie dough makes it
easier to shape into 1-inch balls—*

2 cups all-purpose flour
1 teaspoon ground
   cinnamon
½ teaspoon baking soda
½ teaspoon salt
1 cup butter *or* margarine
1 cup packed brown sugar
1 egg
2 tablespoons milk
½ teaspoon vanilla
1½ cups quick-cooking
   rolled oats
   Red *or* green candied
   cherries, halved

In a bowl stir together the
flour, ground cinnamon, baking
soda, and salt. In a mixer bowl
beat the butter or margarine on
medium speed of electric mixer
for 30 seconds. Add the brown
sugar and beat till fluffy. Add
the egg, the milk, and vanilla;
beat well. Add the dry ingredients to the beaten mixture and
beat till well combined. Stir in
the rolled oats. Cover and chill
thoroughly.

Shape into 1-inch balls. Place
2 inches apart on an ungreased
cookie sheet. Press a red or
green candied cherry half atop
each cookie.

Bake in a 375° oven for 8 to
10 minutes or till done. Cool
about 1 minute; remove to
a wire rack. Cool completely.
Makes about 60 cookies.

ROOT BEER POPCORN BALLS

14 cups popped popcorn
   (about ⅔ cup
   unpopped)
1 cup peanuts
   Butter *or* margarine
1 cup sugar
1 cup water
½ cup light corn syrup
¼ cup butter *or* margarine
¼ teaspoon salt
1 teaspoon root beer extract

Remove all unpopped kernels
from the popped popcorn. Put
the popcorn and the peanuts in
a large roasting pan; keep
warm in a 300° oven.

Butter the sides of a medium
saucepan. In saucepan combine
the sugar, water, light corn syrup, the ¼ cup butter or margarine, and the salt. Cook to 238°
(soft-ball stage), stirring frequently. (The sugar mixture
should boil gently over the entire surface.)

Remove from heat; stir in
the root beer extract. Slowly
pour the sugar mixture over
the heated popcorn mixture.
Stir just till mixed. Cool about
5 minutes or till easily handled.

Butter hands lightly; using a
buttered cup, scoop up the popcorn mixture. Shape with buttered hands into 3-inch balls.
Wrap each ball in clear plastic
wrap. Makes about 12 balls.

CANDY CANE BREAD

2 cups all-purpose flour
¼ cup packed brown sugar
2 teaspoons baking powder
½ teaspoon salt
½ cup butter *or* margarine
¼ cup chopped peanuts
1 beaten egg
½ cup milk
　　Powdered Sugar Icing
　　Red and green decorator
　　　icing (optional)
　　Red cinnamon candies
　　　(optional)

Grease a baking sheet; set aside. Stir together the flour, brown sugar, baking powder, and salt. Cut in the butter or margarine till the mixture resembles coarse crumbs. Add the peanuts. Combine the egg and the milk. Stir into the flour mixture just till moistened.

On a lightly floured surface pat the dough into a 10x7-inch rectangle. Cut crosswise into 1-inch-wide strips. Twist each strip by holding both ends. Bend one end to form a candy cane. Place several inches apart on the greased baking sheet.

Bake in a 425° oven for 10 minutes or till light brown. Carefully remove to a wire rack; cool. Frost the candy canes with the Powdered Sugar Icing. If desired, decorate frosted candy canes with red and green decorator icing and cinnamon candies. Makes 10 candy canes.

POWDERED SUGAR ICING: In a small mixing bowl combine 2 cups sifted *powdered sugar* and enough *milk* to make of drizzling consistency (about 3 tablespoons).

THUMBPRINT SWEET ROLLS

1 13¾-ounce package hot
　roll mix
2 tablespoons sugar
¾ cup orange juice
1 egg
　　All-purpose flour
1 cup chopped mixed dried
　fruit
1¼ cups water
¼ cup chopped walnuts
3 tablespoons sugar
1½ teaspoons butter *or*
　margarine
¼ teaspoon ground nutmeg
1 cup sifted powdered
　sugar
¼ teaspoon vanilla
　Milk

Grease a baking sheet; set aside. Set aside yeast packet from hot roll mix. In a mixing bowl combine remaining mix and the 2 tablespoons sugar. In a small saucepan heat orange juice till warm (115° to 120°). Remove from heat. Sprinkle the yeast from the hot roll mix over orange juice; stir to dissolve yeast. Stir into the flour mixture. Add egg and stir till well combined. Cover with clear plastic wrap. Let rise till double (30 to 45 minutes).

Punch down. Turn out onto a lightly floured surface. Knead for 1 to 2 minutes or till dough is smooth and no longer sticky. Add additional flour, if needed.

Divide dough in half. Divide each half into 8 pieces. Shape the pieces into balls. Place 3 inches apart on baking sheet. Press each ball into a 3-inch circle. Cover; let rise till double (30 to 45 minutes).

For filling, in a saucepan combine dried fruit and water. Heat to boiling. Reduce heat; simmer, uncovered, for 10 minutes. Remove from heat; drain.

Return fruit to saucepan. Stir in walnuts, 3 tablespoons sugar, butter, and nutmeg.

With your thumb, press a hole in the center of each roll. Spoon about *1 tablespoon* of the fruit filling into *each* hole. Bake in a 375° oven for 10 to 12 minutes or till golden. Remove to a wire rack.

For the icing, stir together the powdered sugar and vanilla. Stir in enough milk (about 1½ tablespoons) to make of drizzling consistency; drizzle over warm rolls. Makes 16.

PEPPERMINT BONBONS

1 pound vanilla-flavored
　confectioner's coating
½ cup whipping cream
1¼ teaspoons peppermint
　extract
　Striped round
　　peppermint candies,
　　crushed (2 ounces)

In a small heavy saucepan melt the vanilla-flavored confectioner's coating over low heat, stirring often. Turn into a mixer bowl. Add the whipping cream and peppermint extract. Beat on high speed of electric mixer till smooth. Chill in the freezer for 20 to 30 minutes or just till the candy mixture is stiff enough to be shaped. Shape into balls, using 2 teaspoons of the candy mixture for each. Roll in the crushed peppermint candies. Store in the refrigerator. Makes 3½ dozen.

FRUIT 'N' GRANOLA PARFAITS

Eat the granola alone or team it with your favorite fruit in a parfait glass—

- 2 cups quick-cooking rolled oats
- ⅔ cup shredded coconut
- ½ cup toasted wheat germ
- ½ cup peanuts
- ¼ cup cooking oil
- ¼ cup honey
- ¼ cup water
- ¼ teaspoon ground allspice
- ⅔ cup raisins
  Desired fresh fruit, such as pineapple chunks, grapes, sliced bananas, apples, *or* pears
  Whipped cream *or* fruit-flavored yogurt (optional)

In a mixing bowl combine the oats, coconut, toasted wheat germ, and peanuts; set aside.

In a screw-top jar combine the cooking oil, honey, water, and allspice. Cover and shake to mix well; stir into the oat mixture. Spread out evenly in a 15x10x1-inch shallow baking pan. Bake in a 300° oven about 25 minutes or till light brown, stirring twice. Remove from oven; cool on a wire rack. Stir in the raisins.

To make a parfait, spoon alternate layers of the granola and the desired fresh fruit into a parfait glass, layering twice. If desired, dollop with whipped cream or yogurt. Store granola in tightly covered jars or plastic bags. Makes 4 cups granola.

PEANUT BUTTER AND JELLY PARFAITS

- 1 1½-ounce envelope dessert topping mix
- 1 3-ounce package cream cheese, softened
- ¼ cup peanut butter
- 1 tablespoon milk
- ¼ cup chopped peanuts
- ¼ cup jelly

Prepare the dessert topping mix according to package directions. In a small mixing bowl combine cream cheese, peanut butter, and milk; beat till creamy. Stir in the chopped peanuts. Fold in *half* of the dessert topping mix. Spoon alternate layers of the peanut mixture and the remaining dessert topping into 4 parfait glasses, layering twice. Cover and chill. At serving time, spoon *1 tablespoon* of the jelly atop *each* parfait. Makes 4 parfaits.

CHUNKY PEANUT BUTTER SPREAD

- 1 4-ounce container soft-style cream cheese
- ½ cup chunk-style peanut butter
- 2 tablespoons milk
- 1 tablespoon honey
- ½ cup finely snipped raisins *or* dried apricots
  Assorted crackers

In a small mixing bowl stir together the cream cheese and the peanut butter. Add the milk and honey; stir till well combined. Stir in the raisins or dried apricots. Cover and chill. Serve with assorted crackers. Makes 1½ cups.

BERRY FROSTY SHAKE

- 1 8-ounce carton strawberry yogurt
- 1 cup milk
- 1 cup fresh *or* frozen strawberries
- 1 egg
- 2 teaspoons sugar
- ¼ teaspoon vanilla
- 2 to 3 ice cubes

In a blender container combine the yogurt, milk, strawberries, egg, sugar, and vanilla. Cover and blend till smooth. With lid slightly ajar, add ice cubes, one at a time, while blending; blend till smooth. Pour into tall glasses. Makes 4 (6-ounce) servings.

CRUNCHY MARSHMALLOW BALLS

Pictured on page 220—

- 6 1¹⁄₁₆-ounce bars chocolate-coated English toffee, broken up
- 1 14-ounce can (1¼ cups) Eagle Brand sweetened condensed milk
- ½ cup butter *or* margarine
- 24 marshmallows
- 2 cups crisp rice cereal, coarsely crushed

In a saucepan combine toffee, sweetened condensed milk, and butter. Cook over medium-low heat, stirring frequently, about 25 minutes or till toffee melts. Cool slightly.

Roll marshmallows in the toffee mixture, then in cereal. Arrange on a baking sheet. Store in refrigerator. Makes 24.

BABY'S FIRST CHRISTMAS

*T*he first Christmas with a new baby is always excit-ing—for children and grown-ups alike. To celebrate this memorable event, plan a family get-together, like the one above, to make child-oriented trims for your home. Then needlepoint a colorful snowman stocking, top, for the newest family member.

*T*his holiday workshop begins with a group of hand-print wrapping papers, above and opposite, and Christmas drawings made by your children. The drawings form the master patterns for ornaments, puppets, dolls, and pillows, opposite and above. You can even turn a child's interpretation of the Christmas story into a soft-sculpture Nativity scene, below.

Enlarge or reduce drawings to a suitable size, then cut matching shapes from colorful fabrics and attach them with fusible webbing to felt or fabric backgrounds. Outlines of machine embroidery add the details.

BABY'S FIRST CHRISTMAS

***P**urchased name tapes and made-to-order rubber stamps are the focal points of the spirited ornaments, trims, and package wraps, below. Calico scraps, ribbons, and embroidered trims add the color.*

*O*rdinary muslin that's been stamped with a newborn's name forms the fabric for the bunting, above. Leftover bits of colorful trims personalize a toddler's overalls, right, and embellish a generously sized stocking, below.

*N*ame tapes (available from mail order supply houses) double as ribbon on the calico ornaments, above. The drawstring gift bags also sport the tapes, creatively wrapping hard-to-disguise gifts for the whole family.

BABY'S FIRST CHRISTMAS

*T*he charming name tags (or tree ornaments), left, are designed with little folks in mind. Because they're worked on perforated paper, you can just cut out the shapes when the stitching is done.

Additional cross-stitched motifs are used on baby's knitted bunting, opposite. The pair of dolls features yarn bodies and easy-to-stitch clothing. And the baby afghan, made with a simple shell stitch, works up in a hurry.

*T*he paper doll cards and wall plaque, above, and the painted wooden blocks, right, are thoughtful yet quick-to-make projects.

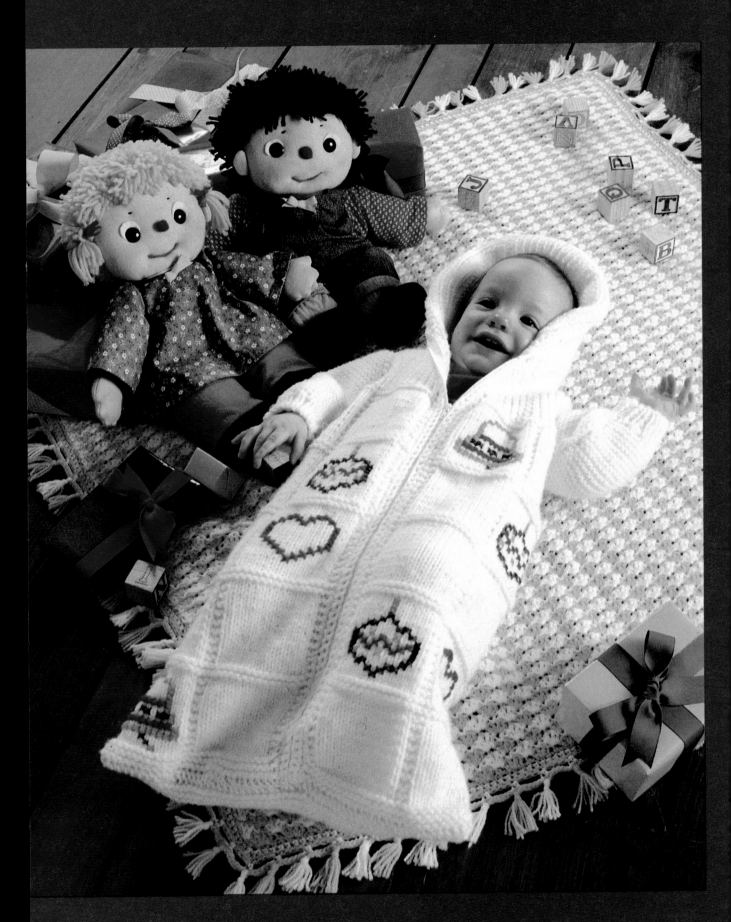

Snowman Stocking
Pictured on page 232

MATERIALS: 16x22 inches *each* 10-count needlepoint canvas and backing fabric; 32-inch strands of 5-ply Persian yarn in these amounts and colors: 10 dark red, 18 light red, 10 dark green, 20 light green, 10 dark blue, 25 light blue, 10 light orange, 3 yellow; 32-inch strands of 3-ply yarn in these amounts and colors: 50 white, 12 black, 4 yellow, 1 pink, 15 dark orange.

INSTRUCTIONS: Using mosaic stitches and three plies of yarn, work the pattern, *below.* Leave 2 inches of unworked canvas around the design. Block finished needlepoint by steam-pressing with a warm iron on the wrong side.

Trim excess canvas ½ inch beyond the needlepoint. Cut back to match front. With right sides facing, sew back to front. Turn, press, and sew 2-inch-wide facing to stocking top; turn to inside. Embellish side seam with twisted cord made of remaining red yarn.

Children's Projects
Pictured on pages 232-233

Original children's drawings are the basis of the projects shown (except wrapping paper). To make similar projects, use your own children's pictures drawn especially for ornaments and decorations, artwork brought from school, or sketches drawn for fun. Also, you may spot an object or two in a drawing that would make a wonderful doll, toy, or decoration all by itself. Directions for turning artwork into decorations and gifts follow.

Here are some tips to help guide your children in drawing designs:
• Provide crayons or felt pens. Suggest that kids use black for outlines and colors for filling shapes, so designs may be interpreted in fabric.
• For these projects, simple shapes are best—hearts, stars, trees, candy canes, and snowmen, for example.
• Enlarging designs simplifies shapes and produces bold, dramatic results. If drawings are small, make them larger by using a grid similar to grids on patterns in this book. If necessary, eliminate small details or execute them in embroidery. Make tissue paper patterns from drawings.
• *To make ornaments,* ask youngsters to draw simple tree ornaments for you to execute in fabric. Have the kids make several drawings of each shape, then choose ones that can be worked easily in cut fabrics.

For each ornament, cut the background shape from black felt. Cut inner colored shapes from fabric scraps. Trim the edges of the colored shapes so black felt will show, giving the impression of black lines. Using fusible webbing, iron colored shapes onto back and front of felt.

Add facial features and other details using permanent felt-tip pens.
• *To make dolls and toys,* choose simple shapes without too many difficult projections. You may need to alter the youngster's drawing slightly to make it work in fabric.

Enlarge and simplify the drawing, if necessary, then transfer outlines to fabric that is the same basic color as the doll front. Cut out and fuse appliqués to doll front, then machine-satin-stitch around appliqués.

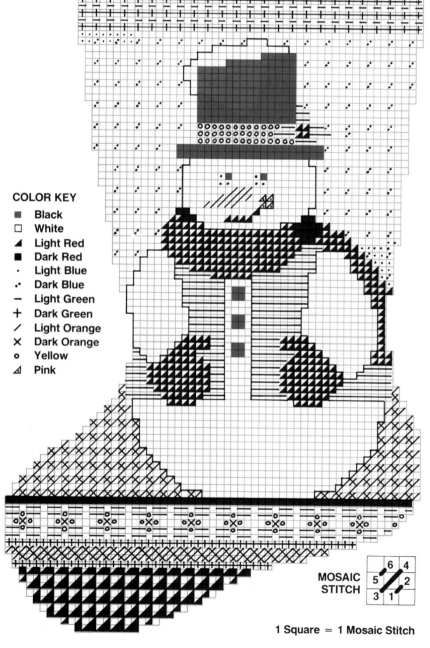

COLOR KEY
- ■ Black
- □ White
- ◢ Light Red
- ■ Dark Red
- · Light Blue
- ·· Dark Blue
- — Light Green
- + Dark Green
- / Light Orange
- × Dark Orange
- ○ Yellow
- ◿ Pink

MOSAIC STITCH

```
  6 4
5     2
  3 1
```

1 Square = 1 Mosaic Stitch

Embroider details. Cut out doll and satin-stitch to felt backing, leaving an opening wherever needed for stuffing. Stuff; satin-stitch openings closed. Trim felt backing, leaving ¼-inch edge bordering toy.

• *For a crèche,* make quilted pillows by tracing outlines of drawing onto muslin. Using the original drawing as a guide for colors and details, re-create the picture in your favorite needlework techniques, such as appliqué, embroidery, and quilting. Cut a muslin back to match the front; sew sides and top of front to back (leave the bottom open). Cut an oval of fabric for the bottom of each piece; stitch in place, leaving an opening. Turn; stuff firmly and close opening.

Handprint Gift Wrap
Pictured on pages 232-233

MATERIALS: Powdered tempera paints in colors of your choice; cake pan; white butcher paper.

INSTRUCTIONS: Mix tempera paints with water to the consistency of heavy cream. Pour a small amount into the cake pan; swirl to leave a thin film on the bottom of the pan.

Lay your child's hand flat in the pan to pick up paint, then lay hand flat on paper to print. Make random prints on paper.

Name Stamp Projects
Pictured on pages 234-235

MATERIALS: Shelf paper (gift wrap) and muslin (ornaments, dolls, and baby bunting) in sufficient quantity for the project you wish to make; fiberfill (dolls); rubber name stamps (available from stationery stores or mail order suppliers) in assorted sizes; foam stamp pads; stamp pad inks in colors of your choice.

• *For bunting:* Quilt batting; 2 yards flannel (lining); blanket binding; 18-inch-long zipper; 20 inches of ½-inch-wide elastic.

Note: Use nontoxic inks and paints on projects for children.

INSTRUCTIONS: To print fabric or paper, cover the work surface with newspaper or paper toweling. Lay fabric or paper on top and print with the desired stamp. (Practice on scrap fabric or paper first so you know how much ink to use.) Print in straight rows, using a ruler as a guide; create designs by varying the direction or color of the stamp.

After the ink is dry, press fabric with a warm iron to set colors. Then complete your project.

• *Ornaments and dolls:* Enlarge the pattern, *below.* For dolls, use a scale of 1 square equals ¾ inch (6-inch doll), 1½ inches (12-inch doll), or 2¼ inches (18-inch doll). Trace pattern front and back onto muslin, adding ½-inch seam allowances.

Print names on right side of fabric, *opposite* the penciled outline.

Cut out pattern pieces, pin fronts to backs (printed sides facing), and sew around outlines. Leave an opening for turning. Clip curves, trim seams, turn, and stuff. Slip-stitch openings closed. Embellish ornaments or dolls with bows, buttons, or trims of your choice.

• *For baby bunting:* Baste 1¼ yards of unbleached muslin to a matching piece of quilt batting. Machine-quilt in 5-inch-square diamonds; stamp baby's name in centers of diamonds.

Enlarge pattern, *right;* cut pieces from fabrics. Cut a 3x42-inch piece of flannel for hood casing. With wrong sides facing, fold casing in

half lengthwise; press. Pin and stitch casing to top of prequilted fabric (leaving ends open) to form hood. Insert elastic and secure the ends.

Stitch zipper to front of bunting. With right sides facing, sew bunting to lining; leave center front open. Trim seams and turn. Slip-stitch lining to center front.

With right sides facing, sew the two bottom pieces together, leaving an opening for turning. Trim seams and turn. With right sides facing, pin and stitch the bottom piece to the bunting, easing the corners.

Name Tape Projects
Pictured on pages 234-235

MATERIALS: Name tapes (purchased from mail order suppliers) imprinted with names or holiday greetings; embroidered trims; *continued*

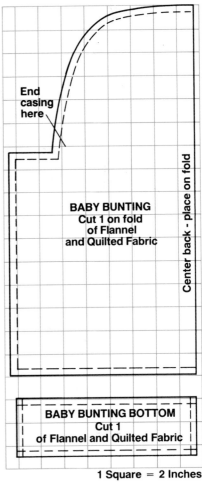

End casing here

BABY BUNTING Cut 1 on fold of Flannel and Quilted Fabric

Center back - place on fold

BABY BUNTING BOTTOM Cut 1 of Flannel and Quilted Fabric

1 Square = 2 Inches

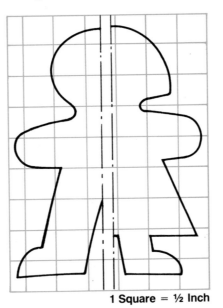

1 Square = ½ Inch

239

ribbons; purchased appliqués; fusible webbing; child's overalls; ½ yard *each* of green wool and muslin (stocking); fabric scraps (gift bags, ornaments); plastic foam balls, pins, fabric glue, and wire (ornaments).

INSTRUCTIONS: For overalls, pin, baste, and then hand- or machine-appliqué lengths of name tape, ribbon, and embroidered trims to the straps, seam lines, and bib of a child's overalls.

Appliqué letters of the child's name to the front bib pocket.

• *For personalized stocking,* design your own stocking pattern or use one of the patterns in this book. Cut stocking front and back from wool, adding ¼-inch seam allowances.

Appliqué bands of embroidered trim, ribbon, and name tapes across calf and toe sections of stocking. Sew a purchased star appliqué or other motif to the center of the heel; frame with bands of embroidered trim to define the heel.

Sew stocking front to back. Trim seams, clip curves, turn, and press. From muslin, cut stocking lining. Stitch and insert in stocking; slip-stitch to stocking along top.

• *For gift bags,* cut fabrics into rectangles of various sizes. Hem one long edge (top). Three inches above the remaining long edge, begin stitching rows of trim, ribbon, and name tape; or, apply trims and tapes with fusible webbing. Leave bottom 3 inches of rectangle empty.

With right sides facing, sew short sides of rectangle together. Center seam at back of bag, then stitch bottom edges together. Next, make a 1-inch gusset in each corner of the bottom of the bag to make a flat bottom. Tuck gifts into the bag and tie with name tape ribbon.

• *For personalized ornaments,* enlarge pattern, *right;* cut six shapes from calico. Appliqué shapes to 4-inch-diameter foam balls, using pins and fabric glue (adjust size of pattern for larger or smaller balls).

Cover overlaps between fabric pieces with lengths of name tapes, taking care to center name on curve of the ball. Attach bows of name tape "ribbon" to the top of each ball with straight pins and add a U-shaped loop of wire or a hairpin to the top of each ball for hanging. Glue foil stars at random on balls.

Embroidered Paper Tags and Trims
Pictured on page 236

MATERIALS: Perforated paper; embroidery floss; tapestry needle.

INSTRUCTIONS: Using the charts, *opposite, below,* and *on page 242,*

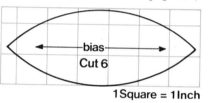

1 Square = 1 Inch

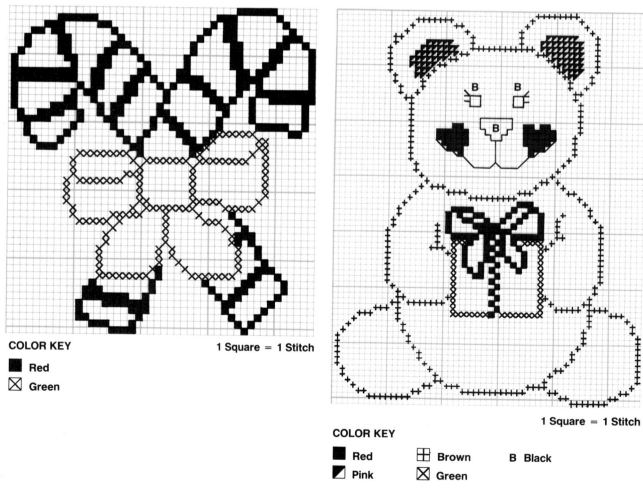

COLOR KEY   1 Square = 1 Stitch

■ Red

☒ Green

COLOR KEY

■ Red   ⊞ Brown   B Black

◸ Pink   ☒ Green

cross-stitch each design on paper using two strands of floss. Outline some areas using backstitches.

When embroidery is finished, carefully cut away excess paper from around the designs. Leave a margin equivalent to one "row" of stitches around the designs. Trims may be used as package decorations or mounted on colored card stock to use as greeting cards or ornaments.

Paper Doll Picture and Cards
Pictured on page 236

MATERIALS: 8½-inch square of tissue paper ("First Christmas" cutout); construction paper (cards); single-edge razor blades; sharp scissors; frame; foam-core board.

INSTRUCTIONS: *To make the cutout,* fold tissue square into 16ths. Using patterns *(page 243),* cut away shaded areas. Unfold circle; cut letters from center using a razor blade (see pattern, *page 243*). If baby's name is too long for the center, substitute "Baby's" for the name. Secure cutout between glass and foam-core board; frame as desired.

For cards, use pattern, *page 243,* for small sizes; enlarge pattern for larger sizes. Fold paper; cut outline plus apron or overall motifs.

Baby Blocks
Pictured on page 236

MATERIALS: Leftover scraps of ½-inch-thick plywood or pine; wood glue; primer paint; acrylic paints.

INSTRUCTIONS: For each block, cut six 5-inch squares of wood. Miter all edges, then glue edges together, making blocks.

Sand and prime blocks; paint designs using acrylics.

Yarn Dolls
Pictured on page 237

MATERIALS (for two): Three skeins pink Coats & Clark craft yarn; ¼ yard pink jersey; 1 skein *each* of brown and yellow Coats & Clark 4-ply Wintuk yarn; 7x8-inch piece *each* of brown and yellow felt; four ¾-inch black buttons; two red pompons; white, navy felt; black and red embroidery floss; fiberfill; darning needle; 13x18 inches of cardboard.
continued

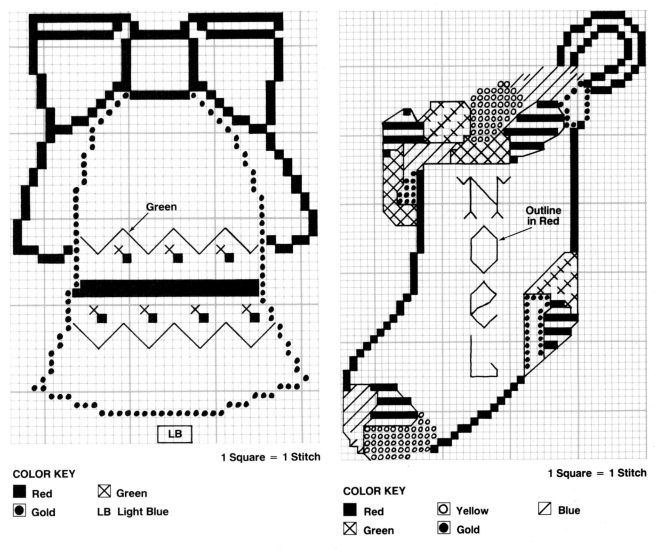

Green

1 Square = 1 Stitch

LB

COLOR KEY

■ Red   ⊠ Green

● Gold   LB Light Blue

Outline in Red

1 Square = 1 Stitch

COLOR KEY

■ Red   ◯ Yellow   ⁄ Blue

⊠ Green   ● Gold

INSTRUCTIONS: Cut eight 10-inch pieces of pink yarn; wind remainder of skein lengthwise around cardboard (body). Tie both ends with 10-inch pieces of yarn; slip yarn off card. Tie off head 4 inches from the top. Wind second pink skein widthwise around cardboard (arms). Tie the two ends and slip yarn off card. Slip arms through body; tie off at waist. Untie piece at bottom of body; divide yarn in two. Tie each with a 10-inch yarn strand.

On a 3-inch square of paper, draw a hand pattern. Cut four pink jersey hands for each doll. With right sides facing, sew two hands together using ¼-inch seams; leave wrist open. Turn; stuff. Turn raw edges under; sew hand to arm, covering yarn tie.

Cut navy blue shoes (3x3½-inch ovals); follow instructions for hands to make two. Tack center tops of shoes to legs.

Cut two 7-inch pink jersey circles (head). Sew heads together; leave neck open. Turn; slip head onto yarn. Stuff head with fiberfill to shape. Turn raw edges under; sew neck to yarn to secure head to body.

Sew button eyes in place, starting from the back and stitching through entire thickness of head. Embroider mouth and eyebrows, using red and black floss. Add a red pompon nose. Accent eyes with circles of white felt around buttons.

For hair, make wig base from 6x7-inch oval of felt. Cut several darts in front of felt piece; whipstitch edges together so felt curves to fit head.

Cut brown or yellow yarn into 3- and 4-inch pieces. Fold each piece of yarn in half; sew yarn to felt, alternating lengths. Fill felt piece with rows of yarn, spacing rows ¼ inch apart. Leave ⅜ inch of felt around edges for attaching wig to head.

Cut twelve 8-inch pieces of yellow yarn, fold each piece in half, and sew six pieces to each side of the girl doll's face. Tie the ends of the strands with red ribbon. Stitch wigs to heads; trim yarn ends if necessary.

Cut four 1x1½-inch oval pink jersey ears for each doll. Sew together, turn, and sew to head.

Make simple clothing for dolls by sewing squares and rectangles together to make shirt, skirt, pants, or vest. Bind raw edges with tape, hem, or add decorative trims.

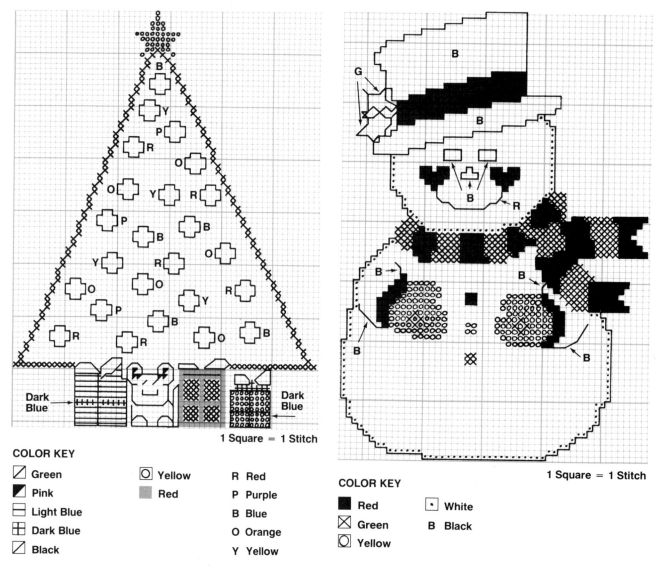

1 Square = 1 Stitch

1 Square = 1 Stitch

COLOR KEY

	Green		Yellow	R	Red
	Pink		Red	P	Purple
	Light Blue			B	Blue
	Dark Blue			O	Orange
	Black			Y	Yellow

COLOR KEY

	Red	•	White
	Green	B	Black
	Yellow		

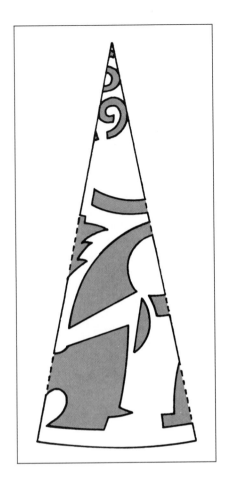

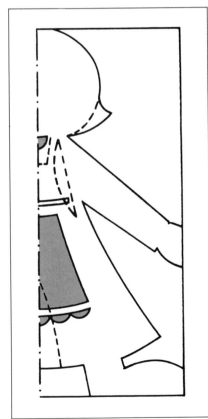

JUSTIN'S FIRST CHRISTMAS 1981

Crocheted Baby Afghan
Pictured on page 237

MATERIALS: Coats & Clark Red Heart Sport Yarn: 10 ounces *each* of No. 225 daffodil and No. 1 white; Size F aluminum crochet hook, or size to obtain gauge.

Abbreviations: Page 310.

Gauge: 5 shells = 6 inches; 3 rows = 1 inch.

INSTRUCTIONS: Beg at narrow edge with daffodil, make a 40-inch-long ch, with 5 ch sts to 1 inch.

Row 1: 2 dc in 4th ch from hook, sk next 2 ch, sc in next ch, * sk next 2 ch; *4 dc in next ch—shell made;* sk next 2 ch, sc in next ch. Rep from * 29 times more. Drop lp from hook, do not turn. Cut off rem ch.

Row 2: Join white to top of ch-3 at beg of last row worked, ch 1, sc in same place where yarn was joined, * shell in next sc, sc bet 2nd and 3rd dc on next shell. Rep from * to last sc, 2 dc in last sc, yo and draw up a lp in same st where last 2 dc were made, yo and draw through 2 lps; drop white, pick up dropped daffodil lp and draw through all lps on hook to complete last dc. With daffodil, ch 1, turn.

Row 3: Sc in first dc, * shell in next sc, sc bet 2nd and 3rd dc of next shell. Rep from * to last sc, 3 dc in last sc. Drop lp from hook; do not turn. *Row 4:* At beg of last row worked, pick up white and draw up a lp in first sc, ch 3, 2 dc in same st where yarn was drawn up, * sc bet

2nd and 3rd dc of next shell, shell in next sc. Rep from * to last 3 dc, sk next 2 dc, draw up a lp in next dc; drop white, pick up dropped daffodil lp and draw through all lps on hook to complete last sc. With daffodil, ch 3, turn.

Row 5: Make 2 dc in first sc, * sc bet 2nd and 3rd dc of next shell, shell in next sc. Rep from * to last 2 dc and ch-3, sk next 2 dc, sc in top of ch-3. Drop lp from hook, do not turn. *Row 6:* At beg of last row worked, pick up white and draw up a lp in top of ch-3, then work as for Row 2; ch 1, turn.

Rep Rows 3-6 for pat until length is about 38 inches. End with a row worked with daffodil. Fasten off.

Edging: Rnd 1: Join daffodil to any corner, ch 1, in same place where yarn was joined make sc, ch 1, and sc for corner; being careful to keep work flat, sc evenly to next corner. In corner make sc, ch 1, and sc. Work across rem edges and corners to correspond, having the same number of sc bet corners as on opposite side. The total number of sts should be divisible by 4, plus 3. Join with sl st to first sc. Fasten off.

Rnd 2: Join white to first st worked on last rnd, ch 1, sc in joining; making 3 sc in each ch-1 corner sp, sc in each sc around. Join to first sc. Fasten off. *Rnd 3:* Join daffodil to first st worked on last rnd, ch 1, sc in joining and in each sc around. Join to first sc. Fasten off.

continued

243

Rnd 4: Join white to first st worked on last rnd, ch 1, sc in joining, * ch 6, sk next 3 sc, sc in next sc. Rep from * around, ending with ch-6. Join to first sc. Fasten off.

Rnd 5: Join daffodil to any sc on last rnd, ch 1, sc in joining, * sl st in next 6 ch, sc in next sc. Rep from * around. Join to first sc. Fasten off.

Fringe: Wind daffodil 50 times around a 2½-inch square of cardboard; cut at one edge, making 5-inch strands. Make white strands in same way. Hold six strands daffodil tog and fold in half, forming a lp. Insert hook from back to front in any sc on last rnd of edging and draw lp of strands through; draw loose ends through lp on hook and pull tightly to knot. In next sc knot six strands of white. Alternating colors, work fringe around entire outer edge. Continue to cut strands as needed. Trim fringe to 1½ inches.

Knitted Bunting
Pictured on page 237

MATERIALS: Coats & Clark Red Heart 4-ply hand-knitting yarn (or a suitable substitute): 13 ounces of No. 1 white; 18-inch-long white J & P Coats Flexzip all-purpose zipper; Sizes 7 and 8 knitting needles, or size to obtain gauge below; Size G aluminum crochet hook.

Abbreviations: Page 310.

Gauge: With larger needles over st st, 4 sts = 1 inch; 6 rows = 1 inch. With smaller needles over garter st, 9 sts = 2 inches; 9 rows = 1 inch.

INSTRUCTIONS: *Note*—Work bunting in one piece to underarm.

Beg at lower edge with larger needles, cast on 114 sts. K 6 rows. Now work in pat as follows: *Row 1* (right side): K across. *Row 2:* K 2, * p 14, k 2. Rep from * across. *Rows 3-18:* Rep Rows 1 and 2 alternately. *Rows 19-22:* K across. Rep Rows 1-22 four times more, inc 1 st on last row—115 sts. Change to smaller needles.

Yoke: Row 1: K in back of first st—twisted st made; * p 1, k in back of next st. Rep from * across.

Row 2: P 1, * k 1, p 1. Rep from * across. These 2 rows form rib pat.

Dividing row: Work in rib pat across first 27 sts and sl to a holder for right upper front; cast off next 4 sts for underarm, work in rib until there are 53 sts on right-hand needle and sl these sts to a holder for upper back; cast off next 4 sts for underarm; complete row.

Upper left front: Working over the 27 sts on needle only and keeping to rib pat as established, dec 1 st at armhole edge on next row and every other row until 25 sts rem; then work even until length from first row of yoke is 3½ inches, ending at armhole edge. *Next row:* Work across 14 sts, sl rem 11 sts to a holder. Working over the 14 sts on needle only, dec 1 st at neck edge on every row until 9 sts rem; then work even until total length from dividing row is 5 inches, ending with a wrong-side row. Cast off in pat.

Upper right front: Sl the 27 sts from right front holder onto smaller needle. With wrong side facing, join yarn at armhole edge. Keeping to rib pat as established, dec 1 st at armhole on next row and every other row until 25 sts rem; then work even until length from dividing row is 3½ inches; end at neck edge. *Next row:* Work across first 11 sts; sl these sts to a holder. Work across rem 14 sts. Complete as for other side.

Back: Sl the 53 sts on back holder to smaller needle. With wrong side facing, join yarn at first st. Keeping to rib pat as established, dec 1 st at each end of next row and every other row until 49 sts rem. Work even until length from dividing row is 4½ inches; end with a wrong-side row.

Shoulder shaping: Cast off 9 sts at beg of next 2 rows. Sl rem 31 sts to a holder.

Sleeves: Beg at lower edge with smaller needles, cast on 26 sts. Work k 1, p 1 ribbing for 1½ inches, inc 10 sts evenly spaced across last row—36 sts. Work in garter st, inc 1 st at each end on every 8th row until there are 42 sts on needle. Work even until length is 6½ inches, ending with a wrong-side row.

Top shaping: Cast off 2 sts at beg of next 2 rows, dec 1 st at each end of next row and every 4th row until

28 sts rem; then dec 1 st at each end of every other row until 18 sts rem. Work 1 row even. Cast off.

Sew shoulder seams.

Hood: Sl the 11 sts from the right front holder to smaller needle; place a marker on needle; join yarn and pick up and k 12 sts along right front edge for garter st panel. Place another marker on needle; work in established rib pat across the 31 sts on back holder, place another marker on needle; pick up and k 12 sts along left neck edge for other garter st panel, place another marker on needle; work in rib pat as established across the 11 sts on left front holder—77 sts.

With a yarn scrap, mark beg and end of this row. Sl markers bet panels on every row, work each panel in pat until length is 7½ inches.

Cast off 26 sts at beg of next 2 rows, then continue in rib pat over rem 25 center sts until strip measures same length as cast-off sts. Cast off in pat. Sew side edges of center strip to cast-off edges.

Edging: With right side facing and crochet hook, join yarn to corner of right front edge. *Row 1:* Keeping work flat, sc in same place where yarn was joined, sc evenly across right front edge, hook edge and left front edge; ch 1, turn. *Row 2:* Sc in each sc across. Fasten off.

Now work along front edge of hood as follows: With right side facing, join yarn to st in line with right front marker. *Row 1:* Ch 1, *draw up a lp in same sc where yarn was joined, draw up a lp in next sc, yo and draw through all lps on hook—dec made;* sc in each sc to within sc before left front neckline marker, dec over next 2 sc; ch 1, turn. Do not work over rem sts.

Row 2: Make a dec over first 2 sts, sc in each sc to last 2 sts, dec over last 2 sts. Fasten off.

Beg at marked sts on fronts, sew zipper in place, then sew rem front seam. Sew lower edges tog. Sew sleeve seams; sew in sleeves.

Referring to the photograph for ideas, cross-stitch simple holiday motifs (heart, bell, ornament, and so forth) in some of the squares with 4-ply knitting-worsted yarns in bright primary colors.

OLD-COUNTRY
CUSTOMS
TO CHERISH

*Luckily we Americans have been heir
to the Christmas customs of
many countries. Practiced for generations,
these treasured traditions of faraway
lands are celebrated today in the hearts
and homes of many families,
regardless of nationality. These cherished
folkways are especially evident
in the things we make for the holidays.
This Christmas, add that special
Old World spirit to your own celebrations
by making the gifts, toys, decorations, and
food found in this section of
old-country handcrafts and recipes.*

OLD-COUNTRY CUSTOMS TO CHERISH

Traditional Old World Trims and Gifts

A passion for the robust, a love of the traditional, a delight in the handmade—such stirrings are part of the rich Old World heritage of America. Especially at Christmas, the naive spirit of European country ways can add warmth and vitality to your own holiday celebrations. Throughout this section, you'll find a lively array of projects and ideas inspired by festive folk art. Tree trims, toys, clothing, gifts, and all manner of cherished things take on the patina of Old World charm.

The spirit of an old-country Christmas can be seen in this festive spectacle brimming with trims and gifts crafted in the mood and manner of the Old World. The tree sports pristine crocheted snowflakes, folded white paper birds, and painted pinecones.

To herald the holidays, cross-stitch a Christmas greeting in German—or the language of your choice—and attach it to a tea towel. Embroider fanciful flowers onto a heart-shape hearth ornament, *opposite.* Or stitch a hostess apron using upholstery or drapery fabrics.

Instructions for projects in this section begin on page 256.

The making and sharing of handcrafted gifts is a Christmas custom cherished by many cultures. Join in this joyous tradition by presenting your family and friends with handmade gifts.

To give Old World gifts that touch of "something extra," tuck tiny treats into the felt-appliquéd stocking and woodburned and painted box, *below*. The hand-painted peasant folk, *below left*, are actually breadboards—and so charming you'll want to make a set for yourself as well as one to give. To personalize package wraps, stamp "Merry Christmas" on plain paper in a dozen languages.

250

The quaint woodburned village and forest, shown *above* and on the mantel *opposite*, are crafted from one-inch-thick pine and populated with four friendly residents and their barnyard animals. Cut the simply shaped pieces with a jigsaw. Then etch the stylized folk motifs and other details using a woodburning tool.

Whether you make the wool horse on the windowsill, *above*, as a toy or holiday trim, it's sure to capture the imagination of all who are young at heart. Stitch this sturdy steed from an Army blanket or coat-weight wool. Decorate with felt and yarn.

The dolls in the wagon are members of a Bavarian dollhouse family that's described in detail in the following section.

Traditional Old World Trims and Gifts

Add zest and joy to holiday decorating with such striking Old-World accessories as the red-and-white Hungarian cloth, *opposite*, embroidered entirely in buttonhole stitches. Or fashion a festive folk tablecloth in a jiffy by fastening felt scraps and novelty yarns to a wool army blanket, *left*.

Kids and adults alike will treasure the stenciled peasant dolls, *below*. You make each doll using the same pattern but vary the skirt designs.

The pineapple doily, *below left*, is a lovely rendition of the lacy designs long favored by old-country crocheters.

Traditional Old World Trims and Gifts

In Northern Europe, children traditionally decorate a tree with treats for the birds at Christmastime. Share this custom with your youngsters by trimming an evergreen tree with orange slices; alphabet breadsticks; cranberry, carrot, and popcorn garlands; and bread "cookies" spread with colored peanut butter, *opposite.*

The exuberance of peasant-style craftsmanship can be seen in the embroidered vests worn by the young nature lovers on this page and the wool bonnet, *opposite.* The vests are fashioned from felt and embroidered with crewel yarns. Felt appliqués and embroidery accent the bonnet.

Nature's motifs are celebrated in the printed gift wrap, *opposite,* crafted from brown paper and linoleum blocks.

Make the sprightly red-and-white stocking, *below,* by couching craft cording and crewel yarns to felt.

Hostess Apron
Pictured on page 248

MATERIALS: Apron pattern; drapery fabrics to match yardage on pattern (we used a dark floral and bird print for bodice and pockets, a grid pattern for skirt and midriff); quilt batting; ribbon and lace trims.

INSTRUCTIONS: Cut pattern pieces from fabrics; decorate midriff and pockets with ribbon and lace trims. Back bodice front with batting and machine-quilt around the printed design. Construct garment following pattern instructions.

Paper Bird Ornaments
Pictured on page 248

MATERIALS: Heavy white paper (such as watercolor paper); straight edge; cutting knife; white glue; paper clips.

INSTRUCTIONS: Enlarge pattern, *below;* transfer to heavy paper and cut out. Slit sides of bird along dotted lines. To assemble, slip wing tips through slots from *underside* of bird. Pull wings through until bird body is drawn together. Glue beak tips together; clip until dry.

Snowflake Ornaments
Pictured on page 248

MATERIALS: Coats & Clark "Big Ball" crochet cotton, Size 20 (one 400-yard ball is sufficient for 12-14 ornaments); Size 8 steel crochet hook; white glue.

Abbreviations: See page 310.

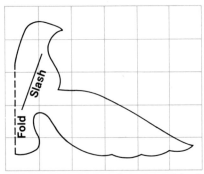

1 Square = 1 Inch

INSTRUCTIONS: There are five snowflake designs.

• *Design 1:* Ch 5; join with sl st to form ring. *Rnd 1:* Ch 3, 13 dc in ring; join with sl st to top of beg ch-3—14 dc, counting beg ch-3 as dc.

Rnd 2: Ch 4, dc in next dc, ch 1, (dc in next dc, ch 1) 12 times; join to 3rd ch of beg ch-4—14 ch-1 sps.

Rnd 3: Sl st into ch-1 sp, ch 3, in same sp work dc, ch 2, 2 dc; in each ch-1 sp around work 2 dc, ch 2, 2 dc; join to top of beg ch-3.

Rnd 4: Sl st into next dc and ch-2 sp; ch 1, in same sp and in every ch-2 sp around work sc, hdc, 3 dc, hdc, and sc; join to first sc—14 petals made. *Rnd 5:* Sl st into hdc and next 2 dc; ch 1, sc in same st as last sl st, * ch 5, sl st in top of next petal (center st of 3-dc grp). Rep from * around; join last ch-5 to first sc at beg of rnd.

Rnd 6: Sl st into ch-5 lp, ch 4, 7 trc in same lp; in each ch-5 lp around work 8 trc; join to top of beg ch-4.

Rnd 7: Ch 1, sc in same st as joining; ch 7, sk next 6 trc, sc in sp bet next 2 trc, * ch 7, sk next 7 trc, sc in sp bet next 2 trc. Rep from * around; join last ch-7 to first sc.

Rnd 8: In each ch-7 lp around work sc, hdc, 9 dc, hdc, and sc. Fasten off.

• *Design 2:* Ch 7; join with sl st to form ring. *Rnd 1:* Ch 3, 23 dc in ring; join with sl st to top of beg ch-3—24 dc. *Rnd 2:* Ch 1, sc in same st as joining, sc in each dc around; join with sl st to first sc.

Rnd 3: Ch 1, in same st as joining work sc, ch 2, and sc; sc in each of next 2 sc, (in next sc work sc, ch 2, sc; sc in next 2 sc) 7 times; join to first sc—8 ch-2 lps. *Rnd 4:* Sl st into ch-2 sp, ch 1, sc in same sp, (ch 5, sc in next ch-2 sp) 7 times; ch 5; join to first sc—8 ch-5 lps.

Rnd 5: In each ch-5 lp around work 4 sc, ch 3, and 4 sc; join to first sc—8 ch-3 lps. *Rnd 6:* Sl st in next 3 sc and ch-3 lp; ch 6, dc in same lp, (ch 7, sc in next ch-3 lp, ch 7, in next ch-3 lp work dc, ch 3 dc) 3 times; ch 7, sc in next ch-3 lp, ch 7; join with sl st to 3rd ch of beg ch-6.

Rnd 7: Sl st into ch-3 lp, ch 4, 11 trc in same lp, (ch 5, sc in next sc, ch 5, 12 trc in next ch-3 lp) 3 times; ch 5, sc in next sc, ch 5; join with sl st to top of beg ch-4.

Rnd 8: Ch 4, dc in next trc, (ch 1, dc in next trc) 10 times; * ch 4, sc in next sc, ch 4, dc in next trc, (ch 1, dc in next trc) 11 times. Rep from * 2 times more; ch 4, sc in next sc, ch 4; join with sl st to 3rd ch of beg ch-4.

Rnd 9: Ch 5, dc in next dc, (ch 2, dc in next dc) 10 times; * ch 3, sc in next sc, ch 3, dc in next dc, (ch 2, dc in next dc) 11 times. Rep from * 2 times more; ch 3, sc in next sc, ch 3; join with sl st to 3rd ch of beg ch-5.

Rnd 10: In each ch-lp around work 2 sc, ch 3, sl st in 3rd ch from hook for picot, and 2 sc. Fasten off.

• *Design 3:* Ch 7; join with sl st to form ring. *Rnd 1:* Ch 3, 17 dc in ring; join with sl st to top of ch-3—14 dc, counting beg ch-3 as dc.

Rnd 2: Ch 5, dc in next dc, * ch 2, dc in next dc. Rep from * around; join last ch-2 to 3rd ch of beg ch-5.

Rnd 3: Ch 3, work 4 dc in same st as joining; drop hook from work, insert hook from front to back in top of beg ch-3 and draw the dropped lp through, ch 1—beg popcorn made; * 2 dc in next ch-2 sp; 5 dc in next dc, drop hook from work, insert hook from front to back in first dc of the 5-dc grp and draw dropped lp through—popcorn (pc) made. Rep from * around; join to top of first pc.

Rnd 4: Ch 1, sc in same st as joining, * sc in next 2 dc, sc in next pc. Rep from * around; join to first sc.

Rnd 5: Ch 1, sc in same st as joining, ch 6, * sk 2 sc, sc in next sc, ch 6. Rep from * around; join last ch-6 to first sc of rnd.

Rnd 6: In each ch-6 lp around work 9 sc; join to first sc—18 9-sc grps.

Rnd 7: Sl st in each of next 4 sc; ch 1, sc in same st as last sl st, * ch 5, sc in center of next 9-sc grp. Rep from * around; join to first sc at beg of rnd. *Rnd 8:* Ch 1, sc in same st as joining, * 7 sc in next ch-5 lp, sc in next sc. Rep from * around; join to first sc at beg of rnd.

Rnd 9: Ch 1, sc in same st as joining, * ch 2, sk 3 sc; in next sc work 3 dc, ch 2, 3 dc; ch 2, sk 3 sc, sc in next sc. Rep from * around; join to first sc at beg of rnd. Fasten off.

• *Design 4:* Ch 6; join with sl st to form ring. *Rnd 1:* Ch 1, 16 sc in ring; join with sl st to first sc at beg of rnd.

Rnd 2: Ch 1, sc in same st as joining, * ch 3, sk sc, sc in next sc. Rep from * around; join last ch-3 to first sc at beg of rnd—8 ch-3 lps.

Rnd 3: Sl st into ch-3 sp, ch 4, ** yo hook twice, draw up lp in same sp, (yo, draw through 2 lps on hook) twice **. Rep bet ** **s 3 times more; yo, draw through rem 5 lps on hook—5-trc cluster (cl) made; * ch 5, yo hook twice, draw up lp in next ch-3 lp, (yo, draw through 2 lps on hook) twice; ** yo hook twice, draw up lp in same sp, (yo, draw through 2 lps on hook) twice **. Rep bet last set of ** **s 3 times more; yo, draw through rem 6 lps on hook—2nd 5-trc cl made. Rep from * around; join last ch-5 to top of first cl.

Rnd 4: Ch 1, 9 sc in each ch-6 lp around; join to first sc.

Rnd 5: Ch 6, dc in same st as joining, * ch 3, sk next 4 sc, sc in each of next 9 sc, ch 3, sk 4 sc; in next sc work dc, ch 3, dc. Rep from * around; join last ch-3 to 3rd ch of beg ch-6.

Rnd 6: Sl st in next ch-3 sp, ch 4, 7 trc in same sp, * ch 5, sk first sc of 9-sc grp, sc in next 7 sc, ch 5, 8 trc in next ch-3 sp. Rep from * around; join last ch-5 to top of beg ch-4.

Rnd 7: Ch 4, dc in next trc, (ch 1, dc in next trc) 6 times; * ch 6, sk first sc of 7-sc grp, sc in next 5 sc, ch 6, dc in next trc, (ch 1, dc in next trc) 7 times. Rep from * around; join last ch-6 to 3rd ch of beg ch-4.

Rnd 8: Ch 4, dc in next dc, (ch 1, dc in next dc) 6 times; * ch 7, sk first sc of 5-sc grp, sc in next 3 sc, ch 7, dc in next dc, (ch 1, dc in next dc) 7 times. Rep from * around; join last ch-7 to 3rd ch of beg ch-4.

Rnd 9: * (In next ch-1 sp work sc, 2 dc, and sc) 7 times; ch 7, sc in center sc of 3-sc grp, ch 7. Rep from * around; join last ch-7 to first sc. Fasten off.

• *Design 5:* Ch 8; join with sl st to form ring. *Rnd 1:* Ch 3, 23 dc in ring; join with sl st to top of beg ch-3—24 dc, counting ch-3 as dc.

Rnd 2: Ch 1, sc in same sp as joining, * ch 3, sk dc, sc in next dc. Rep from * around; join last ch-3 to first sc of rnd—12 ch-3 lps.

Rnd 3: Sl st into next ch-3 sp, ch 3, 2 dc in same sp, * ch 2, 3 dc in next ch-3 sp. Rep from * around; join last ch-2 to top of beg ch-3.

Rnd 4: Sl st in next dc, ch 1, sc in same st, * sc in next ch-2 sp, ch 15, sc in same sp, sk next dc, sc in next dc. Rep from * around; join with sc in first sc at beg of rnd—12 ch-15 lps.

Rnd 5: * In next ch-15 lp work 2 sc, 2 hdc, 9 dc, 3 trc, 9 dc, 2 hdc, and 2 sc; sl st in next sc (on top of 3-dc grp). Rep from * around; join with sl st in last sc of previous rnd. Fasten off.

Finishing ornaments: Wash ornaments, if necessary, in warm water and mild detergent. Pin shapes out (with rustproof pins) and let dry away from heat and light.

While drying, saturate ornaments with a half-and-half mixture of white glue and water. Let dry completely. Suspend ornaments from monofilament line; tie with ribbon bow.

Stamped Gift Wrap
Pictured on page 250

MATERIALS: Purchased rubber stamps with Christmas greetings in desired language; red, blue, and green stamp pads; large sheets or rolls of brown or white paper.

INSTRUCTIONS: Press stamps onto stamp pads; press onto paper in random design.

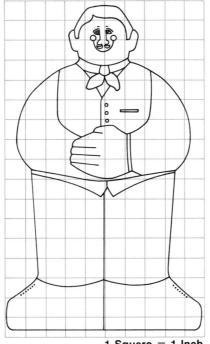

1 Square = 1 Inch

Breadboard Dolls
Pictured on page 250

MATERIALS: 4 feet of 1x12-inch clear hardwood; sandpaper; primer paint; acrylic paints; brushes; satin-finish polyurethane; masking tape; carbon paper; jigsaw.

INSTRUCTIONS: Enlarge patterns, *below.* Trace figures onto hardwood using carbon paper. With a jigsaw, cut out figures. Sand edges.

Cover cutting-board side with masking tape. Coat decorative sides and edges with primer paint.

Paint figures with acrylics. Trim clothing with small flowers, stripes, or dots. (See photograph for ideas.)

When paint is dry, brush painted surfaces with three coats of polyurethane. Dry thoroughly between coats. Remove protective tape from cutting side of board. To hang breadboards, drill holes on cutting sides; hang on nails in wall.

Felt Stocking
Pictured on page 250

MATERIALS: ⅓ yard of 50-inch-wide red-orange felt; scraps of dark red, light orange, and white felt; yellow, black, and khaki crewel yarn; scraps of orange novelty yarn, medium-weight yellow cord; sewing threads, pinking shears.

continued

MOTHER — 1 Square = 1 Inch
DAUGHTER — 1 Square = ¾ Inch

INSTRUCTIONS: Enlarge the stocking pattern, *page 68.* Using pinking shears, cut two stocking shapes from red-orange felt.

Decorate the stocking front with bands, circles, and ovals of felt (see photograph for design and color ideas).

Attach felt "buttons" with single stitches worked in crewel yarn. With sewing thread, whipstitch colored bands in place and couch yarn edgings and scrolls made with yarn or cording to stocking. For additional decoration, use crewel yarns to embroider herringbone bands.

With *wrong* sides facing, sew stocking front to back ½ inch from pinked edges. Add yarn hanger.

Hearth Ornament
Pictured on page 250

MATERIALS: One red and one white 9x12-inch felt rectangle; 1 skein *each* of DMC pearl cotton embroidery floss in the following colors: medium green, dark green, pink, yellow, burgundy, red, magenta, orange, and blue; fiberfill; dressmaker's carbon paper; embroidery needle; embroidery hoop.

INSTRUCTIONS: Enlarge pattern, *right.* To complete the design, flop the pattern along the center line. Then transfer the design to white felt, using dressmaker's carbon paper in a light color. Do not cut it out until embroidery is finished. Mount fabric in a hoop.

Embroider the design using three strands of floss. Use stem stitches for outlines of leaves and flowers, chain stitches for the border, and satin stitches for filling in shapes.

When embroidery is complete, cut out the handle and heart along the zigzag line, using pinking shears. From red felt, cut backing for pieces ½ inch larger all around than fronts.

With wrong sides facing, machine-sew fronts and backs together directly over the chain stitch border. Leave the top of the heart open for stuffing. Stuff the heart lightly with fiberfill, insert handle ends into heart, and sew closed.

Old World Village
Pictured on pages 250-251

MATERIALS: 1-inch-thick pine scraps; sandpaper; carbon paper; jigsaw; woodburning tool.

INSTRUCTIONS: Enlarge the pattern, *opposite.* Using carbon paper, transfer designs to pine. Cut out pieces with a jigsaw; sand smooth. Round edges slightly if small children will be playing with the pieces.

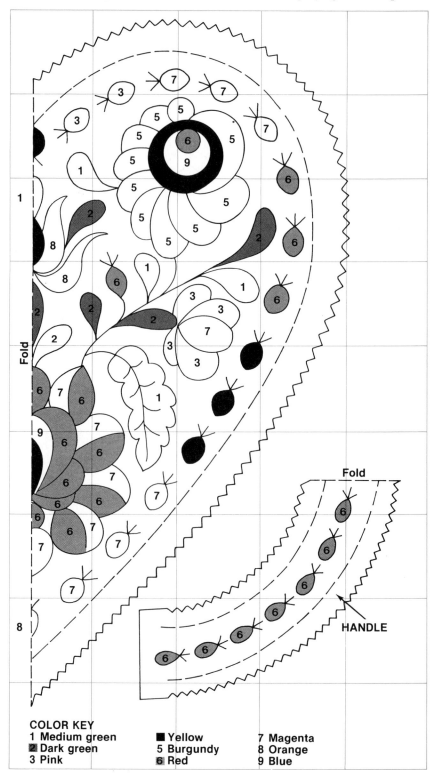

COLOR KEY
1 Medium green
2 Dark green
3 Pink
■ Yellow
5 Burgundy
6 Red
7 Magenta
8 Orange
9 Blue

1 Square = 1 Inch

To decorate the toys, heat the woodburning tool and outline the pieces by running the woodburning point along the edges, darkening them. (Practice on wood scraps first.) Then, on both sides of pieces, outline surface details and fill in the dark shapes indicated on the pattern. (To make dots, stand woodburning tip on end; for larger shapes, use side of the chisel tip.)

Village Gift Wrap
Pictured on pages 249, 255

MATERIALS: Brown wrapping paper; 4x6-inch linoleum blocks; linoleum block cutting blades; carbon paper; water-soluble printing inks; artist's brayer (available in art supply stores); glass plate (palette).

INSTRUCTIONS: Transfer design motifs from toy village, *below,* onto linoleum blocks with carbon paper. Using cutting blades, cut away linoleum around outlines and shapes (see photograph for ideas).

Drop a spoonful of printing ink onto a glass plate; roll out evenly with brayer. Roll ink onto printing block; *firmly* press block onto brown paper. Repeat in rows until desired amount of paper is printed.

continued

1 Square = 1 Inch

Woodburned Box
Pictured on page 250

MATERIALS: Purchased unfinished wooden box; woodburning tool; acrylic paints; brushes; sealer; paper; carbon paper.

INSTRUCTIONS: Enlarge the pattern, *below*. To complete the design, flop the pattern three times along dotted lines.

If necessary, adapt the design to fit the box lid (the one shown is 5x10 inches). Transfer the design to the unfinished box using carbon or graphite paper.

Woodburn all the outlines and paint the shapes with thinned acrylics. When the paint is dry, coat all box surfaces with sealer.

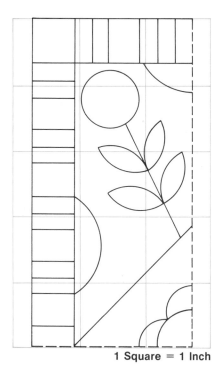

1 Square = 1 Inch

Wool Horse
Pictured on page 251

MATERIALS: Scraps of khaki wool Army blanket or ⅓ yard of coat-weight khaki wool; small piece of red cotton (ear lining); scrap of navy felt (eyes, dots on blanket); white, gold, red, maroon, khaki, and white felt scraps (decorative blanket); white wool yarn; 16 yards of red wool yarn (mane, tail, embroidery); 1 yard of white leather lacing for bridle; fiberfill.

INSTRUCTIONS: Enlarge pattern, *below*. Transfer to fabric; cut out, adding ½-inch seam margins.

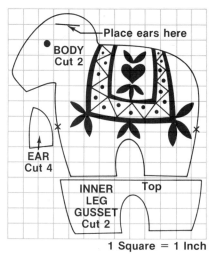

Place ears here

BODY
Cut 2

EAR
Cut 4

INNER
LEG
GUSSET
Cut 2

Top

1 Square = 1 Inch

Cut blanket decorations from felt: Heart is red, blanket center is white, triangles for border are gold, red, and maroon, leaves in center are khaki, and outer leaves are white. Sew blanket to horse. Trim center with couched red yarn; trim outer edge of blanket with couched white yarn. Glue eye in place.

With right sides facing, sew body pieces together around upper portion (between Xs). Pin leg gussets in place. Sew around legs from X to X. Turn legs, firmly stuff horse through opening. Sew opening.

Sew ears to linings; leave open at bottoms. Turn and press. Tuck raw edges inside; sew to head. For mane, cut 5-inch pieces of yarn and tack to head. For tail, cut 30 pieces of yarn each 10 inches long; fold in half and tie at fold with thread. Tack in place.

For bridle, drape leather over nose, under chin, and up over neck; knot to secure.

Embroidered Hungarian Cloth
Pictured on page 252

MATERIALS: 1¼ yards of off-white linen, or any length suitable for your table; red No. 5 pearl cotton thread; embroidery hoop; embroidery needle; purchased red crocheted edging or Size 7 crochet hook (to make your own edging).

INSTRUCTIONS: Enlarge the pattern, *opposite*, reversing as necessary to complete the design; transfer to the fabric. (Adjust the design to fit your tablecloth, if necessary.) Mount fabric in a hoop, if desired.

Using red pearl cotton, work the entire design in buttonhole stitches. When working the flower petals, centers, and dots, lay the stitches side-by-side, with the loop part of each stitch along the outer edge of the shape, as shown in the diagram, *below*. Work stems, scallops, scrolls, and the straight line along the border in double buttonhole stitches, as shown on the stem.

Block the finished embroidery; turn up a narrow hem and add purchased crocheted edging.

Or, work hemstitching over one or two drawn threads around the edge. Then add a lace edge crocheted from red thread following the directions below. (For crochet abbreviations, see page 310.)

• *Scalloped edge: Row 1:* Make sc with ch 1 bet around cloth. End with sl st in first sc.

Row 2: * 2 sc in first ch 1 sp, 2 hdc in next sp, 2 dc in next sp, 2 trc in next sp, 2 dc in next sp, 2 hdc in next sp, 2 sc in next sp, 2 sl st in next sp. Repeat from * around cloth. End with sl st in first sc.

260

Cross-Stitched Towels

Pictured on pages 249, 252

MATERIALS: Purchased linen towels; even-weave fabric to cover towel end; embroidery floss; alphabet chart of your choice.

INSTRUCTIONS: Select letters for a Christmas greeting in English or another language. Embroider according to charts, centering letters on even-weave fabric border.

Machine-sew border to towel, finishing all raw edges.

White Pineapple Doily

Pictured on page 253

MATERIALS: Two 2-ounce skeins of white Coats & Clark Red Heart Lustersheen; Size E aluminum crochet hook. Use Lustersheen for 21-inch doily; for 12-inch doily use 2 balls of white J. & P. Coats Knit Cro-Sheen mercerized cotton (250-yard balls) and a Size 7 steel crochet hook.

Abbreviations: See page 310.

INSTRUCTIONS: Finished diameter is 12 or 21 inches. Ch 10; join with sl st to form ring. *Rnd 1:* Ch 3, dc in ring, (ch 2, 2 dc in ring) 9 times; ch 2, join with sl st to top of beg ch-3. *Rnd 2:* Sl st in dc and in ch-2 sp, *ch 3, dc in same sp, ch 2, 2 dc in same sp—beg shell made;* (in next ch-2 sp make *shell* of 2 dc, ch 2, and 2 dc) 9 times; join to top of ch-3.

Rnd 3: Make beg shell in center of shell, (ch 1, shell in next shell) 9 times; ch 1, join in top of ch-3.

Rnd 4: * Shell in shell, ch 2, make (2 dc, ch 2, 2 dc, ch 2, and 2 dc) in next shell, ch 2. Rep from * around; join. *Rnd 5:* (Shell in shell, ch 3, sk ch-2 sp, shell in each of next 2 ch-2 sps) around; join. *Rnd 6:* (Shell in shell, ch 3) around; join. *Rnd 7:* * (Shell in shell, ch 3) twice, dc in ch-3 sp, ch 3, shell in shell, ch 3. Rep from * around; join. *Rnd 8:* * (Shell in shell, ch 3) twice; make (dc, ch 5, dc) in center dc, ch 3, shell in shell, ch 3. Rep from * around; join.

Rnd 9: * (Shell in shell, ch 3) twice; 10 dc in ch-5 sp, ch 3, shell in shell, ch 3. Rep from * around; join. *Rnd 10:* Make beg shell, then ch 2 and make 2 more dc in same sp, * ch 3, shell in shell, ch 3, dc in first of 10 dc, (ch 1, dc in next dc) 9 times; ch 3, shell in shell, ch 3, make (2 dc, ch 2, 2 dc, ch 2, 2 dc) in next shell. Rep from * around; join.

Rnd 11: * (Shell in shell,) twice, ch 3, shell in shell, ch 3, sc in ch-1 sp, (ch 3, sc in next sp) 8 times; ch 3, shell in shell, ch 3. Rep from * around; join. *Rnd 12:* * (Shell in shell, ch 3) 3 times; sc in ch-3 lp, (ch 3, sc in next lp) 7 times; ch 3, shell in shell, ch 3. Rep from * around; join.

Rnd 13: * Shell in shell, ch 1, 5 dc in ch-3 sp, ch 1, (shell in shell, ch 3) twice; 6 lps across pineapple, ch 3, shell in shell, ch 3. Rep from * around; join. *Rnd 14:* * Shell in shell, ch 1, 2 dc in each of 5 dc, ch 1, (shell in shell, ch 3) twice; 5 lps across pineapple, ch 3, shell in shell, ch 3. Rep from * around; join.

Rnd 15: * Shell in shell, (ch 1, dc in next dc) 10 times; ch 1, (shell in shell, ch 3) twice; 4 lps across pineapple, ch 3, shell in shell, ch 3. Rep from * around; join. *Rnd 16:* * Shell in shell, (ch 2, dc in next dc) 10 times; ch 2, (shell in shell, ch 3) twice; 3 lps across pineapple, ch 3, shell in shell, ch 3. Rep from * around; join. *Rnd 17:* * Shell in shell, (ch 3, dc in next dc) 10 times, (ch 3, shell in shell) twice; ch 3, 2 lps across pineapple, ch 3, shell in shell, ch 3. Rep from * around; join.

Rnd 18: * Shell in shell, (shell in next ch-3 lp) 11 times; (shell in shell, ch 3) twice; 1 lp in pineapple, ch 3, shell in shell, ch 3. Rep from * around; join.

Rnd 19: * (Shell in shell) 13 times; ch 3, shell in shell, ch 3, sc in center lp, ch 3, shell in shell, ch 3. Rep from * around; join. *Rnd 20:* * (Shell in shell) 13 times; ch 3, (shell in shell) twice; ch 3. Rep from * around; join.

1 Square = 1 Inch

continued

Rnd 21: * (Shell in shell) 13 times; (ch 3, 2 dc in center of next shell) twice; ch 3. Rep from * around; join.

Rnd 22: Sl st to center of shell, ch 3 and make dc in same sp, ch 3, sl st in top of dc just made for picot, 2 dc in same sp, * (ch 2, in next shell make 2 dc, picot, 2 dc) 12 times; ch 2, make (2 dc, picot, 2 dc) in each of next 3 ch-3 sps, ch 2, make (2 dc, picot, 2 dc) in next shell. Rep from * around; join with ch-2 at first shell made. Fasten off.

Using wool setting, block very carefully with steam iron on wrong side of work, beg at center of doily and working outward.

Felt-Appliquéd Tablecloth
Pictured on page 253

MATERIALS: Khaki Army blanket or 60-inch square of lightweight wool or felt; ¼ yard of 50-inch-wide orange felt; ⅛ yard each of red, yellow, and white felt; 30 yards of red-orange novelty yarn; matching sewing thread (for couching yarn on tablecloth); black and red buttonhole twist; khaki crewel yarn; 13 yards of yellow medium-weight synthetic cording; fabric glue; large-eyed tapestry needle; pinking shears.

INSTRUCTIONS: Trim wool to 60 inches square; machine-hem all raw edges.

To decorate the tablecloth, refer to photograph for design ideas and placement of trim rows.

• *Outer row:* Cut four 2x50-inch strips of orange felt. Trim one long edge of each strip in a scalloped design, cutting halfway around a quarter to form each scallop. Snip small diamond shapes out of every other scallop.

Position the strips 2 inches above the hemmed edges of tablecloth all around and whipstitch into place. With khaki yarn, work a row of large running stitches ¼ inch from straight edge on orange felt.

Cut ¾-inch-diameter circles from red felt and sew (with a single stitch

of buttonhole twist) between every diamond shape cut from orange felt.
• *Corner:* Cut graduating circles of white (large), orange (medium), and red (small) felt with pinking shears. Stack circles in each corner of cloth and tack in place.

Use sewing thread to couch rows of red-orange yarn in long lines and looped patterns. Between couched rows of yarn, tack a pattern of alternating single and double felt circles.
• *Inner row:* Sew intertwining designs of yellow cord to the tablecloth using red buttonhole twist and running stitches. Inside the loops formed by the twining, tack alternating orange and white circles to the cloth with large black pearl cotton cross-stitches.

Babushka Dolls
Pictured on page 253

MATERIALS: 1 yard of muslin; ½ yard of quilt batting; fiberfill; textile paints; stencil brushes; art knife; stencil paper; fine-point, permanent black marker; sheet of glass approximately 12 inches square.

INSTRUCTIONS: Enlarge pattern, *below*, following scale notations for small, medium, and large dolls.

Using a sharp art knife and waxed stencil paper, cut three stencils (see numbers on patterns) for the doll front and two for the back. Save the circle cut from the face on stencil number 1.

Cut fabric (two pieces for each doll) 5 inches larger all around than front or back. Stretch and tape fabric to a flat surface.

Position stencil 1 atop fabric, centered. Place cut-out face circle on head portion, centering it in the area cut out for the scarf. Secure with pins or double-sided tape.

Stencil in colors of your choice, referring to the photograph for ideas. Repeat for stencils 2 and 3.

When changing colors in cut areas that are close to each other on the same stencil (eyes, cheeks, mouth), cover the areas not to be stenciled with a scrap of paper.

Allow fabric to dry thoroughly before painting another color over a previously painted area (polka dots over apron, flower center over flowers). Set paint according to manufacturer's instructions.

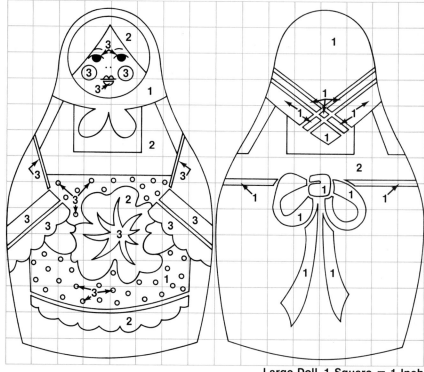

Large Doll 1 Square = 1 Inch
Medium Doll 1 Square = ¾ Inch
Small Doll 1 Square = ⅝ Inch

Vary motifs on doll fronts as shown in photograph. Color mouth on small doll using paint and brush or colored pencil if it is too small to cut on a stencil. Add lines around eyes and dots for nose with fine-point marker.

To assemble dolls, add ½ inch to outlines of dolls (seam allowance); cut out. Cut batting for doll front and back; baste in place. With right sides facing, stitch back to front; leave base open. Clip curves, turn, and stuff.

Cut an oval of fabric and batting for the base; hand-sew in place.

Felt Vests
Pictured on page 254

MATERIALS: Commercial vest pattern; heavy-weight felt in amount specified in pattern; thread; narrow hole punch (⅛-inch holes); hand-spun yarn (for lacing); crewel yarns; dressmaker's carbon paper.

INSTRUCTIONS: Enlarge pattern, *below*.

Using vest pattern, cut fronts and back from felt (cut away all seam allowances except at shoulders and sides). Seam front to back at shoulders and sides; press seams open.

To decorate the vest, punch lacing holes ½ inch from raw edges of vest; space them ½ inch apart. Lace hand-

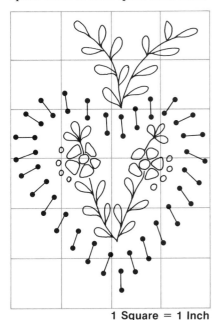

1 Square = 1 Inch

spun yarn through holes. Transfer embroidery design to vest front, altering it to fit if necessary. Punch holes where indicated by pattern. Lace yarn through holes, tying off on wrong side. Embroider flowers by couching heavy yarn to the vest with sewing thread or embroidering in lazy daisy stitches.

Corded Stocking
Pictured on page 254

MATERIALS: ⅓ yard of 50-inch-wide white felt; 4 yards of red medium-weight synthetic cord; red crewel yarns; red thread.

INSTRUCTIONS: Enlarge the stocking pattern, *page 68*. Cut two stockings from felt.

Beginning 1 inch from left edge of stocking front, tack red cord in l-inch-wide loops along left side. Couch loops with thread; baste remainder of cord along outer edge. Couch scrolls and flowers with red yarns at the center and toe of stocking (refer to the photograph for placement).

With wrong sides facing, pin front and back together. Stitch ½-inch-deep buttonhole stitches along left edge of stocking, across sole, and around bottom of toe. Whipstitch stocking front and back together along right side, catching red cording in seam. Whipstitch narrow red cording along top edges of stocking; add hanger.

Old-Country Bonnet
Pictured on pages 254-255

MATERIALS: ¼ yard *each* coat-weight wool, fleece or taffeta lining; 1 yard of ribbon (ties); scraps of crewel yarns for embroidery; scraps of felt.

INSTRUCTIONS: Enlarge pattern, *above right*. Cut the outer pieces from wool and the lining pieces from fleece or taffeta.

Using ⅜-inch seam allowances and easing curves, sew hat sides to top. Press seams open; turn raw edges inside ⅝ inch and press. Dec-

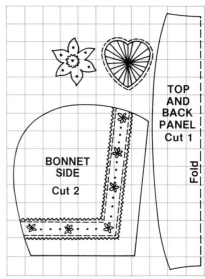

1 Square = 1 Inch

orate bonnet with hand-appliquéd felt shapes and yarn embroidery. Stitch lining pieces together as for bonnet. With wrong sides facing, slip-stitch lining inside bonnet.

A Tree of Treats for the Birds
Pictured on page 255

MATERIALS: Peanut butter; food coloring; stale bread; cookie cutters; popcorn; cranberries; carrots; marshmallows; orange and apple slices; raisins; birdseed; bread pretzels; carpet thread; needle.

INSTRUCTIONS: *To make garlands,* pop the popcorn; thread kernels, marshmallows, and cranberries on carpet thread using a needle. Or, thread carrot slices and cranberries on thread for a colorful garland. Drape on tree.

• *For ornaments,* slice oranges and apples; tie onto branches in places where birds can reach them while perching.

Make "cookies" by cutting stale bread with cookie cutters. With red food coloring (red attracts birds), color peanut butter and spread onto cookie cutouts. Allow to dry overnight. Thread hangers through cookies; attach to tree.

• *For ground feeding,* sprinkle raisins, birdseed, and other treats on ground around tree.

OLD-COUNTRY CUSTOMS TO CHERISH

Storybook Presents for Children

As every child knows, Santa's sack holds all sorts of surprises for good boys and girls. This section, too, is brimming with Christmas delights designed to enchant children of all ages. There are dolls in all shapes and sizes, storybook characters, and other imaginative play-things for you to create.

Each of these gift ideas was inspired by European folk toys. Some are dressed in native cos-tumes, while others are crafted using old-country techniques. Besides providing hours of play, these toys and dolls can intro-duce your youngster to the ways of the Old World.

In the childhood land of enchantment, there's always room for a few more magical residents. Any child would be thrilled on Christmas morning to meet this charming family of Bavarian dolls. And since these diminutive dolls are dressed in the festive garb of the peasant folk, your little one can celebrate the specialness of Christmas all year long.

Construct the dolls' bodies and limbs using pliable chenille stems. Then costume the dolls with cotton and felt in Christmasy colors, adding lace and ribbon trims. Fashion their hair from embroidery floss and embroider their delicate facial features with sewing thread.

Instructions for projects in this section begin on page 274.

Country folk of many lands have a special knack for crafting the most delightful dolls from simple materials. At Christmastime, they enchant their children with such home-spun beauties as the rag and bead dolls shown here.

Create Old World dolls like the appealing pair, *left*, using everyday materials such as wooden beads and coat hangers. Pad the basic wire shapes with quilt batting and clothe the dolls with snippets of fabric and lace. Add special touches such as painted faces and patches on clothing, if desired.

Rag dolls take on a vintage look when they have long braids and provincial costumes. The Alpine country lass dolls, *opposite*, are huggable, lovable, and easy to make. To create these 21-inch-tall dolls, use beige cotton challis for the faces and bodies and yellow Persian yarn for hair. Dress them in Old World prints and fashion boots from felt to complete the folkloric effect.

Storybook Presents for Children

Doll fanciers of all ages will find dozens of different ways to use this charming carriage, *right*. Little ones will love to wheel it around, but you also can fill it with packages and other Christmas goodies and turn it into a delightful holiday decoration.

To convert a plain wicker basket into a winsome doll buggy, simply add wooden wheels and a handle. Almost any basket shape will do. Even if your basket doesn't have a "hood," you can create one by cutting a second basket in half and lacing it in place. Leave the buggy in its natural state or give it a coat of candy-color paint.

Bring a beloved bedtime story to life by stitching the adorable Goldilocks doll and a family of three Tyrolean bears, *opposite*. This stitch-and-stuff set of storybook characters will capture the hearts of all who see them—especially the children.

To give Goldilocks her peaches-and-cream complexion, use cotton fabric in the palest pink. The whimsical teddy bears are fashioned from brown wool and dressed in native Alpine costumes.

268

No matter how old you are, crafting a homespun toy for a child makes you feel young at heart. And once you've put the finishing touches on these lively wooden animals, you will have created something special for that favorite child or grandchild—a handcrafted toy that will be treasured for many years.

The handcrafted puppets pictured here recall the dancing antics of traditional limberjack toys from America's Appalachian mountains. Cut the pieces for each of the four puppets—mule, cow, sheep, and rooster—from pine lumber and fasten them with springs and cotter pins. Then, add simple details like a furry coat for the sheep, a leather tail for the mule, and a ring through the cow's nose.

To play with these puppets, sit on the springboard and hold the dowel fastened to the animal so its feet barely touch the board. Just a tap of the springboard with your finger sets off lively movement of the feet and legs.

271

Fancy prancing ponies like these call to mind imaginary king-doms, complete with castles and knights in shining armor. You can be sure fairy tales will come true on Christmas day when you craft a set of these stalwart steeds for your youngsters.

Use felt combined with novelty yarns and fabrics to fashion these horses. Stitch and stuff each leg individually; then tack the legs to the body pieces and attach a string to each hoof. Secure the strings to wooden dowels and watch the horses gallop and trot marionette-style when you twist and turn the strings. Make a whole stableful of horses using scrap bag materials.

273

Bavarian Dollhouse Family
Pictured on pages 264-265

MATERIALS: ⅛ yard of quality muslin; scraps of fiberfill; thirty-one 12-inch-long chenille stems; ⅛ yard of polyester fleece; 3¾ yards of off-white cotton-filled tubing; off-white single-fold bias tape.

Also: Embroidery floss in the following amounts and colors for dolls' hair: 1½ skeins of dark brown (father); 1½ skeins of medium gray (grandmother); 1½ skeins of light

golden yellow (mother); 1 skein of light golden yellow (boy); 2 skeins of medium brown (girl and baby). *Plus,* for facial features: Red, brown, gray, blue, and flesh-color sewing threads; cake-type rouge.

• *For clothing:* Scraps of fabric (whites and assorted lightweight cotton prints and solids); eyelet lace fabric; lace, embroidered trims, and satin ribbons in narrow widths (⅛ to ½ inch wide); red crochet cotton thread; scraps of black, red, and green felt; fusible webbing; tiny artificial flowers.

INSTRUCTIONS: Follow general directions for the construction of each doll. (Also see tips for making miniature dolls, *opposite.*) Refer to the diagram illustrating the head and body structure, *left,* and the sizing chart, *below,* for individual measurements when cutting chenille stems for body pieces and for shaping each doll's body.

To begin, enlarge the head and clothing patterns, *opposite.*

• *Head:* Cut two head pieces for each head (pattern includes ¼-inch seam allowances). With right sides facing, pin and stitch pieces together along curved stitching line. Use tiny machine stitches. Trim seam allowance, clip curves, turn, and smooth seam with fingertips.

Using a double strand of thread, run a row of gathering stitches ¼ inch from the edge of the top of the head "sack"; leave the needle attached to the thread. Stuff the head firmly, keeping the bottom seam round and smooth. Pull gathers

tight, tuck in raw edges, and whipstitch the opening closed. Tie off.

• *Face:* To embroider faces, use a single strand of sewing thread throughout. (Refer to the photograph for design ideas for faces.)

Use dark tan or brown for the upper eyelids and the eyelashes. Use brown or dark blue for the eyes and shades of red for the lips. Use satin stitches for the eyes and stem stitches for the upper eyelids and the lips. Use straight stitches for the eyelashes and a single small stitch in dark flesh for the nose.

For color on the cheeks, use a cotton swab to lightly apply dry blush. Repeat as needed.

• *Body:* Use one chenille stem for each neck and body piece. Bend the stem in half and twist together. Cut polyester fleece into ⅜-inch-wide strips and wrap the body stem tightly and smoothly with fleece strips, overlapping fleece about every ⅛ inch. Leave ⅜ inch of the bent end of the stem unwrapped. Secure end of fleece.

Remove cotton stuffing from a length of tubing and slip the fleece-wrapped stem into the tubing. Pin the bent end of the stem to the back of the head ⅝ inch below the gathers; whipstitch securely in place.

• *Arms:* Cut two chenille stems to size for each pair of arms and hands. Twist stems together and wrap with fleece, ending ¾ inch from each end. For hands, bend each end back ⅜ inch and twist around stem. Slip stem into emptied strip of tubing, allowing an extra ¼ inch of tubing fabric at each end.

Align center of arm piece atop shoulder position on body stem and tightly wrap stem once around body. Pinch the joining with a pair of pliers to secure.

Turn the extra tubing at the ends of the stem to the inside and slip-stitch openings closed, making slightly rounded hands. Bend stem at each shoulder (refer to measurement chart for width of shoulders).

• *Legs:* Cut two chenille stems for each pair of legs. Twist stems together and wrap with fleece, ending 1 inch from each end. Cover stem with tubing, leaving 1 inch uncovered at each end.

Measurement Chart (in inches):

	Grand-mother	Father/Mother	Boy/Girl	Baby
Finished Height	7½	9	6½	3½
Body*	2¼	2½	2	1
Arms**	10¼	12	9¼	5⅞
Legs**	11¾	14	10½	4⅞
Hips	1¼	1½	1⅛	⅝
Shoulders	2	2⅜	1¾	⅞

* Body measurement is from base of the neck to the crotch.
** Arm and leg measurements are from tip to tip before ends are bent back for the hands and feet, and before limbs are attached to body.

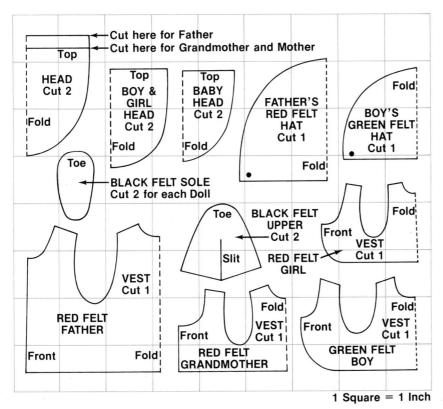

Cut here for Father
Cut here for Grandmother and Mother

Top
HEAD
Cut 2
Fold

Top
BOY &
GIRL
HEAD
Cut 2
Fold

Top
BABY
HEAD
Cut 2
Fold

FATHER'S
RED FELT
HAT
Cut 1
Fold

Fold
BOY'S
GREEN FELT
HAT
Cut 1

Toe
BLACK FELT SOLE
Cut 2 for each Doll

Toe
BLACK FELT
UPPER
Cut 2
Slit
RED FELT
GIRL

Front
VEST
Cut 1
Fold

VEST
Cut 1

RED FELT
FATHER
Front   Fold

Fold
Front
VEST
Cut 1
RED FELT
GRANDMOTHER

Fold
Front
VEST
Cut 1
GREEN FELT
BOY

1 Square = 1 Inch

Center the leg piece across the lower portion of the body. Check the chart for the body length measurement (body length is measured from base of neck to crotch), and tightly wrap the body piece once between the legs. Then wrap remaining portion of the body stem around upper part of body. Pinch the joining with pliers.

Bend leg piece at hip (see construction diagram), and bend the feet flat. Make each foot 1 inch long (except for baby—make baby's feet each ¼ inch long).

To pad the body, wrap it with ⅜-inch-wide strips of polyester fleece, working from top to bottom. Wrap over each shoulder several times; shape the top of the body so it is broader than the bottom, and keep the waist narrow. For the grandmother and mother, make the body somewhat fuller at the bust.

Next, wrap short pieces of bias tape over each shoulder in a V-shape and tack front and back onto body. Also wrap a small piece of tape between legs, securing at center back and front.

Finally, wrap the entire body with bias tape, from chest down to top of legs. Overlap the folds of the bias tape every ¼ inch. Tack the end of the tape in place.

• *Hair:* Use the same basic hair style for each doll (except baby), then add a braid for mother and a bun for grandmother. Work with floss in the original circular shape; *do not cut or unwind the skein.* When instructions call for half a skein, neatly divide and cut as few loops as possible.

For the basic style, use one skein of floss (1½ skeins for the father). Flatten out the skein and stitch across the center (as for a center part). Pin the skein to the head and tack along the stitching.

Keep floss neat and smooth as you wrap the ends of the loops around each side of the head to meet at the back edge of the part. Tack end loops to the head and tack several strands at base of neck, at each side of neck, and at each side of the face (about eye level) to hold the "wig" in place.

Use half of a skein for grandmother's bun; twist into loops. Tack to back of head. For mother's plait, fold half of a skein of yellow in half, divide into three equal parts and braid. Tack around mother's head.

For baby's hair, cut one skein of floss into four equal parts. Stack the strands, and stitch floss together across the center. Tack this "thatch" of hair to the center of the head, with stitching running sideways, from ear to ear. Trim front bangs to frame the face, and trim back hair evenly at base of neck.

Make clothing for dolls following instructions below.

• *Blouses and Shirts:* Cut a rectangle of white fabric as long as the doll's arms from tip to tip, plus 1 inch, and as wide as twice the measurement from neck to crotch, plus ½ inch. Fold rectangle in fourths and cut a ½-inch-radius quarter circle from folded corner for neck opening. Slit one side of fabric to make back opening.

continued

Tips for Making Miniature Dolls

Small dolls require special crafting skills. Here are tips for making your favorite miniatures.

• *Draw around patterns* on double thickness of fabric. Sew over drawn lines; cut close to stitching.

• *Use 20 stitches* per inch for machine-sewing, or sew seams by hand. Trim seams evenly; clip curves at uniform intervals. Iron or finger-press all seams open.

• *Use sewing thread* or one strand of floss to embroider faces.

• *Select prints* for clothes and yarn or threads for hair scaled to the size of the doll.

• *Spot glue* trims and laces in place with fabric glue, then sew.

• *For a hat,* cut handles off tiny straw basket; invert basket. Trim.

• *Make eyeglasses* from florist wire and dip into plastic film.

• *Make buttons* using a paper punch and colored plastic lids and containers. Pierce holes in buttons (for stitching) using a heated needle. Or, use tiny glass beads and seed pearls for buttons.

• *For bows* on costumes, thread narrow ribbon into a needle. Take a stitch in the fabric; pull ribbon through. Remove needle; tie bow.

To shape sleeves, cut a small rectangle from corners as shown *below*.

Open up the blouse or shirt and hand- or machine-stitch bands of lace or embroidered trim and nar-

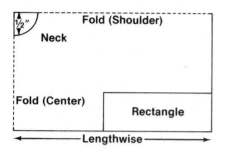

row (⅛-inch) satin ribbon in bands across each sleeve. Then fold blouse or shirt in half, with right sides facing, and stitch up sides and under arms. Turn and press.

Fold under the raw edges ¼ inch along the back opening of the blouse or shirt and on each sleeve, and baste. Turn under the raw edge ⅛ inch at the neck and run a gathering stitch around neck. Leave the needle on the thread.

Fit the blouse or shirt on the doll and pull the gathers tight at the neck; tie off. Tack the blouse/shirt closed down the back.

For each blouse, gather a scrap of lace and tack it around the neck for a collar. For the man's and boy's shirts, tie a bow of ribbon and tack it at the throat.

• *Sleeves:* For shirts, gather edges of sleeves; tack at wrists. For blouses, stitch lace to cuffs. Gather sleeves ½ inch from cuff, fit to wrist, and tie off. Tie narrow ribbons around each wrist for girl's blouse.

Gather waist of shirt or blouse, fit to doll, and tie off. Trim away excess fabric at bottom.

• *Pantaloons (women):* For mother and grandmother, cut a 4¾x7¾-inch rectangle of fine white fabric. Press under one long edge ¼ inch and trim with lace. With right sides facing, stitch the two short ends together. Press the seam open.

To cut legs, place the seam at one side, then slit through both layers of fabric from the bottom, midway between the seam and the folded side. Make the slit 2¾ inches long. Sew

up one side of slit and down the other to make inner leg seams, stitching to a point at the crotch. Clip the seam allowance, turn right side out, and press.

Turn under raw edges at top, gather waistline, fit pantaloons to doll, and tie off. Tack to doll.

For the girl, repeat the above procedure using a 4¼x6¾-inch rectangle of white fabric.

• *Slips:* For mother and grandmother, cut 4¾x16-inch rectangles of white fabric; trim one long edge with lace. Stitch short ends together (¼-inch seam). Turn under the top edge ¼ inch; gather, fit the slip to the doll, and tack in place.

For girl's slip, repeat procedure with a 4¼x15-inch rectangle.

• *Skirts:* Cut 5x19-inch rectangles of print fabric for mother and grandmother. Border one long edge with lace; trim with additional lace or ribbon. Seam short ends, gather, and fit skirt as for slips, above.

For girl's skirt, repeat with 4½x18-inch rectangle of fabric.

• *Aprons:* Cut fabric rectangles—5x9 inches for mother's apron and 3¼x7 inches for girl's. Embellish with ribbons and trims, narrowly hem sides and bottom, and gather the top edge of each apron onto a 16-inch length of ribbon for waistband and ties. Fit apron around waist and knot ties at back. Trim ribbon ties.

• *To complete women's clothing:* Bond two layers of felt together using fusible webbing. Cut daughter's and grandmother's vests (see patterns, *page 275*) from bonded felt. With wrong sides facing, sew vests at shoulders; fit to dolls. Overlap grandmother's vest in front; secure with a row of tiny beads (buttons).

Cut small squares of print fabric for shawls for mother and grandmother. Fringe the edges, fold the squares in half diagonally, and tack around doll's shoulders.

Cut a ½x3½-inch strip of bonded felt for mother's girdle. Stitch two beads to each short end. Wrap belt around doll's waist and tack in place. Then crisscross a length of red crochet thread back and forth between beads to lace belt at front. Tie thread into a bow and clip ends.

For women's hats, cut and hem narrow bands of white fabric; embellish them with ribbons and laces. Gather the lower edge of the mother's headdress and stitch it to her head behind her braid. Trim with red and blue flowers and streamers of narrow ribbon. For grandmother's and girl's hats, tack the embellished strip of fabric to each doll's head at temples; trim with ribbon streamers and flowers, as shown.

• *To finish men's costumes:* Cut a 6x9-inch rectangle of green fabric for the man's trousers, and a 4x8-inch piece of blue for boy's trousers. Construct trousers as for women's pantaloons, above. Cut the center slit 3⅞ inches long for the man's pants, and 2¾ inches long for the boy's pants. Turn under raw edges, gather at waist and ankles, and fit the pants to the dolls' bodies.

Cut man's and boy's vests from bonded felt (as for women's vest, above). Whipstitch vests together at shoulders. Trim man's vest with red soutache braid and take tiny darts beneath armholes (as shown on pattern) to improve fit.

For man's cummerbund, fold a 3x5-inch piece of fabric in half lengthwise; stitch, turn right side out, press, and pleat into a cummerbund. Overlap the edges at the back of the trousers and stitch. Repeat with a 2x4¼-inch piece of fabric for the boy's cummerbund.

• *Men's hats:* Following individual patterns *(page 275)*, cut one hat for each doll from bonded felt. Overlap straight edges to dot and tack together. Fold peak down ¼ inch to back seam and tack in place. Trim each hat with short ribbon streamers and a cluster of flowers.

• *Shoes (for all dolls):* For each doll, cut two soles and two uppers from bonded black felt, following patterns. For women's and girl's shoes, whipstitch soles to uppers. Fit shoes to doll's feet, then whipstitch each back seam closed, catching the doll's heel with a stitch or two to secure.

For father's shoes, first stitch soles to uppers and fit shoes to doll, as for women's shoes. Then, cut two 2x2½-inch rectangles of bonded black felt for boot tops. Trim one long edge of each rectangle with embroidered ribbon. Wrap boot tops around each ankle and whip-stitch along back seam; then whip tops to bottoms of shoes. Trim tops with double bands of satin ribbon and short streamers.

For boy's boots, cut tops measuring ⅝x2¼ inches. Trim and stitch as for man's boots. Embellish boy's boot tops with crossed straps of ribbon (see photograph).

• *Baby's outfit:* First cut a tiny triangle of white flannel or felt for diaper; stitch in place and trim with an appliquéd flower. Next, make baby's slip from a 3x10-inch strip of scalloped eyelet lace. Assemble the slip as for slips of grown-up dolls.

To make dress, trim a 3¼x9½-inch piece of eyelet with embroidered ribbons for skirt. Seam and gather this skirt into a yoke made from two pieces of embroidered trim, each 2½ inches long. Slip the dress onto the doll, and tack the yoke at the shoulders.

Make two sleeves from 2¼x2¾-inch pieces of eyelet lace. Seam short edges of each piece together. Gather the raw edges of each sleeve and stitch them into the shoulders of the yoke. Gather scalloped edge of lace at wrist and tack in place. Tie wrists with bows of red crochet cotton and tack a tiny bow of crochet cotton to the center of the yoke.

For baby's bonnet, cut a 1¾x3½-inch piece of eyelet. Trim with embroidered ribbon, and hem short sides. Turn under raw edge ¼ inch; gather tightly. Seam short sides together about ¾ inch, fitting bonnet to head. Tack in place. Trim bonnet with ribbon streamers and a flower or two. Tack streamers and flowers to baby's hand for a bouquet.

Alpine Doll
Pictured on page 266

MATERIALS: ¼ yard of beige cotton challis (body); ⅓ yard of white cotton (pantaloons, blouse); ¼ yard of navy calico (dress skirt); 6x18-inch pieces of rust fabric and cotton lining (dress bodice); ¼ yard striped fabric (apron); three skeins yellow Persian yarn (hair); scrap of black felt (shoes); 28 inches navy piping; 25 inches of ¼-inch-wide lace; white single-fold bias tape; 33 inches of ¼-inch-wide elastic; three snaps; ½ yard of ½-inch-wide ribbon; ½ yard of ¼-inch-wide black satin ribbon; three heart-shape buttons; ¼-inch-diameter white button; embroidery floss; pink marker.

INSTRUCTIONS: This doll measures 21 inches tall. See the doll-making tips and techniques, *page 281,* before you begin.

Enlarge patterns, *below.* Pieces include ¼-inch seam allowances.

• *For body:* Cut pieces from challis. Satin-stitch eyes with three strands of blue floss; work black French knots for pupils. With gray thread, outline eyebrows, eyelids, and nose. Satin-stitch mouth with pink and color cheeks with pink marker.

Sew the center seam on head back; sew head back to one body section and head front to other body section. Sew the body front to back; leave the bottom open. Turn right side out and stuff firmly, especially the neck. Sew the bottom closed.

Sew arms; leave tops open. Turn; stuff hands loosely and hand-sew finger divisions. Stuff arms, close openings, and sew to body sides.

Sew front and back seams of legs. Sew soles to leg bottoms. Trim seams, turn, and stuff. Sew closed; sew legs to doll bottom.

• *For hair:* Sew bangs on forehead. Cut 21-inch lengths of yarn and sew to head, making a center part all the way down the head back. Braid hair; tie with ½-inch-wide ribbon.

• *For clothing:* Cut pantaloons from white cotton. Hem leg bottoms. Sew bias tape ⅜ inch from hemline to make elastic casings on each leg. Insert 7 inches of elastic through each casing; sew across elastic ends.

With right sides facing, sew front seam. Fold waist edge over ½ inch for casing; stitch. Insert 11 inches of elastic through casing; sew across ends. With right sides facing, sew back seam; sew inseam. Clip curves; trim seams, turn right side out.

• *For blouse:* Cut pieces from white cotton. Narrowly hem sleeves; trim with lace. Insert 4 inches of elastic in each sleeve; sew across elastic ends. Gather curved edges of sleeves.

With right sides facing, sew blouse front to back at shoulders. Gather neckline ¼ inch from raw edge. Sew blouse front seam, leaving a 2-inch opening at top. Finish gathered neck with an 8-inch piece of bias tape. Fasten neck opening with white button and thread loop.

Sew sleeves to armholes; sew underarm and side seams; hem blouse.

• *For dress:* Cut bodice from rust fabric, bodice lining from lining fab-
continued

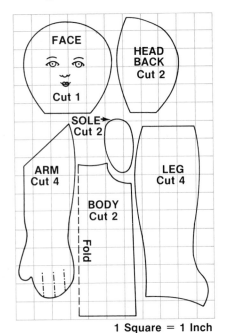

1 Square = 1 Inch

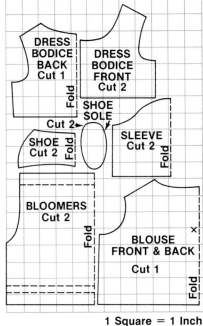

1 Square = 1 Inch

277

ric, and an 8x21-inch piece of navy calico (skirt). Sew bodice shoulder seams. Sew navy piping around center front, neck edge, and arm holes. Sew lining shoulder seams. Sew lining to bodice along piping stitch line. Turn; press. Sew side seams.

Gather skirt top. Sew front seam, leaving a 1½-inch opening at top. Hem skirt. Sew skirt to bodice, placing skirt front opening at bodice front opening. Turn under bottom edge of lining; slip-stitch to skirt. Sew heart buttons on right front of bodice. Overlap left bodice front and sew snaps behind buttons.

• *For apron:* Cut a 7x9-inch piece of striped cotton. Hem lower edge and sides. Gather top edge. Cut a 2x30-inch tie; press under ¼ inch on raw edges. Fold tie in half lengthwise, wrong sides facing; sew to apron, centering it over gathered edge.

• *For shoes:* Cut shoes and soles from felt. Sew front toe seams, leaving ¾ inch open at tops. Sew soles to shoe bottoms. Turn, sew black satin ribbons (ties) at front openings.

Bead Dolls
Pictured on page 267

MATERIALS: Wire hanger with cardboard tube; one 38-mm wooden bead; one 20-mm wooden bead; two 16-mm beads; 18 inches of 18-gauge wire; batting, fabric, and felt scraps; yarn roving (hair); scraps of ribbon, lace, and other trim; glue; acrylic paint; polyurethane; black felt pen; modeling compound.

INSTRUCTIONS: Remove the cardboard tube from wire hanger. Bend hanger (see illustration A, *above right*). Cut leg wire to measure 6 inches.

Draw and paint face on 38-mm bead; outline eyes, eyelashes, and mouth with black felt pen. (For boy, eliminate eyelashes and add freckles.) Finish with polyurethane.

Slip 20-mm bead onto wire for neck; slip head on top. Bend top of wire (illustration B) to form flat hook across top of head. Stuff bead holes with cotton; glue neck and head beads together.

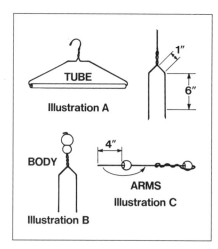

TUBE

Illustration A

BODY

Illustration B

ARMS

Illustration C

Slip 16-mm beads onto ends of 18-gauge wire; twist 4 inches of wire back over bead and around remaining wire (C). Tape center of arm wire to body under neck; wrap strips of batting around arms several times to secure.

Cut cardboard tube to fit legs, allowing ½ inch of wire to extend beyond cardboard. Tape top of each tube to wire to prevent slippage.

Wrap strips of batting around center of body, crossing over and around arms, tops of legs, and hip area. (Do not wrap legs.)

Roll modeling compound into a 2-inch-diameter ball; cut in half. Shape to foot pattern; make ½-inch-deep hole in heel end. Bake according to manufacturer's directions; paint with acrylics. After doll is fully dressed, glue shoes in place.

• *For hair:* For girl, cut six 30-inch strands of roving. Line up strands and machine-sew across center (part). Glue to head. Braid sides; tie with ribbon. For boy, cut eight 5-inch strands. Sew as for girl. Glue to head, placing stitching at side for part; trim for desired length.

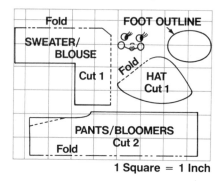

1 Square = 1 Inch

Dress dolls as desired, using pattern guidelines. For sweater and blouse, place wrong sides together; stitch underarm and side seams. For pants and bloomers, place wrong sides together; stitch inside seams, front center, and back center. Hat requires one seam (across top, down side). Add assorted trimmings.

Tyrolean Bears
Pictured on page 269

MATERIALS: ¾ yard of brown wool; fiberfill; four sets of Size 4 snaps for each bear; two round button eyes for each bear; black and brown felt scraps; black floss; carpet thread; darning needle; fabric glue.

• *For clothing:* ¼ yard gray felt or suede cloth (lederhosen); scraps of lace and print fabrics; dark green felt; 3 yards black middy tape; 1¼ yards embroidered ribbon; 1 yard of ¼-inch-wide satin ribbon; 12 inches of red cording; eight red buttons; two heart buttons; three small snaps; four sets of medium-size nylon fastening circles; matching threads.

INSTRUCTIONS: Enlarge patterns, *opposite* and *page 280;* cut out pieces. (Patterns include ¼-inch seam allowances where necessary.)

• *For ears, snout, arms, and legs:* Draw around pattern pieces on wrong side of *double* thickness of brown wool. Sew on drawn lines; leave openings for turning along straight edges or between Xs on patterns. Cut out pieces ¼ inch beyond stitched lines; set aside until needed.

• *For head:* Cut head backs; sew together along center seam. Cut out the head front. Turn the ears right side out; stuff lightly. With right sides facing, pin the ears to the head front, matching the raw edges. Sew the head front to the back; clip curves and turn right side out. Turn under the raw edge of the neck ½ inch and baste. Stuff the head firmly with fiberfill.

• *For snout:* Turn right side out and turn under raw edges ⅛ inch; baste. Stuff firmly; blindstitch to head front. Glue black felt nose in place, embroider mouth with black floss, and sew on button eyes.

• *For body:* Cut out pattern pieces. Sew center back and center front seams. Clip curves. Run double rows of staystitching along top edge of neck on both pieces. With right sides facing, stitch front to back; clip and turn. Stuff firmly. Pin head to body, matching side and center back seams. Blindstitch together.

• *Legs:* With wrong sides facing, sew sole to leg. Turn, stuff, and sew openings. Glue felt pads on soles.

• *Arms:* Turn right side out, stuff, sew openings closed. Sew divisions inside each paw with black floss.

• *To join arms and legs:* Use doubled thread to sew half of snap set to each arm and leg (snap positions are dots on patterns). Sew remainder of snap sets to corresponding parts on body. Snap together.

• *For lederhosen:* For each leg, place pattern atop a *double* thickness of felt or suede cloth; cut out. Sew center seam (A) and side seam (B) for each leg. Turn one leg right side out, slip into other leg, matching center back seam (C). Sew seam. Turn lederhosen right side out. Sew back dart, adjusting to bear's contour if necessary. (Front flap should overlap onto pants about ½ inch.) Turn under ¼ inch at waist (⅜ inch on flap); topstitch with dark green thread.

For flap, glue a double row (single row for baby) of middy tape to sides. Glue a ½-inch-wide green felt strip (cut with pinking shears) across top of flap. Sew buttons at each corner. Glue circles of nylon fastening tape inside flaps and on pants.

For suspenders, cut center crosspiece from green felt with pinking shears. Glue trim behind center. Cut gray felt or suede crosspiece slightly smaller than green crosspiece; cut out oval center. Glue gray atop green crosspiece. Cut two ¾x8½-inch green felt straps with pinking shears; cut two ⅝x8½-inch gray straps; place over green straps, leaving 2½ inches of strap to extend below center crosspiece.

Cut slits in each front strap for a buttonhole. Pin and tack the straps in place on the back; sew buttons at the end of each strap.

• *For Papa's hat:* Cut from felt. Sew top seam (⅛ inch). Turn under bottom ½ inch; topstitch. Whipstitch red cord around hat ½ inch above edge, crisscrossing ends of cord.

• *Baby's tie:* Draw around pattern on double thickness of fabric. Sew on drawn line; leave opening between Xs. Turn, press; sew opening.

• *Mama's dress:* Cut bodice and bodice lining. With right sides facing, sew around neck and center back opening. Clip corners; turn, press. Sew trim around neckline. Baste around armholes. Cut two 3½x12-inch sleeves. Gather sleeves to fit around armholes; sew in place. Hem sleeves; add trim. Sew side seams of sleeve and bodice. Gather lace on sleeve bottom, pulling to fit loosely around arm. Secure thread.

For skirt, cut a 5½x26-inch rectangle. Hem. Sew center back; leave 1¼ inches open at top. Gather and sew to bodice. Sew snaps to back.

For apron, cut a 4x10½-inch rectangle. Hem bottom and sides. Use remaining trim for waistband and ties. Gather apron to middle section of trim. Sew apron around waist.

• *Mama's hat:* Cut from green felt; cut ear slits. Fold up each back corner, matching A to B; tack. Glue ribbon along back edge of hat, leaving 12-inch ties. Slip onto head, pulling ears through slits; tie.

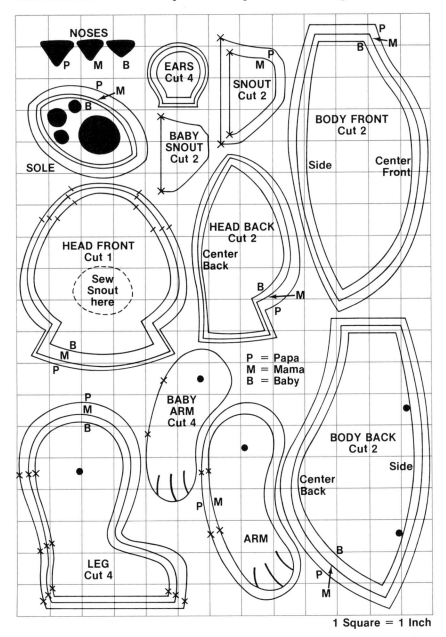

1 Square = 1 Inch

continued

Goldilocks Doll
Pictured on page 269

MATERIALS: ¼ yard of light pink fabric (body); ½ skein of yellow yarn (hair); four sets of Size 4 snaps; fiberfill; darning needle; acrylic paints; fine brushes; black permanent marker; pink floss.

• *For clothing:* Fabric scraps (blouse, dress, bloomers, slip); white knitted fabric (socks); black and gray felt (shoes); felt scrap (cummerbund); ribbon and lace trims; three small snaps; 10 loops from hook-and-eye sets; elastic thread; fabric glue.

INSTRUCTIONS: Enlarge pattern, *opposite.* See doll-making tips, *opposite.* Cut, stitch, and assemble doll's body, arms, and legs as for bears, *pages 278-279.* Use ¼-inch seams unless otherwise stated.

• *For head:* Cut and stack two 4x5-inch pink rectangles, right sides facing. Trace head profile onto wrong side of fabric, lining up bottom of neck with edges of fabric. Stitch. Trim ⅛ inch from stitching; clip curves. Turn to right side; gently push out nose and chin.

Cut out head back. Pin back to front; match dots on back to seam on front. Sew; turn. Turn under edges of neck ¼ inch; baste. Stuff head firmly. Push two cotton balls through neck to round out cheeks.

• *For body:* Sew body pieces together; attach head as for bears. Sew snaps where shown on pattern.

• *For face:* Using full-size pattern, *below,* transfer face to head. Paint with acrylics. Outline eyes and draw eyelashes with marking pen. Sew mouth with pink floss.

• *For hair:* Cut 1x4½-inch strip of pink fabric. Wrap yarn 40 times (lengthwise) around a 5x14-inch piece of cardboard. Slip off yarn; lay across pink strip, centered. Sew yarn to strip with yellow thread. Glue strip to head center, beginning just above eyebrows. Tie into pigtails.

• *For clothing:* Cut bloomers. Hem (edge A). Sew each leg together along B. Turn one leg right side out, slip into other leg. Line up, matching C edges; sew. Turn. Turn under waistline; run elastic through, fitting around doll's waist. Repeat for legs.

For slip, cut a 5½x24-inch rectangle. Sew back seam, hem waist and lower edge. Fit elastic in waistline seam. Trim hem edge with lace.

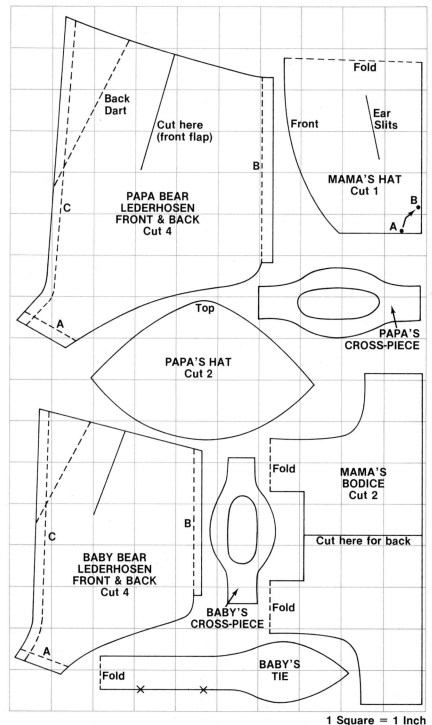

Back Dart

Cut here (front flap)

PAPA BEAR LEDERHOSEN FRONT & BACK Cut 4

Fold

Front

Ear Slits

MAMA'S HAT Cut 1

Top

PAPA'S HAT Cut 2

PAPA'S CROSS-PIECE

Fold

MAMA'S BODICE Cut 2

Cut here for back

BABY BEAR LEDERHOSEN FRONT & BACK Cut 4

BABY'S CROSS-PIECE

Fold

Fold

BABY'S TIE

1 Square = 1 Inch

For dress, follow instructions for mama bear's bodice, *page 279.* For sleeves, use two 4x10-inch rectangles. For skirt, cut fabric 5½x24 inches. Cut cummerbund from felt; sew dart. Sew five hook loops on each side of front edges directly across from each other. Trim edges, using ¼-inch-wide ribbon; thread ⅛-inch-wide ribbon through loops (bottom to top); tie at waist.

For socks, wrap a 6-inch square of knitted fabric snugly around foot and lower half of leg; pin. Pull socks off feet; sew pinned seams. Trim seams; add lace to sock tops. For shoes, cut soles from gray felt; cut uppers from black suede. Seam back edge of uppers with ¼-inch seams. Baste uppers to soles; sew with ⅛-inch seams. Clip curves; turn.

Doll-Making Tips

• *Selecting materials:* For the doll body, choose firm, closely woven fabric. Select high-quality fabric, because the body fabric largely determines the doll's quality. Select body fabric and yarn for the doll's hair first, then use these materials to coordinate fabrics and trims for the clothing. Before beginning construction, lay out all materials to make sure they work well together.

• *Cutting and stitching:* Lay out fabric with right sides facing. Unless otherwise indicated, position the longest part of the pattern piece on the lengthwise grain of the fabric.

Instead of cutting out the fabric *before* stitching, draw around patterns onto a double thickness of fabric. Stitch on the drawn line, leaving openings for turning. Then cut out ⅜ inch away from the stitching.

Set your machine for 15 to 20 stitches per inch; use 20 stitches per inch for tiny areas such as fingers. Press seams flat on both sides, then press open. (Finger-press seams that are too intricate for an iron.) Trim seams evenly; clip curves at even intervals and close to stitching.

• *Attaching arms and legs:* For extra strength, use buttonhole twist or pearl cotton thread to attach limbs to the body.

To add interest, stitch arms to the body with one arm slightly raised or more forward than the other, rather than having them perfectly aligned. Use T-pins, which are longer and stronger than regular pins, to hold arms and legs to the body while determining their positions and while hand-sewing limbs in place.

To make hands more realistic, stitch a small tuck in the palm. On a one-piece hand, create fingers by hand-stitching finger lines.

• *Facial features:* The most important part of a doll is its face, since facial features determine a doll's personality. Designing the perfect face for your doll takes practice and experimentation, but it will be easier with these guidelines.

To shape the features: Study illustrations and dolls you like for different types of facial features. Keep a record of favorite expressions, then simplify them to their basic shapes for adaptation to your dolls.

A plastic template of ovals and circles available at art or crafts stores will provide basic shapes that can be used for many facial features.

Experiment with features by cutting felt into eye, cheek, and mouth shapes. Combine shapes to achieve a variety of expressions.

Pin tracing paper over felt pieces and trace with a pencil, then transfer outlines to the face for painting or embroidery. Or, appliqué felt features directly onto the face.

To position the features: Use the following hints as a general guide.

Eyes: Place halfway between chin and top of head, leaving space equal to the width of one eye between.

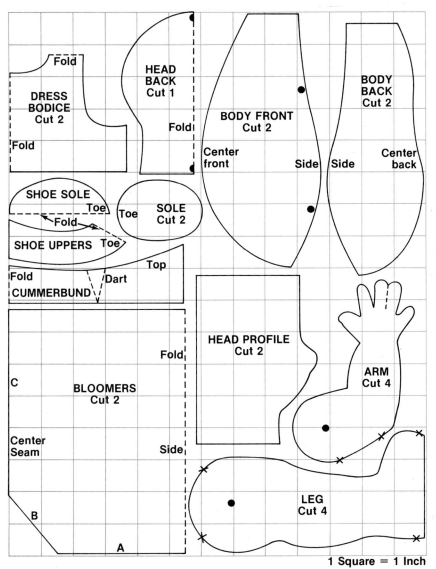

1 Square = 1 Inch

continued

Nose: Place bottom of nose half-way between eyes and chin, or slightly closer to chin.

Mouth: Place it halfway between nose and chin.

Ears: Position tops of ears even with eyebrows, and bottoms even with lower edge of nose.

For a child's face, make eyes rounder and farther apart. Or, place features lower on a rounder face.

To apply features: Use embroidery, paints, appliqué, or a combination of all three.

Embroider small parts (nostrils, eyelashes, eyebrows) with sewing thread or fewer strands of floss.

For cheek color, rub a cotton swab or a small ball of fiberfill into a rouge cake. Blow excess rouge from the ball; lightly rub color on fabric. To keep color from rubbing off, spray *lightly* with hair spray or clear acrylic.

• *Hair:* Blend yarns for special effects, but keep the yarn in scale with the size of the doll.

Use cotton, linen, twine, untwisted rope, and unspun wool for hair for large character dolls. For small dolls, use embroidery floss and crewel yarn.

Make hair slightly longer than necessary so the ends can be trimmed evenly later. To attach hair to the head, couch yarn by sewing over it with matching thread, or use darning needles to stitch wig to doll.

Doll Buggy
Pictured on page 268

MATERIALS: Hooded basket approximately 10x15x18 inches (or two baskets—cut one in half for the hood); ½x6x46-inch pine board (handle sides, wheels); 1x3x20-inch pine board (buggy and wheel supports); two ½x9-inch dowels; 1x12-inch dowel (handlebar); ½x13-inch dowel, four 1-inch-diameter washers (rear wheel assembly); two sets of washers and long screws (front wheel assembly); four long screws (for attaching basket); wood glue; blue enamel.

INSTRUCTIONS: Refer to the diagram, *below,* to cut all pieces. Drill holes for the handlebar and axle dowel as shown. Sand all wood surfaces until smooth.

Assemble the parts, fitting washers where shown. Attach the basket to buggy supports with long screws. Paint with enamel.

For smaller or larger baskets, adjust sizes for buggy supports, wheels, and handles to fit.

Wooden Limberjacks
Pictured on pages 270-271

MATERIALS: Scraps of the following: ¾x3-inch clear white pine; ¼x2-inch pine lath; ¼- and ½-inch-diameter dowels; 6x24-inch piece of

3/16-inch oak or plywood (performance platform).

Also: Scraps of simulated sheepskin, fiberfill, leather, and leather lacing; hemp twine; ¼x1-inch cotter pins; stovepipe wire; short, flexible ¼-inch-diameter springs; instant glue or epoxy; jigsaw; drill and assorted bits; sandpaper; needle-nose pliers.

INSTRUCTIONS: Enlarge patterns, *below* and *opposite;* trace onto wood. Cut body parts from pine; cut hooves, wings, horns, ears, and cow's udder from lath. Cut slits for mouths and details as indicated on patterns. Drill holes as marked. Use a hole-cutter drill for large body openings on cow (optional).

For legs, cut sections as shown on patterns; drill ⅛-inch holes for attachments. Sand all wood parts.

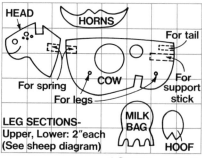

1 Square = 1 Inch

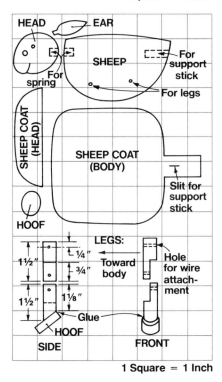

1 Square = 1 Inch

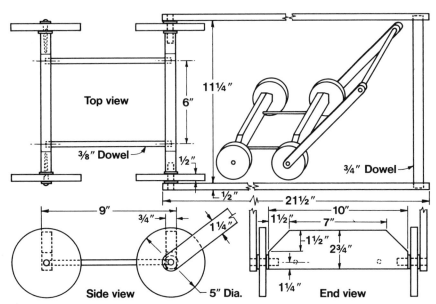

With pliers, snip springs into 1-inch lengths. Using glue or epoxy, insert ends into ¼-inch-diameter holes drilled ¼ inch deep into body and head pieces for sheep, cow, and mule as indicated on patterns.

Insert ears (mule) and horns and udder (cow) into ¼-inch-wide slots on head and body pieces. Glue hooves or feet to lower leg sections for each animal. Use cotter pins to assemble leg sections, allowing enough space at knee joints for legs to remain limber. (Keep heads of pins on outside of limbs.)

Use soft wire to attach assembled legs to torso as follows: With needle-nose pliers, bend one end of wire into small loop. Insert other end through ⅛-inch holes drilled in top of leg, body, and other leg. Trim wire; bend cut end into a small loop, securing legs *loosely* to body. Add details to each animal. Secure (but don't glue) a 20-inch length of ¼-inch dowel into rear support holes.

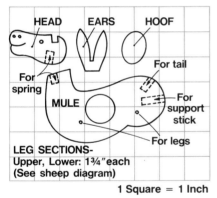

HEAD EARS HOOF

For tail

For spring

MULE

For support stick

For legs

LEG SECTIONS-
Upper, Lower: 1¾"each
(See sheep diagram)

1 Square = 1 Inch

Loose movement-
(Larger hole)-no glue

Dowel

Glue

FRONT VIEW OF HEAD ATTACH- MENT

HEAD

Cut out this section

ROOSTER

For support stick

For legs

Glue

UPPER LEG ATTACH- MENT

FOOT

WING

LEG SECTIONS-
Upper, Lower: 2½"each
(See sheep diagram)

1 Square = 1 Inch

• *For sheep:* Glue sheepskin to one side of body. Using stuffing, pad skin on sides and top of body; glue other edge of skin and tail section in place. Glue ears into holes just behind eyes; glue a bit of wool to head.
• *For cow:* Cut 5½ inches of twine. Fray 1 inch of one end; knot above frayed section; glue other end into body. Bend short piece of thick, flexible wire into circle. Trim with pliers; insert ends through holes in nose. Secure by pressing sides of circle until cut ends meet inside nose.
• *For mule:* Cut four 4-inch lengths of leather lacing. Gather ends together; insert and glue into tail hole.
• *For rooster:* Cut slot for beak and wattles. Insert into slot on head; line up eye holes with hole in insert. Push 1-inch length of ¼-inch dowel through hole. Glue dowel on each side of rooster's head, allowing crown section to rotate freely.

Carrousel Marionettes
Pictured on pages 272-273

MATERIALS: Two 12x12-inch felt squares in matching or contrasting colors; 12 inches of 2-inch-wide satin fringe; felt scraps for saddle, blanket, and decorations; 24 inches of narrow gold cord; gold lamé scraps; stuffing; black fishline; tapestry needle; ¼x6-inch dowel; two ⅛x4-inch dowels; white glue; hole punch; plastic lid; ⅛-inch drill bit.

INSTRUCTIONS: Enlarge pattern, *below;* cut from felt. (Seams, except mane, are on the outside.)
• *For body:* Slit B where indicated; insert 2¾ inches of fringe for mane;

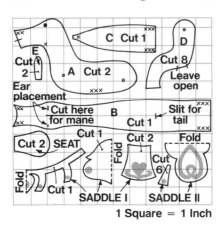

C Cut 1

D

E Cut 2

A Cut 2

Cut 8

Leave open

Ear placement

Cut here for mane

B Cut 1

Slit for tail

Cut 2 SEAT

Fold

Cut 1

Cut 2 Fold

Fold

Cut 6

Fold

Cut 1

SADDLE I

SADDLE II

1 Square = 1 Inch

sew closed. Sew B to side A beginning at nose (XX), sewing over top edge and ending at center bottom of body (XXX). Sew C to body edges between XXX and X. (B and C will overlap ¼ inch at center.) Sew lower jaw closed to line marked on pattern. Separate sections above line mark to form a T from front view; sew closed. Stuff firmly through overlap B and C. Hand-sew closed.

Using small scissors, snip holes in top of head for ears. Fold ears in half; insert; sew closed. Glue small black felt dots in place for eyes.
• *For tail:* Cut ¼x3-inch rectangle from plastic lid. Cut point at one end. Using remaining fringe and beginning at blunt end of plastic, sew through plastic, attaching fringe in upward spiral around plastic to within 1 inch of pointed end. Insert tail into slit in horse back; sew closed.
• *For legs:* Sew leg sections; leave openings. Turn, stuff; sew closed. For leg control lines, thread needle with fishline; pull line through upper portion of leg, through body to opposite leg. Knot securely.

Add saddle seat and saddle decorations. Use gold cord for bridle.
• *For control bar:* Drill ⅛-inch holes in larger dowel ½ inch from ends. Insert two small dowels through ends of larger dowel; glue in center. Drill small hole in ends of three dowels. Attach 8-inch fishlines to body parts, as shown *below.*

MARIONETTE CONTROL

283

INTER-NATIONAL CHRISTMAS HERITAGE

No matter how far from home they may have roamed, when the yuletide season rolls around, young and old alike look forward to sharing special foods, music, and customs with family and friends.

All across America, Christmas is a mixture of Old World traditions and contemporary habits. The secrets for preparing favorite ethnic holiday recipes have been lovingly handed down for generations. So, for this section of our book, we searched for and found some of the best of these traditional ethnic recipes. As you look through them, you'll be transported across oceans, over land, and through time to experience some of the most flavorful of holiday traditions.

Poppy Seed Loaf, Black Forest Cherry Cake, Cinnamon Cookies, and Zagreb Cake (see Index for recipe pages)

PORK ALENTE JANA

1½ cups dry white wine
2 teaspoons paprika
2 cloves garlic, minced
2 bay leaves
2 pounds lean boneless pork, cut into 1-inch pieces
2 pounds clams in shells
2 medium onions, thinly sliced
2 tablespoons olive oil *or* cooking oil
¼ cup chopped pimiento
½ teaspoon salt

For marinade, combine wine, paprika, garlic, and bay leaves. Place pork in a large plastic bag set in a deep bowl. Pour marinade over pork and close bag. Let stand at room temperature for 2 hours or in the refrigerator overnight, turning bag occasionally. Drain pork well, reserving marinade. Pat pork dry with paper toweling.

Cover clams with salted water (use 3 tablespoons salt to 8 cups cold water). Let stand 15 minutes; rinse. Repeat soaking and rinsing twice. Meanwhile, in a Dutch oven brown pork and onion in oil. Drain off fat. Stir in reserved marinade, pimiento, salt, and ¼ teaspoon *pepper.* Simmer, covered, over medium-low heat 35 minutes.

Add clams to pork mixture; cook, uncovered, 10 minutes longer or till clam shells open. Discard any clams that do not open. Skim off fat. Remove bay leaves. Makes 6 to 8 servings.

Portuguese Vegetable Soup (see recipe, page 288), Portuguese Cod-Potato Casserole (see recipe, page 288), and Pork Alente Jana

PORTUGUESE VEGETABLE SOUP

Pictured on pages 286-287—

8 cups water
1 large beef shank crosscut (about 1 pound)
1 cup dry green split peas
3 cloves garlic, minced
1 teaspoon salt
½ pound chorizo links, sliced, *or* Italian sausage links, sliced
3 medium tomatoes, peeled, seeded, and chopped
2 medium carrots, chopped
1 medium onion, chopped
½ cup chopped green pepper
1 cup elbow macaroni

In a large kettle or Dutch oven stir together the water, beef shank crosscut, split peas, garlic, and salt. Bring to boiling. Reduce heat. Simmer mixture, covered, for 1 hour.

Remove beef shank. Cool till meat can be easily handled. Cut meat off bone; discard bone. Chop meat and return to mixture in kettle. Stir in sliced chorizo or Italian sausage, tomatoes, chopped carrots, chopped onion, and chopped green pepper. Simmer, covered, for 20 minutes.

Stir in elbow macaroni. Bring to boiling. Reduce heat; simmer, covered, about 10 minutes or till macaroni is tender. Makes 10 servings.

OLHOS DE SOGRA

3 beaten egg yolks
1 14-ounce can Eagle Brand sweetened condensed milk
1 teaspoon finely shredded lemon peel
2 tablespoons lemon juice
1 12-ounce package pitted, dried prunes
Sifted powdered sugar

In saucepan combine egg yolks, milk, and lemon peel. Cook over medium heat, stirring constantly, till mixture is thickened and bubbly. Continue cooking 2 minutes more. Remove from heat. Stir in lemon juice. Cool. Using a pastry tube and small star tip, fill prunes with lemon mixture. Roll in powdered sugar; set in individual paper cups. Store, covered, in refrigerator. Makes 48.

BROWN SUGAR PRALINES

2 cups packed brown sugar
1 cup light cream
2 tablespoons butter
2 cups pecan halves

In a large saucepan combine sugar and cream; bring to boiling, stirring constantly. Cook to 238° (soft ball stage), stirring as necessary to prevent sticking. Remove from heat; add butter. Stir in pecans. Beat for 1 to 2 minutes or till candy just begins to lose its gloss. Drop by tablespoons onto waxed paper, shaping into patties with back of spoon. If the candy becomes too stiff to drop, add a few drops hot water. Makes 24.

PORTUGUESE COD-POTATO CASSEROLE

Pictured on pages 286-287—

1 pound salt cod
1 cup chopped onion
2 tablespoons olive oil *or* cooking oil
1 10½-ounce can tomato pùree
1 cup chicken broth
¼ cup snipped parsley
⅛ teaspoon pepper
3 medium potatoes, peeled and sliced

In a bowl soak the cod in enough cold water to cover for 12 hours or overnight, changing the water several times. Drain and rinse the cod.

Place the cod in a large saucepan. Add enough cold water to cover the cod. Bring the cod to boiling; reduce heat. Simmer the cod, covered, about 12 minutes or till the cod flakes easily when tested with a fork. Drain off the water.

Meanwhile, in another saucepan cook the chopped onion in the olive oil or cooking oil till the onion is tender but not brown. Stir in the tomato-puree, chicken broth, snipped parsley, and pepper. Simmer the tomato mixture, uncovered, for 15 minutes.

Flake the drained cod with a fork; gently stir into the tomato mixture along with the sliced potatoes. Turn into an ungreased 1½-quart casserole. Bake, covered, in a 350° oven about 1 hour or till the potatoes are tender, stirring once or twice. Makes 4 servings.

CHICKEN IN PEPITORIA

1 2½- to 3-pound broiler-
   fryer chicken, cut up
¼ cup all-purpose flour
1 teaspoon salt
¼ teaspoon pepper
2 tablespoons cooking oil
½ cup sliced green onion
½ cup sliced fresh
   mushrooms
3 cloves garlic, minced
1 cup chicken broth
1 cup dry white wine
1 tablespoon dried parsley
   flakes
1 bay leaf
2 hard-cooked eggs, sieved
¼ cup ground almonds
¼ cup soft bread crumbs
⅛ teaspoon ground saffron
   Hot cooked rice

Rinse chicken pieces; pat dry.
In a paper or plastic bag combine flour, salt, and pepper.
Add chicken, a few pieces at a
time; shake to coat. In a skillet
brown chicken on all sides in
hot oil about 15 minutes. Remove and set aside; reserve oil.

Cook onion, mushrooms, and
garlic in reserved hot oil till onion is tender. Drain off fat. Stir
chicken broth, wine, parsley
flakes, and bay leaf into onion
mixture. Return chicken to skillet. Bring to boiling; reduce
heat. Cover and simmer 45
minutes or till chicken is
tender. Transfer chicken to a
platter; keep warm. Remove
bay leaf; skim off fat.

For sauce, combine sieved
eggs, almonds, bread crumbs,
and saffron; stir into mixture in
skillet. Cook and stir till thickened and bubbly. Pour sauce
over chicken. Serve with hot
cooked rice. Makes 6 servings.

Although the most popular version of Gazpacho is chilled fresh tomato soup, it can be more than that. Some versions are served hot, with meatballs, chicken, or even grapes. Other recipes exclude tomatoes entirely and call for very little liquid. Regardless of the differences, all gazpachos do contain some vegetables and garlic.

SONOMA SANGRIA

4 cups dry red wine
2 cups apple cider *or* apple
   juice
1 cup carbonated water
1 medium apple, cored and
   sliced
1 medium peach, pitted and
   sliced
1 medium orange, sliced
1 cup brandy (optional)
   Ice

In a large pitcher stir together
the wine, cider or juice, and
carbonated water. Add the apple, peach, and orange. Stir in
the brandy, if desired. Pour
over ice to serve. Makes 10 to
12 (6-ounce) servings.

GAZPACHO

If you use the blender to chop the vegetables, cover them with water before blending. Then, drain them well—

1 medium sweet red pepper
½ of a medium red onion
1 medium cucumber
1 46-ounce can tomato juice
3 tablespoons vinegar
2 tablespoons olive oil *or*
   cooking oil
2 cloves garlic, minced
1 teaspoon salt
   Condiments such as
   chopped pimiento,
   chopped red onion,
   chopped cucumber,
   or croutons

In a blender container or food
processor bowl process the
sweet red pepper till chopped.
Remove from container. Process the ½ onion in a blender
container or food processor
bowl till chopped. Remove
from container. Process the 1
medium cucumber in a blender
container or food processor
bowl till chopped.

In a large bowl combine the
chopped red pepper, chopped
½ onion, and chopped medium
cucumber. Stir in tomato juice,
vinegar, olive oil or cooking
oil, garlic, and salt. Cover
and chill.

To serve, spoon the tomato
juice mixture into individual
bowls. Pass the condiments to
sprinkle atop each serving.
Makes 8 to 10 servings.

KOTOPITS IN BÉCHAMEL SAUCE

10 to 12 sheets frozen phyllo
   dough (8 ounces)
1 cup chopped celery
¾ cup chopped onion
1 tablespoon butter *or*
   margarine
2 cups chopped, cooked
   chicken *or* turkey
2 tablespoons water
⅛ teaspoon instant chicken
   bouillon granules
2 teaspoons dried parsley
   flakes
½ teaspoon salt
½ teaspoon ground nutmeg
⅛ teaspoon pepper
1 beaten egg
⅔ cup butter *or* margarine,
   melted
   Hot cooked rice
   (optional)
   Béchamel Sauce

Thaw phyllo dough for 2 hours
at room temperature. Meanwhile, in a skillet cook the
chopped celery and onion in
the 1 tablespoon butter or margarine till vegetables are tender
but not brown, stirring occasionally. Stir in chicken or turkey, water, and chicken
bouillon granules. Cook and
stir, uncovered, till all the liquid is absorbed. Stir in parsley
flakes, salt, nutmeg, and pepper. Remove from heat. Stir in
beaten egg. Set aside.

Spread 1 sheet of the phyllo
dough flat. Brush liberally with
some of the ⅔ cup melted butter or margarine. Top with second sheet; brush liberally with
butter. Repeat stacking and
brushing with butter using 3 or
4 more sheets phyllo dough.
Spoon *half* of the chicken mixture over phyllo layers to within 1 inch of edges.

Turn one short side of the
phyllo over the chicken mixture
about 1 inch; fold in long sides.
Roll up jelly-roll-style starting
with folded short side. Place,
seam side down, in a lightly
greased 13x9x2-inch baking
dish. Repeat with remaining
phyllo, butter, and chicken mixture. Brush the top of each roll
with some additional melted
butter or margarine.

Score each roll into 3 or 4
portions. Bake in a 350° oven
for 30 to 35 minutes or till the
rolls are brown and crisp. Cut
rolls where scored. Arrange on
a serving platter with hot
cooked rice, if desired. Spoon
some of the Béchamel Sauce
over rolls. Pass remaining
sauce. Makes 6 to 8 servings.

BÉCHAMEL SAUCE: In a
small saucepan melt 2 tablespoons *butter or margarine*. Stir in
2 tablespoons *all-purpose flour*
and dash *salt*. Add 1¼ cups
chicken broth all at once. Cook
and stir over medium heat till
the mixture is thickened and
bubbly. Cook and stir 1 minute
more. Stir together 2 beaten *egg
yolks* and 4 teaspoons *lemon juice*.
Stir about *half* of the hot mixture into the egg yolk mixture.
Return all to the saucepan.
Cook and stir over medium
heat for 2 minutes more.
Makes 1½ cups sauce.

*Kotopits in Béchamel Sauce, Lemon-
Basil Carrots, and Karidopeta (see
recipes, page 292)*

*A*ll across America, people celebrate Christmas with the food and fellowship styles of their ancestors. On this page and page 291, you'll find the recipes for a traditional Greek Christmas meal—Kotopits in Béchamel Sauce served on a bed of rice, Lemon-Basil Carrots, and Karidopeta.

LEMON-BASIL CARROTS

Pictured on pages 290-291—

- 1 pound baby carrots *or* medium carrots, cut into 2½-inch pieces
- 1 tablespoon butter *or* margarine
- 1½ teaspoons lemon juice
- ¼ teaspoon garlic salt
- ¼ teaspoon dried basil, crushed
  Dash pepper

In a medium saucepan cook carrots in boiling salted water, covered, for 10 to 20 minutes or till tender. Drain.

In a small saucepan melt the butter or margarine. Stir in the lemon juice, garlic salt, dried basil, and pepper. Drizzle butter mixture over the carrots; toss to coat. Makes 6 servings.

KARIDOPETA

Pictured on pages 290-291—

- 8 egg yolks
- 1 cup sugar
- 2 cups ground walnuts (about 8 ounces)
- 1 cup finely crushed zwieback (11 to 12 slices)
- 1½ teaspoons baking powder
- 1 teaspoon ground cinnamon
- 8 egg whites
  Thin lemon slices, halved
- ⅓ cup water
- ⅓ cup sugar
- 2 tablespoons lemon juice

In a small mixer bowl beat together egg yolks and the 1 cup sugar on high speed of electric mixer about 5 minutes or till very thick and lemon-colored.

Stir together ground walnuts, crushed zwieback, baking powder, and cinnamon; set aside. Thoroughly wash beaters. In a large mixer bowl beat egg whites till stiff peaks form (tips stand straight). Fold in egg yolk mixture; fold in ground walnut mixture. Pour batter into a greased and floured 13x9x2-inch baking pan. Bake in a 350° oven for 30 to 35 minutes or till done. Cool in the pan on a wire rack. Score the top of the cake into diamonds. Top each diamond with a halved lemon slice.

In a small saucepan combine water, ⅓ cup sugar, and lemon juice. Bring to boiling; reduce heat. Simmer, uncovered, for 5 minutes. Pour hot mixture over cooled cake. Cut cake into diamonds along score lines. Makes 20 to 24 pieces.

KOURABIEDES

Sometimes these tender, rich cookies are garnished with a few whole cloves before they are baked—

- 2¼ cups all-purpose flour
- ½ teaspoon baking powder
- 1 cup butter *or* margarine
- ½ cup sifted powdered sugar
- 1 beaten egg yolk
- 2 tablespoons brandy
- ½ teaspoon vanilla
- ⅓ cup finely chopped almonds
  Powdered sugar

In a bowl stir together the flour and baking powder. Set dry ingredients aside.

In a mixer bowl beat the butter or margarine on medium speed of an electric mixer for 30 seconds. Add the ½ cup powdered sugar and beat till the mixture is fluffy. Add the beaten egg yolk, brandy, and vanilla; beat well. Stir in the finely chopped almonds.

Add the dry ingredients to the beaten mixture and stir till well combined. Cover and chill the dough for 30 minutes.

Shape the chilled cookie dough into 1-inch balls or ovals. Place on an ungreased cookie sheet. Bake in a 325° oven for 25 to 30 minutes or till cookies are a light sandy color. Remove from cookie sheet; cool on a wire rack. Roll in powdered sugar. Makes about 36 cookies.

SEAFOOD-STUFFED CAPON

½ pound fresh *or* frozen
   shrimp
½ pound fresh *or* frozen
   scallops
6 to 8 clams in shells,
   rinsed
1 cup chopped onion
½ cup dry white wine
1 teaspoon snipped parsley
½ teaspoon dried thyme,
   crushed
   Dash pepper
2 tablespoons butter *or*
   margarine
1 cup chopped celery
1 cup chopped onion
2 tablespoons butter *or*
   margarine
¼ cup snipped parsley
¼ cup snipped chives
½ teaspoon dried oregano,
   crushed
⅛ teaspoon ground red
   pepper
1 beaten egg
5 cups dry bread cubes
½ cup chopped filberts,
   toasted
½ cup grated Parmesan
   cheese
1 tablespoon lemon juice
1 6- to 8-pound capon
   Cooking oil
   Butter Sauce

Thaw shrimp and scallops, if frozen. In a saucepan combine clams, 1 cup chopped onion, wine, 1 teaspoon parsley, thyme, and pepper. Bring to boiling. Reduce heat; cover and simmer mixture about 5 minutes or till clams open. Discard any clams that do not open. Cool; remove clams from shells and finely chop. Discard shells. Strain liquid and reserve.

Finely chop shrimp and scallops. Cook in 2 tablespoons butter or margarine about 2 minutes or till nearly done. Remove from heat; set aside. Cook celery and 1 cup onion in 2 tablespoons butter or margarine till tender but not brown. Stir in ¼ cup snipped parsley, chives, oregano, and red pepper; remove from heat. In a large bowl combine egg, bread cubes, filberts, Parmesan, lemon juice, clam meat, shrimp mixture, and onion mixture. Add enough reserved clam liquid to moisten mixture.

Rinse capon; pat dry with paper toweling. Season body cavity with salt, if desired. Spoon stuffing loosely into neck and body cavities; pull the neck skin to back of bird. Twist wing tips under back, holding skin in place. Tie legs to tail. Place, breast side up, on a rack in a shallow roasting pan. Brush with cooking oil. Insert meat thermometer in the center of the inside thigh muscle, making sure the bulb does not touch bone. Bake in a 375° oven about 2 hours or till thermometer registers 185° and the drumstick moves easily in its socket. (Bake any remaining stuffing in a covered casserole for the last 35 minutes of the roasting time.)

Transfer capon to a platter. Prepare Butter Sauce. Pass Butter Sauce with capon. Makes 10 to 12 servings.

BUTTER SAUCE: Skim fat from pan drippings. Melt ¼ cup *butter*. Stir in pan drippings. Add 4 ounces fresh or frozen, thawed, chopped *shrimp* and 4 ounces fresh or frozen, thawed, chopped *scallops*. Cook and stir about 2 minutes or just till done. Stir together ¼ cup dry *white wine* and 1 tablespoon *cornstarch*; add along with 1 cup *chicken broth* to mixture in saucepan. Cook and stir till bubbly. Continue 2 minutes more. Makes about 2 cups sauce.

CRISP GOLDEN PIZZELLES

You usually can purchase or rent a hand-held or electric pizzelle iron from a kitchen equipment store—

3½ cups all-purpose flour
2 tablespoons baking
   powder
3 eggs
1 cup sugar
½ cup butter *or*
   margarine, melted and
   cooled
1 teaspoon vanilla

In a bowl stir together the flour and baking powder. Set aside.

In a mixer bowl beat eggs on high speed of an electric mixer till foamy; stir in the sugar. Add the cooled, melted butter or margarine and vanilla; mix well. Stir in the dry ingredients. Chill the dough for several hours or overnight.

Shape the dough into balls, using 2 tablespoons dough for each ball. Heat a seasoned pizzelle iron over medium-high heat on the top of the range.

Place one ball of dough on the iron. Squeeze the lid to close the iron. Bake the dough over medium-high heat for 1 to 2 minutes on each side or till the pizzelle is golden brown. (Or, use an electric pizzelle iron according to the manufacturer's directions.) Open the pizzelle iron and turn the wafer out onto a wire rack to cool. Repeat with remaining balls of dough. Makes 24.

COD MATELOTE

1 16-ounce package frozen
    cod fillets
2 slices bacon
1 cup whole fresh
    mushrooms, quartered
1 medium onion, sliced and
    separated into rings
1 clove garlic, minced
1 tablespoon all-purpose
    flour
1 teaspoon instant chicken
    bouillon granules
¼ teaspoon dried thyme,
    crushed
⅛ teaspoon pepper
    Dash ground allspice
1 8-ounce bottle (1 cup)
    clam juice
1 cup dry white wine
1 bay leaf
1 9-ounce package frozen
    Italian green beans,
    thawed
    Croutons (optional)

Let cod fillets stand at room
temperature for 20 to 30 minutes. Cut into 1-inch pieces. Set
aside. Meanwhile, in a saucepan
cook bacon till crisp; drain,
reserving drippings. Crumble
bacon and set aside.

Cook mushrooms, onion, and
garlic in the reserved drippings
till tender. Stir in flour, bouillon granules, thyme, pepper,
and allspice. Add the clam juice
and wine all at once. Add bay
leaf. Cook and stir till thickened and bubbly. Reduce heat;
simmer, uncovered, for 15 minutes. Add the fish and green
beans; return to boiling. Reduce heat; simmer, covered, for
10 to 12 minutes or till fish
flakes easily when tested with a

fork and green beans are
tender. Remove bay leaf. Stir
in bacon. Serve with Croutons,
if desired. Makes 4 servings.

CROUTONS: Remove crust
from four ½-inch-thick slices of
French bread. Cut each slice into
scalloped shapes, triangles, or
other decorative shapes. In skillet fry the bread in *butter or margarine* on both sides till golden.
Keep warm.

PEACH-GLAZED SAVARIN

2 cups all-purpose flour
1 package active dry yeast
⅔ cup milk
⅓ cup butter *or* margarine
2 tablespoons sugar
½ teaspoon salt
3 eggs
    Savarin Syrup
    Peach Glaze
    Desired fruits such as red
    grapes, strawberries, *or*
    sectioned oranges
    Crème Chantilly
    (optional)

In a large mixer bowl combine
1½ cups of the flour and the
yeast. In a small saucepan heat
the milk, butter or margarine,
sugar, and salt just till warm
(115° to 120°) and the butter
or margarine is almost melted,
stirring constantly. Add the
milk mixture to the flour mixture; add the eggs. Beat on low
speed of an electric mixer for

½ minute, scraping sides of
bowl constantly. Beat on high
speed for 3 minutes.

Stir in the remaining flour
with a spoon. Cover; let rest 10
minutes. Spoon batter into a
well-greased 6-cup savarin mold
or ring mold. Cover; place in
oven. Turn oven on to 250°;
turn oven off after 1 minute.
Open oven door slightly; let
dough rise till nearly doubled
(about 40 minutes). Remove
from oven; preheat oven to
350°. Bake in a 350° oven for
25 to 35 minutes or till done.
Cool 5 minutes, then remove
from pan onto a wire rack
placed over waxed paper.

With fork, prick top of ring
at 1-inch intervals. Gradually
drizzle Savarin Syrup over
warm ring till all syrup is absorbed. Let stand 30 minutes.
Spoon on Peach Glaze. To
serve, fill center of ring with
desired fruits. Serve with
Crème Chantilly, if desired.
Makes 10 servings.

SAVARIN SYRUP: In a
small saucepan stir together 1½
cups *peach nectar* and ½ cup
sugar. Bring nectar mixture to
boiling; remove from heat. Stir
in ½ cup *rum*.

PEACH GLAZE: In a sauce-
pan heat one 12-ounce jar *peach
jam* over low heat till melted,
stirring constantly.

CRÈME CHANTILLY: In a
mixer bowl beat 1 cup *whipping
cream* with 1 tablespoon *powdered
sugar* and 1 teaspoon *vanilla* on
high speed of an electric mixer
till soft peaks form.

Cod Matelote and Croutons

ROAST GOOSE WITH APPLE STUFFING

1 7- to 9-pound domestic
  goose
1 cup chopped onion
2 tablespoons butter *or*
  margarine
5 cups dry bread cubes
2 cups chopped, peeled
  apple
¼ cup snipped parsley
¾ teaspoon dried sage,
  crushed
½ teaspoon salt
⅛ teaspoon pepper
2 beaten eggs
½ cup chicken broth

Remove liver from the goose
and chop. Rinse the goose and
pat dry with paper toweling.
Set goose aside.

  Cook liver and onion in butter or margarine till liver is
done and onion is tender. In a
large bowl combine liver mixture, bread cubes, apple, parsley, sage, salt, and pepper. Stir
together eggs and chicken
broth. Add egg mixture to
bread cube mixture and toss.

  Lightly stuff the body cavity
of the goose with bread mixture. Tie legs to tail. Twist
wing tips under back. Prick
legs and wings with fork. Place
goose, breast side up, on a rack
in shallow roasting pan. Insert
meat thermometer in center of
inside thigh muscle, making
sure bulb does not touch bone.
Roast the goose in a 350° oven
about 2½ hours or till thermometer registers 185° and the
drumstick moves easily in its
socket; spoon off fat. Makes 10
to 12 servings.

DARK FRUITCAKE

3 cups raisins
2 cups pitted, dried prunes,
  cooked and chopped
2 cups diced mixed candied
  fruits and peels
1½ cups broken walnuts
1 cup chopped red candied
  cherries
½ cup chopped candied
  pineapple wedges
1½ teaspoons finely shredded
  orange peel
¼ cup burgundy
2¼ cups all-purpose flour
1½ teaspoons baking powder
1½ teaspoons ground
  cinnamon
1 teaspoon ground cloves
1 teaspoon ground mace
½ teaspoon salt
½ teaspoon ground allspice
1 cup butter *or* margarine
1 cup sugar
½ cup packed brown sugar
5 eggs
1½ teaspoons vanilla
½ cup brandy
½ cup light rum

Grease a 10-inch tube pan.
Line bottom and sides of pan
with brown paper; grease paper. In large bowl combine raisins, prunes, fruits and peels,
walnuts, cherries, pineapple,
and orange peel. Pour burgundy over and set aside.

  Stir together flour, baking
powder, cinnamon, cloves,
mace, salt, and allspice; mix *half*
of the flour mixture with fruit
mixture. In mixer bowl beat
butter or margarine on medium
speed of electric mixer for 30
seconds. Add sugar and brown
sugar; beat till fluffy. Add eggs,
one at a time, beating well after
each addition. Add vanilla. Mix
in remaining flour mixture.
Pour over fruit mixture; stir to
mix well. Turn batter into prepared pan. Bake in a 300° oven

about 2 hours or till done.
Cover loosely with foil after 1
hour of baking to prevent overbrowning. Cool in pan for 20
minutes. Remove from pan and
cool completely. Combine ¼
cup each of the brandy and
rum; use to moisten several layers of cheesecloth. Wrap fruitcake in cheesecloth, then in
foil. Store fruitcake in refrigerator 2 or 3 days. Moisten
cheesecloth again with remaining brandy and rum. Rewrap
fruitcake and refrigerate 2 to 6
weeks. Makes 1 fruitcake.

STANDING RIB ROAST WITH YORKSHIRE PUDDING

1 4-pound beef rib roast
4 eggs
2 cups milk
2 cups all-purpose flour
¾ teaspoon salt

Place roast, fat side up, in a
13x9x2-inch baking pan. Season with salt and pepper. Insert
a meat thermometer. Roast, uncovered, in a 325° oven for 2½
to 3¼ hours or till meat thermometer registers 140° for
rare, 160° for medium, or 170°
for well done. Remove roast
from pan. Cover roast with foil;
keep warm. Reserve ¼ cup
drippings. Increase oven temperature to 400°.

  In a mixer bowl beat eggs on
low speed of an electric mixer
for ½ minute. Add the milk;
beat for 15 seconds. Add flour
and salt; beat till combined,
then beat for 2 minutes.

  Return reserved drippings to
13x9x2-inch baking pan. Pour
egg mixture into pan. Bake in
400° oven for 30 minutes. Cut
into squares. Serve with roast.
Makes 8 servings.

EASY PLUM PUDDING

1 16-ounce can whole, unpitted purple plums
1 14½-ounce package gingerbread mix
1 cup light raisins
½ cup chopped walnuts
2 tablespoons sugar
2 tablespoons cornstarch
1 tablespoon lemon juice
   Fluffy Hard Sauce

Generously grease a 6-cup fluted tube pan. Set aside. Drain plums; reserve syrup. Remove pits; chop plums. Prepare gingerbread mix according to package directions. Stir in plums, raisins, and walnuts. Spoon into prepared pan. Bake in a 375° oven about 1 hour or till done. Cool in pan for 10 minutes. Remove from pan by inverting onto a wire rack. Cool slightly.

Meanwhile, add water, if necessary, to reserved plum syrup to make 1 cup total liquid. In a small saucepan stir together the sugar and cornstarch. Stir in the 1 cup liquid. Cook and stir till thickened and bubbly. Cook and stir 2 minutes more. Stir in lemon juice. Place warm cake on a serving plate. Pour warm mixture atop. Pass Fluffy Hard Sauce. Makes 10 to 12 servings.

FLUFFY HARD SAUCE: In a mixer bowl beat ½ cup *butter or margarine* on medium speed of an electric mixer for 30 seconds. Add 2 cups sifted *powdered sugar;* beat till mixture is fluffy. Beat in 1 *egg yolk* and 1 teaspoon *vanilla.* Fold 1 stiffly beaten *egg white* into mixture. Chill thoroughly.

HONEY-BUTTERED WINE

2 cups dry white wine
3 tablespoons orange liqueur
3 tablespoons honey
1 tablespoon sugar
4 teaspoons butter *or* margarine
   Lemon slices
   Cinnamon sticks

In a medium saucepan combine wine, orange liqueur, honey, and sugar. Heat to boiling; pour into four small mugs. Top *each* serving with *1 teaspoon* of the butter or margarine.

Garnish with lemon slices and cinnamon stick stirrers. Makes 4 (4-ounce) servings.

WASSAIL PUNCH

2 cups water
1 cup sugar
12 inches stick cinnamon
6 cups orange juice
1 1.5-liter bottle burgundy
3 cups unsweetened pineapple juice
   Lemon slices *or* orange slices

In a large saucepan combine water, sugar, and cinnamon. Bring to boiling. Reduce heat; cover and simmer for 5 minutes. Remove cinnamon. Stir in orange juice, burgundy, and pineapple juice. Cook over medium-low heat just till mixture almost boils. Pour into heatproof punch bowl. Float lemon or orange slices atop. Makes about 30 (5-ounce) servings.

CHEESE STRAWS

1 cup all-purpose flour
¼ teaspoon salt
½ cup shredded cheddar cheese (2 ounces)
¼ cup butter *or* margarine
4 to 5 tablespoons cold water
1 teaspoon Worcestershire sauce
2 tablespoons sesame seed

In a mixing bowl stir together the flour and the salt. Cut in the shredded cheddar cheese and butter or margarine till the mixture resembles coarse crumbs. Sprinkle *1 tablespoon* of the water over part of the mixture; gently toss with a fork. Push to side of bowl. Repeat till all is moistened. Form dough into a ball. Wrap in waxed paper; chill in the refrigerator for 1 hour.

On a floured surface roll the dough into a 12-inch square. Brush with the Worcestershire sauce. Sprinkle with the sesame seed. Fold 2 opposite sides of the square to the middle then fold the remaining two sides to the middle. Roll out the pastry into a 12x6-inch rectangle.

Use a knife to cut the dough into 3x½-inch strips. Twist each strip and place on a greased and floured baking sheet. Bake in a 400° oven about 10 minutes or till lightly browned. Remove from pan to a wire rack; cool. Makes 48.

STOLLEN BREAD

4 to 4½ cups all-purpose
   flour
1 package active dry yeast
¼ teaspoon ground
   cardamom
1¼ cups milk
½ cup butter *or* margarine
¼ cup sugar
1 egg
2 tablespoons finely
   shredded orange peel
1 tablespoon finely
   shredded lemon peel
1¼ cups raisins
¼ cup diced mixed candied
   fruits and peels,
   chopped
¼ cup chopped blanched
   almonds
1 cup sifted powdered
   sugar

Combine *2 cups* flour, yeast,
and cardamom. Heat milk, butter, sugar, and 1 teaspoon *salt*
just till warm (115° to 120°);
stir constantly. Add to flour
mixture; add egg, orange peel,
and lemon peel. Beat on low
speed of electric mixer for ½
minute, scraping bowl. Beat for
3 minutes on high speed. Stir
in raisins, candied fruits, and
almonds. Stir in as much of the
remaining flour as you can.

On a floured surface knead
in enough remaining flour to
make a moderately soft dough
that is smooth and elastic (3 to
5 minutes total). Shape into a
ball. Place into a greased bowl;
turn once. Cover; let rise till
double (about 1¾ hours).

Punch down; divide into
thirds. Cover; let rest 10 minutes. Roll *one-third* of the dough
into a 10x6-inch rectangle.
Without stretching, fold a long
side over to within 2 inches of
opposite side; seal. Place onto a
greased baking sheet. Repeat
with remaining dough. Cover;

let rise till nearly double (about
1 hour). Bake in a 375° oven
for 18 to 20 minutes or till
done. Combine powdered sugar and 2 tablespoons *hot water;*
brush onto warm bread. Cool
on wire racks. Makes 3.

THREE KINGS RING

2¾ to 3¼ cups all-purpose
   flour
1 package active dry yeast
¼ teaspoon ground
   cinnamon
⅔ cup milk
¼ cup butter *or* margarine
¼ cup sugar
½ teaspoon salt
2 eggs
2 teaspoons finely shredded
   orange peel
½ teaspoon finely shredded
   lemon peel
½ cup chopped walnuts
½ cup diced mixed candied
   fruits and peels,
   chopped
   Icing

In a mixer bowl combine *1½
cups* flour, yeast, and cinnamon.
In a saucepan heat milk, butter,
sugar, and salt just till warm
(115° to 120°); stir constantly.
Add to flour mixture; add eggs,
orange peel, and lemon peel.
Beat on low speed of electric
mixer for ½ minute, scraping
bowl. Beat for 3 minutes on
high speed. Stir in nuts and
fruits. Stir in as much of the remaining flour as you can.

On a well-floured surface
knead in enough remaining
flour to make a moderately soft
dough that is smooth and elastic (3 to 5 minutes total). Shape
into a ball. Place into a greased
bowl; turn once. Cover; let rise
till double (1 to 1½ hours).

Punch dough down. Roll
into a 25-inch-long rope; seal
ends together to form a ring.
Place onto a greased baking
sheet. Cover; let rise in a warm
place till nearly double (about
40 minutes). Bake in a 375°
oven about 25 minutes or till
done, covering with foil the last
5 minutes. Cool. Prepare Icing;
drizzle over bread. If desired,
decorate with candied fruit
"poinsettias" centered with walnut halves. Makes 1 ring.

ICING: Combine 1 cup sifted *powdered sugar* and enough
milk (about 1½ tablespoons) to
make of drizzling consistency.

GINGER CUTOUTS

Pictured on page 300—

5 cups all-purpose flour
2 teaspoons ground ginger
1½ teaspoons baking soda
1 teaspoon ground
   cinnamon
1 teaspoon ground cloves
1 cup shortening
1 cup sugar
1 egg
1 cup molasses
2 tablespoons vinegar

Combine flour, ginger, soda,
cinnamon, cloves, and ½ teaspoon *salt*. Beat shortening with
electric mixer for 30 seconds.
Add sugar; beat till fluffy. Add
egg, molasses, and vinegar;
beat well. Add dry ingredients;
beat till combined. Divide into
thirds. Cover; chill for 3 hours.
Roll dough, one-third at a time,
to ⅛-inch thickness. Cut into
desired shapes; place onto a
greased cookie sheet. Bake in a
375° oven for 4 to 6 minutes
or till done. Cool 1 minute before removing to rack. Decorate, if desired. Makes 60.

BLACK FOREST CHERRY CAKE

Pictured on pages 284-285—

Cherry Filling
Chocolate Buttercream
1½ cups all-purpose flour
1½ cups sugar
 1 teaspoon salt
 ¾ teaspoon baking soda
 1 cup milk
 ⅓ cup cooking oil
 2 eggs, separated
 2 squares (2 ounces)
  unsweetened chocolate,
  melted and cooled
 1 teaspoon unflavored
  gelatin
 3 cups whipping cream
 ½ cup Kirsch
 ¾ cup toasted, sliced
  almonds
 1 square (1 ounce)
  semisweet chocolate,
  shaved

Grease and flour three 9x1½-inch round baking pans. Prepare Cherry Filling and Chocolate Buttercream. Set aside. Stir together flour, *1 cup sugar,* salt, and soda. Add *½ cup* milk and the oil; beat 1 minute with electric mixer. Add remaining milk and egg yolks; beat 1 minute more.

Thoroughly wash beaters; beat egg whites till soft peaks form. Gradually add remaining sugar, beating till stiff peaks form. Fold into flour mixture.

Pour *one-third* of the mixture into *one* pan; set aside. Fold chocolate into mixture in bowl; pour into two pans. Bake in a 350° oven for 20 to 25 minutes. Cool for 10 minutes before removing to racks.

Soften gelatin in 2 tablespoons *cold water* for 5 minutes. Stir over low heat just till dissolved. Whip cream till slightly thickened. Add gelatin, beating till soft peaks form.

Place one chocolate cake layer on platter. Fit pastry bag with medium rose point (No. 2F); fill with Chocolate Buttercream. Pipe 3 concentric rings onto cake, ending with last ring on outer edge. Fill area between buttercream rings with some of the Cherry Filling. Spread a thin layer (about 1 cup) of whipped cream over top. Place yellow cake layer atop; drizzle Kirsch *very slowly* over cake. Fit pastry bag with large rosette tip (No. 1C); fill with *2 cups* of the whipped cream. Pipe a band of whipped cream about 2 inches wide around outer edge. Fill center with *some* of the Cherry Filling. Place the second chocolate cake layer over cherries; frost cake with remaining whipped cream. Press almond slices onto side of cake. Spoon remaining Cherry Filling into center. Sprinkle shaved chocolate around edge of top. Chill for 1 to 24 hours. Makes 16 servings.

CHERRY FILLING: Drain two 16-ounce cans *pitted tart red cherries (water pack),* reserving ⅔ cup juice. In a 2-quart saucepan combine reserved juice, ⅔ cup *sugar,* and ¼ cup *cornstarch.* Cook and stir till thickened and bubbly. Add cherries; cook and stir for 2 minutes more. Remove from heat; stir in 1 teaspoon *vanilla.* Cool.

CHOCOLATE BUTTER-CREAM: Beat 3 tablespoons *butter or margarine.* Gradually beat in 1 cup sifted *powdered sugar.* Beat in 1 square (1 ounce) *unsweetened chocolate,* melted and cooled, 2 tablespoons *light cream or milk,* and 1 teaspoon *vanilla.* Gradually beat in 1 cup sifted *powdered sugar* till fluffy. If necessary, stir in enough *light cream or milk* (1 to 2 teaspoons) to make buttercream of piping consistency.

SPRINGERLE

Pictured on page 300—

 2 cups all-purpose flour
 ¼ teaspoon baking soda
 2 eggs
 2⅓ cups sifted powdered
  sugar (about ½ pound)
 10 drops oil of anise

Stir together flour and baking soda; set aside. In a mixer bowl beat eggs on high speed of electric mixer about 5 minutes or till thick and lemon colored. Gradually add powdered sugar, beating till combined. Beat on high speed about 15 minutes more or till mixture is slightly thickened. Stir in oil of anise.

Using a spoon, stir the dry ingredients into beaten mixture (mixture will be stiff). Form the dough into a ball. Cover and let stand for 15 minutes.

Divide dough in half. On a lightly floured surface roll each portion of dough into an 8x6-inch rectangle. Let dough stand for 1 minute.

Dust a springerle mold or springerle rolling pin with additional flour; roll or press hard enough on dough to make a clear design. Using sharp knife or cookie cutter, cut the cookies apart. Place onto a lightly floured surface; cover and let stand for 6 hours or overnight.

Brush excess flour from cookies. With finger, rub bottom of each cookie lightly with cold water. Place cookies onto a greased cookie sheet. Bake in a 300° oven for 15 to 18 minutes or till cookies are a light straw color. Cool on a wire rack. Makes about 36 cookies.

APRICOT LEBKUCHEN

1 cup unblanched almonds
1 cup filberts
2 tablespoons diced
    candied citron
2 tablespoons diced
    candied orange peel
1 tablespoon diced
    candied lemon peel
⅓ cup all-purpose flour
1 teaspoon ground
    cinnamon
¼ teaspoon ground cloves
2 egg whites
⅔ cup sugar
½ cup apricot preserves
1¼ cups blanched whole
    almonds (144)
1 egg white

Grease a cookie sheet. Grind unblanched almonds, filberts, candied citron, orange peel, and lemon peel through fine blade of food grinder or in food processor. In a large mixing bowl stir together the ground nut mixture, flour, cinnamon, and cloves. Set aside.

In a small mixer bowl beat the 2 egg whites till foamy; gradually add sugar, beating till soft peaks form (tips curl over). Fold into nut mixture; stir in apricot preserves.

Drop batter from a tablespoon 3 inches apart onto prepared cookie sheet. Arrange *3* whole almonds atop *each* cookie. Bake in a 325° oven about 15 minutes or till done.

Mix 1 egg white and 1 tablespoon *water;* brush onto cookies. Remove from sheet; cool on wire rack. Makes about 48.

Springerle (see recipe, page 299), Zinsterne (Cinnamon Stars), Ginger Cutouts (see recipe, page 298) decorated with Santa picture, Apricot Lebkuchen, and Florentines

FLORENTINES

1 cup blanched almonds,
    finely chopped
½ cup diced mixed candied
    fruits and peels, finely
    chopped
⅓ cup butter *or* margarine
⅓ cup milk
¼ cup sugar
2 tablespoons honey
¼ cup all-purpose flour
¾ cup semisweet chocolate
    pieces
2 tablespoons shortening

Grease and lightly flour a cookie sheet. In a mixing bowl combine almonds and fruits and peels; set aside. In a saucepan combine butter or margarine, milk, sugar, and honey. Bring to boiling, stirring occasionally. Remove from heat. Stir in almond mixture; stir in flour.

Drop from a tablespoon at least 3 inches apart onto prepared cookie sheet. (Place only 6 cookies at a time on a cookie sheet.) Using back of a spoon, spread into 3-inch circles.

Bake in a 350° oven for 8 to 10 minutes or till done. Cool 1 minute before carefully transferring to waxed paper with a spatula to cool thoroughly. Repeat with remaining batter, greasing and flouring cookie sheet before each batch.

In a small heavy saucepan melt chocolate pieces and shortening over low heat, stirring often. Spread about *1 teaspoon* of the chocolate mixture over the bottom of *each* cookie. When chocolate is almost set, draw wavy lines on it with the tines of a fork. Store, covered, in the refrigerator. Makes 24 cookies.

ZINSTERNE (CINNAMON STARS)

1½ cups toasted almonds,
    ground
¾ cup toasted filberts,
    ground
2 tablespoons all-purpose
    flour
1 teaspoon ground
    cinnamon
¼ teaspoon ground nutmeg
2 egg whites
1 cup sugar
    Powdered sugar
1½ cups sifted powdered
    sugar
1 to 2 tablespoons milk

Grease a cookie sheet. In a mixing bowl stir together almonds, filberts, flour, cinnamon, and nutmeg. In a mixer bowl beat egg whites till soft peaks form (tips curl over). Gradually add sugar, beating till stiff peaks form (tips stand straight). Fold the nut mixture into the beaten egg whites. Cover and let the mixture stand for 30 minutes to let the nuts absorb moisture.

On a surface lightly sprinkled with powdered sugar, roll dough to ¼-inch thickness. Cut with 1½-inch star-shape cookie cutter, dipping cutter into flour between cuts. Place onto prepared cookie sheet. Bake in a 325° oven for 10 to 15 minutes or till done. Remove from sheet; cool on a wire rack.

For frosting, in a mixing bowl combine the 1½ cups sifted powdered sugar and enough milk to make of spreading consistency. Spread frosting on cookies; store in a covered container. Makes about 48 cookies.

NOTE: Dough scraps may be rerolled to ½-inch thickness and cut with a scalloped cutter. Bake in a 325° oven about 20 minutes or till done.

DUTCH APPLE CAKE

2 cups all-purpose flour
1 teaspoon baking soda
1 teaspoon salt
1 teaspoon ground
   cinnamon
2 eggs
1 cup cooking oil
1 teaspoon vanilla
1½ cups sugar
4 cups very finely chopped,
   peeled, tart apples
   (1½ pounds)
1 cup chopped walnuts
   Vanilla Icing

Grease and lightly flour a 10-inch fluted tube pan; set aside. Stir together flour, baking soda, salt, and cinnamon; set aside.

In a large mixer bowl beat eggs on high speed of electric mixer about 2 minutes or till light and fluffy. Add the cooking oil and vanilla; beat about 2 minutes more or till thickened. Gradually add the sugar, beating till dissolved.

Add the dry ingredients and finely chopped apple alternately to the beaten mixture, beating on low speed after each addition till just combined. Beat on medium speed for 3 minutes. Fold in the chopped walnuts.

Turn the batter into prepared pan. Bake in 350° oven for 55 to 60 minutes or till cake tests done. Cool in the pan for 10 to 15 minutes. Remove the cake from pan; cool on a wire rack. Make Vanilla Icing and drizzle over cake. Makes 12 servings.

VANILLA ICING: In a mixing bowl stir together 1 cup sifted *powdered sugar,* 1 teaspoon *vanilla,* and enough *milk* (about 2 tablespoons) to make of drizzling consistency.

ALMOND LEBKUCHEN

4 cups all-purpose flour
2 teaspoons ground allspice
2 teaspoons ground
   cinnamon
1 teaspoon baking soda
1 teaspoon salt
1 teaspoon ground cloves
3 eggs
1½ cups packed brown sugar
¼ cup honey
   Diced candied citron
   (about ⅓ cup)
   Slivered almonds
   (about ⅔ cup)

Stir together flour, allspice, cinnamon, baking soda, salt, and cloves; set aside. In a large mixer bowl beat eggs on high speed of electric mixer about 5 minutes or till thick and lemon colored. Gradually add brown sugar, beating till mixture is fluffy. Stir in honey. Using a spoon, stir flour mixture into beaten mixture. Divide dough in half; wrap each portion in waxed paper. Chill the dough in the refrigerator for several hours or overnight.

On a lightly floured surface roll the dough, half at a time, to ¼-inch thickness. Cut with a 2½-inch round cutter, dipping cutter into flour between cuts. Place onto greased cookie sheet. Place a citron piece in the center of each round. Arrange 6 slivered almonds around each citron piece in a spoke fashion.

Bake in a 400° oven about 7 minutes or till light brown. Remove from cookie sheet; cool on wire rack. Makes about 48.

NOTE: If desired, store baked cookies in a covered container with two or three apple slices to soften.

CRESCENT TARTS

1 cup butter *or* margarine,
   softened
1 8-ounce package cream
   cheese, softened
2 cups all-purpose flour
⅓ to ½ cup orange
   marmalade *or* fruit
   preserves
1 beaten egg
   Powdered sugar

In a large mixing bowl combine butter or margarine and cream cheese; beat on medium speed of electric mixer till mixed. Add flour; beat till smooth. Divide dough in half; wrap each portion in waxed paper. Chill in the refrigerator for several hours or overnight.

On a lightly floured surface roll the dough, half at a time, to ⅛-inch thickness. Cut with a 2½-inch round cutter, dipping cutter into flour between cuts. Place about *½ teaspoon* of the marmalade or fruit preserves in the center of *each* circle. Brush the edges with water. Fold the dough circles in half. Press edges with the tines of a fork to seal. Brush the tops with beaten egg; sprinkle with powdered sugar. Place onto an ungreased cookie sheet.

Bake in a 350° oven about 15 minutes or till done. Transfer the cookies to a wire rack to cool. When cool, sprinkle again with powdered sugar. Makes about 42 cookies.

*C*hristmas is cookie-baking time, especially if you are of Dutch descent. It is a time for young hands to learn how to shape the spicy treats that their grandparents held so dear. Almonds, ginger, cinnamon, and cloves find their way into many Dutch cookies.

ALMOND BARS

1 cup butter *or* margarine
2 cups all-purpose flour
½ cup water
1 8-ounce can almond paste
2 eggs
¾ cup sugar
½ teaspoon vanilla

In a medium mixing bowl cut the butter or margarine into flour till mixture resembles fine crumbs. Add the water; stir till all is moistened. Divide dough in half; wrap each portion in waxed paper. Chill in the refrigerator for several hours or overnight.

Let the dough stand at room temperature about 30 minutes or just till soft enough to handle. Meanwhile, for filling, in a mixer bowl crumble almond paste. Add eggs, sugar, and vanilla; beat on medium speed of electric mixer till combined.

On a lightly floured surface roll the dough, half at a time, into a 14x10-inch rectangle. Lay one rectangle in the bottom and ½ inch up the sides of a 13x9x2-inch baking dish. Spread the almond filling over dough. Lay the remaining dough rectangle atop filling. Fold edges under. Bake in a 400° oven for 30 to 35 minutes or till done. Cool thoroughly in the pan on a wire rack. Cut into bars. Makes 36 bars.

CRISPY SPICE COOKIES

3½ cups all-purpose flour
1 teaspoon baking powder
1 teaspoon ground cinnamon
½ teaspoon ground nutmeg
¼ teaspoon salt
¼ teaspoon ground cloves
1½ cups butter *or* margarine, softened
2 cups packed brown sugar
1 egg
Blanched whole almonds (optional)

Stir together the flour, baking powder, cinnamon, nutmeg, salt, and cloves; set aside. In a mixer bowl beat butter or margarine on medium speed of electric mixer for 30 seconds

Add the brown sugar and beat till fluffy. Add the egg; beat well. Add the dry ingredients to the beaten mixture and beat till combined. (The dough will be somewhat stiff.)

On a lightly floured surface roll the dough, one-third at a time, to slightly less than ¼-inch thickness. Cut into desired shapes with cookie cutters, dipping cutters into flour between cuts. Top each with an almond, if desired. Place cutouts onto an ungreased cookie sheet.

Bake in a 350° oven for 10 to 12 minutes or till done. Cool about 1 minute before transferring to a wire rack. Makes about 96 cookies.

SPICED MILK PUNCH

4 cups milk
2 inches stick cinnamon
4 whole cloves
Dash ground mace
Dash ground saffron (optional)
¼ cup sugar
1 tablespoon cornstarch
4 cinnamon sticks (optional)

In a medium saucepan combine milk, the 2 inches stick cinnamon, cloves, mace, and saffron, if desired. Bring almost to boiling. Reduce heat. Cover and simmer over very low heat for 15 minutes. Remove cinnamon and cloves with a slotted spoon.

Combine sugar and cornstarch; stir into milk mixture. Cook and stir till bubbly. Cook and stir for 2 minutes more. If desired, beat with rotary beater till foamy. Ladle into mugs. Serve warm with cinnamon stick stirrers, if desired. Makes 4 (8-ounce) servings.

LUCIA BUNS

⅛ teaspoon ground saffron
4¼ to 4¾ cups all-purpose
    flour
1 package active dry yeast
1¼ cups milk
½ cup butter *or* margarine
⅓ cup sugar
1 teaspoon salt
1 egg
96 raisins (⅓ cup)
1 slightly beaten egg white

Pour 2 tablespoons *boiling water*
over saffron; let stand. In a
large mixer bowl combine *2
cups* of the flour and the yeast.
In a saucepan heat milk, butter
or margarine, sugar, and salt
just till warm (115° to 120°)
and butter is almost melted,
stirring constantly. Add to flour
mixture; add egg and saffron
mixture. Beat on low speed of
electric mixer for ½ minute,
scraping bowl constantly. Beat
for 3 minutes on high speed.
Using a spoon, stir in as much
remaining flour as you can.

On a floured surface knead
in enough remaining flour to
make a moderately stiff dough
that is smooth and elastic (6 to
8 minutes total). Shape into a
ball. Place into a greased bowl;
turn once. Cover; let rise till
double (about 1½ hours).

Punch down; divide into
quarters. Cover; let rest for 10
minutes. Divide each quarter
into 12 pieces. On a lightly
floured surface roll each piece
into a 12-inch-long rope. On a
lightly greased baking sheet
form one rope into an S-shape,
coiling the ends in snail fashion. Repeat with remaining
ropes. (For double buns, place
two of the S-shaped pieces together to form a cross.) Press a
raisin into the center of each
coil. Cover; let rise till nearly
double (about 40 minutes).

Brush with beaten egg white.
Bake in a 375° oven for 12 to
15 minutes or till done. Cool
on wire racks. Makes 48 single
or 24 double buns.

JULEKAGE

8¼ to 8¾ cups all-purpose
    flour
2 packages active dry yeast
2 teaspoons ground
    cardamom
3 cups milk
½ cup butter *or* margarine
½ cup sugar
2 teaspoons salt
½ cup raisins
½ cup dried currants
½ cup diced candied citron
½ cup diced red candied
    cherries
½ cup diced green candied
    cherries
    Powdered Sugar Icing

In mixer bowl combine *3½ cups*
flour, yeast, and cardamom.
Heat milk, butter, sugar, and
salt just till warm (115° to
120°); stir constantly. Add to
flour mixture. Beat on low
speed of electric mixer for ½
minute, scraping bowl. Beat for
3 minutes on high speed. Stir
in raisins, currants, citron, and
cherries. Stir in as much of the
remaining flour as you can.

On a lightly floured surface
knead in enough of the remaining flour to make a moderately
stiff dough that is smooth and
elastic (6 to 8 minutes total).
Shape into a ball. Place into a
lightly greased bowl; turn once.
Cover; let rise in a warm place
till double (about 1 hour).

Punch dough down; divide
into 3 portions. Cover; let rest
for 10 minutes. Shape each
portion into a round loaf; place
each into a greased 8x1½-inch

round baking pan. Cover; let
rise in a warm place till nearly
double (about 45 minutes).

Bake in a 375° oven about
40 minutes or till done; cover
with foil the last 10 minutes.
Cool. Prepare Powdered Sugar
Icing; drizzle atop loaves. Garnish with red candied cherries,
if desired. Makes 3 loaves.

POWDERED SUGAR
ICING: Combine 2 cups sifted
powdered sugar and enough *milk*
(1 to 2 tablespoons) to make of
drizzling consistency.

GLOGG

3 750-milliliter bottles dry
    red wine
1 cup raisins
¼ cup sweet vermouth
8 inches stick cinnamon,
    broken
6 whole cardamom pods,
    cracked
6 whole cloves
    Peel of 1 orange
1 cup sugar
1 cup blanched whole
    almonds

In a saucepan combine *1 bottle*
of wine, the raisins, and the
vermouth. Place cinnamon, cardamom, and cloves into a
cheesecloth bag; add to the
wine mixture. Simmer, covered, for 15 minutes. Add orange peel; simmer for 5
minutes more. Remove spices
and peel. Stir in the sugar and
remaining wine; heat through.
Add the almonds. Serve warm
with orange slices, if desired.
Makes 24 (4-ounce) servings.

Lucia Buns, Julekage, and Glogg

PIEROGI (STUFFED PASTRIES)

1¾ cups all-purpose flour
½ teaspoon salt
2 beaten eggs
⅓ cup water
  Potato-Cottage Cheese
    Filling *or* Farmer
    Cheese Filling
  Butter *or* margarine,
    melted
  Dairy sour cream
    (optional)
  Snipped fresh dill
    (optional)

Stir together flour and salt. Combine eggs and water; add to flour mixture, stirring till combined (dough should be pliable but not sticky). On a lightly floured surface knead dough gently for 15 to 20 strokes. Cover and let stand for 10 minutes.

Meanwhile, prepare Potato-Cottage Cheese Filling or Farmer Cheese Filling; set aside.

Divide dough in half. On a lightly floured surface roll dough, half at a time, to ⅛-inch thickness. Cut with a 3-inch round cutter, dipping cutter into flour between cuts.

For pierogi, place *1 tablespoon* of the filling onto half of *one* circle. Fold other half of circle over, making a crescent shape. Pinch edges together to seal. Place onto a floured surface; cover. Repeat with remaining dough circles and filling.

In a large saucepan gently slide the pierogi, a few at a time, into boiling water, stirring with a spoon to keep them from sticking. Simmer gently, uncovered, for 4 to 5 minutes or till pierogi rise to surface.

Using a slotted spoon, transfer cooked pierogi to a colander; rinse immediately under hot running water, shaking gently. Turn into a shallow oven-proof bowl. Gently stir in a little melted butter to prevent sticking. Keep warm while cooking remaining pierogi.

To serve, top with additional melted butter or margarine or with sour cream, if desired. Sprinkle with fresh snipped dill, if desired. Makes about 30.

POTATO-COTTAGE CHEESE FILLING: Cook ⅓ cup chopped *onion* in 1 tablespoon hot *butter or margarine* till tender but not brown. Stir in 1½ cups mashed cooked *potatoes,* 1 teaspoon snipped fresh *dill or* ½ teaspoon dried *dillweed,* ¼ teaspoon *salt,* and dash *pepper.* Stir in ⅔ cup *dry cottage cheese.* Makes 2 cups.

FARMER CHEESE FILLING: Beat 2 *eggs* and 2 *egg yolks.* Stir in 2 cups shredded *farmer cheese* (8 ounces), 2 teaspoons *lemon juice,* and ½ teaspoon *salt.* Makes 2 cups.

NOTE: Any leftover pierogi can be chilled and reheated. To reheat, melt a small amount of *butter or margarine* in a skillet. Add pierogi; cover. Cook over low heat till pierogi are golden, turning once.

HAM-FILLED ROULADE

¼ cup butter *or* margarine
½ cup all-purpose flour
¼ teaspoon salt
⅛ teaspoon pepper
2 cups milk
5 egg yolks
5 egg whites
  Ham Filling

Grease a 13x9x2-inch baking pan. Line with waxed paper; grease again. Dust with flour; set aside. In a saucepan melt butter. Stir in the ½ cup flour, salt, and pepper. Add milk; cook and stir till thickened and bubbly. Cook and stir 1 minute more. Remove from heat.

Beat egg yolks on high speed of electric mixer about 5 minutes or till thick and lemon colored. Gradually stir thickened mixture into yolks. Cool slightly, about 5 minutes.

Thoroughly wash beaters. Beat egg whites till stiff peaks form (tips stand straight). Fold into cooled mixture. Pour into prepared pan; spread evenly. Bake in a 400° oven for 25 to 30 minutes or till puffed and brown. Meanwhile, prepare Ham Filling; keep warm.

Immediately turn cake out onto a clean towel. Remove waxed paper. Spread Ham Filling over cake. Roll up jelly-roll style, starting from short side and using towel to help roll. Transfer to platter, seam side down. Makes 6 servings.

HAM FILLING: In a skillet cook 2 tablespoons finely chopped *onion* in 1 tablespoon hot *butter or margarine* till tender but not brown. Stir in 1 cup ground *fully cooked ham,* 2 tablespoons snipped *parsley,* 2 tablespoons *dairy sour cream,* and 1 teaspoon *Dijon-style mustard.* Heat through.

POPPY SEED LOAF

Pictured on pages 284-285—

5¼ to 5¾ cups all-purpose
    flour
2 packages active dry yeast
1½ cups milk
⅓ cup sugar
⅓ cup shortening
3 eggs
¾ cup poppy seed
½ cup chopped walnuts
⅓ cup honey
1 teaspoon finely shredded
    lemon peel
1 stiff-beaten egg white
1 egg yolk

Combine *2 cups* flour and yeast. Heat and stir milk, sugar, shortening, and 1 teaspoon *salt* just till warm (115° to 120°). Add to flour mixture. Add eggs; beat with electric mixer for 3½ minutes. Stir in as much remaining flour as you can.

On a floured surface knead in enough of the remaining flour to make a moderately stiff dough that is smooth and elastic (6 to 8 minutes total). Shape into a ball. Place into a greased bowl; turn once. Cover; let rise till double (1¼ to 1½ hours).

Pour 1 cup *boiling water* over poppy seed; let stand 30 minutes. Drain. In a covered blender container blend till ground. Add to nuts, honey, and peel. Fold in egg white.

Punch dough down; divide in half. Cover; let rest 10 minutes. Roll *half* into a 24x8-inch rectangle; spread with *half* of the nut mixture. Starting from short side, roll up jelly-roll style; seal. Place, seam side down, into a greased 8x4x2-inch loaf pan. Repeat. Cover; let rise till double (30 to 45 minutes). Combine yolk and 1 tablespoon *water;* brush onto dough. Bake in a 350° oven 35 to 40 minutes. Cool. Makes 2.

ZAGREB CAKE

Pictured on pages 284-285—

¾ cup butter *or* margarine,
    softened
⅔ cup sugar
9 egg yolks
5 squares (5 ounces)
    semisweet chocolate,
    melted
2 cups ground filberts *or*
    walnuts
⅓ cup fine dry bread crumbs
2 tablespoons milk
9 stiff-beaten egg whites
    Chocolate Filling
    Chocolate Glaze
    Blanched whole filberts

Grease and lightly flour four 8x1½-inch round baking pans. In a mixer bowl beat butter or margarine and sugar till fluffy. Add egg yolks, one at a time, beating well on medium speed. Add chocolate. Stir in nuts, crumbs, and milk; fold in egg whites. Turn into prepared pans. Bake in a 350° oven for 15 minutes. Cool for 10 minutes on wire racks; remove from pans and cool thoroughly.

Prepare Chocolate Filling and Chocolate Glaze. Spread Chocolate Filling between cake layers. Pour Chocolate Glaze atop. Garnish with whole filberts. Makes 16 to 18 servings.

CHOCOLATE FILLING:
Combine 1 cup sifted *powdered sugar* and 1 tablespoon *all-purpose flour;* gradually stir into 4 beaten *egg yolks*. Stir in ¼ cup *milk*. Cook and stir over medium heat till very thick. Remove from heat; stir in 2 tablespoons *crème d'almond* and 1 teaspoon *vanilla*. Cover surface with waxed paper; cool. Cream ½ cup softened *butter or margarine* and 3 squares (3 ounces) *semisweet chocolate*, melted and cooled. Gradually stir yolk mixture into chocolate mixture.

CHOCOLATE GLAZE:
Melt 1 square (1 ounce) *unsweetened chocolate* and 1 tablespoon *butter or margarine*. Take off heat. Stir in 1 cup sifted *powdered sugar* and 1 teaspoon *vanilla*. Add enough *hot water* (1 to 2 tablespoons) to make of pouring consistency.

CINNAMON COOKIES

Pictured on pages 284-285—

2 cups all-purpose flour
⅓ cup ground almonds
1¼ teaspoons ground
    cinnamon
¼ teaspoon baking powder
⅛ teaspoon salt
¾ cup butter *or* margarine
¾ cup sugar
½ teaspoon vanilla
1 egg
½ teaspoon finely shredded
    lemon peel
1 tablespoon lemon juice
1 cup sifted powdered
    sugar
    Brandy, rum, *or* milk

Stir together flour, almonds, cinnamon, baking powder, and salt. Beat butter for 30 seconds. Add sugar and vanilla; beat till fluffy. Add egg, lemon peel, and lemon juice; beat well. Add dry ingredients to beaten mixture; beat till combined. Cover and chill overnight.

On a floured surface roll into a 12-inch square. Cut into 3x¾-inch strips. On an ungreased cookie sheet bake in a 375° oven for 9 to 11 minutes or till done. Cool. Combine powdered sugar and enough brandy, rum, or milk (1 to 2 tablespoons) to make of spreading consistency; frost cookies. Top with toasted, sliced almonds, if desired. Makes 48.

PUMPKIN EMPANADAS

3 cups all-purpose flour
2 teaspoons baking powder
½ teaspoon salt
½ cup lard *or* shortening
2 beaten eggs
½ cup milk
   Pumpkin Filling
   Cooking oil *or* shortening
     for deep-fat frying
     (optional)
   Powdered sugar *or* sugar
   Milk (optional)

In a mixing bowl stir together flour, baking powder, and salt. Cut in lard or shortening till mixture resembles fine crumbs. Combine eggs and milk; add to flour mixture, stirring till all is moistened (use hands, if necessary). Form into a ball. Cover and chill for 1 hour. Meanwhile, prepare Pumpkin Filling.

Divide dough into 16 portions. On a lightly floured surface roll each portion into a 6-inch circle. Place about *3 tablespoons* of the Pumpkin Filling in the center of *each* circle. Brush edges with water. Fold in half; press edges with tines of fork to seal. Fry or bake as directed below. Makes 16.

TO FRY: Fry empanadas, a few at a time, in deep hot fat (375°) about 4 minutes or till golden, turning once. Drain on paper toweling. Sprinkle with powdered sugar.

TO BAKE: Place empanadas onto a greased baking sheet. Brush tops with milk; sprinkle with sugar. Bake, uncovered, in a 400° oven about 15 minutes or till golden.

PUMPKIN FILLING: In a mixing bowl combine one 16-ounce can *pumpkin,* 1 cup packed *brown sugar,* ¾ cup chopped *walnuts,* ½ cup *raisins,* 1 teaspoon ground *cinnamon,* and ¼ teaspoon ground *cloves.*

CAPIROTADA (APPLE STRATA)

2 cups water
1¼ cups packed brown
   sugar
¾ teaspoon ground
   cinnamon
2 tablespoons butter *or*
   margarine
6 slices white bread, toasted
½ cup raisins
½ cup pine nuts *or* chopped
   almonds
2 apples, peeled, cored, and
   sliced (2 cups)
½ cup shredded Monterey
   Jack cheese (2 ounces)
   Light cream (optional)

In a medium saucepan combine the water, brown sugar, and cinnamon. Bring to boiling; reduce heat. Simmer, uncovered, for 3 minutes. Stir in the butter or margarine.

Cut the toasted bread into 1-inch squares. Fold the toast squares, raisins, and pine nuts or chopped almonds into the brown sugar mixture.

Place *half* of the mixture in the bottom of an 8x8x2-inch baking dish, top with apple slices, then remaining toast mixture. Cover and bake in a 350° oven for 20 minutes. Uncover and sprinkle with the shredded Monterey Jack cheese. Bake, uncovered, about 20 minutes more or till apples are tender. Serve warm with light cream, if desired. Makes 6 servings.

BUÑUELOS

¾ cup milk
¼ cup butter *or* margarine
2 beaten eggs
3 cups all-purpose flour
1 teaspoon baking powder
1 teaspoon salt
   Anise Syrup
   Cooking oil *or* shortening
     for deep-fat frying

In a saucepan combine milk and butter or margarine; bring to boiling. Remove from heat; cool slightly. Stir in beaten eggs. In a mixing bowl stir together flour, baking powder, and salt; add the egg mixture and mix well.

Turn dough out onto a lightly floured surface. Knead for 2 to 3 minutes or till smooth. Shape into 20 balls. Cover and set aside. Prepare Anise Syrup.

On a lightly floured surface roll each ball of dough into a 4-inch circle. Fry, a few at a time, in deep hot fat (375°) for 3 to 4 minutes or till brown, turning once. Drain on paper toweling. Drizzle with Anise Syrup. Makes 20.

ANISE SYRUP: In a 1-quart saucepan combine ½ cup *piloncillo or* packed *dark brown sugar,* and ½ cup *water.* Bring to boiling; reduce heat. Simmer, uncovered, for 8 to 10 minutes or till syrup is thickened. Stir in ⅛ teaspoon *anise extract.*

NOTE: Piloncillo is a dark brown sugar that has been formed into cones. Mexicans grate or shave the cone to obtain brown sugar. You can find piloncillo in Mexican food markets or you can substitute dark brown sugar instead.

Pumpkin Empanadas and Buñuelos

GLOSSARY OF BASIC KNITTING AND CROCHETING STITCHES

KNITTING AND CROCHETING ABBREVIATIONS

beg........................begin(ning)	lp(s) ....loop(s)	sk ....skip
ch.......................................chain	MC ....main color	sl st...............................slip stitch
dc............................ double crochet	p .... purl	sp...space
dec ....decrease	pat...................................pattern	st(s)............................. stitch(es)
dp ....double pointed	psso.............. pass slip stitch over	st st ....stockinette stitch
dtr .... double treble	rem .... remaining	tog .... together
hdc..............half-double crochet	rep .... repeat	yo .... yarn over
inc ....increase	rnd .... round	* ....repeat from * as indicated
k ....knit	sc ....single crochet	

KNITTING

CASTING ON

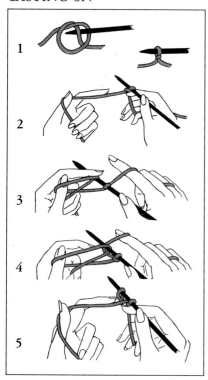

Wind yarn from the ball under and over the needle; draw it through the loop, leaving the stitch on the needle (5). Tighten the stitches on the needle; bring the yarn end around your thumb. Repeat steps (2) through (5) for the desired number of stitches. Switch hands so the stitches are on your left.

KNITTING

PURLING

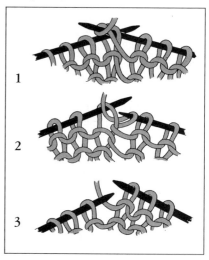

Repeat these three steps (explained below left) until you have transferred all the stitches from the left needle to the right needle. This completes one row. When you are working the next row, move the needle holding the stitches to the left hand, and move the other needle to the right hand.

Make a slipknot around the needle at a distance from the yarn end that equals 1 inch for each stitch to be cast on (see diagram 1, *above*). Hold the needle with the slipknot in your right hand; make a loop of the short length of yarn around your left thumb (2).

Insert the point of the needle in your right hand under the loop on your left thumb (3). Loop yarn from the ball over the fingers of your right hand (4).

Hold the needle with the stitches on it in your left hand and the other needle in your right hand. Insert the right needle through the stitch on the left needle from the front to the back. Pass the yarn around the point of the right needle to form a loop (see diagram 1, *above*).

Pull this loop through the center of the stitch on the left needle; draw the loop onto the right needle (2).

Now, slip the stitch completely off the left needle (3).

Hold needle with stitches in your left hand and the other needle in your right hand. Insert right needle through stitch on left needle from back to front. Wind the yarn around the point of the right needle to form a loop (1, *above*). Draw a loop through the stitch on the needle in your left hand; transfer it to the needle in your right hand (2). Slip the stitch completely off left needle (3). Repeat these steps until all loops are transferred to right needle.

INCREASING AND DECREASING

To increase, knit or purl; do not slip stitch off left needle. Insert right needle into back of stitch; knit or purl into stitch again. Slip both onto right needle. To decrease, knit or purl two stitches together. To slip a stitch, insert right needle into stitch on left needle from the back, as if to purl. Slip stitch onto right needle.

BINDING OFF

Work two stitches in pattern. With left needle, lift first stitch over second and off right needle. Repeat for required number of stitches.

CROCHETING

CHAIN STITCH

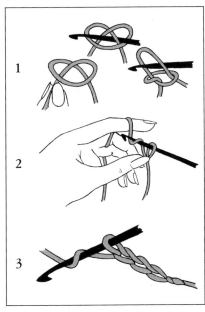

Make a slipknot on the crochet hook about 6 inches from the end of the yarn (1, *above*). Pull one end to tighten the knot. Hold the hook between your right index finger and thumb, as you would a pencil. Wrap yarn over your ring finger, under the middle finger, and over the index finger; hold the short end between your thumb and index finger. For more tension, wrap yarn around little finger. Insert hook under and over strand of yarn (2).

To make a foundation chain, catch the strand of yarn with the hook; draw through the loop (3). Make chain the length pattern calls for.

SINGLE CROCHET

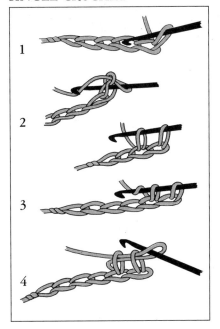

Insert the hook into the second chain from the hook, under the two upper strands of yarn (1, *above*). Draw up a loop (2). Draw the yarn over the hook (3). Pull the yarn through two loops, making a single crochet stitch (4). Insert the hook into the next stitch; repeat the steps explained above.

HALF-DOUBLE CROCHET

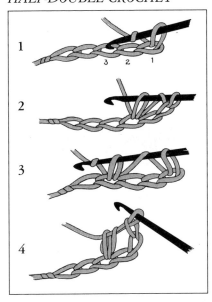

With yarn over the hook, insert the crochet hook into the third chain, under the two upper strands of yarn (see diagram 1, *above*). Draw

up a loop (2, *below left*). Draw the yarn over the hook (3). Pull through three loops, completing a half-double crochet stitch (4).

DOUBLE CROCHET

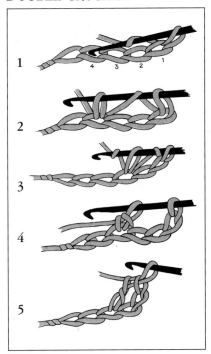

Holding the yarn over the hook, insert the crochet hook into the fourth chain, under the two upper strands of yarn (diagram 1, *above*).

Draw up a loop (2). Wrap the yarn over the hook (3). Draw yarn through two loops as shown (4). Then, yarn over again and draw through the last two loops on the hook (5). This completes the double crochet stitch.

SLIP STITCH

After you have made the foundation chain, insert the hook under the top strand of the second chain from the hook, and yarn over. With a single motion, pull yarn through the stitch *and* the loop on the hook. Insert hook into next chain; yarn over and draw yarn through stitch and loop on hook. This stitch also may be used for decreasing.

GLOSSARY OF
BASIC EMBROIDERY STITCHES

BACKSTITCH

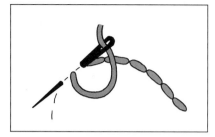

BUTTONHOLE STITCH

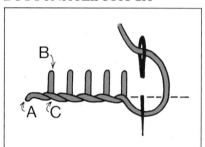

CHAIN STITCH

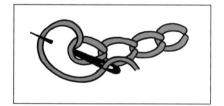

COUCHING STITCH

LAID WORK

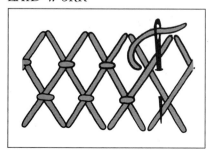

FEATHERSTITCH

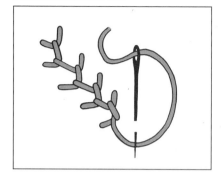

FRENCH KNOT

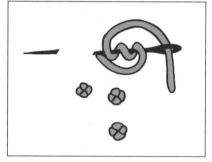

OUTLINE (OR STEM) STITCH

LONG-AND-SHORT STITCH

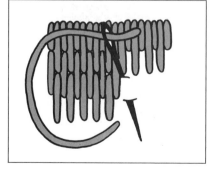

RUNNING STITCH

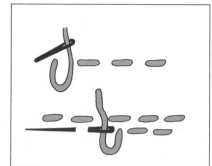

SATIN STITCH

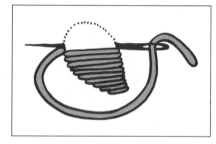

SEED STITCH

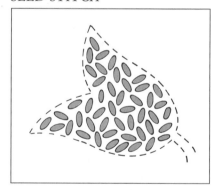

STRAIGHT STITCH

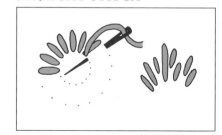

312

GLOSSARY OF
BASIC NEEDLEPOINT STITCHES

BARGELLO STITCH

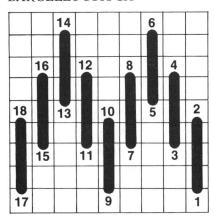

BASKET-WEAVE STITCH

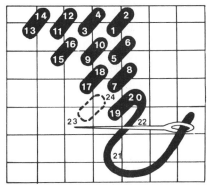

CASHMERE STITCH

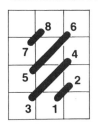 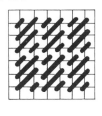

CONTINENTAL STITCH

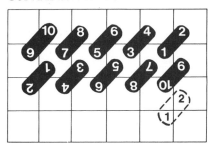

CROSS-STITCH

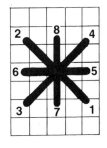

DIAMOND EYELET STITCH

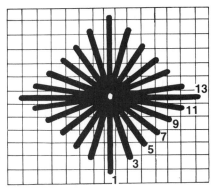

MOSAIC STITCH

 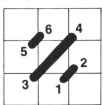

SCOTCH STITCH

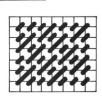

SMYRNA STITCH

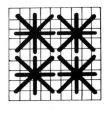

SLANTING GOBELIN STITCH

STRAIGHT GOBELIN STITCH

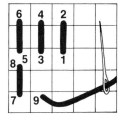

UPRIGHT CROSS-STITCH

 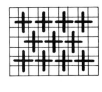

WASTE KNOT

313

CRAFT DESIGN AND PHOTOGRAPHY CREDITS

For her special contribution to this book, we offer our heartfelt thanks and appreciation to Arlette Gosieski, an artist who works in fabric. Her appliqué paintings appear on the cover and on pages 6-7, 40-41, 128-129, 200-201, and 246-247.

We also are happy to acknowledge our indebtedness and extend our sincere thanks to all of the talented people who contributed craft designs to this book.

The numbers in each listing refer to the page or pages on which the color photograph appears.

Jan Anderson—nutshell ornaments, 206-207.

David Ashe, The Design Concern—wooden mosaic, candle holder, 133; wooden sled, 205.

Pauline Asmus—snowflakes, 176-177.

Arlene Aune—cookie cutter trims, 8-9.

Mary Becker—angel, 146.

Linda Bender—wagons, 136.

Mary Blaylock—doll furniture, 60.

Vicki Bluth—country family dolls, 28-29; breadboard dolls, 250.

Curt Boehringer—pillow, 77.

Tess Boernke—Bavarian dollhouse family, 264-265.

Gary Boling—place mats, 18-19.

Susan Booth—baskets, lace ornaments, 150-151.

Sue Bruni—dolls, 206.

Patty Burrets—pine shaving ornaments, 135.

Helen Clark—stamped ornaments, 77.

Janet Collins—apron, 130.

Jackie Davis—soft dolls, 232-233.

Jane DiTeresa—angel ornaments, 8-9; Mrs. Claus doll, 30; carrousel marionettes, 272-273.

Neil DiTeresa—grapevine wreath, 14; limberjacks, 270-271.

Hughie Dufresne—knitted doll, 10.

Deborah Dugan—village gift wrap, 249.

Phyllis Dunstan—bistro bears, 65; collars, cuffs, and apron ornamentation, 108-109; plain and fancy dolls, 150; tree-shape ornament, 174; T-shirt, 203; pinwheel ornaments, 205; babushka dolls, 253; bead dolls, 267; Tyrolean bears, Goldilocks doll, 269.

Linda Emmerson—floorcloth, pillows, 78; paper cutout, 236.

Mary Engelbreit—quilt, dolls, pillows, 210-211.

Dorothy and John Everds—picture, 149; banner, puppets, cards, 177.

Dixie Falls—knitted bonnet, 105.

Jan Farley, Country Folks, Ltd.—wreath, 75.

Pat Gardner—ceramic plate, tiles, 179.

Ilone Gilmore—country dolls, 60.

Kay Gleason—plate, tiles, 179.

Su Graves—Advent calendar, candle dolls, 148.

Sara Gutierrez—needlepoint snowman stocking, 232.

Carol Vanderpool Hall—pillows, 176.

Mary Hardy—clown, 177.

Lezli Harris—tablecloth edging, 12.

Ron Hawbaker—cutting board, 17; birds, trees, 18-19; doll chest, 31.

Helen Hayes—candle ornament, 178.

Laura Holtorf—doily stocking, 44; wool ornaments, 61; heart place mats, 63; sampler, 110; quilted boxes, 148.

Adam Jerdee—tree ornaments, hand puppets, soft dolls, story pillows, soft crèche, 232-233.

Amy Jerdee—story pillows, 232; bird treats, 255.

Rebecca Jerdee—doll chest, 31; rocking horse, 33; hostess apron, floral decal boxes, 62; crèche, 151; angel and shepherd costumes, 207-208; crèche, 208; tree ornaments, hand puppets, 232-233; hostess apron, 248; felt stocking, 250.

Gail Kinkead—white pineapple doily, 253.

Ann Marie Kocherga—papier-mâché ornaments, 176-177. Pat Kraus—towels, 14-15; heart-shape pillow, 58; appliquéd jacket, 104; baskets, lace ornaments, 150-151.

Mary Sue Kuhn—tatted wreath, candy canes, 176-177.

Alla Ladyzensky—cross-stitched stockings, 10.

Roxine Lawton—cow, rooster, 73; apron, tea cozy, 76; animal ornaments, 77.

For their cooperation and courtesy, we extend a special thanks to the following companies, institutions, and individuals.

Curtis Alvey

American Thread Co.—crocheted baskets, 42-43.

Berea College, Kentucky

Coats and Clark—knitted doll, 10; knitted gauntlets, 104; dolls, bunting, and blanket, 237.

Manos del Uruguay—patterned sweaters, 106.

Judy Murphy—Amish quilt, 131.

Murphy's Landing, Shakopee, Minnesota.

Pella Historical Society, Pella, Iowa.

Stencil Magic—apron, 31.

Unger Yarn Co.—reindeer sweater, 11.

We also extend our thanks to the following photographers, whose creative talents and technical skills contributed much to this book.

Mike Dieter—42-43, 45, 108, 109, 150-151, 179, 210, 211.

Hedrich-Blessing—Cover, 6-7, 8, 9, 10, 11, 12, 13, 14, 15, 16, 17, 18, 19, 28-29, 30, 31, 32, 33, 40-41, 46, 47, 48, 49, 104, 105, 128-129, 200-201, 232, 246-247, 248, 249, 250, 251, 252, 253, 254, 255.

Thomas Hooper—58, 59, 60, 61, 62, 63, 64, 65, 106, 107, 110.

Hopkins Associates—72, 73, 74, 75, 76, 77, 78, 79, 146, 147, 148, 149, 174, 176, 177, 178, 204, 205, 206, 207, 208, 232, 233, 234, 235, 236, 237.

Scott Little—176.

Maris/Semel—130, 131, 132, 133, 134, 135, 136, 137, 178.

Bradley Olman—174, 175, 202.

Perry Struse—111, 202, 203.

RECIPE INDEX

A-B

C-D

CRAFT INDEX

The numbers in bold type refer to the pages on which photographs appear. Italic numbers refer to instructions.